CONSPIRATOR

CONSPIRATOR

LENIN IN EXILE

Helen Rappaport

BASIC BOOKS

A Member of the Perseus Books Group
New York

Copyright © 2010 by Helen Rappaport
Published by Basic Books,
A Member of the Perseus Books Group

All rights reserved. Printed in the United States of America. No part of this book may be reproduced in any manner whatsoever without written permission except in the case of brief quotations embodied in critical articles and reviews. For information, address Basic Books, 387 Park Avenue South, New York, NY 10016-8810.

Books published by Basic Books are available at special discounts for bulk purchases in the United States by corporations, institutions, and other organizations. For more information, please contact the Special Markets Department at the Perseus Books Group, 2300 Chestnut Street, Suite 200, Philadelphia, PA 19103, or call (800) 810-4145, ext. 5000, or e-mail special.markets@perseusbooks.com.

Designed by Jeff Williams

Library of Congress Cataloging-in-Publication Data
Rappaport, Helen.
    Conspirator : Lenin in exile / Helen Rappaport.
        p. cm.
    Includes bibliographical references and index.
    ISBN 978-0-465-01395-1
    1. Lenin, Vladimir Il'ich, 1870-1924—Travel—Europe. 2. Lenin, Vladimir Il'ich, 1870-1924—Exile—Russia (Federation)—Siberia. 3. Revolutionaries—Russia—Biography. 4. Conspiracies—Russia—History—20th century. 5. Russia—Politics and government—1894-1917. 6. Europe—Politics and government—1871-1918. I. Title.

DK254.L443R37 2009
947.084'1092—dc22
[B]
                                                                                2009039494

10 9 8 7 6 5 4 3 2 1

For Christina

CONTENTS

POLONIUS: What do you read, my lord?

HAMLET: Words, words, words.

Shakespeare,
Hamlet, Act 2, Scene 2

INTRODUCTION

Shlisselburg Fortress, 1887

———— ❧ ————

F IVE OF THEM WERE TO BE TAKEN to Shlisselburg that night, May 5, 1887—the five leading conspirators in the latest foiled assassination attempt against a Russian czar. This time, only six years after revolutionaries had successfully blown up Alexander II, his son Alexander III, who had instituted a highly reactionary and oppressive government in the wake of his father's murder, had been the target. They called themselves the "Terrorist Section" of The People's Will (Narodnaya Volya). Even though this organization had effectively been driven out of existence by widespread arrests, the Terrorist Section had nevertheless dedicated themselves to carrying forward the aspirations of The People's Will for the liberation of Russians from autocratic rule. They had no experience of terrorism, let alone of making bombs. As conspirators they were inept to say the least. It was only their youth—the youngest was only twenty—and their bungling incompetence that had saved St Petersburg's Nevsky Prospekt from yet another outrage. A spot check on two of the conspirators by suspicious police agents had uncovered the crude bomb filled with bullets dipped in strychnine that one of them carried inside a copy of Grinberg's *Dictionary of Medical Terminology.*

It might sound like the stuff of tragicomedy, but the plot's perpetrators were in deadly earnest, even if their bomb was defective. But what had driven them to such violent action?

Russia had ever been a country of extremes, a place where the opulence and extravagance of the Imperial Court was matched by its indifference to the privation suffered by Russia's silent and unseen masses. By European standards, nineteenth-century Russia was a backward country, its population largely illiterate and rural, its infrastructure—roads, railways, and industry—lagging far behind that of the West. In an empire covering one-fifth of the world's surface the vast majority of Russia's multinational population of 180 million (by World War I) had been enslaved by serfdom until 1861. But emancipation had done little to liberate the peasantry from illiteracy, poverty, and land hunger, or to assuage the social conscience of a growing intelligentsia that passionately sought to redress the imbalances of the old order.

Official corruption and repression in Russia drove young people to seek political answers to the questions that so tormented them about Russia's position in the world. They wanted to work toward a better political and economic future, in which the peasantry and the urban proletariat would play key roles. For a while hopes were pinned on the model of the existing village communes providing a shortcut to socialism and the institution of a democratic system. But the populist To the People movement of 1873–1875—an ill judged propaganda drive by the intelligentsia among the peasants of rural Russia—had collapsed amid widespread peasant mistrust of these newcomers and had ended in thousands of arrests, and exile for many to Siberia.

The response to official repression was the establishment in 1876 of Land and Freedom (Zemlya i Volya), the first political party to openly advocate political change in Russia. But before long the party was divided. Some members embraced the peaceful path of agrarian reform and worked for local government in rural areas, while in 1879 a more extreme group formed The People's Will faction, embracing terrorism as a political weapon. But such extreme methods were short-lived; by the time the would-be assassins were arrested in 1887 The People's Will was a spent force. Arrested in March, the five men were held for two months in solitary confinement in the grim Trubetskoy Bastion of the Peter and Paul Fortress in St. Petersburg. After their five-day trial in April, they were condemned to death.

The other prisoners on the isolation wing of the Trubetskoy Bastion heard the cell doors being unlocked the night the men were taken away to their place of execution; even the thick stone walls could not muffle the resonant tread of footsteps matched by the ominous clank of the chains which bound the men hand and foot. The five men's shadows flickered and fell as they passed along the dark prison walls by the light of dingy kerosene lamps and were led out across the cobbled courtyard to the iron gate. Here police vans—little more than cages on wheels—waited for them. This would be the last time they would see the city. Just out of sight, the River Neva lapped softly along its long, flat embankment, where a steamship waited on the dark and deserted quayside, its tiny cabin windows curtaining the outside world from view.

The men were on their way to Shlisselburg—a forbidding medieval fortress built on a small island looking out over Lake Ladoga, thirty-five miles from St. Petersburg along the Neva. Every Russian revolutionary knew about Shlisselburg; it was the Russian Bastille and few survived incarceration there. Built in the fourteenth century by the people of Novgorod, it was later captured by the Swedes and then recaptured by Peter the Great. It had gained notoriety when Ivan VI was held and murdered there in 1764. In the 1820s it became a staging post for conspirators in the Decembrist uprising on their way to exile in Siberia. But since 1884 it had served a much more specific purpose, when a special isolation prison was built within its ancient walls for the incarceration of forty of the country's highest security political prisoners. Shlisselburg was a place, it was said, from which people were only carried out; they very rarely walked. If they took you there it was either to hang you or because your death sentence had been commuted to life imprisonment. And life meant life. One way or another, you'd die at Shlisselburg.

After the steamship had traveled for five hours, the green, iridescent waters of the River Neva suddenly broadened out into the lagoons of Lake Ladoga. Here Shlisselburg with its white walls and limestone towers loomed into view in the early dawn. At the top of a tall spire shone the gilded key that had given the fortress its German name from the word *Schlussel*.

As the five men passed through the high white walls of the main entrance, the huge, two-headed imperial eagle looked down on them as though ready to swoop. Inside everything seemed white and quiet and orderly—like a tiny village with its own small white church at one end. But beyond this seemingly peaceful setting there stood a two-story red brick building with dirty windows and two tall chimneys—the special wing for political prisoners. Inside, the poorly lit first and second floors were divided by a net to prevent suicide attempts from the top floor; connecting the two levels from one side to the other, there was a narrow walkway—a Russian Bridge of Sighs.

Ranged around the circumference were forty black iron doors opening into forty isolation cells—set like a row of coffins standing on end, for incarceration here was a living death—with only the fuzzy outline of the far horizon beyond each cell's opaque windowpane. Inside there was nothing but the overpowering stillness of solitary confinement—where the real becomes unreal and the imaginary can become so vivid that it takes on a life that confuses the senses and drives men mad. The only sound breaking the silence was the hissing of water in pipes somewhere far below, or, from the distance, a faint tubercular cough of another prisoner. Sometimes there was the soft tap-tap of prisoners communicating with each other by an improvised code. And sooner or later, the rattle at the door, as the gendarme slid open the peephole.

Three days later, on May 8, having been lulled into a false sense of security that their sentences would be commuted, the men were woken at 3:30 AM and informed that they were to be executed in half an hour. The prison officials had constructed the gallows in such secrecy that none of the prisoners in the isolation block had known. There was room for only three gallows, which had been built in sections outside the prison and silently assembled near the main entrance, without so much as a single blow of an axe being heard.

As the rest of the prisoners slept the heavy sleep of those with an eternity on their hands, the commandant, priest, and guards accompanied the five prisoners in single file to the place of execution. The condemned men were offered the consolation of a priest but refused. There being only three gallows, they had to hang them in two batches: Vasily Generalov, Pakhomiy Andreyushkin, and Vasily Osipanov embraced each other and cried out "Long Live the People's Will" before the sack was thrown over their heads and the stools kicked from under them. The condemned in Russia were not yet accorded the merciful death of the trapdoor, but a slower one, by strangulation.

After their three corpses had been taken down, the other two men were brought forward. Petr Shevyrov, the ringleader of the conspiracy, pushed away the cross as the priest offered it to him, but the last man, with absolute composure, stopped and kissed it before they hanged him too.

His name was Aleksandr Ulyanov.

In provincial Simbirsk, 935 miles away, Ulyanov's younger brother was studying hard that day for his final school examinations, unaware of what had taken place. That sixteen-year-old boy was the man who became Vladimir Ilyich Lenin.

ALEKSANDR ULYANOV'S CORPSE had already been consigned to a common grave with his fellow conspirators on the Shlisselburg grounds before his mother Mariya, who had been lobbying the authorities for weeks to commute his sentence, learned that her son had been executed—in an announcement in a broadsheet handed out on the streets of St. Petersburg. Mariya's natural stoicism saw her through. Her emotional control and fortitude at a time when one of her daughters, Anna, was also in police custody in the city, implicated in the same plot, was extraordinary. It would enable her to endure many years of anxiety as, one by one, all of her children suffered arrest and exile. More importantly, it was a characteristic inherited by her younger son Vladimir.

In the weeks leading up to his execution, Aleksandr and his fellow conspirators were encouraged to appeal to the czar for mercy but refused. All he asked for in his final days was a volume of verse by his favorite poet, Heinrich Heine. He was in fact not one of those designated to throw the bomb (although as a student of natural science, he had manufactured the nitroglycerin) and would almost certainly have been reprieved had he petitioned for clemency. But he would not compromise his beliefs.

Aleksandr wanted to take on himself the burden of responsibility for the conspiracy, to be a martyr and die an exemplary death. Czar Alexander found his frankness "touching" but did not commute the death sentence. Shortly after the executions, students at Aleksandr's university brought out their own statement on the heroism of the five hanged men who had died for the "common cause." They had fulfilled their duty with absolute integrity and had "firmly upheld the banner of struggle for freedom and justice."

Aleksandr Ulyanov was one of the last of a generation of romantic idealists devoted to the cause of the downtrodden masses, who espoused the Russian populist movement and found themselves drawn into desperate acts of terrorism. But despite scoring some spectacular murders of senior officials and the czar himself in 1881, The People's Will had ultimately been ineffectual in forcing constitutional change in Russia through the use of terrorism. In later years, Lenin, in an extremely rare public allusion to his brother's death, would state that such an act of martyrdom as Aleksandr's had not and never could achieve the conspirators' immediate and passionate aim: "awakening a popular revolution." A year before his death, Aleksandr had won a gold medal for his dissertation entitled "The Segmentation and Sexual Organs of Freshwater Annula." The young Vladimir had watched him at home, huddled over his microscope from the early hours of the morning examining slides. "No, my brother won't make a revolutionary, I thought then," he later told his wife Nadezhda. "A revolutionary cannot devote so much time to the study of worms."

In the unequal struggle between a repressive autocracy that banned all political opposition and small groups of disaffected and disorganized intellectuals who shared no common doctrine, sporadic acts of self-immolation made little difference. Even the five corpses on the gallows at Shlisselburg, and before them the six People's Will leaders hanged in front of 100,000 people in St. Petersburg's Semenovsky Square in April 1881, had succeeded only in provoking an entrenchment of official reaction. True, such events drew attention to the importance of the legal process and the responsibility of judges and lawyers. But the proliferation of committees, clubs, and secret and mutual aid societies, as well as the torrent of resolutions and exhortations that accompanied their inception, did not even dent the oppressive machinery of the state. For Vladimir Ilyich Ulyanov there would have to be another way.

Like many of his peers Vladimir saw the answer in Marxism, as pioneered and interpreted by its Russian "father," Georgy Plekhanov. Marxism provided a sound and scientific rationale for political change, as opposed to the emotional, anarchistic idealism of the populists. It defined history as class struggle: capitalism had replaced the old feudal system and with time would be the means of its own destruction, leading to the ideal, classless society. The working classes would be capitalism's nemesis.

Plekhanov's interpretation of Marx within the Russian context offered young radicals an objective philosophy based on economics and the belief that sooner or later a major clash between the capitalist bourgeoisie and the proletariat would bring about political change. But to arrive at this objective democratically—with the masses being sufficiently enlightened to accept change and willingly take part in it—knowledge, patience, and careful preparation would be needed. The key to Plekhanov's Marxist vision—which inspired so many young Russians from the 1880s onward—was the need for tactics based not on sentiment but on scientific training and a widespread program of political education among the Russian population at large.

In the coming revolutionary struggle, therefore, heroism, self-sacrifice, the unshakeable power of belief—none of these would ever be sufficient to effect real change. As Plekhanov's pupil, Vladimir Ilyich Ulyanov would soon so forcefully demonstrate, what was required was a unique kind of iron-clad, remorseless will.

CHAPTER ONE

Leaving Shushenskoe

SIBERIA: JANUARY 1900

—⚬⚬⚬—

THE SKY IS BIG AT SHUSHENSKOE. No other place in the world is so far from the sea as this remote region in south central Siberia. On the right bank of the great Yenisey River this now forgotten village of exile once sprawled in a huddle of low wooden houses. Beyond the broad expanses of the river loom the dazzling, snow-capped Sayan Mountains. The wastes of Outer Mongolia lie unseen on the other side. In the old days Shusha, as the local peasants called it, seemed so remote that those great shimmering mountains seemed to them "the very edge of the world itself."

For many centuries this remote region, unmapped by geographers, was inhabited only by fur traders and Cossacks. During the nineteenth century the czarist authorities found a new use for Shushenskoe as a suitably remote destination for political exiles. Closed to the outside world, the area was hundreds of miles from the railroad and accessible only to the intrepid few.

Siberian exile for political prisoners in those days did not have the ominous overtones it acquired under Stalin, when the prospect of Siberia and the Gulag became a virtual death sentence. For those lucky enough to be sent to Shushenskoe under the czars, however, life was not always unpleasant or arduous. The climate here was kinder than in the primeval, frozen east of Siberia, where prisoners endured appalling conditions. In comparison to the repressive prison system the Soviets would later institute, Shushenskoe was a virtual holiday camp. No wonder that part of the Minusinsk district where the village lay came to be called the Siberian Italy.

On January 31, 1900, the Russian revolutionary Vladimir Ilyich Ulyanov prepared to leave Shushenskoe after spending three years there as a political exile. It was a timely moment in the new century and in the life of an extraordinary man whose political thinking would come to dominate most of the century.

In many ways Vladimir was sorry to leave. After ten years as an activist in the Russian revolutionary underground with all the uncertainties that such a life involved, he had found a degree of peace here and, paradoxically, freedom. Police surveillance had been lax and there were few restrictions on movement. Although short on money, he had recovered his often febrile health and had grown fit and well as he enjoyed vigorous outdoor pursuits such as hunting, shooting, ice skating, and swimming in the nearby River Shush during the short-lived Siberian summers. And he had benefited too from the comfort and companionship of his wife and political comrade Nadezhda Krupskaya, herself an exile.

———— ❦ ————

THE PATH TO SHUSHENSKOE had been a long one. The man who became Lenin did not turn into a revolutionary overnight. On the day his brother was executed in 1887, he finished his math exam early and was the first to leave the examination hall. At school he remained an exemplary pupil; at home he was always the first to finish his homework. In June, only a month after his brother's death, he was awarded the gold medal for academic excellence. Headmaster Fedor Kerensky noted in the citation that Vladimir was "diligent, prompt, and reliable" and that there was "no single instance on record either inside school or outside of it" of his behavior inviting adverse criticism. Perceptively, Kerensky noted that "rational discipline" seemed to be the young man's guiding light, as well as a marked preference for solitude and "a certain unsociability."

There was no reason for the robust and boisterous Volodya, as he was known in the family, to be other than ordinary, for he came from a loving, stable home that valued learning and respected intellectual enlightenment. His early life as one of six children—Anna, Aleksandr, Vladimir, Olga, Dmitri, and Mariya (two others had died young)—had been far from rebellious or controversial. However, after the revolution, and particularly after Lenin's death in 1924, Soviet hagiography suppressed the true details of the great leader's less than working-class ancestry.

Vladimir Ulyanov was not a full-blooded Russian; the narrow, Asiatic-looking eyes always gave him away. The man who became Lenin, like many other Russians, was of mixed race, his ancestors being Jewish, German, Swedish, Slav, and Kalmyk. On his father Ilya's side, Vladimir's grandfather, Nikolay Vasil'evich Ulyanov, was possibly of Tatar or Kalmyk descent. The son of a former serf, Nikolay Vasil'evich had worked as a tailor in Astrakhan and married a Kalmyk woman. Vladimir's mother, whom Ilya had married in 1863, had more upwardly mobile antecedents. She was born Mariya Aleksandrovna Blank to a family of good Lutheran merchants from Germany and Sweden on one side and middle-class Jewish converts on the other. Vladimir's Jewish grandfather, Aleksandr Blank, was a medical man with progressive if somewhat eccentric views on hydropathy who imposed his water cures on his children. Strict, authoritarian, and frugal, he bought an estate at Kokushkino near Kazan, complete with serfs. With its flower beds, fruit bushes, and graceful linden trees, it would become a happy holiday home for the Ulyanov children as they grew up, a place where the young Volodya reveled in the bucolic pleasures of the Russian country estate, as epitomized in the novels of his favorite writer, Ivan Turgenev.

Ilya Nikolaevich Ulyanov attained the status of minor nobleman, as did many others in Russia in the nineteenth century, by dutiful service to the state. He was in many ways that archetypal Chekhovian figure, a loyal *chinovnik*, one of a breed of czarist bureaucrats who ran the vast, antiquated machinery of state. After completing his studies at the University of Kazan, he had started out as a math and physics teacher. He went on to serve as a primary school inspector and then from 1874 as director of public schools in Simbirsk province. In later years he was promoted through the fourteen ranks of the Russian civil service to number four and was accorded the honorific of Actual State Counselor (the civilian equivalent of a major general) in later years. With the honorific came the right to be addressed as "Your Excellency." One of the perks of the system was that the father's entitlements extended to his sons, thus ensuring that Vladimir could later claim noble status to lessen the harshness of his exile in Siberia.

Photographs of Ilya Nikolaevich sitting in his high-buttoned uniform reveal that Vladimir inherited his high cheekbones, domed Socratic forehead, and patrician look, as well as a strong work ethic, and with it the stern mentality of the pedagogue and the moral puritan. Both parents were well educated and politically enlightened. They supported the liberal reforms of Alexander II, who had emancipated the peasants in 1861. Ilya Nikolaevich was a devout member of the Russian Orthodox Church, a staunch patriot, and a conscientious public servant loyal to his czar. Mariya Ulyanova was less religiously observant but thrifty and long-suffering. The Ulyanov family believed in self-education and the liberating power of scientific progress. The Ulyanov children were encouraged to be curious about the world.

From both parents Vladimir learned to be frugal and unostentatious, to work hard and persevere, despite a propensity to be loud and clumsy, with a habit of breaking things. From his cultured mother he learned to appreciate music. She taught him languages—French, German, and English; his sisters Anna, Mariya, and Olga played the piano and sang. There was much joy and laughter and shared amusement in their young lives.

A humane and conscientious man with a mission to modernize the czarist school system, Vladimir's father drove himself relentlessly at the expense of his health. His work involved long periods away from home. Yet the reward for his diligence in trying to raise education standards throughout Simbirsk province was to be forced into early retirement in 1885, as a result of the political retreat that occurred after Alexander II was murdered. Ilya Ulyanov's dedicated, progressive work was suddenly cut short. His premature death in 1886 spared him the agony and humiliation of his son Aleksandr's involvement in a plot against the czar. Years of overwork and stress culminated in a cerebral hemorrhage that carried him off at fifty-three.

Vladimir Ulyanov's early life in Simbirsk, a regional trading port of 30,000 inhabitants stretched out along the slopes of the River Volga, was uneventful. Life in the Russian provinces in the nineteenth century was legendary for its hidebound tradition and lethargy. But being stuck in a provincial backwater did not seem to worry Vladimir, nor did the fact that his family was not rich enough to live on the leafier, more salubrious side of town where nightingales sang in the apple and cherry orchards. His attachment to the broad flowing waters of the Volga dominated his early years and would stay with him throughout his life, as would a love of the outdoors. Being out in the natural world became for the adult Lenin an essential release from stress and anxiety, as well as the setting for vigorous and regular exercise. But such moments became increasingly few and far between as he grew older. His mind, his time, and his prodigious energy were, from young adulthood, focused entirely on his work and the demands of an exacting classical curriculum.

Quiet, studious, and solitary, he absorbed himself in his books and had few friends. He gave up his favorite subject, Latin, because it got in the way of his more important political and economic studies. He even abandoned ice skating until he rediscovered it in Siberia. Such interests were "dangerous addictions." As he grew older, with his highly rational and logical mind he developed his great passion for statistics.

At school he garnered the respect of his peers and teachers, if not their affection, for his diligence. His family losses—Aleksandr's execution, his father's death, and the tragic death in 1888 of his favorite and extremely gifted sister Olga from typhoid—crushed his natural joviality and drew down the shutters on all discussions of his personal life, creating a lifelong reticence in him. He became, as his younger brother Dmitri later observed, "grimly restrained, strict, closed up in himself, highly focussed." He was crippled by remorse about the strained relationship he had with his older brother, whom he had tried to emulate. The truth was that Vladimir and the dreamy, ascetic Aleksandr had been rivals. Aleksandr was revered in the family for his quiet intelligence, modesty, and moral integrity, and finding his brother too disruptive, had been offended by Volodya's arrogance and his rudeness toward their mother.

Despite this, Vladimir took his brother's death in pursuit of political change very hard and became bitter when his loyal mother and siblings were subsequently ostracized in Simbirsk. The situation prompted the family to move to the Blank estate at Kokushkino near Kazan. Here Vladimir enjoyed the rural pleasures of hunting, swimming, sailing, and walking, combined, as always, with extensive reading, shut away in his sparsely furnished room. In August 1887 he moved into the city of Kazan to study law. Four months later his involvement in relatively low-key student demonstrations against a university inspector ensured his prompt expulsion from the university and banishment by the Ministry of Internal Affairs back to Kokushkino, where his elder sister Anna had already been confined for political activities. As the brother of a would-be regicide, Vladimir would remain under close police surveillance.

Moving into Kazan in September 1888, Vladimir associated with a clandestine political discussion group led by Nikolay Fedoseev, which prompted his first study of Karl Marx's *Das Kapital* in his search for answers to the pressing social and political questions facing Russia. For a pragmatist like Vladimir, Marx's book held enormous appeal on rational, scientific grounds. But his guiding light in this early period was undoubtedly the "plodding genius" of a homegrown Russian social thinker—Nikolay Chernyshevsky.

Chernyshevsky's didactic novel *What Is to Be Done?*, written in prison from 1862 to 1863, presented a vision of a socialist utopia based around communes of politically like-minded young people living and working together for the common good. Its revolutionary heroes, the feminist Vera Pavlovna, doyenne of a cooperative of seamstresses, and the dark and driven activist, Rakhmetov, had become icons to a whole generation of idealistic Russian revolutionaries, including Aleksandr Ulyanov. In Rakhmetov, known to his revolutionary comrades as "the rigorist," Chernyshevsky presented a man with the austerity of a religious fanatic who lived life pared to the bone: "No luxury, no caprices; nothing but the necessary," as he put it. His Spartan existence was dominated by the strict use of his time. There was no room in his highly disciplined schedule for "minor affairs" or personal matters; his only indulgence was time set aside for physical exercise to maintain his strength and energy for the revolutionary struggle to come. In the rationalistic, enigmatic Rakhmetov the young Vladimir saw a man of ruthless dedication on the road to self-perfection and revolution. He read the novel five times, convinced that "every right-thinking and really honest man must be a revolutionary," and adopted similar self-denying precepts in his own life. The book was, so he later claimed, "a work which gives one a charge for a whole life."

Worried about the dangerous political influences to which her son was succumbing in Kazan and dreading that he would follow the same path as his brother, Mariya Ulyanova sold the family home in Simbirsk and her share in Kokushkino in 1889. With this money and some other family legacies she bought an estate at Alakaevka, 150 miles south of Kazan. Here she tried to divert Vladimir's interests into farm management. He did not take to it. Worrying about a neighbor's cattle trampling the Ulyanovs' crops was no substitute for the political literature he was now devouring at a prodigious rate. Thanks to his mother's petitioning of the authorities (she would spend a lifetime doing so on behalf of all her politically active children), Vladimir, after kicking his heels as an idle country squire, was finally allowed to return to St. Petersburg in March 1891 to complete his law studies. With his characteristic ferocious intellectual energy he crammed three years' worth of study into one year. Despite his mother's perennial anxieties that he was overexerting his brain, just as his poor father had done, he emerged with top marks as a qualified lawyer in January 1892. But a career as a provincial lawyer defending peasants and artisans accused of petty offenses would not challenge a man of his exceptional intellectual ability.

By now Vladimir was caught up in studying Karl Marx and preparing a riposte to traditional Russian populist thinking. There was enough money in the family fund to subsidize his continuing political work, and he soon abandoned the legal appointment he took up in September 1893 in St. Petersburg. He concentrated his energy on turning out political pamphlets expounding a Marxist view of Russian economic development and agriculture and engaging in regular debate at illegal political meetings. His life as an active revolutionary would be subsidized thereafter by his mother's income, party funds, and handouts from sympathizers.

In 1894 in St. Petersburg, one of many political activists to be impressed by the intellectual ascendancy of this "learned Marxist who had arrived from the Volga" was twenty-five-year-old Nadezhda Konstantinovna Krupskaya. A teacher and activist among workers in the Nevsky factory district, she was impressed by Ulyanov's lively manner and his skill in setting out political theory backed up by a wealth of statistical evidence. He had the knack of making complex political ideas simple, of describing the objectives of the revolutionary struggle with clarity and sobriety. Their paths crossed at various study circles, with Vladimir at that time propagandizing among workers at the British-owned Thornton textile mill and local shoe factories. Through their shared political views Vladimir and Nadya developed a mutual respect and sense of comradeship and crucially, for a man of Vladimir's pathologically suspicious nature, enduring trust.

By now Vladimir had grown used to a life on the move. In barely two years—from 1893 to 1895—with the Russian secret police always on his tail, he changed his address eight times. The Department for the Protection of Order and Public Security was better known by its acronym, Okhrana.

It operated from its base at 16 Ulitsa Fontanka in St. Petersburg, ably assisted by uniformed police known as the Special Corps of Gendarmes who specialized in the surveillance of politicals in provincial towns. Ulyanov reveled in the daily game of cat and mouse with the Okhrana and was already familiar with the maze of back alleys and courtyards where he could give them the slip. Evasion and subterfuge along with codes and false names and passports would become, for the mature Lenin, the revolutionary art par excellence.

Within St. Petersburg revolutionary circles he disseminated his conspiratorial skills, learned from a close study of the methods of Narodnaya Volya. He was rapidly making his mark as the *starik*—the old man—as though his youth had long since been sucked out of him. Ulyanov was only young according to his identity papers, as his political associate Aleksandr Potresov observed. He had gone bald in his early twenties. Another colleague, Ivan Babushkin, remembered that "we used to say among ourselves that he had such big brains that they pushed his hair out." Potresov also noted Vladimir's ordinariness. He could have been "a typical merchant from any north Russian province—there was nothing of the 'radical' intellectual about him." With his neat, reddish beard and his drab clothes he looked like a man who could blend into the background. But the eyes always gave him away: they were quick and shrewd, and betrayed the speed of his thought. They also projected a certain craftiness of manner and, as time went on, a cruel glint. Coupled with an unnerving, laconic laugh, those mocking eyes would unsettle many political associates in later years.

———— ⸙ ————

In May 1895 Vladimir Ulyanov made the first of many trips abroad, ostensibly for educational reasons but in reality to broaden his knowledge and understanding of socialist thinking in Europe. The Okhrana was not fooled and duly passed on details of his departure to Petr Rachkovsky, head of the organization's Paris Department, charged with the surveillance of Russian political exiles in Europe:

According to information available to the Police Department, the above-mentioned Ulyanov occupies himself with Social Democratic propaganda among Petersburg workers. The objective of his trip is to find ways of bringing into the empire revolutionary literature as well as to establish contact between revolutionary circles and emigrants living abroad.

In Switzerland, Vladimir's primary objective was to visit the father of Russian Marxism, émigré socialist Georgy Plekhanov, who had founded the Emancipation of Labor group there in 1883 to propound his own interpretation of Marxist industrial socialism. Unfortunately he was not at home when Vladimir arrived; but on holiday in the mountains at Les Diablerets above the Rhône Valley. Even now the necessity for subterfuge was paramount in his mind; Vladimir made his way to Les Diablerets on foot by a roundabout route across the Col des Mosses in order to evade any police who might be tailing him. His traveling companion and political colleague on that trip was Aleksandr Potresov, who noted Vladimir's awe for his political master. The sardonic and urbane Plekhanov, despite his sense of moral superiority, was duly taken with Vladimir as "one of the best of our Russian friends." Colleague and fellow exile Pavel Axelrod talked politics with Vladimir at his Alpine retreat in Adoltern and was impressed with the eager, unpretentious young political thinker from Kazan. Vladimir might be unprepossessing in appearance, but there was no doubt in Axelrod's mind about the power of his logic. Vladimir's writing, he remarked to Plekhanov afterward, "had the temperament of a fighting flame." As Russian émigrés of long standing, they both had lost touch with the kind of visceral energy that Ulyanov, the young revolutionary fresh from Russia, exuded.

During this trip Vladimir's health broke down—the first of numerous physical collapses provoked by the relentless pace of his work, his failure to eat properly, and a propensity for bouts of stress-induced insomnia and depression. He suffered from a chronic but ill-defined "nervous stomach"— probably an ulcer—and sought a rest cure for it at a spa in Switzerland. His mother, who was already subsidizing his trip out of her private income, obligingly sent more money from Russia. In Berlin, where Plekhanov had directed him to call on the German social democrat Karl Liebknecht, Vladimir found time for therapeutic bathing in the River Spree. He enjoyed the pleasures of the Tiergarten and went to the theater, while applying himself to political study at the city's Royal Library. In Paris he made a special point of meeting Karl Marx's son-in-law, the socialist journalist Paul Lafargue.

During five months of continuous travel from Switzerland to France and Germany, Vladimir, like other seasoned activists going in and out of Russia, filled the false bottom of his specially made suitcase with illicit political literature that he took back with him. Within weeks of his return, fired with enthusiasm by his European trip, he met up with another idealistic young socialist new to the city, Yuli Martov, a twenty-two-year-old Jew from the middle classes. Together they formed the League of Struggle for the Emancipation of the Working Class, for which Ulyanov began writing illegal propaganda literature.

On December 9 Vladimir's luck ran out. The Okhrana, whose agents had been tailing him for months, finally pounced and arrested him. A short time later, Yuli Martov and other members of the league were also seized. Vladimir took the inevitability of his arrest and imprisonment with calm and equanimity. An arrest was an important rite of passage for any political activist, and Vladimir's lent credibility to his meteoric rise through the ranks of revolutionaries.

Vladimir kept his sanity during incarceration by sticking to a strict routine. Soon he was having messages smuggled out of the house of detention on Shpalernaya Street, using milk as invisible ink kept in inkwells made of bread that could be hastily consumed if the wardens came too close (on one day alone he had to eat six ink pots). Fourteen months of solitary confinement might have been arduous for the average prisoner, but they did not dent Vladimir's sense of purpose or his now entrenched political objectives. If anything, prison allowed him precious time to consolidate his ideas. Life in cell 193 was almost congenial. He was allowed to receive the books he needed, delivered on Wednesdays and Saturdays. So much material arrived that the familiar scraping sound of wardens dragging heavy cases along the corridors meant one thing to the other prisoners: yet more books being delivered to prisoner Ulyanov. Many arrived with secret encryptions, minute dots placed inside letters on the page creating a coded message, or inscriptions in milk that became readable when exposed to a candle flame or dipped in hot tea. Vladimir also learned the prison wall tapping codes, which he used to play games of chess with prisoners in neighboring cells.

More importantly, he now had time on his hands to make considerable headway with his first significant political work—*The Development of Capitalism in Russia*—while turning out articles for the Marxist journal *Novoe Slovo* (New Word) and drafting the program of what would eventually become the Russian Social Democratic Labor Party. He read and wrote feverishly to make full use of his time in jail, barely noticing the prison walls that surrounded him.

Throughout his life, so long as he had books, quiet, and a table to work at, he could function anywhere. His family provided additional food parcels and mineral water for his delicate stomach and even the luxury of pillow cases and towels. Petr Struve, a leading editor of Marxist journals whom he had met in St. Petersburg in 1893, sent books and magazines and procured writing commissions for him. But he also did exercises every day to prevent his joints from stiffening. His advice was passed on to fellow politicals: they should perform fifty "prostrations" a day (touching toes) in their cells. Daily gymnastics and a vigorous rubdown with a wet towel (as advocated by his Jewish grandfather) kept his mind and body sharp. When his cell was icy cold in winter, he moved about vigorously to warm his body so that he could sleep. But even in his sleep the words crowded in on him and he told his sister Anna that he dreamed whole chapters of the book in progress.

In February 1897, after two months in the house of detention, Vladimir Ulyanov was summarily exiled by administrative order from St. Petersburg. Unlike many political exiles before him, he was not subjected to a long forced march to Siberia in chains. As the son of a civil servant promoted to the nobility, he was allowed to arrange his own passage into exile at his own expense. He was even given the luxury of time to arrange what he needed to take with him and to say good-bye to family and friends. He would not be penniless, either, since the government provided eight rubles a month to political prisoners toward their board and lodging.

To get to his place of exile he had to take the Trans-Siberian Railway at an interminable crawl—the farther east it went the slower it got. The thought of exile per se did not trouble him. But he was a man in a constant hurry and the "devilish slowness" of the journey irritated Vladimir, as did the "monotonous, bare and desolate steppe" that passed by his window. Day after day of snow and sky—nothing more. The whole journey proved more uncomfortable and expensive than he had bargained for.

Once he arrived at the provincial capital, Krasnoyarsk on the River Yenisey, Vladimir spent several weeks waiting for the spring weather to melt the ice on the river so that he could carry on by paddle steamer downriver to his place of exile. Although the temperature was 20 degrees below zero, Vladimir knew that the air here was "softer" than in other parts of Siberia. When he was initially ordered to the harsher climate of Irkutsk, he put in an application to be allowed to remain in Krasnoyarsk. His mother petitioned on his behalf too, stating that her son's weak health would not endure the harsher conditions farther east. The request was granted, but it was not until April 24 that Vladimir learned that home for the next three years was to be the village of Shushenskoe.

Vladimir made good use of the time in Krasnoyarsk, as he would do in whatever town, city, or village he would himself visit over the next twenty years. He had been lucky to obtain comfortable lodgings where he was well fed and filled his days with vigorous walks, reading, and study. He knew that on the outskirts of Krasnoyarsk, merchant and bibliophile Gennady Yudin had amassed an extraordinary library of some 80,000 books and periodicals. Armed with a letter of referral, Vladimir had received a "hearty welcome" from Yudin, who allowed him free range of his collection in which he could access the economic data and statistics he needed for his work on *The Development of Capitalism in Russia*. But one library was not enough to satisfy his insatiable appetite for material; back in St. Petersburg his sister Anna was enlisted to seek out books at the Rumyantsev library and send them to him on long loan.

Books alone, however, could not hold at bay the excruciating boredom of life in Krasnoyarsk. He became miserable when letters from home did not arrive and urged his family not to wait for replies from him before writing again. His life took on a monotonous turn of familiarity. "There is nothing new I can write about myself; my life goes on as usual. I stroll to the library outside town, I stroll in the neighborhood, I stroll round to my acquaintances and sleep enough for two—in short, everything is as it should be." The town library provided access to newspapers and journals too, but it frustrated Vladimir that these items took eleven days to arrive.

Always anxious to be on top of the current political situation, he couldn't get used to such old "news."

Leaving Krasnoyarsk at the end of April, he took his time traveling the 280 miles south by horse cart and then paddle steamer down the Yenisey. Beyond Minusinsk he had to travel the final thirty-six miles to Shushenskoe by horse cart. He enjoyed the scenery along the way, particularly the spectacular vistas (some of which reminded him of the view of Mont Blanc from Geneva, Switzerland, which he had seen in 1895), sleeping soundly and breathing in the good air. When he finally arrived he was not disappointed; he knew he was better off than the rest of his arrested comrades:

> Shu-shu-shu is not a bad village. It is true it is in a rather bare locality, but not far away (one and a half to two versts) there is a forest, although much of it has been felled. There is no road to the Yenisey but the River Shush flows right past the village and there is a fairly big tributary of the Yenisey not far away (one or one and a half versts), where you can bathe. The Sayan Mountains or spurs from them are visible on the horizon; some of them are quite white, the snow on them probably never melts.

With the rigor that would characterize his entire career, Vladimir ensured that he did not succumb to the melancholy and lethargy that consumed so many exiles. He planned each day down to the final minute as he had done in prison, allotting set amounts of time for work, rest, and recreation. At this remote spot, populated by a few hardy peasants and a gaggle of geese, ducks, and pigs rooting in muddy puddles, he hunkered down through the howling winds of autumn and the frigid subzero days of winter, grateful for the comfort of his father's heavy bearskin coat. He remained mentally vigorous, engaging nonstop in a voluminous correspondence with activists in St. Petersburg, Moscow, and underground cells across Russia. His network of contacts stretched from Astrakhan to Yakutsk and beyond Russia to the major Russian colonies of exiles abroad in Switzerland. But he also drove himself to distraction wondering where associates were, why they had not been in touch, and what they were getting up to. When letters finally arrived "from every corner of Russia and Siberia," Vladimir experienced a "holiday mood" all day. He was also allowed access to newspapers and journals, which he read voraciously when they arrived in batches, ensuring before he started that they were systematically arranged in date order.

Vladimir also wrote frequent letters home to his mother and sisters requesting a succession of creature comforts: warm socks, a mackintosh cape for hunting. He needed his kid gloves too and his favorite straw hat as protection from mosquitoes during the brief but insect-ridden summer in this boggy region (though a fellow exile told him that the Siberian mosquito would even bite through gloves). He made a point of requesting a certain kind of Harmuth pencil and squared paper, sealing wax, scissors (he had been struggling to make do with the landlord's sheep shears). He needed a pen wiper too, since he had gotten into the bad habit of wiping his pen on his jacket lapel.

Continuing his work and study at a distance from libraries and borrowing books on a six-week turnaround—thanks to the good offices of Anna and Mariya—frustrated Vladimir. It took up to thirty-five days for a letter to reach Moscow or St. Petersburg and a reply to be sent. The delays over receipt of books were a source of endless frustration, and he was particularly irritated when books eventually arrived but proved useless. But he never let up on his demands: books on politics, economics, industrial history, agriculture, statistics, public commissions, and government reports. Book catalogs and "literary manifestations" of every kind were his lifeblood, ensuring that he could keep in touch with all the new writing at home and abroad. Such was his hunger that he told his sister Anna to accept them in exchange for payment for his journal articles and translation work. Otherwise he asked for nothing and only solicited money when his meager income from writing and translating ran out, in order to keep body and soul alive. His letters reveal little about his inner feelings, except to reiterate that life was monotonous and uneventful: "Inwardly day differs from day only because today you are reading one book, tomorrow you will read another; today you take a walk to the right of the village, tomorrow to the left; today you write one article, tomorrow another."

There were, however, opportunities to associate with a dozen or so fellow exiles scattered across a fifty-five-mile radius. He was able to stay in touch with fellow activists from the League of Struggle for the Liberation of the Working Class—Gleb Krzhizhanovsky, Vasily Starkov, and Panteleimon Lepeshinsky—who had also been rounded up and sent into exile at Minusinsk. Krzhizhanovsky was suffering from bouts of melancholy, but Vladimir was worried too about the arduous conditions endured by their other colleague, Yuli Martov, now suffering from tuberculosis in Turukhansk, nine hundred miles to the far north.

When Vladimir managed to tear himself from his books, he found many bucolic pleasures at Shushenskoe: time in the forest, on the river, and in the fields. By the end of September 1897 everybody was telling him how well he looked, how much weight he had put on. His healthy suntan made him look "like a real Siberian." "That is what shooting and village life do for you! All the Petersburg ailments have been shaken off!" he told his mother.

Believing in the need for a well-honed physique, he took to skating again that winter with great aplomb. Gleb Krzhizhanovsky showed him a number of tricks and Vladimir practiced them "with such industry that once I hurt my hand and could not write for two days." He was glad that his "old skill has not been forgotten." He found skating far better than shooting, "when you flounder up to your knees in snow, spoil your gun and rarely see any game!" But he had been keen enough to write asking his brother Dmitri to acquire a gun for him and had no difficulty gaining permits to go on expeditions with other exiles and local peasants to shoot duck and great snipe. Wild goats, sable, bear, deer, and squirrels abounded in the taiga and the mountains around. Hunting was a practical as well as a recreational choice: "Shooting is the only form of amusement here, and some sort of 'loosening up exercise' is necessary because of my sedentary life," as he told his mother, who worried about her son's skill with a gun. Vladimir was never much of a huntsman, but there were so many hares around the little islands on the Yenisey that even he got sick of shooting them. Black grouse, partridge, and gray hen were more of a challenge. But for that he needed a good dog. He borrowed his landlord's while trying to train a local mongrel puppy as a gun dog. But it let him down badly, and eventually he obtained a Gordon setter, Zhenka.

When that first winter in Siberia came, Vladimir sealed up the windows, stoked up the stove, and hunkered down with his books, pleased that he had enough to keep him going as he sat at his high desk through the long, dark days. "I am in no hurry for books," he told his mother at Christmas. "I now have so many that I cannot manage them all, let alone more." Vladimir knew that without work, a man could "go under" in exile. Troubling stories filtered through to him of quarrelling and backbiting among comrades elsewhere in the region. The stress of exile provoked despair, poor health, madness, and even suicide (including that of his close friend Fedoseev in the following year, 1898).

On Sundays he offered free legal advice to local peasants, but the bulk of his time was devoted to completing *The Development of Capitalism in Russia*. This forty-page economic treatise would be the first pioneering work on Marxism that preached a socialist revolution to come in Russia, preceded by a capitalist stage of development. It was published in a print run of twelve hundred copies, thanks to the good offices of Petr Struve in St. Petersburg in April 1899, under the pseudonym Vladimir Ilyin. But Vladimir was never satisfied and always worried that control over the final publication was out of his hands. He was obsessive about misprints and the quality of the proofreading of his work and whether the final article would measure up to his own meticulous standards. Distortions of his very specific meaning and trifling issues over semantics troubled him greatly, as did endless problems over late payments.

⸺⸺

THE COLD WESTERLY WIND that howled across from the Yenisey, so strong it blew down pine and birch trees, persisted well into May 1898, as did the heavy spring rains. The last vestiges of the cold had finally begun their slow and reluctant retreat when Nadezhda Krupskaya arrived in Shushenskoe by steamer from Sorokino, the boat making slow headway against the high floodwaters of spring. She had come to share Vladimir's exile but was sick and ailing, loaded down like a packhorse with the books he had instructed her to bring. And she had brought her mother, Elizaveta Vasil'evna, too. But when they knocked on the door of the house where Vladimir lodged, Nadya found that he was out hunting.

Nadya had been arrested in August 1896 for belonging to an illegal political group. When Vladimir had requested that she be allowed to join him at Shushenskoe from her place of exile at Ufa, the Russian authorities had agreed only on condition the couple marry immediately; otherwise she would be sent back. Vladimir had petitioned the district police superintendent for the requisite documents, but the wheels of the czarist bureaucracy ground slow in Siberia. The two were finally married on July 10 in Shusha's tiny Orthodox church, making do with two rings fashioned from a five-kopeck piece by a fellow exile. Neither partner ever alluded to this being a love match; it was, rather, a collaboration between politically like-minded comrades that grew into love, respect, and mutual dependency as time went on.

The threesome of Volodya, Nadya, and Elizaveta Vasil'evna Krupskaya got on well enough. Nadya struggled with limited cooking and domestic skills. She planted vegetables in the kitchen garden that were bottled and pickled for the long winter months and dragged Volodya out mushroom picking. They were joined by a scraggy little servant girl, Pasha, whom Nadya taught to read and write, and then a kitten. Elizaveta, despite annoying Volodya with her imperious manner and arguing with him about religion, rapidly proved her usefulness as cook, bottle washer, and copyist, and became an almost permanent fixture during the couple's exile in Europe.

Nadya's first task as wife and helpmate was to assist her husband in preparing the final text of *Development of Capitalism in Russia*, as well as a Russian translation of Beatrice and Sidney Webb's substantial tome *The Theory and Practice of Trade Unionism*. They struggled with English geographic and proper names and resorted to the German version (a language they knew better) as invaluable backup. It was an arduous task, requiring them to copy out a thousand pages of translation between them before it could be sent off to the printers. As literary amanuensis, Nadya was following in the tradition of other literary wives, such as Tolstoy's, who also made a lifetime's work of copying out her husband's manuscripts.

Volodya was extremely glad for Nadya's companionship and even his mother-in-law's, and glad to be well away from the "exile scandals" of other colonies in Siberia. But money was always short; when they weren't borrowing it from either of their mothers, they were begging for loans and advances on their publishing work. When books arrived,

Vladimir and Nadya consumed them eagerly. One such in September 1899 was the latest economic thinking of German Marxist writer Eduard Bernstein, who had recently attempted to revise Marxism in a tome entitled *Die Voraussetzungen des Sozialismus und die Aufgaben der Sozialdemokratie*—hardly the stuff of normal recreational reading, but the Ulyanovs weren't like ordinary people. After carefully scrutinizing Bernstein's book, they dismissed it as "unbelievably weak" and "opportunistic."

———

VOLODYA AND NADYA spent Christmas 1898 and Easter 1899 among comrades, skating, playing chess, singing (which Volodya enjoyed with great gusto, drumming out the rhythm with his foot), arguing, and drinking mulled wine by the stove. When his term of exile was up, he left Shushenskoe with few possessions, having accumulated only a gun for shooting, a pair of ice skates, and a very heavy load of books. Five hundred pounds of them were dispatched home from Siberia. As the horses carrying himself, Nadya, and Elizaveta Vasil'evna made their way along the frozen Yenisey north toward Krasnoyarsk, Vladimir Ilyich Ulyanov breathed in the invigorating Siberian winter air for the last time. Three years of enforced isolation at Shushenskoe had produced thirty works of political theory and had clarified and consolidated his political thinking. As he boarded the train at Krasnoyarsk, he could not know that, unlike many of his less fortunate associates in the Russian revolutionary movement, he would not be coming back to Siberia.

He had by now a head full of ideas and political ambitions and was intent on one consuming objective: establishing an underground newspaper as a rallying point for the disparate and poorly organized elements of the revolutionary movement in Russia. He would also set out to combat all forms of political "deviation" and set a clear party line on tactics and objectives, namely, his own.

CHAPTER TWO

Igniting the Spark

MUNICH: 1900–1901

———— ⌘ ————

O N FEBRUARY 18, 1900, Volodya and Nadya, with her mother in tow, arrived in the town of Ufa in western Siberia, still hundreds of miles from Moscow and St. Petersburg. It was as far as Nadya was allowed to travel under the terms of her exile, which still had a year to run. For Volodya, however, Ufa was too far from the center of things. He was too restless to sit out the months with her, even though her health was poor and she needed his moral support. However, as a political comrade first and foremost, she recognized that Volodya had important things to do.

His fellow exiles Yuli Martov and Aleksandr Potresov, now also on their way out of Siberia, fully supported his plans for a newspaper, and the influential Petr Struve had arranged the publication of some of Volodya's articles while he had been in exile. In return for his support Struve was guaranteed a voice in the paper. But how could Volodya launch a major newspaper when the terms of his release banned him from Moscow and St. Petersburg and all major Russian cities? St. Petersburg had long been the Mecca for revolutionaries, "the laboratory of ideas, the centre of life, movement, and activity," as the revolutionary Vera Zasulich described it. And so, like other committed revolutionaries, he ignored the ban and made his way illegally to Moscow at the end of February. He took time to visit his mother and sister Anna before traveling to St. Petersburg to meet Vera Zasulich, who had come to Russia undercover from exile in Switzerland specially to meet him. Together they discussed plans for the newspaper, particularly the urgent need for funding. Soon afterward, Ulyanov was obliged to leave or risk arrest.

He settled in Pskov, near the border with modern-day Estonia, and then appealed to the authorities to allow Nadya to complete her term of exile there. But he was refused. Languishing alone in lodgings on Arkhangel-skaya Ulitsa, he went for long walks, eked out fifty kopeks a time for basic German lessons, and headed for the nearest library. But he couldn't concentrate and did little but sit and read the newspapers and send his mother postcards reassuring her that he was in good health; in fact he was plagued by colds, insomnia, and weight loss. Actually Nadya was the sick one, suffering from some kind of gynecological problem, and urgently needed money for medical treatment. He sent what little he could. In May the authorities refused permission for Volodya to go to Ufa to visit her, but relented and allowed him to visit for six weeks at the end of June. He took advantage of the trip, sharing it with his mother and Anna, and enjoyed a memorable cruise down his beloved River Volga.

The Okhrana was watching Ulyanov's every step, but the underground had become his natural habitat and he was hungry for real revolutionary experience. His friend from exile, Panteleimon Lepeshinsky, remembered him during those days in Pskov as being perpetually driven, racing to "gather together the bricks for the great edifice" that he was in the process of constructing. The Okhrana could not prevent him from ducking surveillance agents to secure secret meetings with Martov and Potresov in April about raising funds to cover the costs of printing their newspaper, to be called *Iskra* (The Spark). An estimated 30,000 rubles would be needed to get the paper under way. Struve came to Pskov to consult with Ulyanov and supplied some funding, but the bulk of it came from a rich philanthropist and bookseller, Aleksandra Kalmykova, code-named "Auntie" among revolutionists. Kalmykova's grand apartment on St. Petersburg's Liteinaya Ulitsa had become a safe haven for their meetings. Ulyanov drafted a declaration of the paper's putative editorial board and then he and Martov made another trip to St. Petersburg in early June with a suitcase full of illegal literature.

They had no sooner offloaded it than they were picked up by the police, interrogated, and imprisoned for ten days. They were released after Ulyanov's mother once more fell on her knees before the authorities on his behalf. Also, the two men were more valuable to the police when they were free, since their links to other revolutionaries could be watched and tracked. Ulyanov and Martov got out of jail with the two thousand rubles they had been carrying (a recent donation from Kalmykova that Ulyanov managed to persuade the police was payment for his publishing work) and a list of European contacts and addresses in invisible ink. Ulyanov's arrest once again underlined the impossibility of running an underground newspaper in Russia. It would put far too many people at risk of discovery and arrest. Police surveillance was just too close, and sooner or later they would all land back in Siberia.

After further talks with Marxist circles in Samara and Smolensk, Ulyanov resolved to establish his newspaper abroad. He sent Potresov on ahead to Switzerland for talks with Plekhanov and Axelrod. As the founding fathers of Russian Marxism, they had long been revered from afar and would play an important role in the paper. Surprisingly, the authorities responded with a six-month passport when Ulyanov requested to leave the country on the pretext of seeking medical treatment for his stomach problems and furthering his studies. Simultaneously the Okhrana stepped up its surveillance of Ulyanov and Martov, though the police had not yet discovered the planned launch of the journal. Nevertheless, trailing Ulyanov across the revolutionary enclaves of Europe was worth more to the police than keeping him penned up in a provincial town. After seeing his mother and Anna one last time in late July, he boarded a train at Smolensk that would take him out of Russia. He would not see his homeland again for five years.

THE HEARTLAND of the Pale of Settlement—the western borderlands of the Russian empire where Russia's Jewish population was confined—passed by Ulyanov's third-class carriage window as he endured the hard wooden seats all the way past Minsk and Warsaw to Vienna, capital of Austria-Hungary. There he boarded a connecting train to Geneva. By paying a supplement, Ulyanov could travel on the express train, but even that only attained a speed of 35 to 40 miles per hour. This exhausting, thousand-mile trip was the first of a succession of long rail journeys crisscrossing Europe that he would make over the next seventeen years.

When he arrived in Vienna in August 1900, he had to face a summit meeting with Plekhanov at Bellerive outside Geneva. He needed the support of Plekhanov and Axelrod and their Emancipation of Labor group to get the newspaper off the ground, but there were clear divergences in objectives and tactics. The two older men, along with Vera Zasulich, saw the newspaper primarily as a vehicle for the discussion and promotion of Plekhanov's theoretical views on Marxism, while Ulyanov, Martov, and Potresov saw it as nothing less than an instrument of revolution.

The gathering may have agreed amicably on a name for their newspaper—*Iskra* (The Spark)—but otherwise the meeting was characterized by suspicion and distrust, temper tantrums, and Plekhanov's implacable opposition to conciliatory moves toward factional groups within the movement. Intractable and arrogant, he condemned Ulyanov's draft declaration and what he saw as its plodding, unimaginative style. With his inflated sense of superiority, he also resisted the suggestion that *Iskra* be produced three hundred miles away in Munich, with Ulyanov and Potresov as chief editors. After twenty years in exile, as Nadezhda Krupskaya later averred, he had "lost all capacity for directly sensing Russia." He did not want the life of a conspirator in Munich; his residence in Switzerland was legal and reasonably comfortable. He insisted on keeping control of the operation in Geneva and became increasingly dictatorial, throwing up objections to involving Petr Struve's group of legal Marxists (who published only in legal, as opposed to underground, publications) or allowing freedom of expression to detractors of his "orthodox Marxist" message. He also demanded a larger say over fellow editors Axelrod, Zasulich, Ulyanov, Potresov, and Martov.

Soon Plekhanov resigned in a fit of pique. Ulyanov and Potresov followed suit in retaliation, until the ever-pragmatic Ulyanov realized that capitulating to Plekhanov's vanity by giving him two votes on the editorial board was the only viable tactic. For the time being Plekhanov had won the argument, remaining the figurehead of the new publication, but Ulyanov was determined he wasn't going to win the war. After he and Potresov had taken the steamer back down Lake Geneva to their lodgings at Vésenaz, their pent-up feelings got the better of them. "The charged atmosphere burst into a storm. Up and down our little village we paced far into the night; it was quite dark, there was a rumbling of thunder, and constant flashes of lightning rent the air. We walked along, bursting with indignation," Ulyanov wrote.

As for his erstwhile political hero, "Never, never in my life had I regarded any other man with such sincere respect and veneration, never had I stood before any man so 'humbly' and never before had I been so brutally 'kicked.'" As a result, Lenin's "infatuation" with Plekhanov disappeared "as if by magic." A week later he unleashed his rage in a scribbled account of the dispute entitled "How the 'Spark' Was Nearly Extinguished." It remains one of the most emotionally revealing and fluent of his voluminous and often ponderous writings. Historically, it is hugely ironic. In railing against Plekhanov for sweeping him aside unceremoniously and condemning him for trampling his fellow comrades underfoot, Ulyanov derided the kind of ruthless tactics that would soon become the hallmark of his own growing domination over the party. But Ulyanov had learned an important lesson. From here on he would exorcise all personal feeling in his political dealings and trust nobody. One had to "keep a stone in one's sling."

Meanwhile Ulyanov was fighting other pressing theoretical battles with a new faction—the so-called economists led by the respected German socialist Eduard Bernstein. His ideas were echoed in Russia by Ekaterina Kuskova in *Credo*. Bernstein disagreed with Marx's basic tenet that the collapse of capitalism was inevitable and argued that reform could only come about within the existing system. Peaceful political change in Russia could come through parliamentary politics and unionization of the workers in a campaign for social reform, economic freedom, and better pay and working conditions. The idea of accommodating capitalism enraged Ulyanov, as did Kuskova's call for strikes against starvation wages rather than insurrection. In his eyes these arguments were reactionary; they subverted his insistence on relentless class war leading to the violent overthrow of the czarist order. From exile in Siberia he had already issued a written salvo against the economists, fearing that their revisionism would split the Russian social democratic movement. Political heresy such as this sent his stress levels rocketing and provoked a recurrence of his stomach problem. In a long letter to Nadya in August he vented his spleen on the economists at length. He did not inquire about her health or her life in Ufa, nor did he express regret for his own solitary life without her. Politics unfailingly took precedence over intimacy.

After a few lonely weeks in and around Geneva, Ulyanov left Switzerland with Potresov, telling his mother in code (in case the police intercepted his letter) that he was going for a "trip down the Rhine." In fact he was headed for Nuremberg to meet with a leading German social democrat and newspaperman, Adolf Braun, to discuss the technicalities of typesetting and printing *Iskra*. On September 6 he got on the train again, this time for Munich (heading for "Paris," as his mother was told when instructed to send letters via a contact in Prague) to search for an editorial base and a sympathetic printer for his newspaper.

⸺ ∞ ⸺

DURING THE YEARS of reaction after the assassination of Czar Alexander II in 1881, many revolutionaries had decided to carry on their activities from outside Russia. Twenty or so European cities, including Zurich, Geneva, London, Paris, and Berlin, now formed the Russian revolutionary diaspora. None of this deterred the Okhrana, which matched this emigration of politicals out of Russia by setting up its own foreign agency with offices in Paris and the Balkans. At a newly opened office in Berlin approved by the German government, detectives kept the Russians under close surveillance. The police in Munich were waiting for Ulyanov when he arrived. Circular 2104 had already been issued by the Okhrana to look for "a man of medium height, reddish hair, eyebrows and beard, roundish head, high forehead, normal nose, round face, medium-sized mouth." He was, it alleged, a "serious and energetic person" intent on subversive activities.

Since the eighteenth century, German university cities of the European enlightenment such as Heidelberg, Cologne, and Göttingen had offered refuge to Russian political and religious dissidents; by 1900 there were 47,000 Russians living in Germany. The writings of the great German thinkers such as Kant, Fichte, Schelling, Hegel, and more recently Marx had long influenced the development of radical thought in Russia. The active and vocal movement for social democracy that arose in turn of the century Germany encouraged Ulyanov and his associates to launch their first venture there. Munich was well placed on the European rail network for easy access to Zurich, Vienna, Paris, Berlin, and London. Many Russian students had enrolled in Munich's university and polytechnic, seeking the freer educational facilities there, and openly associated with German social democrats. Ulyanov's German colleagues had facilities at their disposal such as illegal printing presses, reading rooms, and meeting halls, and offered advice on smuggling literature through Europe and into Russia.

Ulyanov found lodging in the house of a social democratic sympathizer and beer seller Georg Rittmeyer on the corner of Romerstrasse and Kaiserstrasse in the city's Bohemian quarter, Schwabing. Filled with an assortment of tenants from carpenters to bricklayers and their children, it was hardly an oasis of calm, but here at least he was truly among the workers.

At that time Schwabing was a picturesque suburb of Munich located north of the old medieval city center on either side of the grand, poplar-lined boulevards, Ludwigstrasse and Leopoldstrasse. By the 1900s it had assumed a character akin to that of Paris's Latin Quarter or New York's Greenwich Village. In Schwabing Ulyanov was in the heart of Mitteleuropa, surrounded by a community of leading German and European intellectuals, writers, and artists, many of them gravitating to the area's celebrated café culture at the Café Luitpold or the Café Simplicissimus, the latter home to a leading satirical journal by the same name. The *Jugendstil* art movement (a German form of art nouveau) was founded here; in time, Schwabing offered sanctuary "for the dispossessed and the culturally restless, providing a forgiving and inexpensive environment for radical experiments in art, politics and sexual protocols." Writer Thomas Mann, playwright Frank Wedekind, poet Rainer Maria Rilke, Swiss abstract painter Paul Klee and his Russian counterpart, Wassily Kandinsky, were all embraced in the community. "Anyone who painted behind the thousand atelier windows in Schwabing, who kneaded clay, wrote poetry in the garrets, sang or wrote music, amassed debts at little inns, and proclaimed Nihilism or Aestheticism in the cafés" was welcomed. "The only prerequisite was that the artist had to appear un-bourgeois in both clothing and behaviour," as writer Dirk Heisserer observed.

Vera Zasulich had arrived in Munich from Geneva at around the same time as Ulyanov. She was a woman of considerable revolutionary stature, despite her modest and retiring manner. In 1878 she had shot and wounded General Fedor Trepov, the savage governor of St. Petersburg, in revenge for ordering the flogging of a political prisoner. After a sensational trial and acquittal she fled to Switzerland in order to avoid rearrest. Here she endured lonely years of exile and became greatly attached to

Georgy Plekhanov. Like him, she never stopped yearning for Russia. Under the code name "Elder Sister" she transferred to Munich to help run *Iskra* in a triumvirate with Ulyanov and Martov, but she worried terribly about the growing rift between Ulyanov and Plekhanov. She took an apartment on Schraudolfstrasse that she shared with Potresov and later Martov, which was also used as *Iskra*'s base. Editorial meetings were sometimes held in the Café Norris on Leopoldstrasse, especially when Axelrod and Plekhanov visited from Switzerland.

Although famous as a political assassin of the legendary Narodnaya Volya school, Zasulich shunned public attention. Her private life was shambolic. She had no family and she lived for her revolutionary ideals, her large gray eyes expressive of her undying hope for the coming socialist apocalypse. She cared nothing for herself and her appearance and dressed shabbily, like an old-style nihilist; she chain-smoked and didn't eat properly. By 1900 she was fifty-three, overweight, and disheveled. Reserved, cautious, and introspective, she suffered from depression, often locking herself away for days on end to work and existing on cups of black coffee. Ulyanov held her in great affection despite her idiosyncrasies, a comrade he respected as being "true to the core."

Meetings in Munich were also held at the apartment of a local Russian émigré and radical journalist, Aleksandr Helphand (who wrote under the pseudonym Parvus), on Ungererstrasse. Helphand ran an illegal printing press in his flat. Esteemed by Russian and Polish students in the city, he brought Ulyanov into touch with the wider German movement for social democracy beyond the Russian colony. With Helphand's assistance the first issue of *Iskra* and a subsidiary bimonthly journal *Zarya* (The Dawn) were prepared for publication with advice on the logistics of printing and storage from local German social democrats.

Security was always uppermost in Ulyanov's mind. Whether *Iskra* survived depended on communicating with Plekhanov in Geneva and Axelrod in Zurich on editorial matters and getting information and material for editorials from Russia. To avoid interception, letters to and from Ulyanov in Munich went to safe addresses in Berlin, Hamburg, Königsberg, and Stuttgart and were often diverted yet again through Paris and Prague before reaching Russia. Letters in—from revolutionary circles in key cities such as Kiev, Petersburg, Moscow, Poltava, Samara, and Tula—

were directed to a friend of Helphand's, Dr. Carl Lehmann, who ran his medical practice at 46 Gabelsbergerstrasse in Munich.

In the first half of December Ulyanov went to Stuttgart to prepare *Zarya,* then traveled 270 miles north to Leipzig, where the first issue of *Iskra,* most of it written by him, was typeset on December 11 and printed on Christmas Eve by a Polish typographer, Joseph Blumenfeld. In it, Ulyanov gave pole position to his own article "The Urgent Tasks of Our Movement." In a swipe at the economists, he argued that the economic struggle in Russia was inseparable from the wider political one. Several thousand copies of *Iskra,* printed in a cramped typeface on four pages of onionskin paper, were sent to addresses in Switzerland and Belgium. Echoing the sentiments of the poet Prince Aleksandr Odoevsky in response to the failed Decembrist uprising of 1825, who wrote that "our sorrowful task will not be for nothing; the spark will kindle a flame," the paper's title predicted the creation of a new party. As the precious copies were being sent to Russia, the year 1901 began in fervent hopes that flames of change would spring from this small political spark, igniting revolution in Russia.

CHRISTMAS 1900 had been lonely and purposeless for Ulyanov. He was, he told his mother (pretending to be writing from Prague), "wandering aimlessly in a strange land and still only 'hoping' to put an end to the fuss and bother and settle down to work." In dreary, rain-drenched Munich he missed the great snowy wastes of Siberia. The cold here was different:

> Actually there is no winter at all, it is like a rotten autumn; everything wet and dripping. It is a good thing it is not cold and I can manage quite well without a winter overcoat, but somehow it's not very nice without snow. I am fed up with the slush and recall with pleasure the real Russian winter, the sleigh rides and the clean frosty air.

Nor could he enjoy ice skating as he had on the frozen Yenisey. Here the ice rink was artificial. Back in Russia his mother worried whether her

Volodya needed extra winter woollies sent to him. No, he reassured her. The winters here were positively mild in comparison to Russia. The Germans complained of terrible cold if the temperature was minus 10 or 15 and had no comprehension of how Russians managed to stay alive at minus 20 and 30.

Back in Ufa, where she had endured yet another subzero winter of the kind that Volodya now missed, Nadya had completed her term of exile. She and Volodya had remained in contact via coded messages sent inside books that were circulated to activists in Ufa. She had made the most of her time, translating and writing articles to support herself and maintaining important contacts with exiles passing through on their way back from Siberia. Volodya in the meantime had traveled to Vienna in March to arrange her passport with the Russian consul there, finding time to enjoy a city he found beautiful and lively, visit the Museum of Fine Arts, and see a Viennese operetta (he "did not like it very much," he told his mother).

Leaving her mother behind in Moscow, Nadya made her way across the frontier by train, "looking purposely like an innocent provincial going abroad for the first time" to avoid attracting police attention. She misguidedly set off for Prague on the assumption that the Herr Franz Modraczek she had been writing to at an address there was Volodya under a false name. But he did not meet her at the station and, alone and friendless, she took a cab to the tenement building in the working-class district from which Volodya's letters had been forwarded to her at Ufa, only to encounter the *real* Herr Modraczek. "Oh no," she was told, "you want Herr Rittmeyer and he lives in Munich." So, after sharing some Czech rissoles with Herr Modraczek and his sympathetic wife, Nadya wearily resorted to the invaluable *Henschel's Telegraph* of European train times that Volodya had recommended and boarded yet another train, for Munich, weighed down with baskets and her heavy Russian fur coat.

Once arrived, she left her luggage behind at the station and got on the tram to Kaiserstrasse to seek out "Herr Rittmeyer." The address turned out to be a beer cellar and when she confronted Rittmeyer, he was not Volodya but a burly German publican. "Ah, you want Herr *Meyer*," the publican's wife told Nadya and escorted her across a yard to a small room at the back containing only a minimum of furniture. At that point Nadya discovered that her husband had been going to the station several times a day in hopes she would be on a train. The book he had sent her concealing his real address in Munich had never been redirected to her.

Having overcome her annoyance at being sent on a wild goose chase, Nadya unpacked the English pen nibs she had been instructed to bring Volodya from Russia (the German ones were useless, he said) and took over the important day-to-day correspondence of the underground organization on his behalf, especially the key work of sending and receiving information in code. When her mother joined them a month later, Nadya was able to devote more time to her role as secretary to the board of *Iskra*, a post engineered for her by Volodya to ensure his close control over things.

To protect their work from Okhrana infiltration, Zasulich, Martov, Potresov, and the reunited Ulyanovs were living illegally in Munich on fake Bulgarian passports, as well as fake names. To their landlords Volodya and Nadya were Dr. and Mrs. Meyer, but they also went under a Bulgarian passport in the name of Jordan K. Jordanov, a doctor of law supposedly from Sofia (the real owner of the passport had died in Varna in 1890), and his wife Maritza.

Although Volodya was, after years of revolutionary training, highly self-sufficient—he was naturally tidy, kept his clothes neat, and could sew on a button—there is no doubt that Nadya's presence was hugely calming and reassuring for him. Until then he had been living on cups of tea from a tin mug and his landlady's dodgy food. He never cooked, though he knew where to find things in the pantry when he was hungry. Nadya's expertise in the kitchen was limited to egg concoctions, and she often burned things. Yet even she blanched at the slovenly habits of Vera Zasulich, who once cooked herself some meat and then "clipp[ed] off pieces to eat with a pair of scissors."

Volodya endured Nadya's attempts at home cooking with surprisingly good grace, having very simple needs. Certain foods aggravated his stomach problem anyway, and he had always been one of those who eat to live rather live to eat. Even in the Kremlin, he would often be happy with a late night snack of herring and black bread. When work overtook him, he often forgot to eat at all. During their exile, when money allowed, Nadya sometimes offloaded some of her domestic duties and paid her landladies to change the beds and wash their dishes. On other occasions, such as in Siberia and later in Finland and Galicia, she hired local girls to come in and cook for them. On the rare occasions when they had money to spare, the couple treated themselves to meals in cheap eating houses. Volodya enjoyed a glass of German beer but took no part in the *Bierkeller* culture of the city and never gave himself long to sit and relax and enjoy it. Under pressure from colleagues he occasionally frequented some of Munich's cafés, such as the Café Altschwabing on Schellingstrasse and the Osteria Italiana nearby.

For a month after Nadya's arrival the couple lived in lodgings farther west on Schleissheimerstrasse (where a couple of doors down in 1911 a certain Adolf Hitler came to live). Here they made do with a single room in a small apartment occupied by the Kaisers, a working-class family with six children, who crammed into the other room and the kitchen. Such close proximity didn't seem to bother Volodya. He liked mingling with poor workers more than he did with other revolutionaries, as Nadya later observed. The weather that April and May was cold, and Hans Kaiser noticed that his Russian tenants kept to their room. It turned out that they were too poor to buy a stove. Taking pity on them, Kaiser rigged up a special tube to circulate warm air from his own apartment below. He liked the Meyers, as he knew them; they were serious-minded, genuine people, forever huddled at their work tables. They were sociable too and clearly loved small children, taking an interest in the landlord's own. Only occasionally, however, did they venture out to the Zur Frankenburg snack bar across the road.

But Volodya was sick with influenza, and their accommodation was dreadfully small. Nadya would creep around trying not to clatter the dishes as she prepared meals, while her husband paced back and forth on tiptoe muttering as he gathered his thoughts. When asked in later life why Volodya walked in this way, Nadya asserted that he didn't want his foot-steps to disturb his train of thought. After a month they rented a small house on Siegfriedstrasse in the heart of Schwabing, furnishing it with the basic necessities bought secondhand. Quiet, modest, and homely, Nadya never complained about her enormous workload and put up with inter-minable late-night discussions around her kitchen table when Volodya had editorial meetings with Zasulich and Martov. In March 1901 the team was joined by Martov's sister Lidiya and her husband Fedor Dan.

Martov, the dreamy intellectual with the mournful face and the pince-nez, was Volodya's physical and polar opposite. An archetypal bohemian revolutionary, he was unmarried and was "by predilection a haunter of cafes, indifferent to comfort, perpetually arguing." He was an eccentric émigré *intelligent* of the restless, distracted kind later epitomized in Joseph Conrad's *Under Western Eyes* and *The Secret Agent*. When he joined the communal life in Munich, he took his turn at the washing up, as did Ulyanov, longing for the day when someone would design crockery that could be thrown away after use. Martov loved to stay up all night talking with fellow émigrés. On occasion, when Volodya threw in the towel after five or six hours of Martov's exhausting company and went to bed, the insomniac would take Zasulich off to continue their dialogue as they sat rolling their own cigarettes in all-night cafés. Ulyanov disapproved of talking in places like the Café Luitpold, where they might be overheard.

After much traveling back and forth across Europe, Ulyanov was eager to get down to his writing. Between May 1901 and February 1902 he worked hard on a major new essay, "What Is to Be Done?" He hated delegating. He wanted to see *everything* himself and be the first to do so, but that was clearly impractical. So Lidiya Dan helped Nadya with the daily task of sorting the mail once it had been picked up from Dr. Lehmann's flat. Nadya would iron letters written in invisible ink to reveal the words, which Lidiya then decoded. Ulyanov got very annoyed if the decoding was unclear, although the original writing was often obscure and difficult to read. But worse, and this was something Ulyanov considered virtually "a crime against revolutionary ethics," was when letter writers were slow to respond to instructions or inquiries from the *Iskra* board. He was soon insisting that each letter sent out should say on it in invisible ink "Please reply on day of receipt." And he was infuriated by the way Martov would snatch up the latest copies of newspapers from Russia. He already spent every evening sitting in the Café Luitpold reading them. Wasn't that enough?

There would always be conflicts in a group where one member was as disciplined as Ulyanov and the other as slovenly as Martov, and where one of the triumvirate—Zasulich—was devoted to Plekhanov. "She would have jumped off a cliff for him," observed Lidiya Dan. While Ulyanov could be a martinet, Lidiya found Nadya easy to get on with. She was neither intellectual nor beautiful, but her plainness was illuminated by her charm. She was warm and kind, "a very honest, good person." Ulyanov clearly held her in high regard but "she was entirely under his spell." Privately Ulyanov's mother-in-law, Elizaveta, complained to Lidiya about how stern and bad-tempered he could be. With time, Lidiya came to the conclusion that Nadya only ever saw things Volodya's way and slavishly deferred to him as always being right.

Throughout his life in exile Ulyanov opted to live in cities where foreigners were easily assimilated, while eschewing the disorderly, noisy lives of Russian exiles, fueled by idleness and too little to eat. He and Nadya did not engage with local life or make non-Russian friends. They relied on letters from home to dispel their loneliness. Work was their life and they stuck to the small extended family of illegals gathered around them in Munich—Zasulich (to whom Nadya became particularly attached), Martov, Potresov, and the Dans. As a group, they had a sense of mutual responsibility and their closeness would prove to be a golden time before major rifts in the party in 1903 destroyed that sense of unity forever.

Life settled into a familiar, reassuring pattern with Nadya around. She had the gift of being a good listener, of being unobtrusive when needed. If late nights and overwork wore Volodya out, she took him out of himself for long walks in Munich's famous Englischer Garten off Leopoldstrasse or along the more remote stretches of the River Isar. In summer they went swimming in the Ungererbad, the municipal pool. Before Nadya's arrival, Volodya had enjoyed watching the carnival procession in Munich; he had indulged his long-standing love of opera by going alone to the Bavarian Royal Opera to see a French opera, *La Juive* (The Jewess) by J. F. Halévy. After Nadya arrived they enjoyed the occasional trip to a concert or the *Volkstheater* when money allowed, but their lives remained pretty isolated, with few visitors. Nadya's mother, who had been sick on and off all summer, was bored and talked of returning to St. Petersburg. And what was this, they asked in a letter, about a new play from Anton Chekhov—*Three Sisters*? They had heard such wonderful reports of it at the Art Theater in Moscow. Yes, it was hard being so cut off from Mother Russia. "To get the most out of a foreign country," Nadya wrote, "you have to go there when you are young and are interested in every little thing."

By now Ulyanov's sense of frustration and isolation was matched by increasing disenchantment with Plekhanov and alienation from his former colleague Petr Struve, who visited him in Munich. Struve's liberal sentiments and advocacy of constitutional reform were clearly out of tune with radical Marxism. Ulyanov refused to see him on his second visit, abandoning him to Vera and Nadya. Struve was deeply wounded. The atmosphere, Nadya recalled, "was as tense as a scene from Dostoievsky." Struve came away convinced of his and Ulyanov's irreconcilability—morally, politically, and socially. Both Ulyanov and Plekhanov had been brusque, to the point of mockery, in their rejection of him, but he found something unnerving and "repulsively cold" in Ulyanov's behavior. Such coldness was "organic," a characteristic of Ulyanov's love of power and his dealing so contemptuously with people once he had fallen out with them. In Ulyanov's view Struve had betrayed orthodox Marxism with the "bourgeois apologetics" of his conciliatory legal Marxism. He was nothing but "a politico, an artful dodger, a huckster, and an impudent boor" and had tried to best him. Such crudely worded and violent character assassination became a hallmark of Ulyanov's writings as he struggled to impose his vision on a fractured movement. Soon after, Struve set up a rival journal, *Osvobozhdenie* (Liberation), and moved increasingly away from Marxism toward constitutional liberalism.

Life in Munich was stagnating and money was very tight until a check arrived from Ulyanov's publisher in Russia. *Iskra* was now being distributed on a regular basis, but the burden of masterminding it all was taking its toll on his health, as was the constant need to protect it from seizure by the German police. In collaboration with social democrats in Berlin, copies of *Iskra* were being sent to the warehouse of their own newspaper, before being taken in double-sided and double-bottomed trunks, or even in smaller numbers in specially lined jackets, by legal "Sunday travelers" into Russia via East Prussia, Upper Silesia, and Austrian Galicia. Once delivered to an agent on the Russian side, such as the Ulyanovs' good friends from Siberian exile, Panteleimon Lepeshinsky and his wife Ol'ga in Pskov, or Martov's brother, Sergey Tsederbaum, a first-rate organizer in Poltava, they were collected by others for distribution locally in the various cities. Issue 2 had already been printed at Helphand's flat in Schwabing before Ulyanov heard the bad news: three thousand copies of the first issue smuggled across the Russian frontier at Memel in East Prussia in January had been seized at Polangen. Another thousand copies did, however, find their way into safe hands in false-bottom trunks.

Once the second issue, printed in Munich, had evaded the Prussian police and arrived safely, the groundswell of demand for copies on a regular basis grew inside Russia. Starved of political literature and vehicles for expressing their discontent, people—particularly out in the Urals at Ekaterinburg and Perm—were writing to the *Iskra* office begging for more. *Iskra* had indeed ignited the voice of political protest in Russia. But in 1901–1902 there was enormous police surveillance and repression inside Russia in the wake of a new tide of opposition to the czarist state, with student and worker demonstrations in major cities, nationalist discontent in Poland and Finland, and professionals in local government protesting proposed restrictions of their reforming powers. Such events exhilarated Ulyanov with their promise of change, but he could not bear the lack of detailed information. "The devil knows what is happening in Russia," he wrote to Axelrod on March 20, 1901, "demonstrations in St. Petersburg, Moscow, Kharkov, Kazan; martial law in Moscow (by the way, they arrested my youngest sister there and even my brother-in-law, who had never taken part in anything!); bloody battles; prisons crammed full, and so on."

With Mariya in solitary confinement and Anna's husband Mark Yelizarov also in jail, Anna was forced to flee to Europe and settled in Berlin, where she was now organizing the dispatch of *Iskra* into Russia. Ulyanov wrote with a rising sense of frustration: they had to do something to improve *transportirovka*—the dispatch of copies into Russia—which was irregular and random. The constant uncertainty of copies not getting through or achieving results was very stressful. Ulyanov bombarded his agents in Russia with complaints:

Things with us are going none too well. We are badly off financially, Russia gives almost nothing. Shipping is still unorganised and haphazard. . . . Our daily bread, by which we barely manage to keep alive, consists as before solely of suitcases. For a couple of them we pay about a hundred rubles, and the chance nature of the persons sent entails a vast amount of delay, carelessness, loss, etc.

Running costs were now up to 1,599 German marks per month for every issue of eight thousand copies. A more disciplined and covert distribution network of *Iskrovitsy* (Iskra-ites) was desperately needed closer to the frontier to raise money for the paper, obtain false passports, and provide safe houses for conspiratorial meetings and decoy addresses for correspondence.

CHAPTER THREE

Konspiratsiya

RUSSIA: 1901–1902

———◦◦◦———

WHILE VLADIMIR ULYANOV and Nadezhda Krupskaya were issuing meticulous instructions on organization, codes, and tactics from their refuge in Munich, a mass of *praktiki*—party agents—inside and outside Russia were living with the real and present dangers of work in the revolutionary underground. They were spreading the word of *Iskra* as well as printing and disseminating other illegal literature on crudely made presses hidden in safe houses. And they were taking enormous risks. They lived on false papers, had no fixed place of abode, and often endured extreme penury. The specter of arrest, imprisonment, and Siberian exile loomed perpetually over their lives and would come at least once for many of them.

Political and industrial unrest, as well as a new wave of student activism, was now reinforcing the revolutionary will in Russia. Students caught taking part in strikes or demonstrations could be summarily conscripted into the army. In the winter of 1901, 183 students from Kiev University were punished in this way for acts of protest. More students suffered arrest and were killed in a demonstration in Kazan two months later in support of the Kiev students.

The radical tradition now rising once more from the ashes of the 1881 repressions in fact dated back to the 1820s, when intellectual discussion groups and secret societies had first sprung up in Russia. Such societies had thrived in an atmosphere of secret debate, and by the 1860s had mutated into organized conspiracy against the czars, encouraged from a distance by exile Alexander Herzen through his socialist journal *Kolokol* (The Bell) and assisted by fellow exiles Nikolay Ogarev and Mikhail Bakunin.

Leadership of the movement for democratic change in Russia came from a distance for much of the nineteenth century.

By the 1900s, such were the levels of state censorship in Russia that a huge range of activities in Russia had to be authorized by the police, from setting up a Sunday school or medical practice to selling books and newspapers. A list of 1,896 political and social issues was expressly removed from public discussion. Even the most innocuous-seeming literary and discussion groups for workers were subject to raids by the police and rightly so, for they were the recruiting grounds for revolutionists and now *Iskra* agents. Even chess clubs were used as cover for seditious activities.

The objectives of the dedicated revolutionary had been laid down in a pamphlet written in 1869 by the nihilist Sergey Nechaev in collaboration with Bakunin. *The Revolutionary's Catechism* asserted that conspirators should operate in small, self-sufficient cells of no more than six people in order to prevent infiltration by spies and betrayal of the wider network. Like Rakhmetov in the Chernyshevsky novel so admired by Ulyanov, the ideal revolutionist described by Nechaev must submit himself to the collective will. He should have no personal life, feelings, or attachments, "not even a name." He should shut out all self-indulgent thoughts of kindness, love, sentiment, or romance and have only one single-minded passion—revolution. His overriding intellectual commitment should be to the "science of destruction." And all this, paradoxically, in the pursuit of the "complete liberation and happiness" of the people.

By 1901 Ulyanov was having serious doubts about the effectiveness of the still embryonic *Iskra* network in effecting change. It was too diverse, too lacking in unifying objectives and overall control. The Marxism of its participants was vague and elusive, the party as a whole fragmented, harassed by police, and demoralized by provocateurs. The stress and worry of seeing his carefully laid instructions go awry gave him many sleepless nights. He worried constantly that *Iskra* would be undermined by splinter groups and rival factions in the Russian regions, working without authorization from the center and thus outside his control. He feared endlessly that his agents would desert to rival political organs. There was carelessness: ciphered letters often proved unreadable because keys had not been properly used, the paper was too poor quality, the handwriting illegible. Important agents failed to carry out directives correctly or meet their deadlines in communicating; others proved downright inadequate. And worse, the methods of importing *Iskra* into Russia were inadequate; huge numbers of copies languished for lack of an effective system of distribution.

In Ulyanov's view the revolutionary movement was at a turning point, facing a tough battle against a powerful modern state that was "straining every nerve in order to crush socialism and democracy." It now needed an injection of power and legitimacy. Back in 1897 he had written that "to be able to conduct a systematic battle against the government, we must raise the revolutionary organization, discipline and conspiratorial technique to the highest level of perfection." But he and those around him in Munich knew that the party in Russia had a membership that varied greatly in ability and caliber, and it needed to be channeled and directed. Although the *Iskra* network was a good vehicle for organizing activists, it also opened the party to the constant risk of infiltration by double agents and informers.

The success of the whole operation in Russia now rested on what, to Ulyanov, was the most crucial element: *konspiratsiya*. The word in Russian does not mean conspiracy or plotting as we know it, but rather secrecy or stealth in avoiding detection. The principles of *konspiratsiya* had been tested during the years of Narodnaya Volya's guerrilla activities and its campaign of political assassination up to 1881. This example had since become Ulyanov's guiding principle: a necessary foundation to all other revolutionary work. Economy, brevity, and punctuality were Ulyanov's watchwords: economy of words and actions in public so as not to give oneself away, brevity in verbal communication, and the prompt fulfillment of assignments. His instructions were clear: "When you are taken up with secret, conspiratorial matters, you must not speak with those whom you normally converse, nor about the things you usually talk about, but only with those you need to talk to and only about things you need to talk about."

Hundreds of activists working covertly in Russia's big cities had given up their personal lives and gone underground. Although they worked as full-time, professional revolutionaries, they received no wages as such. The movement relied on funds raised from sympathetic and wealthy donors to help support them, but the bulk of this money was spent on costly *tekhnika*—mainly printing equipment, paper, and ink. The agents lived from hand to mouth, depending on the goodwill and kindness of others. In the city they operated as illegals—living in safe houses without work permits on false identity papers and using a string of code names. Ulyanov's friend and the leader of the Pskov group, Panteleimon Lepeshinsky, went by the names of Lapot, Bychkov, and even a numerical alias—2a3b. Leonid Krasin, an engineer and explosives expert and a key agent in charge of a printing press in Baku, was known as Vinter, Zimin, Johanson, and simply "The Horse." Another major contact in Moscow, Bauman, was known as "Victor," "The Tree," and "The Rook." Sometimes the introductory codes between agents were risible; Cecilia Bobrovskaya used "We are the swallows of the coming spring." Another was devised to greet a Norwegian contact who knew no Russian: "Ich bin der Freund von Herrn Anders," positively the stuff of schoolboy comic book spies.

All the codes, secret knocks, and passwords employed by illegals, however inept, were essential in the attempt to preserve the operation's secrecy. Underground activists lived insular lives, rarely communicating beyond their own close-knit world and often knowing little about the identity and location of others beyond their own groups. Agents on their way to meetings or delivery points were forbidden from carrying anything in their hands and had to hide items in their clothes. To print leaflets on crude hectograph machines, they had to make a mixture of gelatin and glycerin. Because the latter was only available in small quantities, dozens of agents were needed to buy supplies across a wide area. Paper too had to be bought in small amounts from many outlets in order to avoid arousing suspicion. If safe places could not be found to meet, agents would go out into the woods to hold meetings under guise of picnics or mushroom-picking expeditions or boat trips downriver. One group in Kiev met in a laundry; another in Chernigov was offered the waiting room of a sympathetic doctor. The eminent Russian painter Ilya Repin, a family friend of agent Elena Stasova, allowed the use of his studio at the Academy of Arts. Meetings could always be held at legal workers clubs or in the offices of trade unions. But with the police always on the lookout for seditious activity, these were held at greater risk of discovery.

The clandestine cells were always prepared for the inevitable police raids and circulated an informational pamphlet, *How to Conduct Oneself*

Under Interrogation. In such situations the utmost loyalty toward colleagues was demanded. Anyone who did not master conspiratorial techniques was considered a *kustar*—an amateur. Amateurism was anathema to Ulyanov and he was obsessive about eradicating it.

Even so, as the movement grew, it urgently needed fresh converts from the working classes in Russia's growing urban centers. Distributing *Iskra* (known as "sowing") and other propaganda with it was the quickest means of recruitment. Although the paper was aimed at Marxists with a degree of political acumen and literacy, there was such a strong demand for radical literature in Russia that everybody wanted to read it. There were never enough copies to go round. *Iskra* was read avidly by workers to illiterate coworkers and then passed on from one group to the next until the worn copies literally fell apart. Other propaganda leaflets produced by the *Iskra* board were disseminated by agents who took enormous risks going into theaters in Moscow and St. Petersburg and showering leaflets on audiences. They also distributed them on factory courtyards near the water pumps where people congregated, at army barracks, and along the city streets. Sometimes the leaflets would be surreptitiously pasted on walls, but with so many police on the streets this was highly dangerous.

Such dangers were welcomed by the eager young *Iskra* agents who had committed themselves to the challenge. Underground work, and with it the threat of arrest, gave them a sense of comradeship and purpose. It also offered a unique environment where women took equal risks with the men. Like Nadezhda Krupskaya, they took little credit for the work they did, performing an important but subordinate function as couriers, helping produce and distribute propaganda leaflets, and providing valuable financial and physical backup. They learned how to make bombs and shoot guns, but they did not appear in the ranks of the party's theoreticians. The Russian revolutionary movement did not encourage women to promote themselves, as exemplified by the increasingly slovenly Vera Zasulich. But it valued their "plodding, tireless work," as Nadya described it, and nominally treated them as equals. There was no traditional division of labor between males and females within cells; a good female activist learned to forgo sleep and food, just like the men, and no concessions were made to her sex. And she never complained. Ulyanov's devoted sisters Anna and

Mariya understood this and belonged to the network of female activists who kept him going through the long years of exile. Anna had already been arrested and confined to the family estate at Kokushkino in the 1880s, only to go straight back into the underground on her release, raising money and helping to circulate illegal literature, as well as arranging secret meetings and passing on news and instructions from Ulyanov in Europe. In 1899 Mariya had been arrested in Moscow and then kept in solitary confinement for seven months. She spent the next three years exiled in Samara, but this did not prevent her from continuing her revolutionary work. Meanwhile, Anna in Berlin was now playing an important role in copying and coding letters to and from the *Iskra* board and its agents in Russia.

By the time Lidiya Dan arrived in Moscow in January 1901 on an undercover mission for Ulyanov to consolidate *Iskra*'s position after a series of police raids and arrests, she found that the enclave in Munich seriously underestimated the growth of the socialist movement back home and its now explosive tenor. It was a "seething cauldron," she reported. The students in the city were beginning to stir and Moscow was becoming "a hotbed of provocation." She had arrived one evening, unannounced, on a passport generously given to her by a Jewish student in the Russian colony in Berne. Her only place of refuge in the city was her sister-in-law's apartment, but she would not take the risk of putting Lidiya up.

Lidiya's only option, as night fell, was to get on a train going somewhere, anywhere, to avoid walking the streets. There were gendarmes watching the stations for precisely this ploy. Some illegals lived for weeks riding the trains back and forth across Russia and sleeping in railway station toilets. But it was a risk Lidiya had to take. For about a month, she was endlessly and aimlessly crisscrossing on trains, occasionally being offered a room for the night in the apartments of sympathetic strangers (never her own relatives), making sure she arrived at around the time people usually returned from the theater—when her arrival would not appear conspicuous to the concierges on duty. She could never risk staying late at workers meetings; an illegal was not safe out on the streets after 11:00 PM. Occasionally she would be allowed back to her sister-in-law's for a change of clothes; other times she went to the public baths, where she could hire a room for a ruble and wash, rest, and change. During this time Lidiya managed to hold meetings with activists at safe "bourgeois" apartments or medical clinics. Here anyone who knew the password could come to talk. But she soon realized that the level of personnel and organization in Moscow was extremely poor and people were demoralized by the ongoing police raids and arrests. There were few facilities for organizing and printing leaflets, and it took an inordinate amount of effort and risk for Lidiya to obtain just 250 copies of one.

One night Lidiya was caught out late at a meeting and could not get back to her safe house on time. Her only option was to go out onto Tsvetnoy Boulevard and bribe a prostitute to take her back to her place for the night, assuring her she was not a lesbian but was running away from an abusive husband. The prostitute offered to share her bed, but Lydiya balked at the suggestion and spent an uncomfortable night in an armchair. She left first thing the next morning, being sure to leave a five ruble note on the table. Her socialist conscience would not allow her to leave the woman's loss of earnings unrewarded. In May 1902 Lydiya was arrested on the street as she met another activist. She was sent to Butyrki prison and then exiled to Olekminsk on the River Lena in Siberia. She was out of circulation for three years before escaping to Geneva.

Another devoted female activist, and one on whom Ulyanov in later years greatly relied, was Elena Stasova. In St. Petersburg she became legendary as a master of *tekhnika*—the essential business of running an organization—information gathering, distributing illegal literature, arranging safe houses for meetings and hiding revolutionaries on the run, and liaising with other groups across Russia and in Europe. Stasova shared with Ulyanov the classic conspiratorial qualities of self-discipline, energy, and austerity as well as a photographic memory for names, aliases, and addresses. She had chosen the alias "Absolute," Ulyanov thinking it most appropriate since Stasova's unquestioning loyalty could always be counted on. She came from a comfortable, privileged background (as did several other women activists) and received financial support in her underground work from her family, making use of their country estate as a safe house for meetings and a hiding place for illegal literature. Stasova's parents also allowed the use of their spacious St. Petersburg apartment for evening lectures—ostensibly on uncontroversial subjects—where considerable covert fund-raising went on for *Iskra*. Her

parents posted bail for her when she was arrested and sent money to exiles in financial need.

For Stasova, as for many other young women at this time, the party became her family and she bonded strongly with her fellow activists. Some
of these women married, but most of those who formed relationships
opted to live together, always privileging the cause over and above personal and emotional concerns. There was never any question in Stasova's
mind of where her primary loyalties lay, no matter how great the parental
pressure to give up: "My life is in this, in this and only in this," she was
to write from prison. "No other work can give me the strength to live . . .
without this work of mine I cannot live. This is the flesh of my flesh."
Stasova's dedication brought spectacular results. By 1902 the St. Petersburg group under her direction was printing and distributing political
broadsides weekly, often in print runs of 10,000 copies, as well as smuggling in large supplies of books and newspapers from abroad.

One of Stasova's close associates in the illegal transportation of *Iskra*
and other Marxist literature from Europe was Nikolay Burenin. He remembered how copies of *Iskra* were sent into Russia pasted together to
create the boards of children's books, using a special glue invented by a
Swiss bookbinder. The covers had to be soaked in warm water to disen-
gage the material, which was then painstakingly peeled apart page by
page and dried. The method also worked successfully for cartons and the
backing to pictures and even ornaments. One *Iskra* agent fashioned cheap
plaster figurines for smuggling literature, which were then sold in markets
after they had served their purpose.

One of the most dramatic close shaves experienced by a courier was
that of Lidiya Gobi, the daughter of an eminent botanist and professor at
St. Petersburg University. Gobi was one of the devoted female agents of the
"repentant privileged classes" who dedicated themselves to "righting the
emotional wrongs of Russia." Her svelte appearance belied her passionate revolutionary fervor. She was every inch the elegant lady: tall, beautifully dressed, and aristocratic. When carrying illegal literature on the
street, she passed by the police unnoticed. Indeed, so good was her classy
cover that she became one of the group's best agents in St. Petersburg, and
her family dacha at Piki-Ruki on the Vyborg side of St. Petersburg was

used as a safe house. Ulyanov stayed there during one of his illegal visits to the city.

On one occasion Lidiya was sent south to Kiev with orders for local activists from the Petersburg committee. She got off the train, convinced that no one was following her, and headed straight for her secret assignation. She handed over her documents and received others to take back to St. Petersburg. But outside on the street she suddenly noticed she was being followed. Pretending that she had come out for a stroll, she made her way to the nearby public park but soon noticed that the *shpik* (spook—an Okhrana agent) who was following her had been joined by another. Not only that, they were tailing her openly. Lidiya resolved to destroy everything she was carrying the minute she got back to the train. But now, as she left the park, there were three men on her tail. If she went to the station, she'd be caught like a mouse in a trap. As she walked through the old Podil district of Kiev, her brain was racing. The three men were closing in when she noticed an old house with a garden leading down to the edge of the cliff above the Dnipro River and headed toward it. It was a long way down and all she could see below was dense undergrowth. She was wearing a large fur cloak that day—perfect for hiding the illegal literature she had brought. Unflinching, she sat on the edge of the cliff, pulled her cloak tightly around her, and let herself fall.

Much to her amazement Lidiya landed safely at the feet of startled onlookers below. Such was her self-possession that she picked herself up, apologized for landing so unexpectedly in their midst, and refused all offers of medical help. Her bulky fur cloak had saved her from injury. After tidying herself up in a nearby house, she was on the next train out of Kiev.

———

BY THE END OF 1901 *Iskra* was getting into Russia via the border areas of Poland and Lithuania, especially the town of Vilna (these areas were then part of the Austro-Hungarian and Russian empires), thanks in part to the assistance of the Bund—a Jewish socialist organization founded in Vilna in 1897 that promoted Jewish nationhood and culture within the Pale of Settlement. Other copies came by the most roundabout but safest route through Persia via Tavriz and Alexandria. French and sometimes

Russian steamers brought copies from Marseilles to the Black Sea ports of Batumi and Baku, or Odessa in the Crimea. From there, wrapped in waterproofing, they were dumped overboard, then picked up and taken across the Caucasus and on into Russia. By far the most dependable route was that via Romania and the border town of Teofipol. For a short time political literature was smuggled from Vardo in Finnmarken in the extreme north of Norway, wrapped in greaseproof paper inside boxes of salted fish. These transports, arranged by the Norwegian social democrat Adam Egede-Nissen, arrived at the Russian seaport Archangel. When this method was discovered, Nissen began sending literature with sympathetic Russian sailors arriving at Vardo and returning to Russia via the White Sea.

The northern route into Russia via Sweden and Finland proved extremely efficient. It was the brainchild of the Russian activist Vladimir Smirnov, who was married to Karin Strindberg, daughter of the famous Swedish playwright. With a Finnish mother and fluency in Swedish and Russian, Smirnov had many socialist contacts in Finland. As ardent patriots, the Finns opposed the Russianization of their country and played important roles not just in the distribution of *Iskra* but the Russian revolutionary movement as a whole, particularly in the border towns of Terijoki and Kuokkala, located on the railway line into St. Petersburg. Initially, illegal literature arriving from Berlin and Geneva at Stockholm was packaged up and sent hidden in loads of coal on steamships plying the service between Sweden and the southwestern archipelago of Finland near Åbo (now Turku). But from the autumn of 1902 Smirnov's main middleman was the Finnish journalist and socialist Konni Zilliacus, who organized a network of smugglers (many of them women) to take copies of *Iskra* from Sweden into Finland by train and by steamship, hidden in their clothes and luggage. Zilliacus also used his yacht for smuggling copies. The Okhrana soon became aware of his activities, but Zilliacus constantly slipped the net; anyone who did not know the six thousand tiny skerries and islands around Åbo inside out was easily eluded.

In addition to helping organize the sea routes for *Iskra* smuggling, Vladimir Smirnov carried out able work on the ground via his home in Helsingfors (now Helsinki). His elderly mother, Virginiya, often traveled into St. Petersburg on the train, her basket filled with illegal literature and lists of coded addresses hidden under her knitting. What policeman would think to stop and question such a kindly old lady who looked like any other St. Petersburg children's nurse? And who would suspect the notable Finnish opera star, Aino Akte, another sympathizer and Finnish patriot, of smuggling copies of *Iskra* into Finland among her elegant luggage after a tour to Paris?

With so much material coming in via Finland, Smirnov and his fellow *Iskra* agents had to rely on Finnish workers on the railway line into St. Petersburg from the northern suburbs of Vyborg to ensure the safe transfer of illegal literature hidden in boxes of apples and potatoes. Other items were hidden in the deep skirt pockets or corsets of women agents or special undervests worn by men who crossed into Vyborg to collect the literature from the homes of railway workers. Later they used Nikolay Burenin's country estate at Kiriasali, on the Finnish border, as a way station for illegal literature traveling in both directions. Transports would arrive at the Raivola railway station, and Burenin and his colleagues, dressed up as hunters, would travel by horse cart to pick them up, hiding the copies of *Iskra* under straw in the back of the carts.

Back in Petersburg at his family's fashionable apartment on Ruzovskaya Ulitsa, Burenin used his profession as a pianist as a front for illegal transports, forever treading a delicate line of subterfuge to conceal his activities from his mother. Their apartment was a regular venue for musical gatherings and rehearsals. The regular coming and going of "musicians" with instrument cases duped the vigilant porter. Like many others in St. Petersburg at the time, he was under instructions from the secret police to keep an eye open for gatherings of illegals. On such occasions, as a recital was being held in the drawing room overseen by Burenin's mother, small groups of activists slipped away and congregated in Burenin's room nearby to smoke and plot revolution. But he was always on his guard and kept the packets of illegal literature in a pile ready to be doused in kerosene and burned in the stove should the police knock at the door.

The most dangerous work, however, was carried out by those who ran the illegal printing presses. Most of them were hidden in legitimate shops and businesses, and the people who operated them lived the life of troglodytes, working away in the dark. The press locations were known to only a tight-knit circle of people, and the texts to be printed were passed from agent to agent at public places full of people—such as art exhibitions—

where agents rendezvoused at prearranged paintings to surreptitiously pass on material. The most successful printing press was located far from Russia in Baku, Georgia. Here illegal literature had been reproduced from crude cardboard stencils smuggled from Europe and Russia inside scientific and technical books; then metal stereotype blocks were cast from the stencils. By September 1901 a local Georgian activist, Lado Ketskhoveli, had obtained a more efficient rotary stereotype press and set it up in the Muslim quarter of Tiflis. But it had to be moved constantly to elude the Tiflis branch of the Okhrana, which tried hard to locate it. In the end they caught up with Ketskhoveli, who refused under torture to reveal the location of the press and was shot in his cell. Leonid Krasin took over running the press and vastly improved its techniques. For the next four years, "Nina"—as the press was code-named throughout the Russian underground—proved invaluable to the *Iskra* organization.

———

As THE REVOLUTIONARY movement across Russia entered a dramatic upswing, so too did the activities of the Okhrana, now engaged in its own massive recruitment drive for spies and double agents. Across Russia Okhrana "spooks" were deployed as porters, newspaper sellers, and cabbies, watching railway stations and hotels for strangers and any sign of illegal activities.

Having repressed the extremism of the Narodnaya Volya years with a wave of arrests and executions in the 1880s, the Okhrana was increasingly intercepting letters and telegrams (a practice known as *perlyustratsiya* "perlustration") to and from the *Iskra* board. Working with the Department of Posts and Telegraphs, popularly known as the Chernyi Kabinet (Black Cabinet), the Okhrana tracked mail going through the main post offices of Moscow, St. Petersburg, Warsaw, Odessa, Kiev, Kharkov, and Tiflis, intercepting and copying thousands of letters a year.

Although *Iskra* agents followed carefully laid down procedures, many of their codes were careless and naive, which made them easy for the Black Cabinet's expert cryptographers to crack. Many codes had been adapted from tapping codes that activists devised, with considerable perseverance and ingenuity, in prison. The number of taps referred to a simple checkerboard (or Polybius square) of 5 by 5 rows of letters of the old Russian alphabet. Prisoners memorized this universal system in order to "talk" to each other wherever they found themselves in jail, achieving speeds of ten to fifteen words a minute. The tapping had then been adapted to dots and dashes that were used to conceal messages inside individual letters on particular pages of innocuous-looking books or letters. The key to these codes was found by referring to a specific page, line, and pair of numbers indicating a particular letter of the alphabet on a previously agreed book, such as the journal *Family Pictures*, a biography of Spinoza, and a volume of poetry by Nekrasov, all used by Ulyanov and Nadya to send messages to *Iskra* members at this time. In their correspondence with Elena Stasova in St. Petersburg, they used one of Ivan Krylov's animal fables. Stasova became so adept that she coded and sent hundreds of letters a month by it. Other messages could be conveyed through Aesopian language and allusion in seemingly legitimate published literature or innocuous letters. Thus references to "illness" meant arrest and "hospital" meant prison; any inquiry about people's health was about their imprisonment. If an "epidemic" broke out in a particular town, this was a warning that there had been a series of police raids and arrests and agents should steer clear.

Once coded letters were intercepted and decoded, often thanks to the help of double agents and infiltrators, all names were extracted and recorded in a vast card index. Okhrana specialists were allegedly able to identify suspicious letters merely by the handwriting on the envelopes; once opened and read, such letters were marked with a discreet black mark known as a "fly" (*mukha*).

Throughout the period leading up to the revolution the Okhrana maintained a high success rate in its perlustration activities, thanks to the *Iskra* movement's continuing underestimation of the skills it was up against and its lack of sophisticated codes. Nadezhda Krupskaya, who was at the heart of the operation and responsible for as many as three hundred coded letters a week, was the first to admit the amateurishness of those early days:

All those letters about handkerchiefs (passports), brewing beer [propaganda shipments via Sweden and Finland], warm fur (illegal literature), all those code names for towns beginning with the same letters as the name of the town (Ossip for Odessa, Terenty for Tver, Petya for Poltava, Pasha–Pskov)—substitution of woman's names for men's and vice versa—all this was transparent in the extreme.

One such inexperienced agent, Osip Pyatnitsky, was arrested not long after joining the *Iskra* network. Taken to the Lukyanovka prison in Kiev, he discovered that it was a holding center for other *Iskra* agents (a dozen or more had been arrested in a roundup in February 1902), where they would be systematically interrogated by the notorious General Vasily Novitsky, head of the Kiev gendarmerie, who was already planning a great state trial for them. The arrests were a serious blow to *Iskra,* and Ulyanov was greatly disturbed when he received the news. But inside their prison the *Iskra* agents were quick to apply the methods of their mentor.

They made the most of their time in prison, exploiting its lax regime and turning their cells into classrooms, reading all the political literature they could lay hands on, teaching themselves languages, and debating among themselves. Prison for many new recruits such as Pyatnitsky served as a university and a Marxist training ground. But for the revolutionaries confined with him in Kiev that summer, imprisonment was also a torment, keeping them from taking part in the wave of demonstrations and strikes going on across Russia's cities. When they heard it would be months before their trials came to court, eleven of them resolved on an escape plan. Security was so poor that they smuggled in everything they needed: false passports, one hundred rubles each in money, and vodka and sleeping powder to dope the guards. An iron grapple to get over the twenty-five-foot prison wall (using rope ladders made from bedsheets) arrived hidden inside a basket of flowers for a prisoner's birthday. The prisoners practiced making human pyramids during their exercise period in the yard in order to gauge the height of the walls they would have to scale and plotted the route they would take across neighboring fields to a series of safe houses set up for them. They practiced the best techniques for tying up the guards and began inviting them to share drinks in a softening up campaign. On August 18, 1902, they effected their escape as planned.

Although the Okhrana sent out urgent alerts to all border posts and 295 Russian cities, Pyatnitsky and all but one of the ten others managed to get across the Russian frontier and rendezvous with the other *Iskra* escapees at a restaurant in Berlin. Here, from the cold damp cellar of the German social democratic journal *Vorvärts,* Pyatnitsky worked for *Iskra* under the code name "Freitag," investing huge energy and commitment to his key role and earning the respect of his German counterparts. The Germans, by comparison, complained that their social democratic ranks contained "too many bureaucrats and not enough revolutionaries." The building was under constant surveillance by both the Russian secret police and the Germans, yet Pyatnitsky, who became one of the Bolsheviks' most wily underground operators in Berlin, engaged in regular contraband trips back and forth across the border. He also helped Russian activists get in and out of the country undercover. Eventually he returned to undertake valuable party work in Russia, based in Odessa and Moscow.

CHAPTER FOUR

Becoming Lenin

MUNICH: 1902

⚬⚬⚬

IN THE AUTUMN OF 1902, when a delighted *Iskra* board published details of the mass breakout of activists from Kiev prison, it reported that the mission to free them had cost the party 1,795 rubles. *Iskra*'s objective of raising the profile of the Russian revolutionary movement at home and abroad was beginning to bear fruit. Shortly after the Kiev escape, letters of support and donations rolled in from all over Russia and Europe, including eleven pounds from the British-based Friends of Russian Freedom. But Vladimir Ulyanov was never content with small successes.

In September Ulyanov and Nadya traveled to Zurich to attend a conference of the League of Russian Social Democrats Abroad. The league had been founded on Ulyanov's initiative in 1901 to promote unity among the various revolutionary cells in Russia. He made the most of the trip by speaking to a group of Russian émigré students at the University of Zurich hoping to recruit more *Iskra* agents. He urged them to consider interrupting their studies and going back home to take up the struggle. Many of those present that day were infected by the power of Ulyanov's argument, his charisma, and his sense of purpose. They sat late into the night discussing his theories. *Iskra* offered new hope; its message was the gospel truth and Ulyanov, the prophet of revolution. Some of the students in Zurich who heard Ulyanov that night decided to return home.

Ulyanov continued to be fueled by rage against amateurism and the threat of heresy in the *Iskra* movement. His invective was as colorful as it was crude: "To hell with all conciliators, people of 'elusive views' and shilly-shallyers! Better a small fish than a big beetle. Better two or three energetic and wholly devoted people than a dozen dawdlers," he raged. He was now looking to print every third or fourth copy of *Iskra* inside Russia to spread its message throughout the country. There had been "arrests galore" recently in Voronezh and Ufa, and his sense of urgency was escalating. It was of paramount importance to get the *Iskra* group's "own *reliable* people" into the largest possible number of revolutionary committees.

Since the previous autumn he had been laboring long and hard on a new work: *What Is to Be Done?* It was printed in Stuttgart in March 1902, its title a deliberate allusion to Chernyshevsky's novel of the same name. Its torrent of political argumentation conveyed the author's characteristic energy and sense of urgency. At times violently hectoring and witheringly dismissive of political opponents, it went from the kind of crude invective that Ulyanov was now making his own, to rousing political oratory, to messianic prophecy. Ulyanov and his shock troops were relentlessly moving forward into history, leaving the rest of the world behind. There was no room for compromise with the enemies of Ulyanov's own brand of Marxism. Groups such as Bernstein's economists, Struve's liberals, and the newly established Socialist Revolutionaries (who advocated a return to old-style terrorism in support of their brand of agrarian socialism) all came under savage attack. While aimed at bringing such heretics into line, Ulyanov's essay also laid out, in suitably conspiratorial language, what the work's subtitle suggested were "The Burning Questions of Our Movement": the need to dispense with flabby thinking and the lethargy and carelessness of loosely knit political groups, in favor of a highly disciplined and centralized party with a clearly defined program.

What Is to Be Done? would henceforth be taken as Ulyanov's defining interpretation of Russian Marxism, based on the conditions then prevailing in Russia, although many hundreds of thousands of words would pour from his pen over the next twenty-two years. In Ulyanov's view, Russia was a profoundly backward country lacking a mass movement toward spontaneous revolution; the socialist conscience of the Russian proletariat had yet to be properly awakened and marshaled. Even among politicized urban workers the trade union mentality still prevailed and would continue to do so in the absence of effective leadership. Ulyanov had no faith in the mass movement of the proletariat per se as a force for change. If left to its own devices, it would inevitably become preoccupied with everyday bourgeois issues.

Education—or more correctly indoctrination—was the key. The masses had to be educated into class consciousness and a proper awareness of the battle ahead. But even with this level of political awareness they could achieve nothing in the wider arena without the leadership of an elite, scientifically informed, Marxist intelligentsia, whose role was to organize in the vanguard, secretly. True political struggle had to be orchestrated by hardened, experienced professionals who would think for the masses. The proletariat would remain an amorphous mass, the collective instrument of the party's elitist will. Having been indoctrinated by the party into a new, revolutionary class consciousness, the masses would eventually give rise to the great socialist vision: the dictatorship of the proletariat. This would be the culminating triumph of Ulyanov's all-consuming socialist experiment. But it would be political thinking in a test tube, far removed from the realities of Russia and the Russian masses, detached from them as he was by long years in exile.

In the interest of revolutionary change, no factionalism or infighting would be countenanced. Ulyanov demanded a slavish uniformity of thought and objectives from all his associates, sowing the seeds of later dissent and political rivalry. Iron discipline was necessary, he argued, in the defense of Marxist orthodoxy and the revolution to come. The movement had to operate as a conspiratorial one, in the Jacobin tradition of the French Revolution and its Russian successor, The People's Will, whose inner core would initiate the revolution from above. The vast majority of working-class supporters would find their place—just as Nadya had accepted her own role—as willing but anonymous "cog[s] in the revolutionary machine."

The imposition of a rational, calculated "Germanic method," inspired in no small part by the disciplined social democratic movement he had observed in Germany, was a logical extension of Ulyanov's pragmatic approach. It would knock the amateurism and indiscipline of the traditional Russian revolutionary spirit out of its romantic idealism. Ulyanov was there to lead the way, as *What Is to Be Done?* announced loudly and clearly.

The chaotic first two years of *Iskra* production had proven that training, discipline, and tactics were paramount in the underground network. In this respect *What Is to Be Done?* provided the blueprint for future activism. A broad grassroots movement of uncoordinated and undisciplined groups would remain prey to endless police infiltration. Such "broad democracy," argued Ulyanov, "amidst the gloom of the autocracy and the domination of the gendarmerie, is nothing more than a *useless and harmful toy.*" His demand for an elitist, professional leadership in Russia was highly logical at the time, given the high incidence of the arrest and imprisonment of activists. But, as history was to show after 1917, once the edifice of a revolutionary elite was firmly in place, the leap from centralized control to ultimate dictatorship was a very small one.

On paper *Iskra* continued as a collaborative effort. Even while Ulyanov continued to pay lip service to Plekhanov as figurehead of the movement, *What Is to Be Done?* sounded the death knell of his turbulent partnership with the Marxist old guard, which emphasized theory rather than practical action. After twenty years as a crusading Marxist in exile, Plekhanov was out of touch with the rapidly changing situation in Russia and failed to recognize the need to adapt to the more sophisticated surveillance tactics used by the Okhrana.

Ulyanov now began distancing himself from Plekhanov, Axelrod, Martov, and Zasulich. It was time to move on, not just theoretically but physically too. When it first arrived in Munich in 1901, the *Iskra* board had kept a low profile and had stayed away from the Russian émigré colony, hoping not to attract attention. But its presence in the city had become common knowledge within the close-knit community of émigré Russian students, many of whom had become radicalized in Germany and hung on every scrap of news about the revolutionary movement back home. They sought out their revolutionary heroes, following them around and trying to engage in conversation with them in cafés. This in turn attracted the Bavarian police, which Ulyanov's German socialist colleagues worried would in turn cause problems for them.

A recent agreement between the Russian and Bavarian police on the exchange of political prisoners put the whole *Iskra* Munich operation in jeopardy. The Okhrana had tracked down the whereabouts of the *Iskra* board in Schwabing with the help of the German police, and *Iskra*'s German printer bowed out. Ulyanov sensed that arrest was imminent. The group would have to relocate to a larger city that offered greater anonymity. Plekhanov and Axelrod once more argued vigorously for Switzerland. But Ulyanov, determined to distance himself from Plekhanov's interference, insisted on moving the operation to London.

He and Nadya packed up their few possessions and sent their books on ahead in care of a Russian colleague, Nikolay Alekseev, who lived near Kings Cross, and sold off their few sticks of furniture for a paltry twelve marks. From Munich station they took the train to Stuttgart and then Frankfurt. They stopped off to admire Cologne's historic medieval cathedral before entraining for Belgium and from there, the Channel crossing from Ostend to Dover. Before leaving mainland Europe they spent a couple of days in Liège and Brussels, where an old friend of Nadya's, Nikolay Meshcheryakov, showed them around the city. Having eagerly anticipated meeting his political hero, Meshcheryakov was disappointed that Ulyanov did not cut a more romantic figure. He had "the most ordinary, Russian, rather Asiatic face," he recalled. "There was only one striking thing about it—the eyes. There was no evading their gaze. They were extraordinarily penetrating." Ulyanov's interest had been aroused when he heard about a recent clash between police and striking workers in Liège. Eager to know more about ongoing tension in the workers' district where it had occurred, he went to visit the scene of the confrontation. He loved being in the thick of such things. When Plekhanov passed through some months later, ever the aesthete, all he wanted to do, noted Meshcheryakov, was to see the art galleries.

There was now little time for culture in Ulyanov's scheme of things. As a political leader he had passed a point of transition. His political writings had created a rationale for the Russian Social Democratic Labor Party, founded in 1898 during his Siberian exile, and he now needed to take control of it. With the battle for ideological leadership in the party escalating, he took issue with Plekhanov's constant critiques of his editorials in *Iskra*, tartly accusing him of making their "common work impossible." The discord between them was briefly patched up but resurfaced later in 1902 as their personal relationship degenerated.

The time had come for Vladimir Ulyanov to become independent of Plekhanov and the old guard, and to do so he needed to establish a consistent and unmistakable identity of his own. For years, like all political dissidents in the tradition of *konspiratsiya,* he had used a confusing succession of pseudonyms (more than 150 during the years to 1917). These ranged from mere initials (including variants such as V., V.I., V.U., V. UL., V. Il.) to favored names such as Tulin, William Frey (interchangeable with a Germanized form as Wilhelm Frei), Meyer, Richter, Karpov, and Petrov. V. Ilyn or Ilin (from his patronymic Ilyich) was a favorite, and he even signed his nickname Starik (the old man) to some letters. By early 1901, Ulyanov had taken up a new pseudonym that gained favor within *Iskra*: Lenin.

In January 1901 he first wrote to Plekhanov in Zurich signing himself "Lenin," and in December he published the first four chapters of a pamphlet on the agrarian question in *Zarya* under the same name. He favored the name again in March 1902, when *What Is to Be Done?* appeared under the same pseudonym—N. Lenin, the N. signifying literally nothing but widely misread in the West as representing the name Nikolay. However, even Nadezhda Krupskaya was later unable to explain where he got the name from. It bore echoes of other two-syllable pseudonyms that became fashionable in the party, beginning with Plekhanov's early use of "Volgin" (from the River Volga; many suggested Lenin's was taken from the River Lena in Siberia as a reverential nod to his then mentor) and ending with Josef Dzhugashvili's adoption of "Stalin" in 1913. Whatever the origins, there was a certain pleasing congruence about all of them.

To his wife, Vladimir Ilyich Ulyanov would affectionately remain Volodya, as he would to his family. Publicly Nadya would increasingly refer to him as Vladimir Ilyich or just plain Ilyich, the use of the patronymic being less familiar and projecting a degree of respect. Although the name "Lenin" rapidly gained currency at home and abroad, Lenin's close comrades among the Bolsheviks would likewise address him as Ilyich. As the years went on, particularly after he came to power, Lenin would also become, for the many millions who adored their "great leader and teacher" but never met him, simply Ilyich.

By 1902 history was moving too slowly for Lenin, and so he decided to give it a push. "Give us an organization of revolutionaries," he exhorted in *What Is to Be Done?,* "and we shall overturn the whole of Russia." This clarion call struck a nerve with activists back home such as Lenin's fellow Siberian exile Gleb Krzhizhanovsky, who greeted his messianic vision for the revolutionary movement with great enthusiasm. *What Is to Be Done?* came at an opportune moment, tapping into the intelligentsia's thirst for active work in Russia after years of repression. Its treatise on organization offered the movement a program for achieving practical supremacy over its ill-equipped opponents. But while devotees rapidly inculcated its principles and its Leninist political jargon, others were more skeptical about the less than democratic arguments it contained for a revolutionary elite.

Nevertheless, committees in the major cities such as St. Petersburg and Moscow, Nizhniy Novgorod, Saratov, and Kharkov began acknowledging *Iskra* as the "leading organ of the party" and publishing declarations of loyalty to Lenin's theoretical hegemony and his leadership of the *Iskra* organization. Lenin had shown he was a man of serious intent and action, not just an empty theorist of revolution. *What Is to Be Done?* prepared for the revolution that he was convinced was to come. And now he was about to carry the movement toward revolution into a new venue: London, the very "stronghold of capitalism."

As Lenin and Nadya made their way across Europe on a succession of trains to their next transitory home, in St. Petersburg, the Okhrana opened a new file—number 872—on the subject of one N. Lenin, having noted the publication of his pamphlet abroad and the "great sensation" that it had aroused. In brackets below this comment a dutiful officer added, "This undoubtedly is the pseudonym of Ulyanov." But Lenin was now the man to watch.

CHAPTER FIVE

Dr. and Mrs. Richter

LONDON, 1902–1903

———

O N A DISMAL, FOGGY MORNING in April 1902 an undistinguished-looking couple emerged from London's Charing Cross station into the hectic thoroughfare of the Strand. Dr. and Mrs. Jacob Richter, fresh from the leafier environs of Munich, arriving as ever on false passports, had their senses assaulted by the hubbub of the great British metropolis and the stink of a highly industrialized city. The air was thick with the smoke of thousands of chimneys as the busy thoroughfares lay before them enshrouded in the thick gloom of an English fog. London, the great Leviathan, had a population of around 6.6 million at the time—double that of Paris. The scene was quite a shock for Lenin and Nadya after the solitude of Shushenskoe and the relatively bucolic delights of Schwabing.

At Charing Cross they were glad to see the familiar face of Russian colleague Nikolay Alekseev, who had fled Siberian exile in December 1899 and was living on Frederick Street off Gray's Inn Road. Alekseev escorted the couple to busy Pentonville Road near Kings Cross Station. This noisy and overcrowded part of north London, with its crush of horse-drawn omnibuses and trams and the nearby rackety open cutting of the Kings Cross to Faringdon Circle Line, was to be their home for the next year.

England—and notably London—had a long tradition of offering refuge and freedom of speech to the politically and racially oppressed. Russian and German political exiles such as Marx, Engels, and Herzen had taken refuge here in the 1840s and 1850s, as had the revolutionists Louis Blanc from France, Lajos Kossuth from Hungary, and Giuseppe Mazzini from Italy later in the century. The Italian anarchists who arrived toward the end of the nineteenth century called it "the most comfortable place in the world."

British sympathy for the Russians stemmed largely from respect for their culture and literature and contempt for the repressive nature of czarism. The welcome was extended even to perceived extremists such as Prince Peter Kropotkin, the father of Russian anarchism, who turned out to be a kindly and genial old man who lived amid piles of books in a tiny house in Highgate. Political assassins such as Sergey Kravchinsky (also known as Stepniak), who murdered the hated head of the Russian Corps of Gendarmes in St. Petersburg in 1878, had also been given refuge, seen as a romantic figure fighting a cruel and despotic system. He and other Russian émigrés were taken under the wing of the Society of Friends of Free Russia—established by British socialists and sympathizers in 1890—which campaigned tirelessly for an end to political repression in Russia. The society exposed flogging in the Siberian prison camps, raised funds for Russian famine victims and strikers, and protested the persecution of Russian Jews and even the 1892 construction of Russian prison ships at British yards on the Clyde. It frequently challenged apologists for the czarist regime in the British press and did its best to inform the public about the political situation inside Russia. It all belied the claim of czarist apologist Olga Novikoff that "as a rule the only thing known in England about Russians is that they take lemon with their tea."

The British police force—in particular Special Branch created in 1887 to monitor terrorist activities among Irish nationalists—took a jaundiced but tolerant view of "all the foreign scallywags in the world" that seemed to be congregating in London in the 1900s. Halfhearted attempts to control the entry of aliens in 1892 and 1894 had not been successful. The British police had been "shadowing" or "housing" the activities of foreigners in their refugee clubs and cafés across the city since the 1880s, but they were left alone as long as they didn't cause trouble. The Okhrana solicited the help of Special Branch in flushing out Russian political émigrés, frequently advising it that some undesirable or other was on his way to England. But often, as Detective Inspector Brust of Scotland Yard later recalled, "a wholly false and perfectly dreadful catalogue of crimes would be tacked on to a man's record with a view to earning his disfavour with the British police," a tactic that proved self-defeating, for the British "attached not the slightest importance to what they said."

By the 1900s London had a thriving Russo-Jewish community in the poor East End communities of Stepney, Whitechapel, and Hackney, many immigrants having arrived in the 1880s in the wake of pogroms provoked by the assassination of Alexander II. Here, among the immigrant slipper makers and tailors, cabinetmakers, seamstresses, skin dressers, and boot makers, bow makers and milliners who crammed into the dilapidated tenements of Whitechapel, there lurked an inner circle of highly politicized Jewish revolutionaries. Despite a period of violent anarchist activity in the 1890s emanating from the East End, Britain continued to hold to its liberal reputation of offering safe refuge to the politically oppressed, even while recognizing that the new Russian émigrés, "even of the higher order," were fundamentally "socialists at heart" and had a propensity to "preach the 'Religion of the Future' with the fervour of the Apostles." The British could not help but admire their passionate commitment and ability to endure suffering. The educated Russian exile was seen as "poor, and noble and proud," having little "but his books and few enjoyments."

Lenin and Nadya must have seemed the archetypal new immigrants, modest and frugal, yet passionate about their socialist beliefs. Although they now found themselves in the freer environs of London, old habits died hard. In their correspondence Lenin and Nadya continued to refer to their location as "Munich" or "Prague" in an attempt to confuse the Russian secret police. With none of the usual demands for identity papers made wherever they went, they soon realized that working for the party in London could not have been better "from the conspiratorial point of view."

The couple's first lodgings—a cramped bed-sitter in a row of terraced houses off Gray's Inn Road at 20 Sidmouth Street—were abandoned within a week for something slightly better. Lenin firmly rejected any talk of living in a revolutionary commune with his comrades Martov and Zasulich, soon to arrive from Germany. He could not work with anyone around him other than his self-effacing wife (and mother-in-law who joined them later). The British weather, with its indeterminate drizzling rain and endless fogs, depressed him, and Lenin initially disliked the place. "At first glance, it makes a foul impression," he told Plekhanov in Geneva.

But the situation improved within days, when another Russian couple, Konstantin Takhtarev and his wife Apollinariya, who had fled to London in 1898, helped Lenin and Nadya find their way around. On April 23, they persuaded the landlady of 30 Holford Square into taking them as tenants. The new lodgings seemed the perfect solution. They were only a few minutes' walk from Alekseev on Frederick Street, and the area, although within sight and smell of the choking smoke and din of Kings Cross, was decidedly more welcoming. The house, one in a row of brick-built Victorian terraced houses fronted by iron railings, faced a communal garden square. The slums of Kings Cross might be a couple of minutes' walk away, but the denizens of Holford Square considered themselves decent, respectable people.

Lenin and Nadya's new landlady was forty-eight-year-old Emma Louise Yeo, a dressmaker who had been widowed a few weeks previously. Living at home with her were a daughter and four sons, three of whom worked as printer compositors. The loss of her husband's wages prompted her to take in lodgers, but after her first talk with the strange Dr. Richter about rooms, Mrs. Yeo, so her son later recalled, was so worried by his "foreignness" and broken English that she fainted.

In return for twenty shillings a week rent, Lenin and Nadya had the use of two small rooms on the first floor—one facing the street, the other the backyard. The back room served as both kitchen and dining room and was where Nadya's mother Elizaveta Vasil'evna slept when she joined them later in the year. The other was where Lenin worked and he and Nadya slept, crammed in with their books and writing materials. As the rooms were unfurnished, they had to go out and buy the minimum of cheap furniture on the Tottenham Court Road: two tables, a couple of chairs, a pair of iron bedsteads, and a few pieces of cutlery and crockery. They bought linoleum to cover the floors, but no pictures or decorations.

As paid party workers, Lenin and Nadya had only ten shillings to live on after they paid their rent. They made no concessions to comfort of any kind: they had to bring their coal and water up from the basement and carry their dirty wash water back downstairs to dispose of in the yard outside. The family laughed at Dr. Richter's inability to light a coal fire in an iron grate (quite different from a Russian wood-burning stove), and Mrs. Yeo had to show him how to do it.

Once settled at Holford Square, Nadya was anxious to begin cooking in order to save money. The kind of food on the menu in local working-class restaurants where they had been obliged to eat during their first few days—oxtail stew, skate fried in lard, and indigestible cakes—turned their Russian stomachs, accustomed as they were to very plain fare. Soon Nadya was cooking as best she could on the open fire in their rooms or a tiny primus stove. When she encountered domestic difficulties, she marshaled her few words of English to ask "Muzza" (as she called the motherly Mrs. Yeo) for help. But for the most part, Lenin was the mediator with their landlady, grateful for her instruction in the ways of English shopping. He never took umbrage and was always willing to learn.

He needed to be, for Mrs. Yeo was a paragon of bourgeois respectability. She might have been alarmed at the strange habits of her "German" tenants (as she thought them to be), but she did not hesitate to lay down the law about acceptable standards of behavior. Where was Mrs. Richter's wedding ring? she asked. It was not the done thing to be without one. Takhtarev assured her that the couple were indeed married according to Russian law. But whatever was Dr. Richter doing hanging curtains on their bare windows on a Sunday of all days? Mrs. Yeo did not approve, any more than she did when she saw Dr. Richter walking across Holford Square on a Sunday morning with an unwrapped loaf of French bread under his arm. She wasted no time in telling him such things were not done in England.

In every other respect, however, as Leonard Yeo later insisted, the Richters kept to themselves and were "good, quiet tenants," although "completely unused to English ways." They were always respectful to his mother and always paid their rent on time. "Mrs. Richter" was a sweet, kind lady who became very fond of their tabby cat, talked to it often, and taught it to shake hands and meow good morning to her. As for the studious Dr. Richter, Leonard could not fail to notice his highly educated manner and quickness of thought and action. "His face was alive with great intelligence," though in every other respect he seemed a "most ordinary little man."

As time went on, Mrs. Yeo became increasingly alarmed at the procession of foreigners with peculiar black beards coming in heavy topcoats for meetings at the Richters' rooms in the evening—so many that there weren't enough chairs. To her horror, they sat on the floor. Even more perplexing was the fact that they were all too poor to eat or drink and did nothing but sit and talk late into the night. It seemed that words, indulged in the free environment of London, were sufficient food to them. But such visitations caused trouble for Mrs. Yeo with her neighbors. They didn't like all the comings and goings of these suspicious foreigners in their respectable neighborhood. And the visits increased with the arrival of Martov and Zasulich a couple of weeks later.

Alekseev rented five small rooms on two floors of a house at 14 Sidmouth Street to serve as an editorial office for the *Iskra* board and a base for agents visiting from Europe, as well as a clearinghouse for illegal propaganda. Here they also produced crudely faked passports for comrades from Russia. The rooms quickly became untidy and shambolic, with the smell of boiling soup pervading the air. Lenin visited every day for editorial meetings but was quick to retreat to the Spartan and orderly conditions back at Holford Square. When Ivan Babushkin, who had just escaped from Ekaterinoslav prison by sawing through the bars of his cell, joined the commune in September he did his best to clean the rooms, but grumbled that "the Russian intellectual is always dirty. He needs a servant as he is himself incapable of tidying up." Babushkin's tidying did not help, and the other working-class tenants in the house remained hostile to the Russians. A couple of months later, the landlord at Sidmouth Street gave notice to the commune, having become irritated with the scruffy foreigners who bedded down on the landings and floors and filled the place with the stink of cigarettes. The commune moved a few streets away to 23 Percy Circus, close to Lenin's lodgings on Holford Square.

The strongest argument for bringing the *Iskra* operation to London had been the socialist-run Twentieth Century Press in Clerkenwell, a short walk from Lenin's lodgings which was sympathetic to the Russian revolutionary cause. The press operated from a cramped, run-down building at 37 Clerkenwell Green that had been a center of socialist activism since the days of the Chartists in the 1840s, when workingmen's clubs had met here. Political demonstrations and trade union rallies had been held on the green outside. From the 1850s the press had been a supporter of Karl Marx when he settled in London. The first Marxist group in Britain, the

Social Democratic Federation, was established here in 1881, one of its early members being the socialist writer and painter William Morris. The Twentieth Century Press had printed some of the first translations of Marxist theory, as well as a range of speeches and socialist pamphlets by leading Continental socialists. In 1884 it established its own weekly journal *Justice*, edited from the 1890s by the able and likeable Harry Quelch. After being approached by Alekseev, as well as the German émigré Max Beer to whom Lenin had brought a letter of introduction, Quelch did not hesitate to offer Lenin use of the facilities. Upstairs a corner of the printing room was partitioned off to create a tiny editorial office where Lenin could read and correct the proofs. There was only enough room for himself, a desk, and a chair. Here the "small, stocky, ginger-haired young man" was often observed hard at work by Quelch's son Tom.

Once the editorial work was complete, the paper had to be sent to an East End printer for the Cyrillic letters to be typeset by *Iskra*'s own compositor, Blumenfeld (one of the escapees from the Kiev prison). It was then returned to Clerkenwell Green and run off on the Twentieth Century Press's flatbed machine. That the press operated on such a modest scale seemed strange to Osip Pyatnitsky, given that Britain was a free country where they could have maximized output. Here was a British socialist organization publishing a journal—*Justice*—not much bigger than their illegal one, produced far from home under considerable financial difficulty.

On arriving in London, Lenin accessed the facilities of "the richest library in the world," the domed reading room at the British Museum in Bloomsbury. Before leaving Munich, he had, with his usual punctiliousness, carefully checked the maps of London to work out the quickest route on foot to the library from the Pentonville area, where he knew he would be living. This was as much out of financial necessity—to save money on buses—as it was for personal fitness. He was given a letter of recommendation by Isaac Mitchell, secretary of the General Federation of Trade Unions, and filled in the required application form for admission to the library in late April, explaining that he had come from Russia to "study the land question." A British Museum reader's card, A 72453, was duly issued to Dr. Jacob Richter, LLD, on April 29.

The library was Lenin's lifeline during his time in London. His daily visits gave shape and routine to his life. He retreated to the sanity and peace of the library whenever he wished to escape the endless stream of "comrades from Russia" and elsewhere who regularly beat a path to his door and would "pester him in the Russian fashion" for hours at a time. "What do they think we're here for—a holiday!" he would say in annoyance. Such encounters always deteriorated into interminable debates and the "émigré gossip and empty chatter" that he so despised. All he wanted to do was lock himself away and get on with his own serious theoretical studies, leaving the bulk of the day-to-day editorial work on *Iskra* to Martov. By September 1902 Lenin was complaining of a "crowd of people here and altogether too much commotion," with yet more people arriving in the next few days—a reference to the escapees from Kiev prison who were now on their way to England to seek him out. But in the British Museum, in the comfort of a solid leather chair and a desk complete with ink and blotting paper and reading lamp, he could set to work uninterrupted.

Marx, Blanc, and Mazzini had all resorted to this oasis of peace and scholarship during their time in London. Officials at the British Museum would come to remember the modest Russian well. Fellow Russian émigré Theodore Rothstein often encountered Lenin at the library and was impressed by his "amazing capacity for work." The attendants too observed how Dr. Richter "simply swallows books." No one else, they asserted, asked for such vast quantities. At lunchtime, Lenin would stop for a brief meal at a nearby café on Great Russell Street before walking back for his regular 1:30 meeting with Martov and Zasulich at Sidmouth Street; then home and more hours of reading and writing.

A problem that had made itself felt as soon as they arrived in London was the quality of Lenin and Nadya's English. It was one thing to translate Sidney and Beatrice Webb on the page with the help of dictionaries, as they had done in Shushenskoe, but quite another attuning the ear to the peculiar cadences of English, especially as spoken by the working classes. "We found we could not understand a thing, nor could anybody understand us," remembered Nadya. Vera Zasulich never even tried to learn English, shut away as she was with other transient Russians in Sidmouth Street. But Lenin, determined as always to do things properly, resolved to improve. He placed a small ad in *Athenaeum* magazine: "A Russian LL.D (and his wife) would like to exchange Russian lessons for English with an

English Gentleman (or Lady)." A clerk called Williams and a workman, Mr. Young, responded, as well as the venerable-looking Mr. Henry Rayment (whom Alekseev thought not unlike Charles Darwin in appearance), who worked for the publishers George Bell & Sons. Lenin apparently developed a particular friendship with Rayment, whose aptitude for several foreign languages, including Russian, proved invaluable.

Meanwhile the best way of learning the language was to go out and about and hear it spoken. The best place to do this, in Lenin's opinion, was Speakers' Corner at Hyde Park on a Sunday morning, an area designated in the 1870s for anyone desiring to speak in front of an impromptu audience. They were sometimes accompanied by the British socialist Zelda Kahan, who noticed how intently Lenin listened to the speakers at the atheist and socialist platforms, as well as the Christian evidence and Salvation Army ones, in order to access British socialist thinking of the day. A speaker with an Irish accent was easier for him to understand than the others; it may well have been the young George Bernard Shaw, who often spoke in Hyde Park in defense of civil liberties at that time. But often, as Kahan observed, Lenin paid more attention to the crowds than the speakers.

Having read much on the economic history of Britain, including the writings of Marx and Engels on the subject, Lenin studied London with the forensic approach of a scientist. Contemporary London and its working people were of far more interest to him than its museums and galleries, which he found tedious. Wherever he went, Lenin was eager to get to the heart of the working classes and their language and culture—in pubs, in clubs and churches, and at socialist meetings. Once he had learned to accept the vagaries of the English weather, he came to appreciate the immensity of London and loved riding in the open-topped omnibuses. It was not the city's tourist sights that attracted him but rather the sharp contrasts between Britain's "two nations"—the rich and poor. But he and Nadya knew that not everything could be seen from the top of a bus.

After studying detailed maps of the city, they went out exploring the working-class areas on foot. They often went walking along the filthy, winding back streets with washing strung up across them, where pale, sickly children played in the gutter and drunken workmen consorted with prostitutes outside cheap public houses. They visited the reading rooms for poor immigrants (such as the Free Russian Library on Church Lane off Commercial Road, which stayed open until ten at night). When they got hungry and could afford it, they ate in cheap restaurants. They came to like fish and chips from the Little Inn Restaurant or Adam's Chop House on Gray's Inn Road. Indeed Lenin came to know the backstreets of London better than his English tutor, Mr. Rayment, did. He took him out to Whitechapel, a part of London that Rayment had never visited, to see firsthand how the immigrant Russo-Jewish poor lived. He also walked the streets at night with Takhtarev, observing the throng of traders with their market stalls lit up by naphtha tubes. The traffic was extraordinary, the energy and vitality of London life—albeit capitalistic—thrilling. For here, all around him, Lenin could grasp at the raw material of socialist argument and mold it to his own purpose.

Although Lenin was not a drinker, he realized that the public house culture of London and its music halls was an important facet of working-class life. Not far from Holford Square, the Pindar of Wakefield on Gray's Inn Road, with its Aba Daba Music Hall in a room at the back, was conveniently placed for the occasional meeting with Russian colleagues visiting Sidmouth Street. The Crown and Woolpack and Old Red Lion on nearby St. John Street also became regular venues for the Russians. Sometimes Lenin bought himself lunch at the Crown on Clerkenwell Green opposite his *Iskra* offices and looked in at its music hall. The culture of popular musical theater intrigued him—not just in London but also in Munich, Paris, Zurich, and many of the other cities he visited. There was something about the subversiveness of British music hall—in its use of innuendo and often savage satire to make fun of public figures and issues in the news—that particularly appealed. Yet when it came to translating his response into words, Lenin was hamstrung by the clumsy jargon that infected all his work: "In the London music halls there is a certain satirical or skeptical attitude towards the conventional," he wrote rather starchily, that "attempts to turn conventions inside out, to distrust it somewhat, to point up the illogicality of the everyday."

Throughout their long exile getting into the countryside was the most important aspect of Lenin and Nadya's life. The countryside was free, and whenever the weather was fine and they had the time, they sought out their favorite haunt, Primrose Hill. It was only sixpence on the bus from Kings Cross, and they could visit Karl Marx's grave in nearby Highgate cemetery before standing on the hilltop to view the "smoke wreathed city" stretched out below them. But this wasn't sufficient for the energetic Lenin, and often they took their sandwiches and went beyond the suburbs in search of field paths into the real English countryside. All that good clean air went to Lenin's head, and sometimes, as he told his mother, he had to lie down and recover. He was perpetually disappointed that his lethargic fellow exiles did not follow their example: "We are the only ones of the comrades here who are studying the country round London."

Another essential component of Lenin's life in London was seeking out political debate. There was no shortage of clubs and discussion groups for foreign immigrants in the East End; nearer to Lenin at Holford Square there was the Working Men's Institute and Club—better known as the Communist Club—at 49 Tottenham Street off Tottenham Court Road. It had been established back in 1840 as the Educational Society for German Working Men and offered a main room for conferences as well as smaller meeting rooms, a library, a billiard room, card rooms, and a cheap restaurant that sold good German beer. Always full and buzzing with debate, it was increasingly frequented by Russian émigrés from all over London by the time Lenin arrived.

In his search for political debate, Lenin was soon attracted to Toynbee Hall in Whitechapel. Established in 1884 as a settlement house where volunteers offered advice and practical help to the area's largely immigrant Irish and Jewish population, it had become an important rallying point for social reform in Britain. Its Thursday Smoking Conferences attracted political refugees who worked in the East End or the local docks, whose consuming passion was Marxist revolutionary socialism.

One evening in November 1902, journalist and politician John Morley was to debate the subject of foreign policy at Toynbee Hall. As the members gathered in a haze of thick cigarette smoke, a shabby-looking stranger with a short reddish beard who was "Oriental in appearance" took his place among them. One of the settlement workers, William Bowman, thought the man looked "sick and impoverished" and took no further notice of him. After Morley had spoken, the man, announcing himself as Richter, got up to speak in broken English. "What is the use of you coming to the East End and talking about your foreign policy?" he challenged Morley. "Go down to Limehouse or Shadwell and see how the people live. Their slums, bad food, low wages, impoverishment, degradation, and prostitution—that's where your foreign policy should lie. They are the victims of your capitalist organization." By the time Lenin finished delivering an extended criticism of the English social system, everyone had taken notice of him and a heated but friendly debate ensued.

Days later Dean Robinson, head of Balliol House where some of the Toynbee Hall volunteers lived, announced that he had "invited that Russian fellow, Richter" to tea on the coming Saturday and asked Bowman to join them. Lenin turned up, as shabby-looking as before. He tucked into the plate of toasted and buttered muffins offered him with the enthusiasm of a very hungry man. He told them he found English food unpleasant, but he liked the muffins. Despite wrinkling his nose if anyone smoked at 30 Holford Square—though he had to tolerate his mother-in-law's occasional cigarette—he happily accepted a pipe as the three men drew their chairs around the fire to smoke and talk.

Once more, and despite his broken English, the ever-confident "Richter," self-appointed champion of the British dispossessed, vigorously attacked British imperialism, insisting that it would inevitably "dissolve." And when that happened, he warned, "you will have to live on your own industry or else starve." As for organized religion, that, in his view, was "an opiate used by the capitalist classes to dope the people." The Bible was "just a lot of old Jewish fairy-tales . . . of no value to anyone." As Christian pacifists, the mild-mannered Dean Robinson and Bowman were rather disconcerted by Richter's arrogant, if platitudinous statement. There was no mistaking his insistence that *his* point of view was the right one. Nor did he make any attempt to conceal his distaste for their brand of socialist evangelism. When he left, so he said, to visit his "friends down in Limehouse," Richter reiterated his conviction that no great change in society would ever be brought about "without the shedding of blood and revolution." Soon it would be Russia's turn and Britain's too—he was convinced of that.

Wherever he went around London, Lenin was scathing about speakers who "talked rot." To his mind, many educated British socialists were in fact supporters of the liberal bourgeoisie, isolated from the mass of the proletariat. (Strangely, he does not seem to have noted his own isolation from the Russian masses at this time.) He dismissed trade unionism in Britain as parochial and petty, but he was impressed by the class instincts of the British workers who attended some of the meetings he went to. Socialism, he asserted, was "simply oozing from them" and in their responses they laid bare "the essence of Capitalist Society." Nevertheless, Lenin did have some contact with members of the British Social Democratic Federation aside from Harry Quelch at Clerkenwell Green. He often visited Theodore Rothstein at his home at 6 Clapton Square in Hackney. Rothstein's sister-in-law Zelda Kahan (a leading light in the Whitechapel branch of the British Social Democratic Federation) also lived there and remembered Lenin's visits with affection. She recalled his fondness for Theodore and her sister Anne's children and the casual way he played with them. On one occasion she found him "playing at bears" with them, "covered with a fur coat beneath the table." Although the Rothsteins and Kahans become good friends, Lenin made no attempt to mix with other British socialists while he was in London. Consequently British socialists between 1902 and 1903 remained largely oblivious to his presence in London. "Richter" was just one of many shadowy Russians who came and went at that time.

Meanwhile, the rigors of Lenin and Nadya's life at the center of *Iskra* and the emergent party took their toll. By summer the draft program of the RSDLP was finally published in *Iskra,* but Lenin's nerves were "worn to shreds." So, in the second half of June, he took a month's holiday at Loguivy in Brittany on the northern coast of France, where he met up with his mother from Russia and his sister Anna from Berlin. He enjoyed his stay, paid for by his mother and sister, but was still under par when he returned to London at the end of July. The stress of keeping in contact with the network of *Iskra* agents was unending. He admitted to feeling "all done up" and poured out his frustrations about the network in a letter to a colleague in Zurich on August 4. It was nothing less than a tragedy that the movement, for lack of numbers, had "recruited too 'lightly.'" He was frustrated that he could not control the caliber, selection, and training of every recruit: the "'creaking' of the machinery," he declared, was causing him enormous stress. But there was nothing for it: agents volunteering to go into Russia undercover had to be taken on trust:

> More often than not we can't even get letters, and *in nine cases out of ten* (I speak from experience) all our plans in regard to the future activity of the "agent" end in smoke *as soon as the frontier is crossed*, and the agent muddles along just anyhow. Believe me, I am literally losing all faith in routes, plans, etc., made here, because I know beforehand that nothing will come of it all. We "have to" make frantic efforts *doing (for lack of suitable people)* other people's jobs. In order to appoint agents, to look after them, to *answer* for them, to unite and guide them *in practice*—it is necessary to be everywhere, to rush about, to see all of them on the job, at work.

The organization's failings seemed to underline the arguments in *What Is to Be Done?* for a dedicated team of "practical organizers and leaders" to take over all but the most basic initiatives.

—∞—

ALL WAS QUIET on Holford Square early one morning in October 1902 when a hansom cab drew up outside number 30. A young man with a mass of thick, curly hair, wrapped in a cloak and wearing pince-nez, approached the front door and knocked loudly and purposefully. Alert to the coded knocks employed in the Russian underground, Nadezhda Krupskaya leaped out of bed and opened the door. There before her, all the way from Verkholensk in far Siberia, having escaped a few months before, stood one of the party's brightest and most ambitious new activists. She knew him by his code name "Pero"—the pen. His real name was Lev Bronstein, but he went down in history as Leon Trotsky. He had escaped exile hidden under a load of hay in a peasant cart, leaving behind a dummy in his bed. With a change of clothes and false passport provided by friends in the underground at Irkutsk, he had boarded the Trans-Siberian railway and traveled to *Iskra* regional headquarters in Samara. Gleb Krzhizhanovsky then sent him on to Vienna, Zurich, and finally London.

Trotsky had no compunction about disturbing the household early in the morning; he'd roused Axelrod in the middle of the night in Zurich. He was twenty-two and bursting with self-confidence and had come a long way to meet Lenin, having being sent on Krzhizhanovsky's recommendation. Axelrod had given him enough money to get to London via Paris, but he was now penniless. Nadya went down to settle with the cabbie as Lenin emerged, still half asleep. Soon he was engrossed in the arrival's news from Russia as they sat over tea and a frugal breakfast. Lenin interrogated Trotsky on the strengths and weaknesses of the Russian underground as he had observed it in Kiev, Kharkov, and Poltava (where Krzhizhanovsky had sent him prior to his departure). He was anxious to hear about what effects on the party the conflict created by the heretical Bernstein's economists was having, as well as the activities of the newly emergent Socialist Revolutionaries, who were threatening a renewed terror campaign. Trotsky told how he and his colleagues in prison and exile had studied Lenin's every written word, especially his *Development of Capitalism in Russia,* and were impressed by the wealth of statistical evidence he mustered.

Trotsky returned the next day, after spending the night in the commune on Sidmouth Street, for a walking tour of the capitalist sights of London—the Tower of London and Westminster Abbey—the aristocracy and old order that Lenin so despised. Lenin was sounding out Trotsky's political and intellectual acumen, and his clever young protégée was quick to respond. Later Lenin took him for a subject lesson in that strange brand of British conservatism—prevalent even among the working classes—that allowed socialist sympathies to coexist alongside religious belief. In a socialist church at Seven Sisters in Tottenham, North London, they observed how exhortations to God to end the gulf between rich and poor came hot on the heels of political speeches on social revolution, as though worshipers were hedging their bets by keeping a foot in both the temporal and the spiritual camps.

Although he spent most of his time with Lenin, Trotsky did not fail to notice the self-effacing Nadya, forever hunched over her desk organizing contacts, issuing instructions, coding and decoding letters to and from the *Iskra* board. He remembered how there was always a "faint smell of paper warmed up over a flame" in her room.

The "state of rank disorder" at Sidmouth Street where Martov and Zasulich lived was a marked contrast. Trotsky was charmed by the endearing idiosyncrasies of Zasulich, whom he found an "exceptional person," although her slovenly food handling left much to be desired. Vera appeared to live on tobacco and thin slices of ham spread with copious amounts of mustard. Poor Vera, observed Trotsky, she found writing a torment, and public speaking was hard for her too. Her "diffuse radicalism, her subjectivity and her turbulence" irritated the punctilious Lenin. She paced about in threadbare slippers and shapeless clothing, rolling cigarettes, dropping ashes everywhere, and tossing her cigarette butts about randomly, while Martov absentmindedly dropped tobacco in the sugar bowl. Both of them were romantic, old-school bohemians who were rapidly becoming redundant in the hard-edged party envisaged by Lenin.

Lenin encouraged Trotsky to give a public lecture at Whitechapel, where he debated politics in Russian with other exiles. Lenin participated in a workers study circle for Russian immigrants set up by Alekseev and carefully walked them through the recently finalized program of the Russian Social Democratic Labor Party. In November he gave another lecture at a Whitechapel workers club in which he attacked the program and tactics of the Socialist Revolutionaries. On March 21, 1903, he took great pleasure in addressing a meeting at the New Alexandra Hall in Whitechapel on the anniversary of the Paris Commune, which he greatly admired. And then there was a May Day rally in 1903 at the Alexandra Palace, as Lenin addressed the crowd in Russian, German, Italian, Polish, French, and Spanish.

Despite Trotsky's youth and inexperience Lenin was impressed with his energy and abilities. More importantly, he sensed that this forceful young man had grasped the essential, conspiratorial nature of the party. His approval was echoed by Martov and Zasulich. By March 1903 he suggested bringing Trotsky onto the board of *Iskra*. Having seven members would simplify the voting and avoid hung votes, as often happened, with Axelrod and Zasulich invariably siding with Plekhanov. But the haughty Plekhanov disliked Trotsky's flowery writing style and opposed giving this brash *arriviste* a foothold on the board. With Plekhanov vetoing Trotsky, Lenin sent his protégé to Paris on a lecture tour on behalf of *Iskra*. But confrontation with Plekhanov was brewing once again.

Meanwhile, Lenin couldn't get used to the mild, damp winter weather of London, and he could not bear the time wasted during the Christmas hiatus: "Few meetings, the Reading Room will be closed and it will not be easy to get into the theatres, because everything is crowded out." By the spring of 1903 things were no different. He and Nadya were "jogging along as usual." Her mother Elizaveta Vasil'evna was sick a lot, but they had at least managed to go to a concert at Queen's Hall, where they heard Tchaikovsky's latest symphony—the *Pathétique*—followed by a visit to the German theater.

By February 1903 Lenin was in Paris to deliver a lecture at the Russian Social Sciences Higher School, followed by four more in February on "Marxist Views on the Agrarian Problem in Europe and in Russia," and one to the Paris *Iskra* group. By the time he returned to London in early March, change was in the air. Plekhanov was once more lobbying to move *Iskra* to Geneva, and Lenin was opposing the move. It would mean a dramatic loss of his political independence from the rest of the board, which he had so fiercely defended. The stress and worry brought on terrible insomnia and made him very ill.

But his health was already worn down by overwork, and the paper was suffering from a lack of efficient personnel. Zasulich remained hopelessly disorganized. Potresov had fallen ill with tuberculosis and was in a sanatorium on the Continent while the restless Martov, who hated London, had decamped for the cafés of Paris. He was delighted when *Iskra* was relocated, since he could return to his old haunts in Geneva. The relocation also meant that Lenin's increasing stranglehold over the editorial board could be weakened. More and more of the burden had devolved to Lenin and Nadya even as he was undertaking the complex preparatory work for the second party congress, to be held that year.

When he lost the vote over the relocation to Geneva, Lenin was reluctant to leave Holford Square. He and Nadya were happy and settled, "like cats which get used to a particular spot," as she told Lenin's mother in Russia. But in April 1903 they departed, leaving behind them only a pile of papers in Russian. Sensibly, the Yeo family burned them all in the backyard. But Lenin did not forget his English landlady. After he and Nadya arrived in Switzerland, he sent a book of views of Geneva, dedicated "to the good kind lady, Mrs Emma Yeo." She treasured it, remembering Mr. Richter as a lodger who had been "far better to deal with than many an Englishman." But she and her children never did work out what those long visits from strange foreigners amounted to, nor did they ever suspect their highly seditious objectives. Nadya had observed the "naive perplexity" that their odd émigré way of life inspired in the British and their incredulity at the fact that she, a woman, had gone to jail for her political beliefs. Years later, Leonard Yeo still found it hard to believe that "such a quietly good-natured little man" who looked like a student went on to become "such a world shaker."

But there was one thing the Yeos did remember—their distinctive and emphatic three Russian knocks at the front door.

CHAPTER SIX

"The Dirty Squabble Abroad"

Geneva–Brussels–London–Geneva: April–December 1903

LENIN ARRIVED IN GENEVA a sick man. The stress of his escalating workload in London had resulted in a painful red rash on his back and chest. Consulting a medical dictionary, he and Nadya diagnosed it as a viral infection of the nerve endings commonly known as "holy fire." Since they did not have the guinea needed to consult an English doctor before they left, Nadya dabbed the inflamed area with iodine, causing Lenin excruciating pain. For the first two weeks in Geneva he was, to his intense frustration, confined to bed at the Pension Morhard on avenue de Mail. He was thin and pale, but his condition didn't stop him from working. The pension was a regular haunt of visiting Russian revolutionaries, and colleagues streamed to his bedside. No matter how sick he felt, Lenin insisted that everyone arriving from Russia come and describe the latest political developments in minute detail.

As soon as he recovered, he went out looking for somewhere to live. An activist named Kulyabko, who was visiting from Russia, bumped into him out flat hunting one day. "Was Lenin happy to be back in Switzerland?" Kulyabko asked, his first, brief visit having been in 1895. "No, not much," was the response. He liked the scenery and it was a good country for walking. The mountains of course were wonderful and reminded him of Russia. But Geneva itself had nothing attractive about it. Kulyabko was surprised that someone as busy as Lenin was out looking for a place to live. Surely there were others who could do that for him? "Oh no," responded Lenin. He had factored in time out of his busy schedule expressly for the purpose.

Lenin's schedule was, as always, crammed with activity. When Kulyabko arrived one day to collect a couple of articles from him for the printer, he was told, "I'll have one for you today, it's already in my inkwell, but I don't even have the other one in my head as yet." When Lenin and Nadya had moved to a small two-story house on Chemin privé du Foyer in the working-class suburb of Secheron, they unpacked only their manuscripts, books, and newspaper clippings. They didn't seem to mind using packing cases as improvised furniture; at least here there was no landlady laying down the law. The day Kulyabko turned up, all he saw in Lenin's bleak little room was a mattress and pillow on the floor, a rickety stool with a candle in a bottle, and a large glass inkwell. Downstairs, Elizaveta Vasil'evna was squeezed into a tiny room off the kitchen, where she had taken command of the domestic chores, complaining that all Vladimir Ilyich and her daughter did was "pore over their books and notebooks." Her son-in-law was worrying himself to death over his work, she was convinced of it, and Nadya was worn out. Unsurprisingly, the three of them lived in a state of transit until July.

The large enamel kettle was always boiling on the kitchen range. Tea and conversation were always on offer to visitors; but not much more as Lenin and Nadya were now extremely short of money. Ever a creature of habit, Lenin went daily to his editorial office located in a print shop on rue de la Coulouvrenière. But most of his time was taken up with preparations for the coming party congress: drafting rules and procedures and preparing a report on the *Iskra* operation. Lenin was determined to rally as many supporters to his political point of view as he could, which is why, uncharacteristically, he welcomed so many visitors to his home at this time. Nadya meanwhile was working long hours corresponding with the *Iskra* network. There were endless editorial meetings with Martov and Potresov, and Trotsky had now arrived from Paris. As delegates for the congress began congregating in Geneva and making their way to Lenin's house, the talk in the small, stuffy kitchen at Secheron became noisy and heated. It often had to be continued in the more calming atmosphere of Mon-Repos Park on the edge of Lake Geneva, with spectacular views of snowy Mont Blanc in the distance.

Within three months Lenin and Nadya were on the move again, this time to Brussels, where the party congress would be held. They found lodging with a Belgian workingwoman. Delegates arriving from Russia and elsewhere were told to congregate at Comrade Koltsov's flat in the city to register for the congress. But the procession of suspicious-looking Eastern Europeans soon provoked a predictable response from Koltsov's landlady: she objected to these strange men banging on the door. Koltsov and his wife were told to find some other rendezvous, and the congregating delegates decamped to the Coq d'Or hotel. Here the exuberant Russians, intoxicated by the freedom of Belgium, often indulged in rowdy singsongs after their evening meal, drawing attention to their presence in the city. Their exuberance was partly a reaction to the stress of getting to Brussels illegally from Russia and then finding themselves in the free world. Back home, scores of social democrats had been arrested, including two or three of Lenin's delegates, almost wrecking his plans. Elena Stasova in St. Petersburg had worked hard to replace them. Among them was Aleksandr Shotman, one of only three workers to attend the congress among Marxist intellectuals and professional revolutionaries.

On July 30, 1903, fifty-seven delegates representing a cross-section of twenty-six Russian, Jewish, and other organizations—forty-three delegates with voting rights and fourteen with a consultative voice only—assembled for the second congress of the Russian Social Democratic Labor Party. They did so in hopeful secrecy in a large warehouse attached to the Maison du Peuple, a cooperative society in Brussels. Koltsov had selected it with the help of Belgian socialists, in hopes that such a run-down venue would not attract police attention. The congress had been long awaited and everyone hoped that the groundwork of creating party unity on Marxist policies through *Iskra* as the mouthpiece would have brought the various groups at home and abroad to a common political language and shared objectives for the huge task at hand in Russia.

Inside the warehouse, Koltsov had improvised a dais with a table and a couple of chairs; the rest of the delegates had to squeeze together on crudely knocked together planks of rough wood. The main window was draped with red cloth to keep out prying eyes, but it made the place feel like a dark garret. By night, the lamplight gave the whispering group the appearance of conspirators. As soon as the congress started, a strange fidgeting broke out among the delegates. One by one they leaped to their feet and started wrestling with their clothing. To compound their discomfort, they discovered that they were sharing the premises with not just rats but a plague of fleas that had grown fat and comfortable on bales of wool previously stored there.

The congress carried on disjointedly for a few days, constantly changing venues and sitting twice a day, from 9:00 to 1:00 and from 3:00 to 7:00. Each speaker was allowed half an hour, with ten minutes allotted to each respondent from the floor; no one could speak on a single topic more than three times. Even though it was taken for granted that Lenin's *Iskra* group led the party, Lenin frantically tried to control every session. He beat down factions that threatened to jeopardize party unity, particularly the independent minded Jewish Bund—the General Jewish Labour Union—with five delegates and the economists with seven. Another four delegates remained uncommitted.

In deference to Plekhanov's perceived seniority as author of the party program and grand old man of Russian social democracy, Lenin invited him to give the opening address. He fitted the part, impeccable as ever in his neat frockcoat. It was an auspicious moment in the history of the Russian Social Democratic Labor Party, whose first congress in 1898 had amounted to a meeting of eight members in a back room in Minsk to decide on a name and manifesto for their party. As Plekhanov rose to take the rostrum, the long years of emigration seemed to be fading into the past as the gathering he had dreamed of for twenty years began. It was clear that he intended to assert his leadership over the party, but Lenin, elected deputy chairman of the presidium to Plekhanov, was in a combative mood.

Debate raged for the first two days over the membership of the party's Organizational Committee. The Bund, with its powerful support in the Pale of Settlement, objected to its lack of sufficient representation at the congress and demanded autonomy as a separate group. Ironically, it was Jewish delegates—notably Martov and Trotsky—who repudiated Bund demands on the basis that giving special preference to one group would destroy party unity and open the door to demands for similar status from every other national group. The Bundists lost the vote 46 to 5. Although he took a backseat during this clash, Lenin watched approvingly, having already made it clear to his colleague Krzhizhanovsky in April that if necessary they must "make war against the Bund" in order to achieve peace with it: "War at the Congress, war even to the extent of a split—whatever the cost. Only then will the Bund be sure to surrender." The split Lenin predicted would turn out to be far more profound than a quarrel with the Bund.

During the congress Lenin's unorthodox thesis on the party program as outlined in *What Is to Be Done?* became the subject of intense controversy. The economists raised objections to Lenin's plans for a centralized organization, and Trotsky defended Lenin's position, affirming the need for vigilant control of the party. Unfortunately the congress had attracted the unwanted attention of the Belgian police, who had been surprised to see so many Russians arriving in Brussels. They followed delegates to their lodgings, to evening meals at the Coq d'Or, and on walks in the park. They searched the baggage in their rooms in their absence. The Okhrana had supplied the Belgian police with information about several wanted men, and soon four delegates were stopped and summarily told to leave Brussels within twenty-four hours. Surveillance of the remainder was cranked up. The Russians were amused by the heavy-handed police tactics; they were used to giving the police the slip in Russia and took great pleasure in occasionally grabbing the only hansom cab in a street, leaving the spooks to run down the road after them. One day the police stopped Shotman and some friends, demanding to know who they were. One of the men told them in rudimentary Swedish that they were Swedish students. Since the Swedes were the least likely people to be plotting revolution, the gullible police, whose Swedish was equally poor, went away satisfied.

But clearly the congress could not continue with many of the delegates under threat of arrest and extradition back to Russia. The Leninist principles of *konspiratsiya* disintegrated as so many passionate, opinionated Russian radicals gathered together in a confined space were undermining the security of the congress. It would have to decamp, and London seemed the best option. After the thirteenth session on August 6 the group made its way by train to Ostend and the boat to Dover. The crossing was stormy, and many passengers, including Nadya, took to their beds with seasickness. But not Lenin. Reinvigorated by the prospect of a move to familiar London, he pulled his cap down over his head and paced the deck watching the storm.

On arrival in a drizzly and misty London, the delegates were directed to Nikolay Alekseev's flat in a "small square" near Kings Cross (possibly Holford Square, where he appears to have moved late in 1902) and told to make the prerequisite three hard knocks on the door. Martyn Lyadov, a delegate from Saratov making his first trip to London, found the whole experience bewildering, even more because of the squalid conditions in the apartment. Alekseev lived "like a student," the furniture in his small third-floor room consisting of a "broken bed, two chairs barely standing on their legs, and a rickety table." The only other furnishings were piles of Russian and English newspapers. Aleksandr Shotman was similarly appalled; Alekseev lived on canned food, the empty evidence of which lay scattered in every corner of the room. Soon Nadya arrived with Lenin and got the kettle on the boil and plied the delegates with tea as Lenin rushed around organizing cheap places for them to stay. Meticulous as ever, he provided them all with maps for finding their way to wherever the congress was meeting. He also made a point of visiting the delegates in their lodgings in the days that followed to ensure that all was well with them and that their landladies were not giving them any trouble.

On August 11 the congress reconvened with its fourteenth session. This took place at the "English Club," probably another name for the Communist Club, which had recently moved from Tottenham Street to a house at 107 Charlotte Street. Konstantin Takhtarev, who was still living in London, had found alternative venues for the congress, another being an Anglers Club somewhere in the same area, having informed the landlord that it was needed for a "meeting of Belgian trade unionists." This time the principles of *konspiratsiya* prevailed; indeed, so much so that the details of the precise locations used for the 1903 congress—possibly trade union halls and cafes or restaurants with small conference rooms attached—are still not known. One day, however, when members were leaving a session, local street kids—who had been unsettled by foreigners arguing and gesticulating as they came out—threw rotten potatoes and rubbish at them. At the request of the congress, a policeman was put on duty outside the door the following day, the sole British police presence at the time.

The atmosphere at the congress remained tense. There was a constant furor, first hissing, then applause, with everyone clamoring to speak at the same time. In the midst of it all Lenin made frenzied attempts to shout down the opposition. A crisis point was reached on August 15 over a seemingly minor point of interpretation in the very first paragraph of the statute, regarding membership of the RSDLP.

Martov stood up and argued for a broad-based party allowing secondary members and sympathizers who supported the party program and underground activities to be allowed to participate—personally or materially. Lenin, still wedded to the old Jacobin traditions of secrecy, took a more authoritarian line: the party should remain narrow—for professionals only, with all members fulfilling the precondition of "personal work in one of the Party organisations." It all seemed perfectly logical to Lenin, who had already clarified his views on the subject in *What Is to Be Done?* There had to be a firm leadership: "either the 'organized utopia' of Lenin or 99/100 outside the party." The notes scribbled on his copy of the agenda testify to the extent of his ambition.

Many of the delegates gathered in London during those August days viewed Lenin's demands as undemocratic and un-Marxist, sensing the inherent slide to dictatorship in a closed party. As mistrust and recrimination escalated, the initial atmosphere of unity and compromise that existed at the end of July evaporated into suspicion, if not outright enmity. Lenin's relationship with Martov, which had been deteriorating for months, broke down rapidly, as he mauled Martov's perceived softness. Zasulich had remarked that Lenin was a bulldog with a "deadly grip." Aleksandr Shotman pitied the disheveled and shambolic Martov, with his pale face and his sunken cheeks and his pince-nez perpetually sliding down his nose. The pockets of his shapeless suit were stuffed full of papers. He seemed cowed, yet when he spoke, his analytical strength and intellectual passion still shone through.

Despite having Plekhanov's support on the need for discipline in the party, Lenin was defeated by twenty-two votes to Martov's twenty-eight. Many delegates agreed with the broad outlines of Lenin's plan for a tighter and more centralized party, but they had a problem with Lenin's unbridled jockeying for control. It smacked of Bonapartism, and it was mirrored in an attitude shift among supporters who began to manifest their "hardness" in contrast to the "softness" of Martov and his supporters.

Lenin, as he later admitted, fought like "a madman" to impose his view. Antagonized by Lenin's attempts to dominate, the Bundists and the economists had sided with Martov. Worse, Lenin unexpectedly found himself opposed by his newest and brightest acolyte—Trotsky—who also took Martov's side. Lenin's subsequent attempts behind the scenes to talk Trotsky around failed. The split between the hard and soft camps continued for the rest of the congress. But on August 18, during the twenty-seventh session, the Bundists—having failed to win support for their independence within the party from either Martov or Lenin— walked out, followed soon after by the economists. Martov lost his slim majority and the tables were turned.

A meeting on the evening of August 18 saw the final break between the two camps when Lenin revealed his plans to reorganize the *Iskra* editorial board. Nadezhda Krupskaya later claimed that he had been so stressed by the prospect of breaking with his former friends Zasulich, Axelrod, and Potresov that he had sat up all night and shivered. But they were inefficient and had contributed little to either editorial or organizational work. To Lenin's mind the cozy "family character" of the original board of six had been impeding efficiency for the past three years. From the moment that "*Iskra* became the Party and the Party became *Iskra*" Lenin had known such a break was inevitable; it was the best solution to three years of endless wrangling on the board. And so he ruthlessly forced out the three softs—Zasulich, Axelrod, and Potresov.

Trotsky found Lenin's treatment of the venerable pair of Zasulich and Axelrod callous in the extreme. It might be politically right, he conceded, but it was morally wrong. Nevertheless, Lenin (thanks to the exit of the Bundists and the economists, who would have opposed him in this) narrowly won the vote to change the board to the three most "politically decisive" operators—Plekhanov, Martov, and Lenin.

Vera Zasulich accepted her ejection with a strange passivity considering that the *Iskra* board was the main focus of her lonely life in exile. Nadezhda Krupskaya noted that being removed would for her "have meant cutting herself off from Russia again, sinking back into the slough of emigrant life abroad." Her work for *Iskra* was "not a question of ambition, but a matter of life and death." Yet she was reticent about protesting, perhaps out of a desire to avoid further friction. Party unity came first, even at the expense of lifelong dedication.

Elections followed for the three-man Central Committee—a body which would operate inside Russia in consultation with an elected Council of the Party. Lenin's men, Gleb Krzhizhanovsky, Fridrikh Lengnik, and Vladimir Noskov, gained the crucial seats on the Central Committee. Lenin, Plekhanov, and Martov were elected to the new three-man editorial board of *Iskra* based abroad. But Martov, out of loyalty to his ejected colleagues, refused to continue working with Lenin and Plekhanov on *Iskra* and resigned, although he accepted election to the party council. Despite the long political association and mutual respect that had bound Martov and Lenin, the two men were heading for a fatal divergence of views, largely engineered by Lenin, leaving Plekhanov to vacillate uncomfortably between the two. Lenin's "majoritarians" (*bolsheviki*) thereafter lined up in opposition to Martov's "minoritarians" (*mensheviki*), but the final fatal breach between them would not occur for several years.

As the only delegate to attend every session during the twenty-four days—speaking on more than one hundred separate occasions—Lenin had become, by dint of energy and will, the effective leader of the party. During the congress he had never let up in his constant verbal assault—cajoling, arguing, hectoring delegates at every opportunity on party issues, and making careful notes on where their loyalties lay and carefully filing it all away in the card index of his rigorous political mind. "I realise that I often behaved and acted in a state of frightful irritation," he later told Krzhizhanovsky. His manner admittedly had been frenzied. "I am quite willing to admit *this fault of mine to anyone*, if that can be called a fault." But as far as he was concerned, his behavior had been "a natural product of the atmosphere, the reactions, the interjections, the struggle."

Lenin spent several days with the delegates who had taken his side. On August 24 he took them to Karl Marx's grave in Highgate cemetery, having already introduced them to Speakers' Corner at Hyde Park and the British Museum. Lenin now attached great importance to keeping them on his side and sending them back to Russia to recruit more workers for the party—and his faction within it. Pulling the strings of the Russian revolutionary movement from Europe meant that he rarely met agents in person, but Lenin now took full advantage of having his disciples sitting at his knee. Running the revolutionary underground was, as he later wrote, like conducting an orchestra. He needed to know "precisely who is playing which fiddle, and where, and how he does it." If a false note was sounded, he had to understand where and why, "who ought to be shifted, and how and whither." With the mind of an impartial clinician Lenin argued that every "discordant tone" had to be removed.

As far as he was concerned, his split with Martov was superfluous in the greater scheme of things. However, the sacrifice of Zasulich, Axelrod, and even Martov, as it now turned out, was necessary: in the best interests of the revolution. But he had made enemies by showing so little respect for the old guard. And Plekhanov, caught between a rock and a hard place—valuing Lenin's intellectual and editorial skills while watching him undermine Martov and Zasulich—soon came to regret supporting Lenin on the *Iskra* issue. Delegates could not understand how Lenin could behave so dishonorably toward his former colleagues. Where did he get the "supreme self-confidence" that allowed him to ride roughshod over people?

Lenin's intransigence and ruthlessness—though he would call it revolutionary purity—had won the day, but the breach between him and his former *Iskra* colleagues was irreparable, with accusations of chicanery, intrigue, "opportunism," and unscrupulousness being hurled back and forth. As far as Trotsky was concerned, Lenin, with his ominous Jacobin tactics of extreme centralism, was now imposing "a state of siege" on the party with his "iron fist." But there was no denying his gift for leadership. He was, as Trotsky perceptively noted that August, "a man with every fibre of his being bent on one particular end. Lenin alone, and with finality, envisaged 'tomorrow,' with all its stern tasks, its cruel conflicts and countless victims."

In Geneva Lenin's former friend and colleague Aleksandr Potresov took a cynical view of the events of the summer of 1903, at the end of a seven-year friendship with Lenin. As in everything, Lenin had made finding a middle ground impossible—in terms of running *Iskra* and, more ominously, shaping the future direction of the party as a whole. Everything with Lenin boiled down to extremes—of being for him or against him. There was something destructive in his "monolithic, one-note nature," wrote Potresov later, and in particular the way he "oversimplified" the complexities of the human condition, reducing everything to narrow-minded sectarianism.

As Martov and his supporters left London, Lenin and his faction set off for Geneva. Once again, three weeks of enervating debate and factional infighting had left him prostrate from exhaustion and sleeplessness. But the "battle of recriminations" had just begun. And worse, those in the party at large siding with the Martovites were now transferring their crucial financial and practical support to that faction. Lenin's state of physical and mental collapse continued into the autumn and no doubt directly contributed to a serious accident he had in October. When he was out cycling one day on his new bicycle (purchased with money sent by his mother and siblings; Nadya had one too), his wheels got caught in some tram rails and he went headlong into the back of a tram. As he fell, Lenin gashed his head on a stone, just missing his eye and badly bruising his arm and side. Undaunted, he obtained first aid and then went straight to his next appointment—the Conference of the League of Russian Social Democrats Abroad. He entered the Café Landolt, on the corner of the rue de Candolle, with his head swathed in bandages.

The league had been liaising between the different Russian émigré communities in Switzerland, Paris, and London since 1894. But the personal animosities unleashed at the London RSDLP congress were still rankling and inevitably infected the league. Martov, now losing all sense of tactics and moderation, immediately went on the attack, screaming first at Lenin and then at Plekhanov. For the best part of five days pandemonium reigned at the Café Landolt, with Martovites jumping up from their seats shouting and gesticulating, pushing and shoving and threatening with their fists. In the midst of it all Lenin stood calmly adjusting the bandage over his eye. His self-possession amid the chaos only enraged the Martovites further.

Next Plekhanov backtracked on his support for Lenin in London. In an attempt to conciliate, he persuaded the old editorial board to return to the *Iskra* fold. This was the last straw for Lenin; on November 1 he resigned from the board in protest, saying it was impossible for him to work with the Martovites. Having overseen forty-five issues of his brainchild *Iskra* he had now, so it seemed, willfully cut himself off from his own political mouthpiece. The unthinkable was about to happen: *Iskra* would revert to the control of Martov, Zasulich, Axelrod, and Potresov, all now reconciled with the traitorous Plekhanov. It was the lowest moment in Lenin's revolutionary career so far. For him, there could be "no worse a blind alley than to leave work," and for the last three years *Iskra* had been his life.

Getting sidetracked into a blind alley and losing a good friend and political ally, Julius Martov, was a bitter experience. Martov had been one of the few male associates Lenin had ever allowed to get close to him. But Lenin was forced to recognize that an unbridgeable gulf separated his friend's tragic lack of political will and his own iron determination. In a letter to Gleb Krzhizhanovsky, he wrote, "There is no longer any hope, absolutely no hope of peace. You can't imagine even a tenth of the outrages to which the Martovites have sunk here, poisoning the whole atmosphere abroad with their spiteful gossip, encroaching on our contacts, *money*, literary material, etc." For Lenin it was a terrible moment. "War has been declared," he continued, and he and his supporters must now "get ready for the most legal but desperate struggle."

The loss of *Iskra* left Lenin politically isolated and without his all-important platform, despite letters of solidarity from local committees in Russia. He would have to remake his career as a journalist and a professional political analyst as well as build new personal and political alliances. In the meantime he was determined to tell his side of the story and keep the network of *Iskra* agents in Russia on his side. In a pamphlet published in December 1903 he explained why he resigned from the *Iskra* editorial board. He elaborated on his explanation at even greater, self-justifying length in another pamphlet (*One Step Forward, Two Steps Back)* attacking Martov and his hysterical scandalmongers, published the following year.

Lenin relentlessly maneuvered for position, refusing to let go of his vision for the party and the future. In November he contrived to have himself brought onto the Central Committee, thanks to the influence of his friend and committee member, Krzhizhanovsky. It was an undemocratic and underhanded act, but such things did not concern Lenin in the cause of reasserting his position. "We must by all means fill the places on *all* committees without exception with our own people." Krzhizhanovsky regretted being browbeaten into this act, feeling, as many did, that the "old man" should end his quarrel with Martov for the sake of the party. When he continued to try to conciliate with the Martovites, his relationship with Lenin became the inevitable casualty.

Personal conflicts with colleagues and friends took a toll on Lenin's physical health, which throughout his life veered from extremes of high energy to exhaustion. The clashes at the second party congress and its aftermath left him depressed and unable to eat or work. He became thin and sickly, plagued by a recurrence of his old stomach problem, as well as insomnia and migraines. He sought medical advice, but nothing short of total withdrawal from political life would relieve his many physical ills. A specialist diagnosed Lenin with neurasthenia—a catchall for stress. Yet, as Nadya knew only too well, not being able to work was more distressing for her husband than any illness. Not even a severe health warning could derail him from his chosen path toward revolution in Russia.

Political life in Geneva was gloomy until December 12, when the city came alive for four days as workers took to the streets for the annual celebration of *L'Escalade*—"the scaling of the walls." The festival commemorated the day in 1602 when the citizens of Geneva, who had been independent from the French state of Savoy since 1536, heroically repulsed the Duke of Savoy when he attacked to regain control. Genevans took enormous pride in the event and the streets were humming with carousels, a circus, and fairground stalls. At night the streets were ablaze with fireworks and a torch-lit carnival with masked revelers.

The Russians, however, sat indoors, gloomy and discouraged, poring over their political tracts and documents, too preoccupied and too depressed to join the celebration. But then, as one of them later recalled, came a knock at the door. It was Lenin, demanding to know why they were not out on the streets soaking up the atmosphere. "Let's go," he shouted. "You can leave all your important questions till the morning." It was a mild evening, and the streets were full of flickering lights. The River Arve rushed noisily along its course as the group of comrades, laughing and singing, snaked their way down the streets. No one laughed more heartily than Lenin did. Eventually they wound their way to the Café Landolt, which served the best sausages and sauerkraut. Amid the plain wooden tables and chairs, Lenin had his own table—number 40, near the window. Russian political émigrés occasionally held conferences and meetings here in a small room at the back, with its own discreet emergency exit onto a narrow lane.

That evening, the experience of being out among the masses on the streets totally reinvigorated Lenin. He had come this far, but only at the loss of stalwart friends from the early days of his revolutionary career—Martov and Potresov. Together with Plekhanov, Zasulich, and Axelrod, they had formed the heart of the Russian émigré community. But now the party was fractured. Supporters of the two camps back in Russia thought their leaders had gone mad to allow such a schism to occur over technical points of organization. Seeking to conciliate and save the party from further disruption, many regional committee members continued the practical work of the underground as best they could. For Lenin, there was a hard road yet to travel, but his determination persisted on New Year's Eve 1904, when he and a group of friends met again at the Café Landolt and raised their glasses to the growing success of the Russian revolutionary movement back home.

CHAPTER SEVEN

"Strong Talk and Weak Tea"

GENEVA: JANUARY–DECEMBER 1904

⎯⎯⎯∞∞∞⎯⎯⎯

ON DECEMBER 31, 1903, weakened by an eleven-day hunger strike, party activist Nikolay Valentinov emerged blinking from his dark prison cell onto the streets of Kiev. Expecting to be reunited with family and friends, he was warned to leave the city immediately or risk being rearrested and sent to another prison where he would be allowed to die from a hunger strike. Instead of remaining at risk of rearrest in Russia, on the orders of the local RSDLP leader, Gleb Krzhizhanovsky, he was to carry an important letter to Lenin in Geneva. Once in Switzerland he could rest up, get the inside story on the recent party split, take instructions, and return to Russia "as a professional revolutionary." The temperature was 16 degrees below zero the night Valentinov managed to cross the frozen River Dnestr into Galicia in Austria-Hungary by smuggler's sledge, after hiding overnight in a snow drift. From here he picked up the railway line to Vienna and traveled on to Geneva, arriving with nothing but "a toothbrush, a piece of soap, a towel" and Krzhizhanovsky's secret letter in invisible ink sewn into the lining of his coat.

Cold and hungry, he shuffled his way to Lenin's apartment, where Nadya ripped apart his coat to get at the letter while Lenin subjected him to "an avalanche of questions," eager to find out how the party split was being viewed in Russia. Hours later he allowed his exhausted messenger to take to his bed in the cheap hotel on the Plaine de Plainpalais where many of his supporters regularly stayed.

For a while Valentinov (nicknamed Samsonov by Lenin for surviving his hunger strike) found himself welcomed into Lenin's inner circle. Lenin had heard about his activism in Kiev, how he had been beaten with police truncheons and knocked unconscious while taking part in demonstrations, and wanted to know more about the tactics of violence. "The autocracy will not collapse at the sound of the trumpets of Jericho," he assured Valentinov. "One must start destroying it physically by means of mass blows . . . we must learn to smash mugs in the proletarian way!" Valentinov got the idea that when the day came, Lenin would be the first to mount the barricades.

Lidiya Fotieva, who also made her way to the city that spring after being released from prison in Perm, had to give the commander of the frontier post fifteen rubles to allow her to get out of Russia; the border guard who turned a blind eye as she passed was cheaper at only twenty kopeks for a bottle of vodka. Ceciliya Bobrovskaya, another eager acolyte, had arrived from Tver in northern Russia, having been smuggled across the Prussian border for a bribe of ten rubles to a border guard, having shared the filthy hovels of a succession of Jewish, Polish, and German villagers along the way. Ceciliya was eager to meet Lenin, whose writings had exerted a powerful ideological influence over her party work in Tver. She had heard of the "scandalous" party split in London and sided strongly with the Leninists. This estranged her from her former friend and mentor Axelrod, who had sided with the Mensheviks in opposition to Lenin and his "rams." She, like Valentinov, made a good impression on Lenin with her detailed report on party work in Tver and was invited to visit him and Nadya at their home.

Valentinov, Fotieva, and Bobrovskaya were just three young revolutionaries among many who passed through Geneva that year. Located in southwestern Switzerland on the border with France, Geneva had long been the classic heartland of Russian exile and the unacknowledged capital of the Russian revolutionary movement abroad. Like London, it had been welcoming refugees since European Protestants fled there during the Reformation in the sixteenth century. During the nineteenth century Switzerland had become a center for Russian intellectual emigration, especially from the 1860s, although wealthy Russians also chose to live here for access to the spas and the clean air of its mountains. Eventually an émigré community arose known as La Petite Russie, with its own Eglise Russe funded by Grand Duchess Anna Fedorovna. But in following years the links between the city and the exiles were largely political in character. The first three congresses of Marx's First International had been held in Geneva in the 1860s, and after 1871 French Communards fleeing the barricades of Paris had arrived. Finally, in 1883, the Emancipation of Labor group was founded in Geneva, and the city became "a sort of revolutionary Olympus" for the exiled Russians lorded over by the cultured Plekhanov, the acknowledged father of Russian Marxism.

During those years, Geneva witnessed many different types of Russian political exiles from the first populists, to Narodnaya Volya extremists, to nihilists to anarchists and finally to Bolsheviks and Mensheviks, with Lenin's group gravitating to Geneva and Martov's, later, to Zurich.

No sooner had they arrived than the factions set up their own printing presses, lending libraries, reading rooms, and bookshops, which became a center for the dissemination of radical literature. They shared a propensity to physical austerity and an intense preoccupation with science and politics over and above concerns about personal comfort. For many political exiles, to dress, eat, and live better than the working classes back home in Russia whom they championed was positively criminal. A young Italian émigré, Benito Mussolini, who was studying in Geneva in the early 1900s, observed with curiosity and often admiration this "strange, dissolute, eccentric, fantastic group" of nihilists and bohemians, who seemed to him "the last word in fervid, feverish modernity." Nor could he fail to notice the "orgies of strong talk and weak tea" that punctuated the daily round of the Russians' lives and how they would sit up all night talking and arguing, "following along the track of an idea like so many bloodhounds." Whenever Russians came together to talk, they shared a particular commonality of feeling. They were, as the novelist Joseph Conrad observed, haunted always by "the shadow of autocracy," which forever colored "their thoughts, their views, their most intimate feelings, their private life, their public utterances—haunting the secret of their silences." Physically they might be in the free environment of Switzerland, but spiritually and intellectually they were still in Russia.

Calvinist Geneva, sober and orderly, might therefore have seemed the least compatible environment for the turbulent Russians. For Conrad, as a Pole, Geneva seemed passionless and indifferent to the world outside. But by the 1900s it had a burgeoning new Russian heartland in the streets around the southern end of the rue de Carouge, a newly built workers district on the outskirts of the city. This broad thoroughfare of four- and five-story stone houses with trees planted down one side was not far from the River Arve, a fast-flowing tributary of the Rhône that flooded regularly in the spring. Here the new Russian enclave of political émigrés who congregated around the rue de Carouge and the nearby boulevard des Philosophes gave the area its nickname—*karuzhka*. Amid the city's neatly manicured parks with their graceful promenades of plane trees and poplars, their bandstands and cafés, the air of gentility belied the often desperate political machinations of its Russian community. Beyond the steamboat piers on Lake Geneva and the rows of shiny hansom cabs lined up along the public gardens and the efficiency of the new electric trams, the only thing dispelling what Lenin and Conrad both saw as the banality of the city was the power and majesty of the Jura Mountains beyond.

The local response to the Russians was no different here than in London and Brussels. The Russian students were noisy and disruptive, with their "yells of savages fit to wake up the whole city," when they came home late from their long debates and meetings. Their rowdy singsongs in bars and cafés became notorious. During Russia's war with Japan in 1904, they held victory parades along the rue de Carouge every time the army of Nicholas II suffered a defeat. The majority of the Russian community lived a miserable, impoverished existence, doing translation work, giving lessons, waiting on tables, or taking whatever manual labor they could get. They were forced to live in cold, dark attics on the outskirts of the city. As Herzen had earlier observed of his own Russian community in England, these narrow circles increasingly consisted of "inert memories and hopes" that were cut off from home and their source of inspiration and thus "could never be realized."

Homesickness was compounded during this time of uncertainty by much coming and going in the wake of the party split, as the now fractured RSDLP began to realign itself into two opposing groups. So many people were seeking to visit with Lenin that the comrades agreed to call only once a week to allow him to work. So, on Tuesdays or Thursdays, Lenin and Nadya held open house around the kitchen stove out at Secheron. Valentinov was somewhat disturbed by the air of almost religious worship around "Ilych." This unexceptional-looking man, as he saw him, clearly possessed a "hypnotic influence" that was lacking in his rivals Plekhanov and Martov, and it had a very clear effect on many idealistic young revolutionaries such as Ceciliya Bobrovskaya. She was desperate to "go to Ilyich for a chat" as often as possible. Nevertheless, she worried about taking up the leader's precious time and was dismayed that her hero enjoyed so few creature comforts.

Nadya and her mother, who always had plenty of soup on the boil, offered a warm welcome to all. During such convivial gatherings Lenin delighted in good company and would laugh heartily. He always enjoyed being around new arrivals who "breathed of Russia," joining with them in singing revolutionary anthems and Siberian folk songs. The *Internationale* was obligatory, as too the *Marseillaise* and a very popular Russian revolutionary song, "You Have Fallen in the Struggle."

When the comrades performed, Lenin revealed glimpses of a different, private side. Mariya Essen (code-named *zver*, "Wild Animal"), one of Lenin and Nadya's most valued supporters from the Central Committee in St. Petersburg, was also a regular visitor. At Secheron she noticed how much Lenin enjoyed Petr Krasikov's violin rendition of Tchaikovsky's *Barcarolle*. (Krasikov had narrowly escaped arrest in Moscow to get to Geneva, clutching one small suitcase and his violin. For some revolutionists, art was never dispensable.) Lenin listened intently whenever Sergey Gusev sang in his deep baritone; for a moment he would let go, "leaning back on the sofa, his arms around his lifted knees" as though lost in memories—of home and his mother, of what he had left behind in Russia. Perhaps these melodies reminded him of the spiritual life that he had so ruthlessly sacrificed in favor of the relentless world of politics. But if anyone took notice, Lenin shut off his emotions from view. "Lenin's corner," as Valentinov later wrote, "was a very extensive one, and he did not permit anyone to penetrate it."

But Lenin's relaxed moments belied the thoughts now seething inside his head. The party had been torn apart by the split with the "Martovites," and Lenin's support in Geneva—both physical and financial—had been reduced to a handful of loyal followers. The atmosphere that year was very strained, with endless wrangles and squabbles punctuating the life of the revolutionary exile community. Lenin's response as always was highly combative, as he filled his often long and dictatorial letters to party workers in Russia with endless instructions, demanding details of party work in Russia and emphasizing the need for organization and yet more organization. There were constant calls too for money; Lenin and his faction were now virtually without funds.

By March 1904 Lenin had once again worn himself to a shadow, this time writing *One Step Forward, Two Steps Back: The Crisis in Our Party*, his analysis of the second party congress based on his careful examination of the minutes. The pages of this pamphlet reflected his mental turmoil as he openly attacked the Mensheviks as traitors. Their refusal to accept tight organizational discipline had invited anarchy and opportunism—one of Lenin's favorite catchall terms for anyone who opposed him.

In response, Martov proclaimed Lenin "a political corpse" on the pages of *Iskra* in an article entitled "In Lieu of a Funeral Oration." In retaliation, Panteleimon Lepeshinsky, a talented artist, produced a series of cartoons, "How the Mice Buried the Cat," depicting Lenin—"the big tomcat" as Vera Zasulich had nicknamed him—hanging precariously from a beam while being baited by a group of Menshevik mice, including Martov, Zasulich, and Trotsky. Later in the sequence the tomcat, having fallen to the floor, rises up to tear the mice to pieces. Soon the cartoons were being circulated all over Geneva, enraging the Mensheviks.

The community in which the warring Russian exiles now uneasily coexisted was the size of an average London borough. Relations between Lenin's political camp and Martov's became so strained that they were now crossing the road to avoid each other in Geneva's tight-knit Russian community and meeting in separate back rooms at the Café Landolt. By the spring of 1904 the ongoing rift with Plekhanov and Martov had undermined Lenin's health and his belief in himself. Lepeshinsky had never seen him "in such a depressed state." By April he was on the verge of total breakdown. He was so exhausted that he didn't even have the energy to play chess, his one consuming passion.

Valentinov, who spent a great deal of time with Lenin, was convinced that he had arrived at a turning point in his political life. Lenin knew he had to choose between committing totally to his ruthless Bolshevik line or conceding to the Mensheviks for the sake of party unity. Fundamentally, there were no real and telling differences of principle between Lenin and Martov. It all boiled down to the issue of leadership and discipline, of whether or not Lenin should be allowed to wield "the conductor's baton." He truly believed that he was the man for the job: Plekhanov was a great scholar but no better at organization than Axelrod, Zasulich, and Potresov were. As for Martov, he was an "excellent journalist" but a "hysterical intellectual," too soft to be entrusted with the leadership of the party. The conclusion was based on sheer logic and practicality. It was a mark of Lenin's unshakeable faith in his leadership qualities and his inbred sense of destiny.

Valentinov could see that this faith would never be shaken. During the days when Lenin was working on *One Step Forward, Two Steps Back*, Valentinov often joined him for his 4:00 PM walk along the Quai du Mont Blanc by the lakeside. As they walked, Lenin would launch into one of his contemptuous attacks against all the "riff-raff" who diluted the effectiveness of the party, before proceeding to demolish the Martovite objections to his extreme form of centralism. Sometimes while he was raging against the Martovites his face flushed and his eyes became bloodshot as he stopped from time to time, stuck his thumbs in the armholes of his waistcoat, and stamped his foot. He barely took note of Valentinov; in reality he was talking to himself. Valentinov listened patiently as Lenin railed at his rivals' wishy-washy "bourgeois spirit" and their hatred of "proletarian discipline," warning that sooner or later they would break with orthodox Marxism altogether. And that to Lenin was anathema. The fight for a dictatorship of the proletariat was "absolutely meaningless" without a "Jacobin mentality in the people who set it up." So let Plekhanov and Martov accuse him of being a Robespierre in the style of the French Revolution. A true social democrat had to act in that way in order to achieve his ends. It was time for an end to "shilly-shallying" in order to form an "unswervingly revolutionary Marxist party."

Lenin was now very sick, his eyes "heavy and dead-looking" and his eyelids swollen from lack of sleep. By the time *One Step Forward* was published, he had once again shifted his political position, backpedaling on his earlier call for an irrevocable split. This late and limited attempt to compromise was an indication that his energy levels had collapsed, giving way to doubt and taking a toll on his deeply inflexible and intolerant nature. Nadya, who spent her life worrying about her husband's well-being and monitoring his levels of rage, knew she must get him away. She had also become jealous of Lenin's regular walks with Valentinov. Having always considered herself to be Lenin's first and most important political sounding board, she now felt marginalized.

Nadya too needed a break not just from her burden of party work but also from the "constant turmoil" of housekeeping for the stream of visitors at Secheron. So in early July, with her mother away visiting friends in St. Petersburg, she and Lenin gave up their rented house and, leaving Martyn Lyadov in charge of things, set off on a walking tour with their copy of *Baedeker's Switzerland* and not a lot else. By mutual agreement there was to be no talk of work or politics, or business of any kind. "Work," Volodya assured Nadya, "is not a bear and will not escape to the woods." Five days later they sent Lenin's mother a postcard from the mountains with "greetings from the tramps." They took a few books with them but sent most of them back unread to Geneva when they arrived in Lausanne. They had very little money and subsisted on eggs, cheese, and other staples.

The Ulyanovs were accompanied on their trip by Mariya Essen. During the first week the threesome headed on foot along the northern side of Lake Geneva for Lausanne and some mountain walks; then they took the steamer east along the lake to Montreux. Lenin was "indefatigable on outings" and a prodigious walker, according to Mariya. At Montreux they visited the somber, turreted Château de Chillon perched on the lakeside, and the tiny cell where the Swiss patriot François Bonnivard had been held in chains, the inspiration for Lord Byron's 1816 poem *The Prisoner of Chillon*. As a reaction to this oppressive interior and no doubt unpleasant reminders of their own incarceration, the group decided to climb a nearby snowy peak, the Rochers de Naye. It was too much for Nadya with her weak constitution and she went back to the hotel, leaving Lenin and Mariya to continue without her.

The climb was very hard but Vladimir Ilyich, as Mariya recalled, "strode briskly and confidently," chuckling as she struggled to keep up with him. The terrain was so perpendicular that eventually she was reduced to crawling on all fours. But it was worth the effort to take in the view from the top. Below in all their marvelous variety ranged first the brilliant whiteness of the snow, then great ranks of dark green pine trees, and far in the distance the luxuriant Alpine pastures. It was a magical moment; Mariya was moved to recite poetry; something suitably uplifting from Shakespeare or Byron. Lenin too seemed deep in thought. But no flight of poetic fancy fueled his contemplation of so much beauty; the monomania, as usual, was bubbling only just below the surface. "Hmm," he muttered after a pregnant pause, "the Mensheviks are making a fine mess of things."

On the way down Mariya and Lenin agreed not to talk politics "so as not to spoil the landscape." She was touched and surprised when, on entering a field full of wild flowers, Lenin stopped to gather a bunch to take back to Nadya.

From here the party headed south along the Rhône through Bex-les-Bains, turning north again up the valley to Leuk, and then entered the Bernese Oberland via the Gemmi Pass. At some point during this section of the hike Mariya Essen left them to return to Russia, where she was arrested again at the end of the year.

Thereafter Lenin and Nadya walked a deliberately lonely trail down the Kandertal to Frutigen and skirted the shores of the Thuner See and Brienzer See, before arriving in Iseltwald, happy but exhausted. En route they stayed in local farmhouses and inns and ate cheaply with the workers rather than the tourists, collapsing into bed at the end of each day and sleeping for ten hours at a time. But it was impossible for Lenin to cut himself off from party matters altogether; he kept in touch by letter and had newspapers forwarded to him. From Iseltwald they crossed the mountains again in sight of the magnificent Jungfrau and down through the Bernese Oberland to Meiringen.

Holiday or no holiday, Lenin worried increasingly that, with the Mensheviks now running *Iskra*, the absence of a rival Bolshevik newspaper was giving Martov too much of an advantage. For months Lenin had been appealing for supporters in Russia to send in material for a new newspaper, anticipating that sufficient funds would be raised. In July several party members in Russia were arrested, and consequently new members were coopted onto the Central Committee and a reconciliation between Bolsheviks and Mensheviks (his old friend and committee member Gleb Krzhizhanovsky was among the conciliators, now of the opinion that Lenin had lost touch with reality and was an obstacle to party unity) was demanded. One thing was clear: the protracted conflict was dissipating the party's strength. And so, in August, while staying at a pension at the Lac du Bré, Lenin called an urgent, secret conference of his closest associates.

The subsequent Meeting of the Twenty-Two (for such was the limited extent at that time of Lenin's Bolshevik support in Geneva) took place in the back room of a small hotel across the River Arve from the city in a working-class district well away from the Menshevik and other Russian enclaves. One of Lenin's circle, Vladimir Bonch-Bruevich, had hired the venue, supposedly for a meeting of Russians intent on founding a hiking club for walking the Swiss mountains. The Swiss *patron* was flattered by the Russians' interest in alpinism and urged them to link up with the local Swiss society. After the delegates arrived under strict rules of *konspiratsiya*— instructed not to talk to anyone en route or ask directions to the hotel—they agreed to launch an appeal to the party written by Lenin. This document outlined the current crisis and urged that the only hope of overcoming current political differences was to summon a third party congress.

The meeting saw the emergence of two new and significant political allies for Lenin. Aleksandr Bogdanov, a gifted Marxist theoretician, writer, and philosopher, would, despite strong revisionist leanings, become a Bolshevik stalwart for the next six years and an important fund-raiser. The second newcomer, Bogdanov's brother-in-law, was Anatoly Lunacharsky. Primarily a poet and philosopher, he seemed an unlikely recruit with his interests in the wider human aspirations of revolution. Such political romanticism did not square with Lenin's narrow, authoritarian political approach. But right now Lenin needed all the support he could get.

With the meeting of the twenty-two concluded, Lenin and Nadya ended their holiday at the Lac du Bré in mid-September, having walked over 250 miles, by which time the conscientious Nadya was feeling guilty about taking such a long holiday. The effect on Volodya, however, had been transformative: "It was just as though the mountain streams washed away all the cobwebs of petty intrigue." He returned in peak physical condition. The holiday had performed an essential function; to Lenin's logical mind it was his duty, as a revolutionary, to be physically ready for the fight to come.

On their return the couple decided to find a more central residence in Geneva. They rented a small apartment at 91 rue de Carouge, but soon transferred to 3 rue David Dufour so that the apartment on rue de Carouge could be used as an office, party archive, and library for the Bolshevik faction of the RSDLP. At rue David Dufour, they squeezed into two small rooms: Nadya and her mother in one, Lenin in the other. There were, as usual, only the bare necessities—iron bedsteads with bast mattresses, a few chairs, and a plain table. They shared a modest meal at four in the afternoon in the tiny kitchen; Lenin, as Lidiya Fotieva noted on sharing meals with them there, was a hearty eater but it "did not make much difference to him what he ate."

As he had in London, Lenin kept himself apart from the rowdy lifestyle of the other Russian émigrés, eschewing the cafés of Geneva, unless, like the Café Landolt, they served as a necessary venue for meetings. His living accommodation being so cramped he daily decamped to the calm of the city's libraries. The imposing surroundings of the Bibliothèque Publique et Universitaire located in a grand nineteenth-century building on promenade des Bastions might seem the obvious choice, but Lenin preferred the smaller and more intimate Société de Lecture, a private library in the heart of the city at Grand Rue 11, where he registered on his return from holiday as "W. Oulianoff, gentilhomme russe." He went here day after day to work on the bulk of his political articles. The library was quiet and underused, largely the preserve of elderly professors who rarely came, so Lenin had the full range of the reading room to pace up and down as he composed. Soon he became a familiar figure to the librarian there in his shabby trousers "with the bottoms turned up against the mud in Swiss style" and which he often forgot to turn down. Every day he would arrive, "take out the books unfinished the day before . . . about barricade-fighting or the technique of offensives, go over to his usual place by the window, smooth down the thin hair on his bald head with a customary gesture, and bury his nose deep in the books."

He also liked to spend his evenings in the modest, twenty-five-seat RSDLP library that he had established with Vladimir Bonch Bruevich at 91 rue de Carouge. Soon it was carrying a valuable selection of important socialist writings as well as newly published legal and illegal literature from Russia, Paris, and London and a collection of periodicals in sixteen languages. It relied heavily on donations to keep it going, and both readers and staff helped out on a largely voluntary basis. The prime instigator in founding this library, which became known as the Central Russian Library, had been Bonch-Bruevich, who donated many of his own books, as did Lenin. A Tolstoy scholar and writer on religious sects, he seemed an unlikely Leninist. Quiet and intellectual, Bonch-Bruevich had settled in Geneva in 1901. After the party split he and Lenin set up a publishing outlet for the printing and distribution of party literature, coming to an agreement with a group of Russian émigrés who ran a print shop. The newly established publishing house produced its first pamphlet, *Down with Bonapartism* by Mikhail Olminsky, that September; further pamphlets demanded the convocation of a third party congress, notable among them Lenin's "Letter to a Comrade on Our Organizational Tasks." With party committees also lobbying in Russia for another congress, it was now essential that the Bolsheviks produce a newspaper of their own. The party was extremely short of the money needed to fund the paper and its typesetting; Lenin was rigorous: "to spend money on anything else now is the height of folly."

That autumn, with her husband once more obsessively writing and studying, Nadya threw herself back into her party work. It was terribly burdensome. Martyn Lyadov had helped her for a couple of months initially, and when she arrived from Russia, Lidiya Fotieva took over, working daily with Nadya on the voluminous party correspondence. Lyadov and Fotieva both noted how many party workers in Russia were inexpert in coding letters and how Comrade Krupskaya needed hours of patient, tortuous persistence to decipher them; hundreds passed through her hands every month. They could only marvel at her fantastic recall of the names of committee members and their aliases from all over Russia. When problems occurred, having no newspaper of their own, the Bolsheviks resorted to newspaper personal columns. Cryptic messages, intelligible only to the recipients, were placed and "gave directions and suggestions, requested information, acknowledged the receipt of letters or queried answers long overdue," as well as often announcing the failure to decode a particular letter.

Much to Nadya's joy an old friend from her teaching days in St. Petersburg, Ariadna Tyrkova, arrived in Geneva that year for medical treatment. But she was shocked at the poor living circumstances Nadya and her mother endured. Even in St. Petersburg they had had domestic help. Although Ariadna had thrown in her political lot with Petr Struve's liberals, the two women still shared much empathy. It was the first time she had met Lenin and she could not help noticing how Nadya was totally in thrall to her rather small, undistinguished husband with the deep set "Mongolian" eyes. Lenin was very much the master, sitting behind closed doors through which one could just discern the scribbling of his pen and shuffling of his papers. When he emerged to join in their meal, Nadya's plain little face lit up, her large blue eyes shining with a kind of girlish love and admiration. She was totally absorbed in him and his work, even though she had her own very strong personality, quite different from his. She was still the same warm, loving Nadya and Ariadna had to admire the depth of her devotion to a man who at that time was, to all intents and purposes, just another Russian émigré political journalist and pamphleteer. Nikolay Valentinov had also noticed Nadya's total sublimation in Lenin and his work; her speech was littered with her husband's revolutionary truisms. There was "nothing of her own" in anything she said. In his view, "she borrowed everything, from A to Z, from Lenin."

After supper on their last evening together, Nadya asked Lenin to accompany Ariadna to the tram stop as she didn't know her way around Geneva. En route, Lenin berated her for her liberalism and for being a "bourgeois." Ariadna gave as good she got, attacking the Marxists for their lack of understanding of human nature and their desire to drive people like a military machine. Lenin lashed her with his sharp tongue, his words deeply sarcastic and his eyes glittering in a way that Ariadna found disturbing. Then, as the tram came into view, he turned and looked her straight in the eye: "Just you wait," he said with a smile as she boarded the tram, "soon we will be hanging people like you from the lampposts."

Much of the life of the Russian political community in Geneva, and especially that around Lenin, centered at that time on the Russian canteen opened by Panteleimon and Ol'ga Lepeshinsky at 93 rue de Carouge on the corner of quai de l'Arve, next door to the RSDLP library. Panteleimon Lepeshinsky had arrived in December 1903 as an illegal ahead of his wife, who had come on legitimate papers to study medicine at the university. They had borrowed money to set up a canteen to offer food and shelter to impoverished Russian exiles, as well as make a small profit for the party. The canteen opened in September 1904 and quickly became the Bolsheviks' unofficial club and meeting place, a venue for lectures and classes, as well as endless games of chess. The canteen had once been a shop and had a main entrance and two large windows overlooking the street. Inside were ranged six long wooden benches, fifty or so chairs, and a piano (which resident musicians Gusev and Krasikov used for impromptu recitals, accompanied by Lidiya Fotieva). Through an archway beyond the dining area, a kitchen and one small room served as living accommodation for the Lepeshinskys and their five-year-old daughter. The canteen's success became, however, a poisoned chalice for the couple; every day seventy to eighty people crowded in for a "democratic lunch" costing about forty centimes and again for supper and invariably overstayed their welcome. Soon Panteleimon and Ol'ga found themselves unable to extricate their private life from their business one. There were constant interruptions and knocks at the door at all times of the day and night; and in between Ol'ga was still attempting to ride a bicycle to the university every day to continue her medical studies. The canteen's use as a party school was essential to Lenin, for here he held regular meetings and political classes with party activists leaving to take up underground work in Russia. In time the canteen's popularity spread to the international émigré community in Geneva and it became a regular haunt also of Polish, Bulgarian, and Czech political exiles.

At the beginning of November Lenin wrote to Aleksandr Bogdanov describing the desperate need for funds to alleviate "the intolerable, depressing vegetable existence we are leading here." Things were reaching a critical point: "We must get that money if it kills us." Only a few days later his rising anxieties abated a little when Vladimir Bonch-Bruevich secured a deal with a French firm to supply the paper for their newspaper and do the printing on credit. The name *Vpered* (Forward) was chosen when the Bolshevik group met in early December. The editorial board consisted of Lenin, Anatoly Lunacharsky, Vatslav Vorovsky, and Mikhail Olminsky, with Nadya as secretary. Lenin was elated, hoping that his new mouthpiece, the first issue of which appeared on January 4, 1905, would revitalize his leadership and bring many new recruits in Russia.

An incorrigible optimist even with his back against the wall, he stubbornly refused to acknowledge the stark reality of his political position. At the end of 1904 Lenin's hold on the embryonic Bolshevik faction was at best tenuous. According to some, Bolshevism at this time was little more than a library, a restaurant, and a small publishing house in Geneva. Support—both moral and financial—had fallen away since the summer of 1903, and Lenin faced the prospect of rebuilding his element of the party into a new organization. The name *Bolshevik* (from the adjective for "majority") was, effectively, an absurd misnomer, since Martov's "minority" was in fact comfortably in the majority.

Anxious, beleaguered, and broke, Lenin drew in on himself and his reserves. After a brief speaking tour in early December in Paris and Zurich to rally support for his faction, he retreated to the company of the loyal supporters who venerated him: Bonch-Bruevich and his wife Vera, the Lepeshinskys, Martyn Lyadov, and new arrivals Bogdanov and Luna-charsky, as well as his sister Mariya. After spending several months in jail in Russia, she had come to Geneva to recruit activists to go back into Russia.

But by the end of the year Lenin had already fallen out with one of his newest and most promising political apprentices: Nikolay Valentinov. During his time in Geneva Valentinov had become increasingly uneasy at the feuding within the RSDLP and Lenin's inflexible political line. When he had ventured an interest in the scientific philosophy of the Austrian Ernst Mach and his pupil, the German-Swiss Richard Avenarius, he was shocked by Lenin's venomous response. Any straying from the orthodox materialist thinking of Marxism was "primitive and vulgar" in Lenin's view. As far as he was concerned, Marxism, like the Bible for Puritans, answered all questions and there was no need for philosophy. Anything that attempted to go beyond his own brand of orthodoxy was sham and reactionary, "meaningless verbiage," "ignorant chatter," "claptrap."

Lenin's shrill vocabulary revealed the defensive position he always took on even the most tepid challenge to Marxist orthodoxy, surrounding himself with a picket fence of jargon and theory and lashing out at anything that tried, however tenuously, to breach it. After encountering the full brunt of Lenin's savage intolerance of his own broader, humanist views, Valentinov realized that Lenin had marked him off with the "convict's badge" of theoretical heresy and party disloyalty. At a last meeting with Lenin on the quai du Mont-Blanc he learned that Lenin would no longer shake his hand or sit down at table with him. Nor would he help him get back to Russia.

As 1904 came to an end, rumblings of discontent in Russia had been gathering since summer and were now reaching crisis point. The costly imperialist war with Japan had brought a series of crushing defeats ending with the Russian navy under siege at Port Arthur. This exacerbated the economic crisis in Russia that had been gathering since 1900. With prices rising in the shops, calls were mounting to improve factory conditions and wages and regulate the long working day. Students were turning out regularly for mass rallies protesting the abuses of the czarist government. In the south a general strike had broken out and spread to Transcaucasia. With provincial governments in Russia calling up troops to control unrest, and clashes between police and workers in the major cities of St. Petersburg, Odessa, and Moscow, the Okhrana had reported that "universal attention was utterly transfixed by the unusual growth of the anti-governmental, oppositionist and social-revolutionary movement." The reactionary minister of the interior and chief of gendarmes— Vyacheslav von Plehve—had been assassinated on July 28, 1904, warning of things to come. On the streets of St. Petersburg, with calls mounting for civil liberties and constitutional reform, there was the whiff of revolution.

Even the reticent Nicholas II had noticed the dramatic air of change: "It is as if the dam has been broken: in the space of two or three months Russia has been seized with a thirst for change . . . Revolution is banging on the door."

In Geneva too Lenin sensed an approaching storm. But with the RSDLP hamstrung by dissent, what would he or the party have to offer when the moment came?

CHAPTER EIGHT

"On the Eve of Barricades"

St. Petersburg and Geneva:
January–November 1905

❦

IT WAS A QUIET SUNDAY MORNING in St. Petersburg, the air crisp with the kind of frosty winter cold—just 6 degrees below—that invigorated worshipers on their way to the city's great churches and cathedrals for the morning liturgy. However, on this morning, January 22, 1905, the vast majority of pedestrians were not on their way to worship within the great porticos of St. Isaacs Cathedral on Nevsky Prospekt or the other nearby churches whose golden cupolas glinted in the brilliant morning sunshine. They were heading instead toward St. Petersburg's great focal point, Palace Square, in front of the Winter Palace.

St. Petersburg had been seething with expectation for days. A major strike in the Putilov iron foundry in the southwestern part of the city, organized by the Assembly of St. Petersburg Factory and Mill Workers, had spread, crippling industries across the city. One by one the factories and mills and workshops had ground to a halt and the smoke from their chimneys ceased belching forth. By now 125,000 workers were on strike across 625 factories.

The strike had become the rallying point for a major appeal to the czar regarding factory reform, a statutory workday, and a range of long overdue civil liberties. One hundred thousand people from working-class districts all over St. Petersburg signed a heartfelt statement of grievances addressed to the *tsar-batyushka*—their little father—begging for his intercession. Today they intended to march peacefully to the Winter Palace and present to Nicholas their humble petition:

Sire! We workers and people of St. Petersburg . . . our wives, our children and aged and helpless parents, are come to Thee . . . to seek for truth and protection. We are become beggars, bowing under oppression and burdened by toil beyond our powers, scorned, no longer regarded as human beings, treated as slaves who must suffer their bitter lot in silence. And having suffered, we are driven deeper and deeper into the abyss of poverty, lawlessness, and ignorance. We have been strangled by despotism and arbitrary rule, and we have lost our breath. We have no more strength, Sire. The limit of our patience has been reached. There has come for us the grave moment when death is preferable to a continuation of our intolerable torture.

The faithful were making their way to the czar that morning amid an air of almost religious fervor. But they did not know that Nicholas had already decamped to the safety of his palace at Tsarskoe Selo outside the city, having been assured that the situation was well under control. Intent on maintaining public order, the authorities had approved the deployment of 12,000 troops and police to intercept the marchers before they reached the palace.

Early that morning at six assembly points across St. Petersburg, around 200,000 men, women, and children, many in their Sunday best, had gathered around braziers by lantern light to warm themselves before heading off along the major thoroughfares of the city. It was still dark as the first columns moved off, some of them having ten miles to cover before reaching their destination. But in the early hours, their charismatic leader, Father Georgy Gapon, a self-styled worker-priest, had heard a sinister sound out in the streets—the dull thud of soldiers marching and the metallic clang of the czar's elite mounted regiments moving along the cobbled streets.

Father Gapon's contingent had assembled not far from the Putilov Works at the historic Narva Gate—a massive triumphal arch built to honor Czar Alexander I after his heroic victory over Napoleon in 1812. Twenty thousand of them headed off at midday. Gapon, carrying a large cross, took the lead; the workers followed with all the solemnity of a religious procession, their icons, banners, and a large framed portrait of the czar held high at the front of the column. They sang hymns too; it was all part of a deliberate statement of their peaceful intentions, as was the presence of so many women and children. They wanted to appeal to the czar as a family man. Some, it is said, had a profound sense of martyrdom to come.

A mile and a half north of the Narva Gate, Gapon's contingent found its way barred by troops ranged across the road, and in front of them mounted Cossack cavalry with drawn swords. Without warning the cavalry charged the marchers. Gapon saw his followers "dropping to the earth like logs of wood." But that was not the end of it. The Cossacks then turned and cut their way back through the crowd, slashing at them with their sabers like madmen. This attack was followed by several volleys from the troops, the first two over the marchers' heads. A similar pattern followed elsewhere—in the St. Petersburg Quarter, in Alexander Park, on Vasilevsky Island, at Kolpino—as other columns of marchers found their way barred by armed troops. In some cases an initial warning volley was fired over their heads, in others not. Some marchers were so intent on reaching their destination that they recklessly defied orders to halt and rushed straight into direct gun fire. Some stopped to tear open their coats, baring their chests to the soldiers as proof that they were unarmed. As the soldiers fired and the marching columns broke up and regrouped, many still tried to press on toward Palace Square, now finding themselves joined by students, members of the public, and innocent bystanders, all caught up in the terrifying momentum of events. But when they reached Palace Square, they found it was cordoned off by 2,300 mounted troops and infantry. Once again the crowd, now comprising about 60,000 people, was fired on without provocation, this time by the elite Preobrazhensky Guards. At this point "the passion of the mob broke loose like a bursting dam" when they saw the dead, wounded, and dying lying in blood-soaked snow. The *Times* correspondent wrote that what had started as a peaceful protest was "no longer a workman's question," as members of the public pressed forward in horror and indignation at what they had seen. On side streets, students led groups of people in tearing down telegraph poles and dragging up benches to make barricades; here and there red flags appeared as the crowds surged forward inexorably, attempting to mass on the square amid chaotic firing from the troops.

No one knows how many were killed and wounded that day. The official count numbered fewer than fifty, but that figure includes only the bodies taken to public mortuaries. Many more of the dead and injured were carried home by their friends and families. It is thought that there were around a thousand casualties, with as many as five hundred killed. By three o'clock that afternoon a heavy snowfall deadened the noise on the streets as darkness fell and the traumatized survivors struggled to make their way home. Troops wrapped in their heavy greatcoats were bivouacking around campfires on every city street corner, at the Narva Gate and outside all the factories. Looters came out on the streets of St. Petersburg that night, wrecking shops and stealing wine from stores; the sound of breaking windows pervaded the city.

For Gapon and his followers the Bloody Sunday massacre was a defining moment. "There is no God anymore, there is no czar," they shouted bitterly. Later that evening, Gapon, now a wanted man, appeared at a meeting of the Free Economic Society with his hair cut and his beard shaved off. He was visibly shaken and exhausted as he cursed the soldiers who had fired on his fellow workers and the "traitor Czar who had ordered the shedding of innocent blood." He fled Russia for Geneva, where he met with Lenin to organize a smuggling operation to bring guns to the workers back home.

NEWS OF BLOODY SUNDAY reached Geneva the following day. Lenin and Nadya had set off for a day's reading at the Société de Lecture when they saw Lunacharsky and his wife coming toward them down the street, Anna frantically waving her muff at them. Throughout the day the sedate streets of Geneva resounded with the shouts of newspaper boys—Révolution en Russie!—as the daily *Tribune de Genève* ran through five editions. The Russian community rushed out to buy the papers, constantly checking for new editions and incoming telegraph messages from Russia at newspaper offices. Exiles kissed and hugged each other and sang the revolutionary funeral march "You Have Fallen in the Struggle" in honor of the dead of Bloody Sunday. Political exiles of all nationalities and persuasions gathered in Geneva's Eglise Russe to give thanks, a pattern repeated by exile communities in Zurich, Berne, Paris, Munich, and Berlin.

The Russians in Geneva were instinctively drawn to the Lepeshinsky canteen on rue de Carouge. They struggled to find the words to express their shock and excitement. At the *Vpered* print shop Lenin managed to hold the front page of the new issue long enough to insert a banner headline: "Long Live the Revolution!" Late into the night the exhilarated Russians were walking the streets, singing Russian revolutionary songs on Plainpalais Square until they were reprimanded for disturbing the peace. All over Geneva the same words were spoken over and over again: *Nado ekhat v Rossiyu*—we *must* go back to Russia.

The pull of Russia, that peculiarly Russian *toska*—the longing for home—was incredibly powerful. The next day Lenin's followers congregated punctually at Lepeshinsky's canteen for a briefing and were brusquely reprimanded if they were a few seconds late. Others went out collecting funds for the families of the dead and wounded in Russia. Many Geneva émigrés were already packing and heading for home, no matter what they would find when they got there. Each needed a passport and money for the journey, further depleting the party's already meager funds. They all took advantage of their return by carrying illegal literature in double-bottomed suitcases and "breast plates," special pockets sewn inside their clothing.

But Lenin and Nadya did not start packing. The revolutionary leader was not yet ready to risk his personal safety; he believed that he was more valuable to the movement as its leader in the free West.

⸺

BLOODY SUNDAY changed Russia irrevocably. The massacre finally shifted public opinion against Nicholas and his government across all sections of society, providing the long-awaited catalyst for upheaval. Students went out on strike; the government, anticipating further unrest, closed down all institutions of higher learning for the rest of the academic year.

On this, "the eve of barricades," as Lenin described it, a rash of serious industrial strikes broke out in the major cities, but no socialist party stepped forward to marshal this outpouring of public anger and turn it to political advantage. In January the Japanese had taken Port Arthur, a strategically crucial Russian naval base. On February 17 the czar's uncle and brother-in-law, the reactionary Grand Duke Sergey, was assassinated by a Socialist Revolutionary bomber (the same group that had assassinated the despised interior minister, Vyacheslav von Plehve, the previous year). Any lingering confidence in the government was swept away by the destruction of the Russian navy during the battle of Tsushima at the end of May. The humiliated czar was forced to sue for peace soon after; his imperial war had failed to bring a quick victory and turn the tide of public opinion in his favor. Rather the reverse; a month later the crew of the battleship *Potemkin* mutinied in port at Odessa, a city already crippled by civil unrest. And where were the local Bolsheviks when the moment came? Nowhere. Their power base in Odessa, as elsewhere, was almost nonexistent.

As the tumultuous year wore on, it saw a descent into criminal violence in the cities and especially in the countryside, where peasant rent strikes escalated into anarchic bouts of looting and vandalism. Strikes and marches spread to the borderlands of Latvia and Poland and the key industrial cities of Lodz and Warsaw. Even the professional middle classes, such as professors and industrialists, were joining the revolutionary protest. In an article in *Vpered* soon after Bloody Sunday, Lenin wrote that a civil war for freedom was now blazing across Russia. But he made no move to return to his native land to lead it. In Geneva his major preoccupation was still doctrinal rather than practical: the party split still gnawed away at him and with the situation in Russia so volatile he was anxious to reconstruct the RSDLP and consolidate his own position. He did, however, express his regret at the "accursed distance, the disgusting 'beyond-the-frontier' existence of the émigré," which kept him from Russia.

The Bloody Sunday massacre and the popular response to it had not, of course, played to any of the preordained scenarios argued by the political theorists of the Russian diaspora, and none of them seized the moment when it came. In the big cities the Bolsheviks did not have enough worker support to galvanize revolution under their leadership. They were weak and disorganized, still largely made up of intellectuals and students. If anything, the Mensheviks had a broader base of support in Russia at the time and, crucially, more money. Russia had seen moments of spontaneous civil unrest and protest erupt and wither before. Lenin, like many others, did not believe the insurgency would last. The RSDLP had been weakened by factional infighting since the split at the second party congress. Activists in Russia had become demoralized, and support for the Bolsheviks among the workers had fallen away. No one even read the few illegal leaflets they produced. Crucially, the Bolsheviks were also poorly armed. An up-and-coming underground worker, Maxim Litvinov, had written to Lenin from St. Petersburg during the previous December: "The mass of party workers up to now continue to regard us as a handful of disorganizers with no strength of our own. . . . our situation is impossibly rickety and precarious." In the Nevsky district, populated by 30,000 industrial workers, only six or seven Bolshevik underground circles remained, with barely six workers in each. The combined Bolshevik and Menshevik factions in St. Petersburg that January were supported by as few as a thousand workers, while the charismatic Gapon had garnered a massive popular following.

Why did Lenin fail to seize the moment and head for the barricades, as Nikolay Valentinov had anticipated when he met him the previous year in Geneva? When push came to shove, he made no move to travel to St. Petersburg, any more than Plekhanov, Martov, and Axelrod did. Only Trotsky, who had just arrived in Geneva, immediately headed back to Russia under a false passport as "Petr Petrovich." But none of the long-term Marxist theorists of revolution in Russia, who had by now spent as many as twenty years in exile propagating millions of words on the subject, thought the moment would last. They had become too parochial, too preoccupied with their own endless theoretical squabbles.

Ironically, Lenin, a man who loved the outdoors and believed in keeping himself physically fit, was no man of action. Years of exile had turned him into a dedicated career politician and theorist, irredeemably wedded to books. All he could do was spin out his days at the Société de Lecture, reading French and German tomes on military science about barricades and street fighting during the 1848 Revolution or the Paris Commune of 1870–1871, turning out more pamphlets and articles about the *practice* of revolution, without showing any desire to experience the reality.

And so he sat dreaming in Geneva of the proletariat smashing czarism and setting in train the revolutionary conflagration across Europe that he so longed for. Ironically, Lenin did not understand how rapidly events in Russia were actually moving that year. His ultimate preoccupation, even now, as Valentinov had concluded, was to preserve his own position and with it the leadership of the party for the right moment: "He was the chief of the general staff and he never forgot that in times of emergency he had to safeguard the supreme command." Writing from rue David Dufour,

Lenin continued to exhort his supporters in Russia to form fighting units and use whatever weapons they could lay hands on against the state. But for himself, his preferred plan of action was to set about urgent preparations for a third party congress.

LENIN'S INTENTIONS for the new congress were, as always, driven by political self-interest. He was determined to extend his own Bolshevik power base, establish personal contact with delegates from Russia, and send them back to recruit more workers in Russia for an organized, armed insurrection to follow later. At all costs he wanted to head off mounting calls within his own ranks for reconciliation with the Mensheviks. The congress, he declared, "must be simple—like a war council."

Lenin's real intentions soon became clear; although the congress had been formally announced as an RSDLP event, it was in reality a rump Bolshevik congress. The Mensheviks rightly refused to take part (although a handful of delegates did in the end show up). Mistrustful of Lenin, they saw another congress as another forum for more Lenin-led divisions and held their own separate congress in Geneva, with Plekhanov declaring Lenin's congress unlawful.

London again seemed the safest venue for deliberations. The city, as usual, was hidden in a pall of rain and fog, and the stench of coal fires hung heavy in the air when Lenin and Nadya arrived. From April 25 to May 10, thirty-eight delegates from twenty regional Bolshevik committees congregated. Lenin and Nadya stayed in lodgings at 16 Percy Circus just around the corner from their old home at Holford Square. The leafy environs of Percy Circus became something of a Little Russia for the next two weeks, with several delegates taking lodgings here. The houses at 9 Percy Circus and 23 Percy Circus had been specially rented by Alekseev for the purpose. He and Lenin, much as in 1903, did their best to help the newcomers find their way around London and obtain lodgings in Whitechapel for those not accommodated at Percy Circus. Quite a few, however, ended up bedding down as best they could in the pig sty that was Alekseev's tiny two-room flat, sitting and sleeping on piles of English and Russian newspapers. In between sessions there was time for a cheap lunch at a café on Gray's Inn Road or a drink at a German club on Pentonville Road. But otherwise the delegates kept a very low profile. As in 1903, the levels of *konspiratsiya* were high, with the venues for the congress being two or three rented rooms in clubs or the back rooms of pubs around Kings Cross and Gray's Inn Road not far from Percy Circus.

But one thing had changed. By 1905 the Special Political Branch, a division of the Metropolitan Police, took notice of the activities of this new breed of Russian political exile and put them under surveillance. One of the venues rented for the 1905 congress was an upstairs room of the Crown and Woolpack pub on St. John Street, under the laughable guise, as in 1903, of a supposed meeting of the "Foreign Barbers of London." At Scotland Yard one morning that April newly recruited Detective-Constable Herbert Fitch was instructed to investigate a meeting of this group. The pub landlord, Mr. Moore, had tipped off Special Branch about the meeting. Fitch was fluent in German, Russian, and French but since the meeting would be relatively small, there was no way he could infiltrate it in disguise. He consequently decided to squeeze himself into a narrow, airless cupboard built into the wall of the upstairs room booked for the meeting and listen to the proceedings. From here Fitch heard the password "liberty" given in Russian as one by one the delegates entered. As he suffered increasing dizziness crouched inside his cupboard, Fitch heard "Oulyanoff" take the floor and demand "bloodshed on a colossal scale," without mercy, "in Russia first, and then from one side of Europe to the other." The speech was greeted by fierce cheering. Although he could not see Lenin's face, Fitch later wrote that such was the "passionate magnetism" of his voice "that it would have incited a multitude to madness."

At the third congress, as at the second, Lenin interrogated delegates in detail about the state of the party in Russia—what was morale like? How many worker members did they have? From the first of twenty-eight sessions to the last, he threw all his energy into dominating the proceedings, taking the floor more than a hundred times and frequently interrupting the speeches of others. Prior to the congress he had spent considerable time drafting resolutions and listing the major subjects for discussion, which would revolve around three major issues: the crisis in the party; organization, in particular the creation of fighting units in Russia; and insurgency tactics. Even his most loyal followers were shocked by his aggressive attempts to impose his views, as he threw out Martov's loose definition of party membership—the cause of the 1903 split, over which he had lost the vote. They might now agree to drop this resolution, but many still called for reconciliation with the Martovites, particularly at this critical time in Russia.

On May 1—International Workers Day—the Russians were disappointed to see no British workers out parading along the streets of London or clashing with police and troops as was now the case in Russia. Instead, demure young women with flowers and collecting boxes were out raising money for the fight against tuberculosis. In Russia the day was marked by a new wave of industrial strikes, while Lenin and his cohorts gathered in another back room off Kings Cross. Herbert Fitch was still on the case, but this time there was nowhere for him to hide so he shaved off his mustache and disguised himself as a waiter. When he carried a tray of drinks into the room where the meeting was being held, he recognized Lenin immediately by the "devilish sureness in every line of his powerful magnetic face." Fitch managed to catch Lenin out by knocking a pile of agenda papers next to him onto the floor as he served the drinks, hiding one under his linen napkin as he retrieved them. As the meeting progressed Fitch stood on a chair by the door outside, his ear to the fanlight, taking further notes on Lenin's "cut-throat ideas of revolt."

The congress in the end did little more than rubber-stamp Lenin's position as leader of the Bolshevik faction, endorsing his calls for the recruitment of more workers to party committees (eight workers to every two intellectuals was his suggestion), supporting the appeal for an armed uprising in Russia and the urgent acquisition of arms. Lenin was elected to the Central Committee and also voted editor of a new party newspaper, *Proletarii* (Proletarian), to replace *Vpered*. It would be aimed at popularizing recent party decisions at the congress. And from now on the work of the Central Committee and the party newspaper was to be led from St. Petersburg. Many delegates thought the time had come for Lenin to return.

Before leaving London, Lenin took his colleagues to see the British Museum reading room where Marx and Engels had worked, as well as the Natural History Museum and the Zoo in Regent's Park. At the final obligatory pilgrimage to Marx's grave, he warned delegates to look out for British police and Okhrana spooks, who might try to photograph them.

In Paris the group stopped off to see the Eiffel Tower and the Louvre. Now of all times it seemed appropriate to complete their political education with a visit to the Wall of the Communards in Père Lachaise Cemetery where, on May 28, 1871, troops had executed 147 Paris workers involved in the uprising. There was time even for a visit to the Grand Opera and an evening's laughter at the Folies Bergère. For Lenin Russia remained an abstraction, still a long way away.

⟶⟬⟭⟵

BY THE TIME LENIN returned to Geneva in May 1905, the euphoria of the January days had long since dissipated. Despondency ruled, with many exiles unable to go back home or even receive up-to-date news. Lenin wrote to Anatoly Lunacharsky, now in Italy, that his people in Geneva were "down in the dumps," berating them for being "awkward, inactive, clumsy, timid. . . . They're good fellows, but no damn'd good whatever as politicians. They lack tenacity, fighting spirit, nimbleness and speed." The "colonial conditions" of life abroad bred the worst habits in political exiles, who were prone to contracting "the disease of squabbling, gossip and tittle-tattle." The party was short of everything right now: money, weapons, and even good speakers. It was down to Lenin singlehandedly to lift them all "above the Geneva marsh into the sphere of more serious interests and problems." Lenin was certainly doing as much in his urgent missives to party activists in Russia, which were becoming increasingly shrill and impatient: "We have been talking about bombs for more than six months," he railed, "and not a single one has been made." He went on to list every available weapon—bombs, revolvers, grenades—even knives and knuckledusters and crudely made fire bombs of rags in bottles—whatever the Russian underground could lay their hands on. "Form fighting squads at once everywhere!" he commanded—despite having no practical experience of what effect such ad hoc and ill-equipped fighting units might have against the the czar's crack troops.

By Lenin's estimates two or three hundred such brigades (of five or six insurgents each) were needed in St. Petersburg alone to seize the revolutionary opportunity. They should be out on the streets attacking police stations, assassinating spies, robbing banks, and expropriating funds for the revolution. If all else failed, they could beat up policemen. It was of course easy for Lenin to fire off naive directives from the safety of Geneva. And his clarion calls did find recruits: a wide range of striking workers, military deserters, and other denizens of the underclasses, often on the run from the police, joined the fighting groups. But what was needed were people with real frontline experience to lead from the barricades, Communard style.

A hard core of dedicated activists in St. Petersburg was willing to attempt the kind of crazy heroics demanded by Lenin. In January Nikolay Burenin, who had originally been recruited by St. Petersburg party chair Elena Stasova to disseminate illegal literature, had been given responsibility for setting up a fighting technical group to smuggle in arms from Finland and set about bomb making. Burenin was already experienced at organizing safe houses for the storage of literature and illegal printing presses, and now these storehouses made way for weapons, ammunition, dynamite, and other bomb-making materials. He knew something about explosives, for he had developed special belts and corsets for carrying fuses and dynamite and jackets for concealing revolvers.

Carrying dynamite posed considerable difficulties. It had a pungent smell, and when it came into contact with the nervous sweat of the person carrying it, it smelled even worse. Women turned out to be the best couriers, dousing themselves in perfume to conceal the smell. When they had to travel on trains, they stood on the open platform of the end carriage, even in the coldest weather, in order to avoid other passengers.

Female couriers even carried rifles into Russia piecemeal. They would be broken down into barrels and stocks and suspended from pieces of cord around the courier's neck under her clothes. Some female students were able to smuggle up to eight rifles at a time, though they were unable to bend or sit down. One particularly fearless female member of Nikolay Burenin's fighting technical group, Feodosiya Drabkina, went on missions back and forth across the city in the cold and snow that winter, taking her three-year-old daughter Lizka with her as cover. The daughter later remembered puzzling over how her mother would change shape and size from fat to thin as she delivered the smuggled arms she carried under her clothes.

For the bomb-making program, Burenin recruited the scientific expertise of a professor at the Kiev Polytechnic, Mikhail Tikhvinsky, code-named

"Ellipsis," and two St. Petersburg-based chemists "Alpha" and "Omega" (there were only two of them originally in this secret cell, hence the choice of names). Alpha was a young female chemistry student, Lyubov' Peskova; Omega was Mikhail Skosarevsky, a part-time teacher and laboratory worker, both of whom secretly manufactured the components for bombs while they were at work. Finding the right explosives and suitable containers for the bombs under the strict practices of *konspiratisya* was another matter. One day, Burenin arrived at Alpha's lab with an amateurish, volatile bomb made from a large sardine tin hidden under his father's raccoon coat. It was one of a consignment sent by activists in Riga, Latvia, and he wanted her opinion on the workmanship. When Burenin picked it up and shook it, Alpha heard a rattling from the pieces of glass that had been packed inside. The bomb was too small to be effective but dangerous enough to cause injury at close hand. Alpha took one horrified look at the object and advised Burenin to take his bombs—he had two more at home—and get rid of them as quickly as he could. Later that evening, having donned his frockcoat and patent leather shoes for a concert at which he was to perform, Burenin headed out to the Obvodny canal with one of the bombs under his raccoon coat. It was a filthy night and the banks of the canal were slippery and thick with mud as he struggled to reach the water and dispose of his bomb, almost falling in the process. He had to take shelter at a friend's flat to wash before continuing his journey, arriving late for his performance. He was later reprimanded for breaking all the rules of *konspiratsiya* in this foolhardy way.

The bomb makers realized they needed a better template to work from and sought guidance from Macedonian partisans—the Chetniks—who for years had been waging guerrilla war against their Turkish oppressors in Bulgaria. In March Skosarevsky was sent to Lenin in Geneva for a secret briefing on contacts and addresses in Bulgaria before departing on a secret mission to liaise with these activists on bomb making. He later reported to Lenin that progress was greatly hampered by the difficulty of obtaining good quality fuses. Soon Burenin was sent back to Bulgaria to buy large quantities of British Bickford safety fuses from the Chetniks.

Meanwhile in St. Petersburg, all sorts of vessels were being tested as containers for improvised bombs and hand grenades—and rejected: tins from sardines, fruit drops, or preserves, pieces of gas piping. In the end iron casings were obtained from a factory on the Liteiny in St. Petersburg and taken to an innocent-looking factory out of town that made lead soldiers and metal toy trains, where they were remodeled into bombs. The moment there was a suggestion of police curiosity about the toy factory, the bomb-making operation was transferred to a workshop that repaired samovars and other domestic items. With the technical advice of Tikhvinsky, who had headed a successful bomb-making operation in Kiev, Burenin organized the production of dynamite, pyroxilin, and mercury fulminate in a workshop that supposedly made cameras. Those who worked on bombs did so in the strictest isolation, giving up all contact with the outside world. They were not allowed to attend meetings or take part in demonstrations and did not know the identity of those who delivered materials, all in order to maintain the absolute secrecy of the operation. Husbands and wives lived apart—as did Feodosiya Drabkina and her husband who was also a member of the group—and hardly ever saw each other.

When the time came to test their newly made bombs, Alpha and Omega took them by train to a remote country estate at Akhi-Yarvi in the Karelian isthmus of Finland north of St. Petersburg. In order to conceal the bombs from customs officers, they strapped them to their legs and hid them under their clothes, which hindered their ability to walk normally. The estate at Akhi-Yarvi, owned by the family of Aleksandr Ignatiev, a member of the technical group, was secretly producing picric acid, a key component in the explosive agent melinite. The toxic yellow crystals stained everything that came into contact with them—even the whites of the eyes of those who manufactured it. On one occasion agents took a consignment to the station at Raivola and discovered to their horror that the melinite had leaked, leaving a bright yellow trail in the snow—all the way back to Akhi-Yarvi. They set to work trying to disperse the trail, but a heavy snowfall soon after the accident saved them from detection.

———— ∞ ————

BY OCTOBER, Lenin had concluded that the best time for insurrection would be the following spring after the army returned from the Far East, defeated and demoralized. He wrote of this to Mariya Essen, now back in St. Petersburg working for the party. the assumption being that he could control the inchoate train of events unfolding in Russia in the same efficient way he timetabled his own life. "The time of the uprising, I repeat, I would *willingly postpone* until the spring," he wrote, admitting however that "it is difficult, of course, for me to judge from a distance."

For all his polemical and political gifts, Lenin never seemed to appreciate that history does not operate according to any preordained schedule. Time and again he would find himself having to improvise and amend his tactics to fit the changing political situation. Earlier, in August, he had published another densely written treatise, *Two Tactics of Social Democracy*, in which he outlined the reasons why he felt Russia was not yet ready for a full socialist revolution. The first and necessary step was the establishment of a bourgeois-liberal regime that could then be overthrown by the urban workforce allied with the peasantry. Only then, according to Lenin, could the great vision of the "democratic dictatorship of the proletariat and peasantry," led by the intellectual leadership of the RSDLP, come into being.

Yet in the middle of October events once again exploded in Russia. A general strike broke out when the shipbuilding, steel, and rail industries put down their tools and paralyzed the infrastructure and industry. The lights went out all over cities; shops, schools, and theaters closed. The water supply was affected; bread and food stocks began to run out. Even wealthy industrialists and professionals—ballet dancers, doctors, lawyers, stockbrokers—came out in support of the strike, which had spread to every major city within days. Workers took to the streets with banners and marching songs. When the electricity went out in St. Petersburg, all the authorities could do to monitor unrest was to sweep the Nevsky Prospekt by a searchlight mounted on the Admiralty building. Where were the bombs and fighting brigades, railed Lenin in a torrent of demands by letter from Geneva, as he realized he and the party had again failed to catch the *Zeitgeist* in his home country.

It was not Lenin's cadres of professional revolutionaries but the workers themselves who took events into their own hands. And now they were learning how to organize. On October 26 striking workers, with help from the Mensheviks (Lenin's Bolsheviks having chosen not to be involved), set up an elected committee known as the St. Petersburg Soviet of Workers Deputies. The dynamic, twenty-six-year-old Trotsky, having returned from hiding in Finland where he had been forced to flee that summer, was nominated as vice chair. Declaring freedom of the press, the soviet began publishing its own newspaper, *Izvestiya*. It organized trade unions and distributed welfare to strikers, and soon its example was emulated by fifty more soviets, set up in major industrial cities across Russia, including Moscow. The workers were at last organizing themselves without recourse to the out-of-touch theorists of Geneva and the Russian diaspora. It was a heroic venture in which Trotsky, with his outstanding oratorical skills in front of a crowd, unexpectedly took center stage. The soviet only lasted fifty days, but it sowed the seeds for 1917 as a potent opposition force.

The advent of the soviets was the final push needed to force political change on a stubborn and dogmatic czar. On October 30, Nicholas II, still vainly clinging to the principles of absolute monarchy instilled in him by his father, Alexander III, was finally forced to agree to political concessions or face a bloodbath. Even his arch-reactionary cousin, Kaiser Wilhelm of Germany, had advised constitutional reform.

Nicholas's October Manifesto reluctantly created an elected State Duma promising freedom of conscience, speech, and assembly and abolishing censorship, with Count Sergey Witte as head of the Council of Ministers. Strikes and civil unrest abated as law and order was gradually restored, but in the provinces a right-wing backlash against the revolutionaries prompted savage pogroms against the Jews, who were blamed as the instigators of unrest.

In November the Moscow soviet, dominated by textile workers who until now had seemed less militant than the industrial workers of St. Petersburg, after being incited by radicals, made one final political gesture and called another general strike. On December 3 Trotsky was arrested along with most of the executive committee of the St. Petersburg soviet. (In November 1906 he and fourteen others, after languishing in the Peter and Paul Fortress, were condemned to lifelong exile in Siberia.) The strike spread from Moscow to St. Petersburg and other cities, but the main focus of the rebellion was in Moscow. Here, on December 10, the workers in the Presnya district mounted an armed insurrection, manning the barricades with all the fervor and heroism of the Paris Commune of 1871. For a while the infectious atmosphere spread. Students and members of the public rolled up their sleeves and helped to raise barricades on one of the city's main streets, the Tverskaya.

At this time Feodosiya Drabkina was sent to Moscow with a bag full of Chetnik bombs for the insurgents. Before she left, she was sent out with party funds to buy herself a smart outfit and bag on the fashionable Nevsky Prospekt. She traveled by train with her daughter. The child was perfect cover for such a dangerous assignment; little sweet-faced Lizka, nicknamed the party's "conspiracy device" by Nadezhda Krupskaya, deflected suspicion on a train filled with troops. Their destination was the apartment of the popular and fashionably "proletarian" writer Maxim Gorky, who had become an important party fund-raiser and figurehead, having been jailed earlier that year for protesting against Bloody Sunday (his release secured by an unprecedented worldwide protest).

When Feodosiya and Lizka arrived at Moscow's Nikolaevsky station, it was ringed by troops with fixed bayonets. As they crossed the deserted streets, they could hear regular volleys of gunfire. Gorky's apartment was a hive of activity when they got there, having become a nerve center for the insurrection, as well as a bomb-making factory. The dining table was laid with food and the samovar was bubbling as people came and went from all over Moscow with news of the latest situation and took instructions. In a small room off Gorky's study set aside for his aviary (he was a passionate bird keeper) activists were receiving instruction in how to prime the bombs.

For days Moscow resounded with the sound of gunfire. But the insurgents were poorly armed and by December 15 the street fighting was put down by the crack Semenovsky Guards, brought in from St. Petersburg (the authorities fearing the Moscow garrison would mutiny in sympathy if deployed) and backed up by heavy artillery bombardment. In the heavy shelling and conflagration that followed much of the Presnya district was laid waste and as many as one thousand civilians killed.

With new civil rights promised by the czar, including enfranchisement of Russia's urban workforce and a full political amnesty, the strikes across the country were called off as industries were at last allowed to set up their own trade unions. Political parties were emerging into the open, with Lenin's erstwhile colleague Petr Struve founding his own party, the Constitutional Democrats (known as the Kadets).

What Lenin later called the "dress rehearsal" for revolution was over, but Bloody Sunday and the Moscow insurrection provided some important lessons in militancy and street fighting. Lenin now recognized the logic of party unity, offering the olive branch to Plekhanov and the Mensheviks in a last-ditch attempt to end the factional infighting. As a member of the Second International of worldwide socialist groups that had been founded in Paris in 1889 to defend the interests of workers everywhere, he had been coming under increasing pressure from his colleagues in Europe, particularly the German social democrats, to end the discord in the RSDLP. He needed their support and drew on all his political skills in order to lay the ground for the anticipated insurrection the following year and wrote an uncharacteristically flattering letter to Plekhanov at the end of October. In it he stressed the "need for Social-Democratic unity" and his appreciation of the "entire movement's *extreme need* of your guiding, close and immediate participation" and asked for a meeting with him. The ulterior motive was to gain Plekhanov's' respected voice on the editorial board of a new Russian-based newspaper, *Novaya Zhizn* (New Life). But Plekhanov ignored Lenin's letter. In his mind, it was too late for the wolf to lie down with the lamb.

By November 1905, with the political amnesty now in operation, it seemed safe at last for political exiles to return to Russia. Lenin finally had to concede that he could not mastermind armed insurrection from a distance, based on erratic and incomplete reports in Western newspapers, with intelligence gathering from his own activists in Russia subject to constant police surveillance and interception. In mid-November he left Geneva, but not before meticulously sorting through all his papers with Nadya, packing them into a trunk and leaving them with a Bolshevik comrade. En route back into Russia via Stockholm, he met up with a Finnish agent, Ula Kastren, sent by Burenin in St. Petersburg, who provided him with a false passport to enter Russia. Lenin needed to get back quickly; the rail route would take too long—forty-eight hours—and involve risky police checks at the border at Torneo. So on November 17 he and Kastren traveled to Åbo in southwestern Finland on the steamship *Bore II* and the following day took a train to Helsingfors (now Helsinki). After an overnight stay in a safe house owned by Kastren's brother, Lenin took the train into St. Petersburg's Finland station, where Nikolay Burenin was waiting for him. From here he headed straight for a meeting of his local Bolshevik committee. He had been away from Russia for five years.

CHAPTER NINE

Stolypin's Neckties

RUSSIA AND FINLAND:
DECEMBER 1905–APRIL 1907

———⚬⚬⚬———

FOR ONCE, LENIN HAD ARRIVED in Russia on legal papers (using the English name William Frey), now assuming he would be able to move around unimpeded by the police, although he was obliged to report to them daily. Nadya joined him ten days later, but she had been closely followed on the train from Finland by a police spy. For a while the couple tried to live legally in a flat on the Grechesky Prospekt with friends of Lenin's sister Mariya. But the flat had been staked out by Okhrana spooks, whose presence so alarmed their host that he prowled up and down the flat at night with a pistol in his pocket terrified of a police raid. So, after a succession of short-term stopovers in safe houses, often living apart, on December 17 the couple was forced underground again.

Once more they found themselves living under the constraints of *konspiratsiya* at its most difficult and dangerous level, something they had not experienced in the relative tranquillity of Geneva for the past two years. Lenin was terrified of being arrested and rarely appeared in public. Nadya was able to move around more freely and became her husband's "zealous reporter," finding out about events in the city from servant girls and activist friends in Sunday school circles. A bewildered Elizaveta Vasil'evna, who had been alarmed by their sudden departure from Geneva but dutifully followed them back to Russia, complained that she hardly saw either of them: "They passed like comets." Lenin played little or no active role in events, apart from appearing at secret Bolshevik meetings or sneaking out for the occasional meeting with Nadya at the Vienna restaurant on Gogol'skaya.

In later years, in an attempt to defuse the obvious questions about why he had kept such a low profile at the time rather than making his way back to Russia, it would be claimed that the party had expressly forbidden Lenin from taking any personal risks. He lived anxiously, forever watching his back, coming and going from different entrances, constantly moving from one Bolshevik safe house to another and changing false passports every couple of weeks. The rest of his time was consumed by writing for *Novaya Zhizn* (New Life), the first legal Bolshevik newspaper to enjoy the new press freedom. Its leading light was Maxim Gorky, the darling of the Russian literary world who had the ear of powerful, liberal-minded industrialists willing to put money into the journal and the Bolshevik faction. A donation of 15,000 rubles from a wealthy benefactor had set the journal up, with Gorky's common-law wife, actress Mariya Andreeva, as its nominal publisher. The original non-Bolshevik literary contributors, all friends of Andreeva's and Gorky's, were soon ousted when Lenin arrived and was installed as editor, bringing in his own politicized people. The *Novaya Zhizn* editorial offices thereafter became the center of Bolshevik underground activity, as a safe house for visiting activists, for distributing false passports and illegal literature and issuing directives, with Nadya at the administrative helm in her role as coordinator and secretary to the Central Committee. The paper's success was meteoric, building to a circulation of 80,000. Lenin was once more in his element at the center of party propaganda, just as in the old *Iskra* days, and would sit until late at night, obsessively checking the page proofs of his articles.

One evening in a Tatar restaurant in the Nevsky quarter not long after his arrival, Lenin had been introduced by a *Novaya Zhizn* colleague, Petr Rumyantsev, with whom he had been staying on Rozhdestvenskaya, to a cultured and attractive party member, Elizaveta de K. A week later he met her again at the offices of *Novaya Zhizn*. At Rumyantsev's suggestion Elizaveta, who was separated from her husband and came from a comfortable background, offered Lenin the use of her apartment for secret party meetings. Located in a fashionable part of town, the premises offered a good front and were used by Lenin on a dozen or so occasions.

One of the first things Elizaveta noticed was his obsession with security. Arriving "as discreetly as a detective" ahead of his fellow conspirators, he would stand by the window for some time viewing the street below and examining the faces of the people he saw there. He would carefully drill her on the passwords of the day and instruct her to let in only those who gave them correctly. He was always the last to leave after meetings. Elizaveta would watch as he stepped cautiously into the street "as though about to plunge into cold water," casting anxious looks this way and that.

Sometimes Lenin stayed late. She cooked him simple food that he seemed to greatly appreciate. He often helped with the washing up and lighting the samovar, and he seemed to be very domesticated. Occasionally she played the piano for him; Beethoven's *Sonata Pathétique* was a favorite. Whenever she came to the third section she noticed that there was something in the music which Lenin was incapable of resisting emotionally. The perpetual ironic smile, a form of self-protection that always played across his lip, would occasionally slip and a world weariness would descend over him. At times Lenin appeared deeply exhausted and depressed. She could tell that he drove himself hard and there was something in the music that lifted him from the otherwise arid, conspiratorial life he was living. But how mortified Lenin was when he realized he had let his emotional guard slip. On such occasions, Elizaveta had visions of him returning to his secret lodgings to read Marx with that furious, self-flagellating energy of his, in order to drive away his emotional demons.

During those first weeks in St. Petersburg Lenin found that living in other people's homes inhibited his work. Words and arguments were his familiars and his weapons, and it was only in the world of political debate that he found his metier. At the end of December 1905 he left Russia for the first All-Russian Bolshevik Conference. As the insurrection in Moscow was being brought to a brutal close, he arrived in Tammerfors in southern Finland. Now Tampere and Finland's third largest city, it was then known by its old Swedish name. A war between Sweden and Russia in 1808–1809 had resulted in Finland, then under Swedish dominion, being ceded to the Russian empire. It was granted the status of an autonomous Grand Duchy by Czar Alexander I. But in reality, throughout the nineteenth century, it was subject to much of the same censorship and political oppression that prevailed in Russia. The Finns had responded with a campaign of passive resistance to czarist rule. Patriotic feeling ran high, and the Finns resisted a concerted program of Russianization late in the century to prepare Finland for full absorption into the empire. It therefore quickly ignited in the wake of events in 1905, when Finnish social democrats offered their solidarity with the striking workers of Russia and showed themselves eager to join in the action.

In the autumn of 1905, activists in Finland, led by the journalist Konni Zilliacus, editor of the leading underground newspaper *Fria Ord* (Free Words), had organized gun running into St. Petersburg from Europe. Couriers used the old *Iskra* smuggling routes developed by Zilliacus in 1901–1903. But now larger quantities of weapons and explosives were needed and individual couriers could smuggle only small amounts into Russia. A massive arms-gathering campaign was therefore initiated by Zilliacus, who began by obtaining Mausers and Brownings from a firm in Hamburg and Wetterli rifles from Switzerland. Other revolvers as well as explosives were bought in England. Eventually a cache of 15,500 rifles, 250,000 cartridges, 2,500 revolvers, and three tons of explosives were ready for transport into Russia. In collusion with Motojirio Akashi, the Japanese military attaché in Stockholm charged with masterminding subversive action against Russia, Zilliacus organized the purchase in England of a small steamship, the *John Grafton,* and two yachts to run the guns, along with machine guns acquired by Akashi, into the Baltic with a crew of British, Norwegian, and Latvian seamen. But disaster struck when the *John Grafton* proved unseaworthy and ran aground off the coast of Finland on September 7. Some of the arms were evacuated, but the ship had to be blown up in order to prevent it from falling into the hands of Russian customs. Most of the unloaded rifles were seized, and the bulk of the arms scattered around the wreck was salvaged by a Russian naval diving unit. But some Wetterli rifles got through and were put to good use during the general strike in Moscow.

In Finland that autumn, activists had followed the example of the Moscow rebellion and seized control of the Tammerfors town hall on Keskustori, the city's central square. From its belfry they raised the red flag and set up their own strike committee, seeing off the few Russian gendarmes and police based there with no difficulty. Soon they issued their own Red Manifesto echoing the political demands made in Russia. Now, in December 1905, the People's House, a workers meeting place and library a short distance away on Hallituskatu, welcomed Lenin and his delegates on a bitterly cold December 23. The conference was a modest affair. The delegates who reached the meeting despite the railroad strike sat on plain wooden benches ranged around long tables. The major topics for discussion were reunification with the Mensheviks, calls for an armed uprising in Russia to which Lenin still held firm, and a boycott of the first Duma. With events in Russia still unraveling, there was an air of excitement throughout the proceedings and practical skills were emphasized. Between sessions, delegates went out into the woods for target practice with an assortment of Mausers, Brownings, and Winchesters. In gratitude for their solidarity Lenin promised the Finnish social democrats that when the revolution finally came in Russia, Finland would be granted its independence.

At Tammerfors, a promising newly elected party delegate, code-named "Ivanovich," had arrived from the Caucasus. Like Lenin, he operated under numerous pseudonyms; in the Georgian underground he was known as Koba or Soso, but his real name was Josef Dzhugashvili (the name Stalin was adopted later). Dzhugashvili had been greatly impressed by Lenin's *Letter to a Comrade on Our Organizational Tasks* at the time of the party split in 1903. Lenin's bold polemic convinced him that "the Party had a mountain eagle" at its helm. On arrival in Tammerfors, his first trip out of Russia to a party conference, Stalin stood around for a while with the other delegates, waiting for the great leader to make his entrance. It was some time before he realized that the stocky balding man talking animatedly to colleagues nearby was Lenin himself. Stalin's disappointment at his first sight of the party's leader mirrored that of many others in the prerevolutionary years. At a distance, Lenin seemed "the most ordinary man," but when he spoke it was quite a different matter; Stalin could not but be impressed by Lenin's charisma as a speaker and his extraordinary strength of will.

Lenin and Nadya's return to Russia early in 1906 after the Tammerfors conference was discouraging. The inevitable official reaction to the events of December was rapidly setting in. The Moscow insurrection had been poorly organized and armed, with little or no coordination with the party in St. Petersburg. Lenin knew that the time had come to look reality in the face: "We are now confronted with the new work of assimilating and refashioning the experience of the latest forms of struggle," he wrote. "We must definitely, practically get down to the tremendous tasks of a new active movement, preparing for it more tenaciously, more systemically, more persistently." The lessons of 1905 had to be learned. The party must expand, adapt, regroup—and to do this effectively it had no option but to go underground again.

Lenin now channeled his irrepressible nervous energy into his political writing and work on *Novaya Zhizn* at its offices on Nevsky Prospekt and for the next year spent most of his time attending conferences and congresses abroad as well as secret Bolshevik meetings in St. Petersburg and Finland. He wrote obsessively, pouring out over one hundred newspaper articles on party policy, the peasants and the land question, and organization and tactics for *Novaya Zhizn* and a succession of short-lived underground newspapers. Many of the articles, such as "Lessons of the Moscow Uprising," analyzed the events of 1905.

He made only a couple of public speeches at this time, the most notable being on May 22. Under the pseudonym Karpov he slipped into a political meeting at the palace of Countess Sofya Panina, addressed by a member of the Kadet party. When given the floor, Lenin denounced the Kadets for negotiating with the Duma, which he declared a fraud, the czar having thrown out most of its proposed program of trade union and land reform. There were three thousand people present, and Nadya recalled how pale and nervous Lenin had seemed until he began to speak—rightly so, for it was the first large gathering of its kind he had ever addressed. When word got round the audience that Karpov was in fact Lenin, he was given an ovation. However, the breach of his anonymity unnerved him. Although he spoke again in June to the All-Russian Congress of Schoolteachers, venturing forth into public greatly discomfited him.

Lenin had every reason to be nervous. On the rare occasions he did go out he was often followed. Once in March, instead of going back to the flat where he was living with Nadya, he slipped his tail and took the train out of the city to a safe house in Finland. A bewildered Nadya was left to wonder where her husband was until finally told. By now she had become used to the perpetual insecurity of their life together.

Lenin's Finnish refuge was the Villa Wasa, a large and attractive wooden dacha with a covered veranda conveniently located not far from the station at Kuokkala, forty miles from St. Petersburg. Surrounded by a high fence and set in a clearing in dense woodland, it was the perfect conspiratorial location. It had been rented from a sympathetic Finn for party use and Lenin stayed here working undisturbed on resolutions for the next party congress to be held in Stockholm at the end of April.

On paper, the coming meeting was intended to be a reunification congress where Bolsheviks and Mensheviks pledged to bury their differences. The element of reconciliation, however, was entirely cosmetic, with even Nadya later admitting that the proceedings had been "decidedly factional." The location in Sweden remained a well kept secret with Lenin registering in a nearby hotel under the name Weber; Nadya was given status as a consultative delegate representing Kazan. At the congress, the Mensheviks were in the majority with sixty-two mandates to the Bolsheviks' forty-six. Since the debacle of 1905 the Bolsheviks had lost the working-class center of St. Petersburg to the Mensheviks, as reflected in their numbers.

Although Lenin was elected to the congress presidium, he was not voted onto the board of the Central Committee, the balance remaining seven Mensheviks to three Bolsheviks. Being in the minority did not discourage Lenin; adversity never did. He rose to the challenge and with his usual verbal dexterity dominated proceedings, the main topic of which was agrarian policy.

Lenin's proposal that a future social democratic government nationalize the land did not go down well with delegates; even his Bolshevik colleagues objected. Nationalization, they argued, would incense the peasants with their age-old assumption that the land belonged to them. Eventually Lenin was forced to concede that the land should be the property of *all* the people, not the state.

At the Congress Lenin did not capture the majority he had hoped for. The Poles, Latvians, and Bundists increasingly held the balance and forced him, on the surface, to compromise. But having lived by the principles of *konspiratsiya* for so long he was not willing to abandon them now. For all the superficial air of unity, he had every intention of keeping his Bolshevik faction alive. "We won't permit the idea of unity to tie a noose around our necks," he confided to Lunacharsky. "We shall under no circumstances permit the Mensheviks to lead us by the rope." Soon after the congress, he went back on the offensive, trying to whip up animosity toward the Menshevik-led Central Committee. As far as Lenin was concerned, in politics all things were permissible. His objective remained the same: to destroy his opponent, "wipe his organization off the face of the earth."

⌘

AT THE END OF MAY 1906 Lenin returned to Russia via Finland and immediately went into hiding under the name Chkheidze, Nadya's alias being Praskoviya Onegina. On May 10 the first Duma was convened at the Tauride Palace, with the Kadets commanding a majority, the Mensheviks appealing for reconciliation, and Lenin and his Bolsheviks stubbornly boycotting the whole process. The Kadets, for Lenin, were nothing less than "the worms in the grave of the revolution," and he would have no truck with them. As the Duma took its first tentative steps, troops were out on the streets in anticipation of trouble. Cossack units were sent into the countryside to quell peasant unrest, burning villages as they went. An orgy of firing squads, courts-martial, mass floggings, and arrests ensued as the Russian government systematically stamped out protest across the country while offering the supposed olive branch of democracy in St. Petersburg.

The architect of this new wave of repression, appointed in April 1906 and in July promoted to prime minister, was Petr Stolypin, a staunch patriot loyal to the czar and committed to crushing revolt. Suppression first and then reform was Stolypin's motto as he offered land reforms in the countryside with one hand to conciliate the still volatile peasantry and with the other brought in emergency decrees against insurgency. The most draconian of these was the introduction in August of field courts-martial for political crimes and heightened penalties for producing revolutionary propaganda. Stolypin also shut down radical newspapers and abolished many trade unions.

Acts of official revenge against insurgents in the Russian territories in Poland and Latvia were particularly savage under Stolypin. Courts-martial—previously restricted to naval and military mutinies—were ordered to effect the trial and execution of a verdict within seventy-two hours and to quell peasant unrest in the countryside. Under this new provision, 883 executions were carried out between August 1906 and May

1907. Between January 1905 and January 1909 the Police Department would record 3,319 condemnations with 1,435 executions, giving rise to the grim epithet "Stolypin's necktie" for the hangman's noose. The executions were accompanied by a concerted roundup of political activists. By 1909 the number of political prisoners in Russia—many of them sent on the long rail journey to Siberia in "Stolypin's carriages"—had risen from 86,000 in 1905 to 170,000.

Such measures engendered further acts of revenge as levels of Socialist Revolutionary–led terrorist attacks increased, culminating in an attempt on Stolypin's life at his villa in August 1906, when an explosion killed thirty-eight people. Public officials and government ministers were now prime targets, while indiscriminate violence was rapidly becoming part of a desperate new campaign to fund revolutionary groups through bank robberies and other forms of banditry. These operations were euphemistically referred to as "expropriations." Lenin had no problem with any violent means used to raise funds to buy arms for attacks on the police and government. These activities were overseen by one of his most trusted associates, his former *Iskra* agent in Baku, Leonid Krasin, now in charge of the fighting technical groups. Together with gunrunner Maxim Litvinov and expropriators in Georgia led by Stalin, Krasin was responsible for bringing in thousands of rubles to run the party machinery and buy weapons.

That summer the token constitutional experiment of the first Duma stuttered and stalled after Nicholas II rejected most of its proposed reforms; he dissolved it on July 21, 1906, after only forty-two days. A brief flurry of protest, including mutinies at the military bases at Kronstadt and Sveaborg, followed and were dealt with harshly. Lenin did not, however, abandon his calls for mass terror, having demanded a general strike in response to the mutinies. But people did not have the energy or will for another insurrection so soon after the events of 1905. With continuing political repression and the difficulties of life in the underground, Lenin could see that the writing was on the wall: in order to secure the future of the party and his own leadership of it, he would have to transfer the Bolshevik center out of Russia. Southern Finland seemed the best option—not quite in Russia but not quite abroad. On September 2 he moved back to the Villa Wasa, where he held open house for his Bolshevik inner circle and his two closest co-conspirators, Leonid Krasin and the rising star of the Bolshevik faction, Aleksandr Bogdanov, whose organizational and writing skills were being put to good use. The three Bolshevik leaders became popularly known as the "small trinity" or the "board of three." Lenin and Nadya occupied the ground floor of Villa Wasa, she sharing with her mother when she later joined them. Bogdanov and his wife were installed in an adjacent stone building used as the party library.

There were none of the constraints and anxieties of Russia at the Villa Wasa, though Nadya repeatedly ran the gauntlet traveling into St. Petersburg daily to continue her important party work, often returning late at night. She made a point before retiring of leaving milk and bread on the table, as well as bedding for any visitor arriving late from the station. The door was never locked. She and Lenin often awoke in the morning to find newly arrived comrades camping out in the dining room. The villa was always full of people. Couriers came and went daily to deliver mail and newspapers and receive Lenin's latest instructions. Often they were asked to stand and wait as Lenin rattled off an article to go back to St. Petersburg by return without pausing for thought or making any changes.

A colorful visitor to Lenin's hideaway at this time was an agent code-named "Kamo," an Armenian by birth, a notorious and successful expropriator from Georgia. His real name was Semen Ter-Petrosiyan. Between 1905 and 1907, together with Stalin, he graduated from committing acts of banditry and extortion to masterminding a string of violent bank, stagecoach, and train robberies in Baku, Kutaisi, and Tiflis, raising thousands of rubles, the bulk of which were sent to Lenin in Finland. In the autumn of 1906 Stalin even turned his hand to piracy, with a team of bandits wresting 16,000 rubles or more from a steamship off the coast of the Black Sea. Bogdanov had contacts with a Bolshevik fighting unit in the Urals that pulled off more than a hundred robberies, confiscating arms and weapons from government depots, soldiers, and local police, and even expropriating printing presses and equipment from publishers. They also robbed post offices and wine stores, but their exploits paled in comparison with the flamboyant gangsterism of the Georgians. Such banditry attracted the scorn of the Mensheviks, who dubbed Lenin and his cohorts little more than common criminals and "swindlers." How the Bolsheviks used this money was an even more contentious issue;

it seemed to Martov and his colleagues that its primary function was to buy Leninist supremacy over the party at their expense, particularly in the run-up to party congresses. Certainly the Bolshevik St. Petersburg Committee of the RSDLP was now being financed to the tune of a thousand rubles a month. This dirty money also funded the dissemination of Bolshevik literature and supported party activists sent into the provinces to galvanize support and set up bomb-making schools.

The revolutionary trade in contraband arms greatly exercised the Okhrana abroad as it attempted to monitor Russian gun smuggling through the European ports, assisted by local detectives. Their agents reported daily on meetings in Paris, Berlin, and other German cities, where revolutionaries were openly dealing with armaments firms, the supplies being stored all over Europe before being smuggled mainly by sea into Russian ports on the Baltic and Black Sea or, on a smaller scale, by land across the borders with Finland and Latvia into Russia. Greatly unnerved by the *John Grafton* affair, the Okhrana resorted to bribing foreign shipping agents, consulates, and customs houses to pass on information regarding Russian arms smuggling.

Maxim Litvinov was a Polish-born Jew whose real name was Meyer Wallach and whose code names were "Felix," "Maksimovich," and "Papasha." He became a successful gunrunner, managing to fool the Okhrana for some time as to his true identity. From his base in Paris on rue Port Royal he posed as a respectable army officer from the South American state of Ecuador (riven by internecine warfare at the time). Under that persona he traveled through Europe, inspecting and buying up arms. He obtained Mausers in Brussels and bullets for them at a munitions factory in Karlsruhe. In Vienna he purchased the ammunition for rifles acquired in Trieste—and on to Hamburg, Berlin, The Hague, and Liège, where he pulled off a succession of arms deals without arousing the least suspicion. In Karlsruhe, with extraordinary sangfroid, he even attended a live ammunition demonstration alongside officers from the Russian army. He shared a beer with them afterward and handed them his business card as he left.

That autumn Litvinov conspired with Kamo in shipping an arms consignment to Russia. He took great care beforehand to reconnoiter the possible exit ports, visiting Holland, Belgium, France, and Austria-Hungary before finally deciding on the Bulgarian port of Varna on the Black Sea. From there the arms, accompanied by Kamo, would be shipped across to the Georgian port of Batumi. But the Okhrana was now hot on Litvinov's trail and sent telegrams across Europe in an attempt to apprehend this elusive quarry, who was now traveling on a false German passport as "Gustav Graf." Two Okhrana spooks picked up Litvinov's trail by train from Warsaw to Vilna, but Litvinov had already disappeared when the train arrived at its destination. Coded telegrams flew back and forth between the Okhrana offices in Vilna and St. Petersburg: Litvinov must be apprehended at all costs. Two agents managed to pick up his trail when he arrived in St. Petersburg, but once again the clever Litvinov disappeared into thin air. The Okhrana men were beside themselves; as they searched for him, Litvinov made his way to Terijoki in Finland and from there to Varna, where he saw his arms shipment on its way. But, just like the *John Grafton,* the yacht bought for the purpose proved unreliable and it too was wrecked three days later during a storm off the coast of Romania. Kamo, who had rigged up an explosive device to destroy the boat in this eventuality, managed to get away but his device failed to go off. Litvinov rushed to Romania to try and save the cargo but the 2,000 rifles and 650,000 rounds of ammunition were seized by the Romanian authorities.

This debacle did not stop the indefatigable Litvinov, who soon was back in Finland, organizing the shipment of arms via the old *Iskra* routes, with the help of Latvian activists. Soon he was in Berlin, having eluded the Okhrana yet again. Early in January 1908 he found a new safe haven—Camden Town in north London.

As the gunrunners and expropriators went about their dangerous work and Lenin privately encouraged their ongoing experiment in guerrilla warfare, he and Bogdanov remained holed up at the Villa Wasa writing lengthy theoretical pieces. Lenin, now with an eye to the future and to securing his role in it, made inquiries about having his written works legally published. From Kuokkala he did what came best to him: listened and watched, convinced and commanded, keeping the flame of Bolshevism alive as he fought back his own doubts about whether his socialist revolution would ever be achieved. With the government now engaged in systematic repression, he sensed that a period of strategic retreat was looming for the revolutionary movement. The best tactical response would be to reverse his opposition to the Duma and support elections to the second Duma early the following year. Better for the RSDLP to have some kind of political forum in Russia than none at all; the Mensheviks certainly had recognized the wisdom of cooperating with progressive elements in the Duma rather than turning their back on it altogether.

And so he concentrated on his political journalism and party conferences in Tammerfors, St. Petersburg, and Terijoki (Finland), while relentlessly attacking the Mensheviks in print. Eventually his vitriolic assaults brought him into conflict with the RSDLP, and in April 1907 he was arraigned before a party tribunal for undermining party unity. His defense was an arrogant reassertion of his unshakeable belief that anything was justifiable in the cause of the party and the revolution. The Mensheviks were his political enemies; they had willfully split the party, and Lenin was waging "a war of extermination" on them. His words were the "poisoned weapons" that he justifiably employed to this end. In a few days he would once more be on the move—this time to the fifth party congress, to be convened in the more politically enlightened climate of Copenhagen. It would be the biggest RSDLP gathering yet, and he had every intention of imposing his will on it.

CHAPTER TEN

"The Congress of Undesirables"

LONDON: MAY–JUNE, 1907

⁕

THEY ONLY KNEW EACH OTHER by their underground code names—
Bukva, Nikolay, Zakhar, and Skorokhodov—but the four young delegates from Ivanovo-Voznesensk, an industrial city in central Russia, were filled with excitement at the prospect of leaving Russia for the first time to attend an important party congress—destination unknown. When they arrived at their Moscow safe house all they had with them, as instructed, was the clothes on their back. They had been specifically told to wear their smartest clothes—buy new suits if necessary—as well as hats, coats, and ties, in order to look like respectable travelers. The trouble was, as the four traveling companions soon noticed, many of the revolutionaries boarding the train that day were given away by the shabby, worn boots that they couldn't afford to replace. They would be lucky to get out of Russia undetected. They were to leave at night and travel by train to Finland, where they would receive instructions on the location of the congress.

The train was full of delegates from all over the Russian empire—the Urals, Siberia, Ukraine, Odessa, and the Caucasus—all trying to look innocent and not draw attention to themselves. As the four colleagues sweated in their suits in the stuffy third-class carriage, the train passed through the town of Beloostrov. They held their breath as customs officials boarded. Passports were not required because they were still within the Russian empire, but the men were convinced that the gendarmes and customs inspectors who walked up and down the train scrutinizing the passengers would identify them as illegals on their way out. As the train rattled on into the night through the forests of southern Finland, the men sat shoulder to shoulder on the hard wooden seats, unable to lie down and sleep, trying hard to observe the rules of *konspiratsiya* by not acknowledging each other and not engaging in conversation. They recognized some of the other passengers on the train by their underground aliases. Finally, down the line at Hangö (Hanko), where they disembarked and were given false passports by Finnish social democrats, they were told their destination was Copenhagen.

After suffering through a night of seasickness on the steamship from Finland, the delegates had already settled into their cheap hotels when the social democrats in the Danish parliament, under pressure from the Ministry of Justice, suddenly withdrew their offer to host the congress. The government was in an embarrassing situation. The Danish king, Frederick VIII, was Nicholas II's uncle and maintained close links with his sister, the dowager empress Maria Fedorovna, and the Russian court. Blood ties among royals, seemingly, were thicker than solidarity among socialists. The delegates had to leave Denmark within twelve hours or face deportation to Russia, which would mean certain arrest.

Where else could they go? Sweden seemed the next best choice. And so, undaunted, 180 delegates boarded a chartered steamer for Malmo. The Swedish authorities, however, gave them equally short shrift, not wishing for a repetition of the "secret" RSDLP congress held under their noses in Stockholm the previous year. The hungry, exhausted delegates were therefore dispersed in small groups across Malmo's cheap hotels, though some had to spend the night huddled on their pathetic bundles by the statue of King Charles X on Sturtoret Square. The following morning, May 6, they all traipsed back to Copenhagen, where they were again allowed a brief respite while the organizers made last-ditch attempts to find an alternative venue. Lenin sent a telegram to the leader of the Norwegian Labor Party, Oskar Nissen, enlisting his help. But the Norwegian government banned the congress in deference to its Danish and Swedish neighbors.

London now seemed the only option left to the RSDLP. A telegram was sent to John Burns, MP, a trade union radical who was president of the local government board in Henry Campbell-Bannermans's Liberal government. After an agonizing wait, word came back that the British government gave refuge to all political emigrants and was not concerned with what the congress members engaged in, provided they did nothing illegal. However, the additional costs already incurred by many of the im-

poverished delegates as well as the party itself in having to move on from two abortive locations was already creating serious problems; a small delegation was dispatched to Berlin to beg funding from German social democrats, who donated 10,000 marks, though not without their leader August Bebel complaining that "these Russians spend too much time talking at their Congresses; ours last five days flat, but they go on jabbering for a whole month." It was no wonder that the Russians' money ran out.

At noon on May 8 the first group of delegates left the port of Esberg for the Harwich docks, after being given a rousing send-off by Danish socialists singing revolutionary songs and waving red flags from the quayside. During their journey this motley crew of Russians, who appeared to be traveling abroad without baggage, were given disparaging looks by better-dressed passengers and treated with disdain by the ship's crew. At Harwich the gaggle of travelers boarded the train to London's Liverpool Street station. Much to their surprise, unlike the Russian police, the British bobbies took no notice of them. They arrived in London at 9:25 PM that night, cold and tired after their twelve-hour journey. The culture shock of London after the relative tranquility of Copenhagen and Stockholm was enormous. At the station their senses were assaulted by the smoke, steam, and hubbub of London. Outside, the trams and buses, the crowds of people, and the brightly lit shop windows were even more arresting. Some delegates reeled in horror at the prospect of being taken down to the underground for their onward journey. Outside the station, the Russians stood bewildered by the "grandiose fantasmagoria" that was London, waiting patiently at the corner of Aldgate High Street for the bus to Whitechapel.

If the delegates from Eastern Europe, the remainder of whom arrived on May 9 and 10, were bewildered by the great modern metropolis of London, then Londoners were equally alarmed by the biggest gathering of the "alien menace" ever seen. The *Daily Mail* was quick to label it a "congress of undesirables." London might have been oblivious to the presence of Lenin and his associates in 1902–1903, but it now found itself the venue for an extraordinary assemblage of Russian, Polish, Latvian, Caucasian, and Jewish revolutionaries from all over the czarist empire—who between them had served six hundred years of imprisonment and exile.

For the next three weeks Londoners stopped in their tracks at the sight of groups of foreign-looking men—a "nameless army from Russia" that had "forced their unwelcome attentions" on the city. Although many of them wore conventional starched collar and tie and homburg hat, others from the Russian provinces and far-flung republics provoked consternation with their "picturesque" dress and their wild appearance in Caucasian sheepskin hats, dark cloaks, black flowing cravats, and Russian-style working men's tunics and high boots. They seemed the very epitome of conspiracy and intrigue, speaking strange languages and having even stranger manners, as they made their way through the streets of Islington and Whitechapel.

The intellectuals might still be the majority in the RSDLP, but the party ranks now included over one hundred representatives from Russia's burgeoning urban working classes. The four delegates from the textile town of Ivanovo-Vosnesensk were typical. They had all been vetted by the Credentials Commission, in which Nadezhda Krupskaya played a leading role, before they left St. Petersburg for Finland, ensuring they were aware of the elaborate precautionary measures necessary for getting out of Russia undetected. A group of seventeen had found their way to Villa Wasa in hopes of meeting their hero, but Lenin had already left. Nadya offered them food, warmth, and a place to sleep for the night before seeing them on their journey. But she would be staying in Finland to continue her essential work for the party.

Lenin had been far too wary of Okhrana surveillance to travel with the main body of delegates from Copenhagen. Instead, he had taken a train south to Berlin where he met up with his new friend Gorky, and spent time at the theater and relaxing in the Tiergarten with him and Mariya Andreeva before they departed for England.

He enjoyed being back in London but remained deeply ambivalent toward what was to him the most advanced land of bourgeois capitalism. He had to concede, however, that Britain was also a country whose citizens enjoyed full political liberty, which explained why the congress was being tolerated here and nowhere else. On arrival, with his usual frugality, he had found himself a cheap room in Bloomsbury, "just a bit larger than a compartment in a railway carriage," as a colleague observed, where his landlady gave him fish and chips and a cup of coffee for breakfast throughout the congress. Gorky and Mariya Andreeva, as special guests of the congress, were given a room at the Hotel Imperial on Russell Square near to Lenin's lodgings. Concerned for their welfare, he went over to vet the couple's room, which was small, cold, and uncomfortable. The weather in London that May was unseasonably cold and rainy; day after day the springtime sky was obscured by fog. Lenin worried about their damp sheets—not good for the tubercular Gorky, now living on Capri for the sake of his health—and he suggested they air them in front of the gas fire.

Meanwhile the 366 delegates were having difficulty finding places to stay. After registering for the congress at the Polish Socialist Club on the corner of Fulbourne Street in Whitechapel, where they were given maps and issued secret passwords in order to maintain a veil of secrecy over the proceedings, they were sent out to a range of billets. Some were lucky enough to be housed with sympathetic British socialist families; others were taken in by Russo-Polish Jewish immigrants. But most of them were dispersed across cheap boardinghouses, socialist clubs, and overnight shelters in the East End with only two shillings and sixpence per day allocated to each of them for board and lodging. This meant that the majority ended up queuing with London's down-and-outers at the local doss house for their first few nights till better lodgings could be found for them. The most conveniently placed of these was Rowton House, the "monster doss house" writer Jack London described in his classic account of the East End slums in 1902. A temple of Victorian philanthropy, Rowton House offered refuge to as many as 816 men, for sixpence a day each. They could use the various communal facilities and after 7:00 PM had the privilege of squeezing themselves into a tiny cubicle with a horsehair mattress on an iron bedstead. Here the bewildered Russians were obliged to run the gauntlet of London's feral low life—drunks, criminals, and the socially desperate. It was, for delegate Konstantin Gandurin, an unnerving glimpse of people reduced by poverty and unemployment to a brutal existence. Gandurin was extremely relieved to be found accommodation with a Jewish tailor in Whitechapel, where, hearing Russian spoken all around him, he immediately felt more at home. But even here, the abyss of human suffering was all too evident.

Much to their disgust and dismay two of the four unofficial delegates who were there as observers with no voting rights, Joseph Stalin and

Maxim Litvinov, were forced to endure the dubious comforts of Rowton House for a couple of nights before their voluble protests got them a back room at 77 Jubilee Road costing three shillings and sixpence a week. From here they enlisted the services of a local boy, Arthur Bacon, to run errands from house to house for "Mr. Ivanovich" (one of Stalin's many pseudonyms), delivering letters to delegates and raking the ash from his fireplace. The boy also brought Stalin toffees, for which he had developed a great liking. In return, the kindly Mr. Ivanovich paid young Arthur well—sometimes half a crown—not realizing its equivalent value in rubles. But unlike many others present, he had ways of raising the money to fund his own appearance at the congress, as the delegates would later hotly debate.

∞

THE TROUBLEMAKERS' ARRIVAL in London did not go unnoticed. Detectives from the Special Political Branch were well primed this time, watching at a discreet distance from day one, as too were a couple of agents sent over by the Okhrana from its Paris agency. The "Russian problem" had increasingly become an issue in London, since the Revolution of 1905 had led to an influx of immigrants. With the presence of so many Russians, the city seemed to have become the "world's storm-centre of anarchism." The Special Branch, however, was thinly stretched. Some fifteen to twenty officers could hardly keep tabs on over three hundred foreign delegates scattered around the East End for the duration of the Congress, particularly as in 1907 detectives were also monitoring a much more vocal and sometimes violent protest movement—the British militant suffragettes.

Most of the men recruited into the Special Branch were fluent Russian, Yiddish, German, and French speakers, notably Herbert Fitch. Based on his 1905 surveillance of the secret RSDLP congress in London, he was singled out as an expert on Russian extremists. He was one of several detectives sent to monitor meetings of "anarchists" (as all Russian and Jewish revolutionaries were labeled, be they anarchist, nihilist, or social democrat) in parks, pubs, and clubs across London in the run-up to the congress. The most important was the inaugural meeting, held "secretly" on May 10 at the Worker's Friend Club in Whitechapel.

Popularly known as the Anarchist Club, this large two-story building at 165 Jubilee Street had been a Salvation Army depot before German émigré Rudolf Rocker rented it in 1906 as a meeting house with classrooms and a reading room for Jewish immigrant workers. It could house up to eight hundred people in its gas-lit meeting hall on the ground floor. By 1907 it had become a focal point for East End Jewish radicals, with its socialist newspaper *Arbeter Fraint* being printed next door. The Anarchist Club had long been under police surveillance. Special Branch detectives were hovering incognito (or so they thought) outside the day of the meeting, when the legendary émigré anarchist, Prince Peter Kropotkin, arrived as a guest of honor. He immediately recognized Detective Edwin Woodhall outside and motioned to him to approach. "This is my friend Lenin," he said, turning to "a short man with a very intellectual face." This was the man everyone had come to meet. But the detective and his colleagues were wasting their time, asserted Kropotkin. There would be no trouble.

Although Woodhall remained posted outside, Herbert Fitch managed to get past the pickets on the door and into the meeting. He had himself made up to look suitably Eastern European, and after giving the requisite secret handshake at the door he was allowed to enter the hall. He immediately recognized the distinctive figure of Maxim Gorky on the podium—tall and gangly, with his pale face, high cheekbones, darting green-gray eyes, and bushy mustache. Fitch heard him give a passionate speech on the sufferings of political exiles in Siberia and the exploitation of the peasantry, calling not for bloody revolution but for the peaceful deposition of Nicholas II. The speech was followed by a burst of revolutionary exhortations followed by the deep and, even to Fitch's ears, "thrilling" singing of the funeral anthem for executed revolutionaries and Siberian exiles. The intensity of the collective hatred for czardom and an overwhelming determination in that drafty hall to effect revolutionary change in Russia made Fitch shiver.

Gorky was followed by a dynamic young Leon Trotsky, who snarled and shook his fists. He had just made his way to London from Finland after spending four arduous weeks on the run from his second exile in Siberia. Trotsky was followed by young "fresh-faced girls with long plaits" whose demure appearance belied their passionate demands for armed insurrection in Russia. As the meeting echoed to the singing of the "Red Flag," the tone was clearly set for a turbulent congress.

A venue for the congress was not found until the very last minute. British sympathizers in the Social Democratic Federation, including George Lansbury and journalist Henry Brailsford, had settled on the two-hundred-member Brotherhood Church, located on Southgate Road at the junction of the run-down working-class boroughs of Islington, Dalston, and Hackney. This formerly derelict Congregational church had been taken over in 1892 by a Christian socialist group founded by British mystic and Tolstoyan J. Bruce Wallace. More an intellectual forum than a place of worship, its brief Sunday morning services were characterized by Bible readings and political discussion, to the accompaniment of socialist songs rather than the traditional hymnbook. This was followed by an improvised vegetarian meal and ongoing discussion until late into the afternoon. Many members of the congregation, including Labour MP Ramsay MacDonald, were active in the British socialist movement and openly sympathetic to the Russian revolutionary cause. Delegate Konstantin Gandurin could not, however, fail to see the irony of a church offering refuge to the godless and the enemies of organized religion. Nevertheless, Pastor Arthur Baker happily made over the use of the building, except for Sunday morning worship and Wednesday evening prayer services, for the duration of the congress.

When the delegates arrived on the first day, May 13, a police officer was already on duty outside (with half a dozen plainclothes detectives in the vicinity) as they entered by a side door on Balmes Road. Only those with the appropriate signed and countersigned blue admission tickets were allowed in through the zealously guarded door. Inside they crammed into the stuffy little church with its narrow lancet windows and its plain wooden walls and benches ranged on either side, with the pulpit serving as the speaker's rostrum. The Mensheviks, considering themselves to be "the real left-wing of the party," made sure they arrived first and took the pews on the left, forcing the Bolsheviks to the right. The Poles, Bundists, and Latvians rightly held the middle ground in the central pews, while guests and observers took their seats in the galleries to right and left, which were reached by an iron ladder. Guest of honor Maxim Gorky sat downstairs among the Bolshevik contingent for days on end, holed up with them like pupils in the classroom of a charity school. As the debate heated up, their bellies rumbled and the German money started to run out.

The major issue preoccupying members as they greeted each other was "to which faction do you belong?" It was a sign of things to come. Not long after arriving in London, Lenin had jokingly told Gorky how glad he was to have him there. "I believe you're fond of a scrap," he had remarked. Well, "there's going to be a fine old free-for-all here." He was right. The days that followed were "protracted, crowded, stormy and chaotic," as Trotsky later recalled. Russian émigré Angelica Balabanoff, now a leader of the Italian Socialist Party, remembered them being marked by an "all-absorbing, almost fanatical, spirit of factionalism."

Although the windows were shut to prevent outsiders from overhearing the proceedings, the sound of raised voices and revolutionary songs frequently echoed around the neighboring streets. Given a temporary reprieve from oppressive political restrictions and constant police surveillance, the 336 delegates grasped the opportunity for free and open political discussion like hungry prisoners suddenly released from jail.

They did not anticipate, however, the reaction of the British press, which was quick to exploit—in traditional cloak-and-dagger style—the sudden presence of so many alien agitators. Journalists and photographers staked out the Brotherhood Church from the outset with all the intrusive persistence of today's tabloids. As early as May 10 the *Daily Mirror* had alerted readers to the presence of dangerous revolutionists plotting against the Russian throne and relentlessly pursued the secretive and pseudonymous delegates as they came and went at the Brotherhood Church each day, screening their faces with umbrellas, hats, and newspapers.

Despite their unwieldy camera equipment, these forerunners of today's paparazzi tenaciously pursued their prey, until it was pointed out that by photographing the delegates they were playing into the hands of the czarist secret police. In Russia, belonging to a socialist organization would get you sent to Siberia. Nor would the delegates give the press their names: "The Russian police have long ears, and, you see, we shall be going back to Russia," as one of them explained. They also objected to being characterized as anarchists with bombs under their coats.

Nevertheless, sensationalistic stories were fashioned from innocuous delegates, particularly the few women, who were, so the *Daily Mirror* told its readers, practiced at handling revolvers and "drill themselves constantly in front of mirrors by which they become adept in aiming and pulling the trigger." One young female trade union delegate, a cotton weaver from Ivanovo-Vosnesensk, was exposed by the press as in fact being the daughter of a Russian governor-general, "Princess so-and-so," who "carried bombs in her muff" and had personally assassinated several high-profile czarist officials. Even the *Times* thundered that the covert purpose of these social democratic visitors was to "make extensive purchase of arms," an allegation vociferously denied by the socialist *Daily News* as "arrant nonsense." All this was more than enough for local residents, one of whom complained across her fence to a *Daily Mirror* reporter that she hadn't been able to sleep since "them foreigners" arrived. Every day they came out into the yard during breaks "and gabble[d] away something dreadful." They "aren't here for no good, I'm sure," she declared, "and I don't like it."

The press wasn't alone in harassing the delegates. At the end of each day's proceedings, the "hooligan element of the neighbourhood" gathered outside the Brotherhood Church to hurl derisive remarks at delegates as they left. One night Stalin narrowly avoided being set upon by a group of dockers in a pub. From now until the end of the congress uniformed bobbies were also in evidence.

Meanwhile, tensions were rising inside. Lenin had arrived intent on edging the Mensheviks out of their precarious majority on the Central Committee, which they had gained in Stockholm the previous year. Thanks to a concerted recruitment campaign in Russia, his Bolshevik delegation at the congress had gained the edge over Martov's Mensheviks with 105 to 97. Although the stated intention of the congress was, as before, to patch up differences, the battle for control of the party congress was heading for a showdown. Many of the delegates, particularly the inexperienced workers, were unaccustomed to the long hours of debate indulged in by political exiles for whom this had become second nature. No sooner had delegates arrived than they found themselves subjected to three days of mainly incomprehensible, protracted, and stormy arguments between Bolsheviks and Mensheviks over the agenda. As Lenin stonewalled, the Mensheviks raised endless objections and attempted to get him excluded from the presidium (he was eventually voted chairman).

The proceedings went on late into the evening, degenerating into endlessly labored points of order and matters of principle, with Trotsky attempting and failing to mediate between the two factions. At times the proceedings became so heated that they had to be interrupted in order to prevent fist fights from breaking out.

By the time the agenda was agreed, many of the delegates had had enough. Gorky noted that the initial "festive" mood surrounding the congress had evaporated during the protracted wrangles over procedures. "The fury of the disputes," he later wrote, "chilled my enthusiasm." British socialist Zelda Kahan, who had befriended Lenin in 1902 and had helped find accommodations for the delegates, attended as an observer. She too was horrified by the way the Bolsheviks and Mensheviks tore into each other during debates. They had no shame, she recalled, in using, she thought, the most unparliamentary and insulting language. Russian politics was quite another country in comparison with the confrontations between Liberals and Tories at Westminster. But that, Lenin assured her, was because here they were fighting for vital principles that would affect the future happiness "of our people, indeed of all mankind." There was no way he or anybody else could be conciliatory when so much was at stake.

From the outset Lenin took center stage in his inimitable, charismatic way, dominating the podium for hours on end, talking without notes, fighting, arguing, and hectoring through every point on the agenda. Lenin was in his element. Tireless if not effervescent, he enjoyed a good quarrel, standing there stocky and pugnacious, his fingers poked up under his armpits, with a challenging, sardonic look in his eye, his voice unmistakable with its thick guttural r's that he couldn't quite roll properly. The transformative power of Lenin's arguments and his persuasiveness carried all before him during the fifteen sessions of the congress that he energetically chaired.

Maxim Gorky was captivated by Lenin, seduced by his bullish physicality as a speaker and his passionate exhortations to his "comrades." For Gorky, as for many others during those three weeks in May, Lenin's greatness lay in his direct manner. He had the ability to breathe life and logic into complex political questions, treating them "so simply, no striving after eloquent phrases . . . but every word uttered distinctly, and its meaning marvellously plain." In comparison, Gorky remained unmoved by Plekhanov in his fey pince-nez, all "closely buttoned up like a Protestant pastor" in his elegant frock coat and cravat and speaking with the portentousness of a preacher.

The major theoretical bone of contention at the congress was the ongoing disagreement between the Bolsheviks and Mensheviks over the true nature of the Russian bourgeoisie. Lenin was convinced that Marx's concept of an initial, bourgeois-led revolution leading to a republic, followed by a workers revolution instituting a proletarian state, would not be effective. Russian revolutionaries should not take Marx's predictions literally but should work toward an immediate proletarian revolution. The Russian liberal bourgeoisie was in his view treacherous and antirevolutionary; it had sold out to compromise in the Duma by dropping demands for a properly elected constituent assembly. With the Mensheviks still clinging to the ideal of a bourgeoisie-led revolution like the French Revolution in 1789, Lenin continued to argue that the only way a revolution in Russia could succeed was through the united leadership of the urban proletariat and the peasantry. After the events of 1905 a resurgence of armed struggle against the czarist government was now inevitable, as well as the exposure of its pseudodemocratic promises. Party collaboration with the trade unions, which had been on the rise since 1905 in the drive to recruit more workers, had given a lift to activism. But Lenin, seeking to adopt increasingly violent tactics in the face of czarist repression, wanted the party to revert to small underground groups of professional revolutionaries; he put forward a militant agenda for armed insurrection, but the Menseviks, led by Martov, defeated it.

At the end of each day's proceedings, most of the impoverished delegates had little intellectual or cultural curiosity, let alone the money, to explore the huge and oppressive city they found themselves in. Fearing surveillance, they could do little but tramp the streets back to their lodgings in full view of the dark underbelly of the East End before wearily grabbing a night's rest. London was a stark object lesson in the contradictions of the British class system. The Russians were struck by the many prostitutes on the streets—thin, sickly, dressed in torn and dirty clothes, many old and withered before their time. Their desperate brazenness seemed a pitiful manifestation of the torment of the human spirit, standing on the edge of the grave.

During breaks between sessions Lenin was irrepressible. He enjoyed the company of Gorky as often as he was able, on one occasion accompanying him to the music hall, where he had laughed loudly at the clowns' pratfalls. Otherwise, he and his inner circle liked to eat together and review the day's proceedings. "You don't want to risk your weak digestion and waste your money on diplomatic restaurants," he warned one of the Latvian Bolsheviks. He knew just the place—a good wholesome workers restaurant near his lodgings in Kings Cross where they could afford eggs and bacon, or a ham sandwich and a mug of stout or porter.

For the most part, Lenin spent as much time as he could talking to worker delegates in pubs and cheap eating houses. As far as these young, impressionable Russians were concerned, Plekhanov might be "the teacher," the figurehead of the movement, but Lenin was undoubtedly "the comrade and leader." If he had one gift it was being a man of the people when it most counted. On Sundays, eager to educate the young and impressionable delegates, Lenin took them to witness the debates at Speakers' Corner in Hyde Park. Coming from a politically repressive regime, the Russians marveled at Londoners' freedom of speech. How long would it be, Lenin asked his companions, before they would be allowed to meet freely like this in Russia? During a tour of the British Museum he was sure to point out, when admiring the Elgin Marbles and other treasures, that the museum was of course a "hoard of colossal wealth" plundered by Britain from its colonies. Like everything else about this magnificent modern city, the museum was a wonderful example of the corrupting power of the capitalist world.

Inevitably, wherever the delegates went, the British detectives followed. The two camps got to know each other and in the end, with the Russians sanguine about being followed, they invited their tails to share a pint with them so they could find out which side they were working for—the British or the czarist secret police. In the Russian scheme of things *agents provocateurs* and double agents were par for the course. It turned out that the men from Special Branch weren't just watching the congress but were also watching the Russian agents who were watching the delegates. The Okhrana, however, had been knocked off balance when the congress was suddenly diverted to London, since it had spent weeks positioning its agents in Copenhagen. Herbert Fitch of Special Branch had a very poor opinion of them; it seemed to him every Okhrana officer was expected to spy on his fellows, and the "biggest bribe was always the final factor." Even here, at the fifth congress, they had two key agents at work, including one who had infiltrated to the very heart of Lenin's Bolshevik group. It would be several more years before Lenin would find out that Dr. Yakov Zhitomirsky, head of the Bolshevik émigré organization in Europe, was a traitor.

Although the congress was dominated by intense discussion focused on the role of the peasantry in the revolutionary movement and the future of legal parliamentary campaigning in elections for the second Duma, the Mensheviks were preoccupied by the thorny subject of financial resources, which they still technically controlled. They complained bitterly about the Bolsheviks' unfair advantage, made possible by funds raised largely by bank robberies and other "expropriations," as well as private donations (such as the 60,000 rubles bequeathed to the party by industrialist millionaire Savva Morozov). The Bolsheviks had used money from expropriations to fortify their ranks in advance of the congress and to fund widespread activism in Russia in favor of Lenin's faction, enabling the party to send out legions of agents to found journals and distribute pamphlets, all with the objective of obtaining additional mandates for Bolshevik delegates to the congress. Illegally obtained funds had allowed the Bolsheviks to buy power over the party with very little of it going into general funds; hence the present financial shortages.

In Stockholm the presidium had voted to outlaw expropriations, and Lenin tried hard to deflect discussion of the subject. In fact, he had ignored the decision and the "exes" had persisted in the Caucasus and in Moscow, monitored by Lenin's inner circle. Their notoriety had spread, despite repeated Menshevik protests that they were bad publicity for the party.

Money—or the lack of it—dominated behind the scenes too. Ten days into the congress Leo Deutsch, head of the economic committee, announced that funds were almost exhausted and many of the delegates were not getting enough to eat. Concerned that the comrades were hungry, Lenin had asked Mariya Andreeva and Bogdanov's wife to organize supplies of sandwiches, oranges, milk, and a large barrel of beer during the breaks between sittings. The delegates, in any event, had no desire to run the gauntlet of the press gathered outside and go in search of food. Most were stoical. They had all been hungrier in Russia; they could endure a few more days in London if it meant seeing the congress through to its end. Meanwhile, as the Mensheviks talked of closing the congress early for this reason, Leo Deutsch appealed—using celebrity guest Maxim Gorky as the lure—to wealthy British socialists and sympathizers to bail the congress out. In the end the Society of Friends of Russian Freedom suggested a fund-raising dinner featuring personal appeals for support from the leading lights of the congress.

Thus, much to his extreme annoyance, Lenin found himself obliged to endure the social discomforts of a dinner party with rich industrialists and philanthropists held on the evening of Sunday, May 26, by the artist Felix Moscheles at his studio in Chelsea. Neither Lenin nor Gorky owned formal clothes, but they did their best to make themselves presentable. Lenin found the whole experience absolutely excruciating, "a stupid affair" he later grumbled. Although he spoke English, his peculiarly strangled accent was impenetrable to the guests. When he was called on to give a short speech, he did not mince his words—even though speaking in Russian—asserting that "as bourgeois and capitalists" those gathered there, despite being his class enemies, should support the victory of "our revolution" over czarism. It would give them a chance to export more goods to a more cultured and freer Russia.

Although the speech was interpreted by Fanny Stepniak, the solemn, emaciated-looking Russians in their shapeless black suits clearly failed to move the gathering. The glitterati stood around in their evening clothes staring at the Russians as though they were "wild beasts in a zoological garden." Despite the elaborate dinner, and some damage limitation from the elegant Plekhanov with a charming speech in fluent French, the Russians were sent home empty-handed. Lenin, angry and humiliated, vowed he would never beg from capitalists again. But he had at least impressed one of those present: the Russianist Constance Garnett (who had pioneered the first English translations of Chekhov and Turgenev). Despite Lenin's bad temper and gruffness, Garnett recognized him as a "man of tremendously strong character." The other Bolsheviks at the congress, however, were "a set of self-righteous crooks."

It was Lenin's good friend Theodore Rothstein, a Russian émigré who had settled in England in 1890 and become a member of the RSDLP in exile, who finally came up with a solution to the pressing financial needs of the fifth congress. As a journalist for the *Daily News* he worked alongside the left-wing radical and revolutionary sympathizer Henry Brailsford, who had suggested they appeal to the Russian-born American magnate and philanthropist Joseph Fels. He had made a fortune from naphtha laundry soap and was now living in north Kent. Rothstein originally suggested a figure of £500, but on discussion it rapidly became clear that a much larger sum was needed. Fels was sympathetic when approached but asked if he could see the congress in session before agreeing to stump up the £1,700 being asked for. He took a taxi to Southgate Road with Brailsford and Rothstein. An afternoon at the Brotherhood Church and the sight of the young and often inspired faces of the delegates soon persuaded him, as did the charismatic figure of Lenin engaged in a blistering attack on the Mensheviks; he had begun his speech the previous evening, broken off at midnight, and then resumed that morning. It was now 1:00 PM, and he was still on his feet. Fels could not fail to be impressed, even though he was not a socialist but an eccentric proponent of the single tax on land values. He agreed to a loan bond, provided all the delegates signed their names to it, guaranteeing repayment by the following January. Most of the congress members dutifully did so— using their party pseudonyms. Lenin managed a few brusque words of thanks to Fels in German. In response, as he left, Fels pressed one of the single-tax leaflets he always carried into a bemused Lenin's hand.

By the time the congress ended on June 1, the congregation of the Brotherhood Church was feeling less than brotherly toward the argumentative revolutionaries who had taken over their church for so long. With typical British politesse and naïveté they had assumed that Russians did things the way they did and that the congress would last two or three days at the most. Three weeks after seeing their church invaded, they were glad to wrest it back again as the delegates, each clasping a gold sovereign generously donated by Fels in addition to the loan, trailed their various ways back to Liverpool Street and then Harwich.

Lenin left London with a sense of satisfaction; he had as always extracted the maximum political advantage from the situation in his relentless drive to secure his hegemony over the Bolshevik faction. Angelica Balabanoff observed that throughout the congress he had been "the most sedulous delegate, and certainly the most punctual one." Not a single word had escaped him, "not one gesture," as he took notes in his small, cramped handwriting. No one had matched his vigor and assurance, his cool and merciless argumentation. Meanwhile, in a secret meeting held immediately after the congress his faction had elected its own "central bureau" of Bolsheviks to press home their dominion over the Mensheviks.

Martov was profoundly affected by the congress and the now irreconcilable divisions within the party. It effectively marked the end of his political life. Bitterly disillusioned, he was, as Gorky observed, a "lost soul" and settled back in Paris where he would haunt his favorite café, La Rotonde—sitting, talking, and writing about revolution to the end. But he never forgot the "accursed month" in London, when factional infighting had finally brought home to him the hopelessness of ever achieving conciliation and cooperation with Lenin in a united party. It was not just the loss of a once close friendship, nor simply disillusion with the ruthlessness and lack of moral integrity of his former friend that he mourned; the congress also marked the beginning of the end of his own political hopes.

As a nonaligned delegate (he had not been able to raise the five hundred Bolshevik supporters in Georgia to obtain a mandate to vote at the congress), Stalin had remained enigmatically silent throughout, as yet uncertain of his political position. Gorky did not even note his presence in his memoir of the congress. But for Stalin at least, the congress had ended in a victory for Bolshevism and he had seen his hero Lenin triumph in forcing the adoption of the tactics of "irreconcilable proletarian class struggle." The "intellectualist vacillation" of the Mensheviks had been dealt a "mortal blow," except in one area: they had secured a vote condemning bank robberies and "gangsterism" (Stalin was now a master at it, along with his alter ego Kamo) on pain of expulsion from the party. But he wasn't going to take any notice of that. Nor was Lenin, who was only too aware of Stalin's talent for raising illicit funds. A month later, back in Tiflis, Stalin and Kamo staged a spectacular bank heist netting 250,000 rubles, a large proportion of which (about £1.7 million in today's money) found its way to Lenin and Bolshevik funds in Finland.

At the end of the congress, which proved to be the last great gathering of Russian socialists before the Revolution of 1917, Georgy Plekhanov publicly thanked the British people for the freedom they had accorded its delegates. In response, His Majesty's Government was proud to state that throughout the duration it had not interfered with the delegates' political freedom. Like other political refugees, they had enjoyed the protection of the British flag. Behind the scenes, however, the presidium of the congress had complained about the way certain newspapers had harassed delegates for their photographs, as did the socialist journal *Free Russia,* which described the paparazzi at the Brotherhood Church as a "swarm of wasps." Henry Brailsford, reporting the congress for the *Daily News,* had written to Ramsay MacDonald complaining about the number of Special Branch men staking out the congress. One of the detectives had complained to a Reuters reporter outside the Brotherhood Church that he was "very fagged," having spent the last three or four days traipsing all over the East End, under orders to "locate the residences of every delegate in London." The detectives had only just completed their onerous task. He pitied the delegates, however, for "they would have a warm time on their return in Russia." The complaint was passed on to home secretary Herbert Gladstone, who raised questions in Parliament about harassment, but not before the congress was almost at an end.

As the delegates prepared to leave, a specially selected "conspiratorial commission" was given responsibility for seeing them covertly on their way back to Russia via Finland. Lenin stayed on in London for a few days, working at his lodgings with the one and only congress stenographer, ensuring that an accurate written record of the sessions—and particularly of his own numerous speeches—was produced. He also found time to do some reading at the British Library, in between attending a second congress held by the Latvian social democrat contingent in the East End. Then he headed back to Nadya in Finland and the safe house at Kuokkala. Much to her amusement, he arrived sporting a large white straw hat, having clipped his mustache short and shaved off his beard in order to evade identification and arrest.

During his time in London, the British press had paid no particular attention to Lenin. Reports of the congress all had focused on Gorky, as well as Plekhanov, Trotsky, and Kropotkin. Gorky was the person the Western press wanted to know more about, viewing him as the hero of the Russian working classes and "the prophet of revolution." "What Gorki

[sic] thinks to-day Russia will do tomorrow," declared the *Daily Mirror*, adding, "History is now being made in London." That much was true— only back in Russia they saw things somewhat differently.

Lenin may have successfully maintained a low profile in Britain, but in Russia, where his police file stretched back to the 1880s, he was now public enemy number one. A warrant had been issued for the arrest of "Vladimir Ulyanov, alias Lenin," a "writer on economic subjects," now regarded as "the most dangerous and most capable of all the Revolutionary leaders." And also the most elusive; for while the story was being syndicated across the world's newspapers, Lenin once more disappeared from sight. The Russian secret police were now searching for him all over southern Finland.

CHAPTER ELEVEN

On Thin Ice

FINLAND–GENEVA–CAPRI–LONDON: DECEMBER 1907–DECEMBER 1908

———— ∞∞∞ ————

LENIN ARRIVED BACK AT the Villa Wasa exhausted, overwrought, and unable to eat or sleep. A month of sustained, frenetic political debate in London had depleted his energy reserves. Nadya, with her usual calm efficiency, sorted out his things and packed him off to rest and recuperate at the dacha of a comrade, Lidiya Knippovich, at Styrs Udde (Stirsudden), a remote village on the Gulf of Finland. Here he briefly let go: he rode around on a rickety old bicycle, swam, walked alone in the pine forest, and sat by the lighthouse contemplating the sea. But within weeks, having put on weight and recovered his strength, he was on the road again. Two more contentious socialist conferences—at Terijoki and Kotka in Finland—were followed by another interminable incognito train ride across Europe to the International Socialist Congress in Stuttgart, Germany, and then back to Helsingfors for another conference. In June 1907 the second Duma had been dissolved. It was followed by a savage clampdown on opposition groups. Many prominent party workers were arrested and deported to Siberia without trial. Active support for the party in Russia was hemorrhaging fast.

Finland was no longer the haven it had once been for politicals on the run. Since 1905 the czarist authorities had been debating whether or not to infringe the supposedly autonomous status of the Duchy of Finland and arrest revolutionaries hiding there. By the beginning of December 1907 they had begun to close in.

At Villa Wasa, with rumors of a coming police raid, Lenin left Nadya and her mother with the Bogdanovs and went into hiding in a small village,

Åggleby (Oulunkylä), set in woodland on the edge of a hillside near Helsingfors. As he left, Nadya and Natalya Bogdanova began sorting through the party archives and burning great heaps of documents, which scattered ash in the snow around the house. It was now clear to the Bolshevik center that publishing *Proletarii* in Finland was no longer safe, and it would have to be transferred to London or Geneva. But London was more expensive, so production would be returned to Switzerland. The important work of transferring the operation devolved to Nadya. She and Lenin would have to sit things out in Geneva again, since, as Nadya admitted, in Russia "the reaction was going to drag on for years." Lenin's flight out of Finland, however, proved to be one of the most dramatic journeys of his exile.

He was now living as "Professor Müller," a German geologist who was studying the limestone deposits of southwestern Finland. His accommodation, not far from the railway station at Åggleby (so he could leave in a hurry if necessary), was arranged by Vladimir Smirnov (his old colleague in Helsingfors from the *Iskra* smuggling days) at the Pension Gärdobacka owned by the Winsten sisters. The two ladies had little chance to get to know their lodger, since he kept to his room on the first floor. He worked incessantly and rarely ventured out, except for meals, when he spoke a few words of German to them. His room was clean, orderly, and formidably cold, as Nadya recalled after visiting him there once. The Winsten sisters were out at work during the day but during the evenings, as they chatted and played the piano in the sitting room next door, Lenin scribbled away at his latest work, *The Agrarian Program of Social Democracy,* and paced up and down on tiptoes as he composed, to avoid disturbing his train of thought with his own footsteps. Then one day three weeks later Professor Müller was gone. The sisters knew their guest was a political émigré, but it was not until they saw his photograph in the newspaper in the autumn of 1917 that they learned Lenin's true identity.

Lenin originally planned to take the train from Åggleby to Åbo (now Turku, the former capital of Finland) and from there to board a steamship to Sweden by the usual route across the Baltic Sea; the sea lanes were kept open by icebreakers during the winter. In Helsingfors Smirnov operated the underground railroad for Russian politicals in collaboration with

Finnish activists at various staging posts. The key one was Åbo, which was run by local businessman and lawyer Walter Borg, assisted by Santeri Nuorteva—editor of the local party newspaper *Socialist*—and a teacher, Ludwig Lindström. Borg represented several foreign firms in Åbo and had valuable connections with the captains and crews of the steamships that plied the sea route to Sweden.

At the beginning of December Smirnov had contacted the Åbo cell with news that a very important party worker would soon need their help in getting out of Finland. They weren't given his name but they guessed that it was Lenin. A coded message finally came announcing the time Lenin's train would arrive at Åbo; meanwhile, Borg arranged him a berth on the *Bore I,* one of two ships belonging to the Bore Steamship Company that regularly plied the Finland-Sweden route. That night, Walter Borg's two young sons, who were also active in the underground, were sent off to the station to look for a man in a heavy coat with an astrakhan collar and hat clutching a copy of the *Hufvudstadsbladet.* They were to bring "Dr. Müller" to Borg's apartment, where he and others gathered to wait for their famous guest. The frost was very severe that night; the ship was due to sail at 11:00 pm and could only leave port through a very narrow channel, closely following an icebreaker. But the Borg brothers returned at ten o'clock with word that there was no one on the train. Perhaps they had failed to recognize Lenin, thought Borg, who telephoned to check with an anxious Smirnov in Helsingfors that Lenin had indeed left. The brothers were sent back to take another look around the station. Borg, knowing that Lenin had been given his address, hoped he would find his way to his apartment if he had indeed missed the others and set a candle in the window as a sign. Meanwhile, he went down to the quayside to ask the captain of the *Bore I* to delay sailing.

The waiting dragged on into the freezing night as Borg watched the clock tick toward midnight—the latest the captain was prepared to wait. If the passenger missed the boat at Åbo, the captain advised getting across by sledge to Dragsfjärd, where he might pick up the boat when it stopped to take on supplies and coal. But still Lenin did not arrive. By 2:00 A.M. the logical conclusion was the gendarmes had picked him up en route. And then came a soft thud at the window. Down below, standing in the soft white glow of the snow, stood a lonely figure clutching a small suitcase.

Lenin, afraid of knocking on the front door at this time of night, had thrown a snowball at Borg's window to attract his attention.

He had barely escaped falling into the hands of the Okhrana. Leaving Helsingfors by train, he soon spotted two agents tailing him. When he got off the train at Karis to have some supper in the station buffet, the men followed and watched him closely. He had to get away from them or they would arrest him the minute he got off the train at Åbo, the end of the line. So, as the train gathered speed out of the tiny station at Littois (Littoinen), the last before Åbo, he slipped out onto the running board, threw his suitcase ahead of him, and leaped from the train. Luckily a deep snowdrift broke his fall. The two agents decided it was not worth risking their necks to follow, and as he watched the train's red taillights disappear into the night, Lenin heaved a sigh of relief. He picked himself up and trudged off in the crackling frost the seven miles of country road into Åbo, his only point of reference amid the dark looming pine forest.

At Borg's apartment, seeing that Lenin was frozen, hungry, and exhausted, the Finns took off his coat and boots. As he lay on the divan, Borg's wife Ida fed him hot milk with cognac and rubbed spirit on his hands and feet to get the circulation going. Lenin was extremely agitated at the thought of being captured, and as soon as he heard there was still a chance of catching the *Bore I*, he demanded a sledge so that he could leave immediately. Ludwig Lindström, who was to be his guide, told him that it would be very hard finding the way in the snow and the dark and they would have to wait until morning. Lenin was hysterical that the spooks would catch up with him before then. "I've already been in Siberia and I don't want to end up there again!" he exclaimed. If Lindström wasn't prepared to take him, he would set off on foot alone and head north for the Gulf of Bothnia. He'd walk all the way to the northern border with Sweden at Torneo if he had to: "I've walked further distances in Siberia." His only option now was to try to pick up the *Bore* at Dragsfjärd or, failing that, to continue west across the southwest archipelago— a chain of thousands of tree-covered skerries and small islands that stretch out beyond Åbo into the Baltic Sea—and pick up the boat at a more isolated spot. There was no going back to Åbo; the police would be watching the port very closely.

So at 4:00 A.M. that morning Lenin left by sledge with Lindström as his driver. But after crossing the frozen Kustosund to the island of Kirjala, the horse stumbled on the icy road and could go no farther. The one place to find another horse at that hour was the local policeman on Pargas (now Parainen). But beyond Kirjala there were no more bridges across the skerries. On the shore they had to ring a bell summoning someone from the other side to come and lead them across the ice. Two men arrived—Karl and Wilhelm, the sons of a local man, Gustav Fredriksson, who had a farm at Norrgården. The young men helped smuggle revolutionaries out of Finland and would guide Lenin over the ice to the island of Pargas. But when they inspected the ice, they found it was not strong enough; a thaw and a heavy rain a few days earlier had weakened it. Lenin wouldn't make it to Dragsfjärd now. He could do nothing but remain at the Fredriksson house. "Don't worry, you can sleep easy," Gustav reassured him. "No one will take you from here by force." And with that he opened a large cupboard full of rifles and revolvers. Food and hot grog were offered, but Lenin refused the alcohol.

The following day, after an uncomfortable night in a tiny truckle bed, Lenin woke late to a beautiful morning of flurrying snow crystals. But he was anxious to be on the move and was in no mood to admire the scenery. Gustav Fredriksson could see that Lenin was exhausted and needed to rest. He tried to convince his guest that he would be safe there until the next snowfall, when they could head off on skis. Reluctantly, Lenin agreed to hang on at the Fredriksson house for a couple more days. But he was incapable of letting go; the major topic of conversation around the stove with Lindström, even in a winter-bound farmhouse in the wilds of Finland, was politics and more politics.

On the third day, as dusk fell, Lenin and Lindström left Norrgården for Pargas, where they headed off to the cooperative store to meet up with local activist Carl Jeansen. Pargas, a small huddle of clapboard houses not far from the water's edge, for all its remoteness was a hotbed of Finnish resistance and home to a Russian bomb-making school whose instructor went by the code name "Dingo." By the time he arrived, the network at Helsingfors and Åbo had become anxious about Lenin's whereabouts and a series of phone calls had been made to and from

Pargas. As the three men sat there chatting, the local policeman, Walter Rohde, walked in. Since he also ran the village phone exchange, he was curious to know why so many calls had been flying back and forth between Pargas, Helsingfors, and Åbo. Lindström could do only one thing—openly enlist the policeman's sympathy and help in getting his "very important" companion to the next island, Lillmälö. The policeman seemed only too happy to help. He invited Lindstrom and Lenin back to his house just down the lane from the store for tea and hot grog. It was nearly Christmas, after all, and he had stocked up on confiscated alcohol (prohibition being in effect in Finland at that time). But Lenin once again refused to take a drink.

Much against Lenin's anxious protestations about the risk (due to Rohde's inebriated state), Rohde said he would drive them in his own horse and sledge to the crossing point to Lillmälö. That would provide the best possible cover. As the two men walked back to the store to wait for their transport, Lenin suddenly stopped and grasped Lindström by the arm. Now he understood, he said, why the Finns would never be cowed by czarism. Here was a nation where even the police fought against oppression. They would never surrender.

At Pargas, Lindström said good-bye as Lenin, Jeansen, and Rohde continued on to Lenin's next refuge. A pleasant-looking two-story wood farmhouse at Västergården on the island of Lillmälö, it overlooked the vast, frozen expanse of the Örfjärden sound—the final stage in Lenin's escape route across the ice. The owner was a local farmer, Gideon Söderholm. But the next day brought bad news: a strong wind and fierce currents had broken up the ice and it was impossible to cross. Lenin was beside himself. He thought he had reached the end of the road, in more ways than one. Here he was, a prisoner of the weather. All he could do was sit in the company of Söderholm and a relative, Svante Bergman, with whom he could not communicate, and wait for the gendarmes to catch up with him. His hosts were kind enough, but it was Christmas and the two men were getting drunker by the day, laughing and joking in Swedish, and they kept slapping him disconcertingly on the shoulder. Lenin's stress levels about the journey he was to make across the ice rose every time the glasses were refilled. Quite apart from fears for his own safety, he was terrified that too much drink would lead to careless talk and his betrayal. And worse, he couldn't understand a word of what his hosts were saying.

Early on Christmas Day 1907 Söderholm and Bergman went down to the sound to check the strength of the ice with poles and agreed that it was safe for Lenin to make the two-mile journey across to Prostvik on the island of Nagu (Nauvo). Prostvik was the final staging post on the Finnish underground network for smuggling arms, illegal literature, and people out of the country. As he prepared to cross the ice with Söderholm and their guide Gustav Wallstens, a local seaman from Kimito (Kemiö), Lenin said good-bye at the water's edge to Svante and his fourteen-year-old brother Gunnar Bergman. One of them broke off a pine branch and gave it to Lenin to use as a walking stick. For many years afterward, local rumor had it that before stepping out onto the ice, Lenin made the sign of the cross and muttered a prayer. The crossing in the faint light of early morning with a piercing wind cutting into them across the open sound was terrifying. Wallstens, who knew a little English, constantly warned Lenin of the dangers, but at one point the men felt the ice beginning to move away from beneath their feet and they only just managed to extricate themselves in time. Lenin later confided to Nadya that he truly thought his time had come. "Oh, what a silly way to have to die," he had thought, as Wallstens had helped him to struggle to safety.

At Prostvik Lenin was met by Johan Sjöholm, a tailor from Åbo and another local activist in the chain. He owned a summer cottage on the island and knew the terrain like the back of his hand. From here, after being warmed with a hearty bowl of *joulupuuro*—Finnish Christmas rice porridge—Lenin was taken by Sjöholm (either on skis or by sledge) to the remote skerry of Själö, where the steamship from Åbo would pick him up on its way to Stockholm. Late in the afternoon of December 25, 1907, Lenin boarded the *Stella* steamship of the Bore Company for Sweden. It had taken him the best part of six days to make his way the tortuous twenty miles to Nagu from Åbo. His luck stayed with him when he disembarked at Stockholm the next morning. The suspicions of the gendarmes were not aroused by the ordinary little man with the astrakhan collar and hat. He produced a German passport, this time in the name "Wilhelm Frei."

While Lenin was making his way out of Finland, Nadya saw her mother safely back from Villa Wasa to St. Petersburg. Elizaveta Vasil'evna was ailing and did not want a return to a life in transit. Eventually Nadya persuaded her to come and live with them in Geneva, but for now she set off for Stockholm to join Lenin at the Malmsten Hotel. On January 3, 1908, the couple took the train to Trelleborg on the south coast of Sweden, where they picked up the steamer for Sassnitz on the Baltic coast. From here they got on the train again, breaking the rail journey to Geneva in Berlin to pay a call on socialist leader Rosa Luxembourg.

Lenin's time in Russia and its neighboring Finnish duchy had lasted barely a year, with numerous interruptions. His second emigration, which was about to commence, would last nine years, during which he would come to rely heavily on the protection of others.

THE RETURN TO GENEVA was as bleak and cold as the weather. To make matters worse, Lenin and Nadya arrived there on January 7 suffering from a serious bout of food poisoning, which they had picked up from fish in a restaurant in Berlin. Their hotel chambermaid had to call a doctor, and with Nadya then traveling on a false American passport, had asked for an American physician, who overcharged them when he realized that the two were clearly not who they claimed to be.

Lenin was severely depressed about returning to Switzerland: "I feel just as if I'd come here to be buried," he told Nadya in despair. For the first few weeks they rented a cheap room in the house of Madame Kupfer at 17 rue des Deux Ponts. But it was cold and cheerless and they hated sitting there in the evenings after a long day in the library. So they spent what little money they had going to the cinema or the theater, or simply walking around the lake in the dark. Then at the end of April they moved to a larger apartment at 61 rue de Maraîchers, where they were joined by Elizaveta Vasil'evna. Lenin's sister Mariya also arrived, having come to Geneva to continue her studies, and rented an apartment above them in the same block.

Ironically there were more Russians in Geneva than ever before. Though the events of 1905–1906 had sent political refugees flocking back to Switzerland, few of Lenin and Nadya's old circle returned. As the year progressed, a new Geneva Bolshevik circle was established around Lenin, its mainstays being Grigory Zinoviev and his wife Zina, followed soon after by Lev Kamenev and his family. But in general, the streets of Geneva seemed friendless to Lenin and Nadya, and they had no desire to mix with the émigré community. Lenin realized now, even more acutely than before, that émigré politics were a far remove from real activism in Russia: "There is no *live* work or an environment for live work to speak of," he wrote to a colleague. He and Nadya, he complained, now waited more for letters than they received them. To militate against his frustration he slipped back into his old, carefully ordered routine. Theory once more supplanted live politics, as he spent his days writing and studying at the Société de Lecture, which he rejoined in February. Deciding they were in for the long haul and with more time on her hands now that party work was evaporating in Russia, Nadya set about learning French and enrolled in a course at Geneva University. Volodya, she recalled, would calm his overwrought nerves in the evenings by lying in bed and reading her French grammar primers for relaxation.

Occasionally he cycled off to visit Elizaveta de K, who was now also an émigré in Geneva, taking with him a piece of rubber from some old galoshes that he had carried about him since St. Petersburg days, in order to deal with a puncture. They would sit by the lake together and read; he tried to teach her chess but gave up in disgust. By now he had clearly given up trying to indoctrinate the independently minded Elizaveta into his authoritarian way of Marxist thinking: "I have yet to meet a single woman who can do these three things," he complained. "Understand Marx, play chess or make out a railroad timetable." Elizaveta was content to be in his company and let him read, not asking any questions or ever mentioning Nadya as he covered the margins with scribbled notes. But odd moments of relaxation such as this were rare, and Lenin's romantic friendship with Elizaveta petered out once he left Geneva for Paris at the end of the year.

The return to "this damned Geneva" stretched Lenin's resilience to the extreme. The city was "an awful hole," and being stuck there seemed even worse as bad news arrived of the arrest and imprisonment of party workers back in Russia. Political work there had become a "spy infested shambles." As professional revolutionaries were arrested, double agents and spies found it easier to infiltrate surviving cadres. The arrests had spread to Europe as well. In Berlin, Munich, Paris, Copenhagen, Stockholm, and even Geneva key activists involved in laundering the proceeds of the Tiflis bank robbery had been arrested by local police acting on tips from the Okhrana as they tried to pass 500-ruble banknotes. The Russian government was demanding their extradition. All of this bad news compounded the pervasive air of defeatism in the party. The intelligentsia was deserting in droves, and the masses, as Nadya observed, "withdrew into their shell" to take stock of the situation, weary of strikes and insurrection. Party membership plummeted. In Moscow it was down to five hundred members in 1908 and dwindled to a third of that by the end of 1909, as Stolypin's government continued its policy of retrenchment and a third Duma, its voting system rigged to shift the political makeup of delegates, moved further to the right.

Lenin was increasingly worried by how "depression, demoralization, splits, discord, defection and pornography" were taking the place of politics in both Russia and the diaspora. The whole impetus of the revolutionary movement seemed to be going into reverse; the time for revolution in Russia had come and gone. Stolypin, by abolishing the peasant commune and giving land to individual peasants, was steering them toward the bourgeois middle ground. The peasantry—the honest shock troops in Lenin's revolutionary scenario—was being corrupted by the lure of mammon and needed to be saved from itself. His only recourse lay in a return to propaganda—dissemination of a strong party organ to fight against further party disintegration. And so he threw himself back into the editing and production of *Proletarii* at its offices in the old émigré heartland of rue de Carouge. A new print shop had to be established, stretching precious funds. The plan now was to smuggle the newspaper into Russia, with help from Gorky and Andreeva on Capri, via Italian steamships crossing to ports such as Odessa. But the copies reached Russia initially in a pitiful trickle: thirteen copies of the first issue made their way through, and only sixty-two of the second, third, and fourth.

In the cold light of retreat, theoretical differences and the fight against political heresy within the party once more loomed large. Reaction to events in Russia could be seen in the worrying drift away from Lenin's brand of hard-nosed Marxist materialism to the vaguer, and to some increasingly more consoling, disciplines of philosophy, religion, and metaphysics. Revisionism was in the air, and one of its high-profile exponents was Lenin's colleague Aleksandr Bogdanov, with whom he worked on *Proletarii*. Bogdanov and his colleagues had objected to Lenin's support for Bolshevik participation in the Duma elections, even as an outlet for propaganda. They wanted the Bolshevik deputies recalled and the whole tokenistic farce of Duma politics to be denounced, earning themselves the nickname of "recallists" (*otzovists* in Russian). Lenin, however, was loath to let go of what little political influence the Duma allowed him.

Reading the kind of "drivel" written by Bogdanov and others made Lenin swear "like a fishwife," as he admitted to Maxim Gorky. Things came to a head when, without consulting Lenin, Bogdanov, Anatoly Lunacharsky, and others published *Essays on the Philosophy of Marxism* promoting their own heretical views, which contradicted Lenin's. It was like a red cape to a bull. Lenin abhorred all forms of "political decadence" and was incensed by what he saw as an attempt to fuse politics with philosophy and other such dubious nonsense. Back in 1904 he had seen off promising acolyte Nikolay Valentinov for expressing similar interests and now he savagely rounded on Bogdanov, demonstrating his poor understanding and lack of respect for the very real moral issues at the heart of socialist thinking that so preoccupied his opponents. As far as he was concerned, all this drivel by "empirio-critics, empirio-monists and empiro-symbolists" who were "floundering in a bog" attempting to replace scientific knowledge with philosophy and religion was "ridiculous, harmful and philistine." Lenin locked himself away for hours in the library researching and writing his riposte to a new religion of the masses that had been given the name "god building" (*bogostroitel'stvo*). Its major proponents—Bogdanov, Lunacharsky, and Gorky—were now attempting to give a moral and religious dimension to Marxism by elevating the masses to divine status and substituting faith and philosophy for scientific Marxist knowledge. But he had to tread carefully. He liked and respected Gorky and needed to maintain good relations with him as a valuable supporter of the Bolshevik faction and a key figure in raising much needed money for the party; he also wanted him to contribute articles to *Proletarii*. In mid-January Lenin had received an invitation from the writer to visit him and Mariya Andreeva on Capri. Lenin admitted to Gorky that the idea of "dropping in" on them was "delightfully tempting, dash it!" In preparation, he started teaching himself Italian, reprimanding Mariya Andreeva like a naughty schoolgirl for spelling *espresso* incorrectly as *expresso* in a letter to him.

Gorky had invited Lenin to visit him on Capri the previous summer after the fifth party congress, but Lenin had been too busy. He had every intention of taking Nadya with him but in the event, perhaps for financial reasons, she stayed behind in Geneva. The invitation, for all that the two men had established a warm friendship, was a poorly disguised attempt by Gorky to effect reconciliation between Lenin, Bogdanov, and Lunacharsky—now staying with him on Capri—before the rumbling theoretical disagreement between them escalated any further. He had seen enough of fierce political wrangling at the congress to know its potential destructiveness to the party. Lenin, however, left for Capri with no such thoughts in mind, having forewarned Gorky that he would have nothing to do with "people who have set out to propagate unity between scientific socialism and religion."

After taking the train from Geneva across to Milan, he headed south through Italy by rail via Parma and Florence. Having been engrossed by books on the Roman Empire as a child, he stopped off in Rome to look at the Forum and Capitoline Hill and take a walk up the majestic Via Nazionale, before boarding the overnight express to Naples. Gorky and Mariya Andreeva met him off the train and together they crossed the azure waters of the Mediterranean by steamship to the south side of Capri, from there taking the funicular up the steep hillside to Gorky's villa. Lenin could not have wished to be more comfortably accommodated than at the Villa Blaesus o Settanni. Capri, with its fine dry climate and its aromatic mix of myrtle, vines, orange groves, and pine woods, was renowned for its curative powers and had been the refuge of many tuberculosis sufferers like Gorky with the means to settle there. In the 1890s it had become a fashionable watering hole for tourists from Britain, America, Germany, and Scandinavia, as well as affluent Russians such as the opera singer Chaliapin and the novelist Ivan Bunin. Its isolated location also attracted a more bohemian element and homosexual tourists.

The Villa Blaesus had been built in 1900 on the south side of the island by an old Caprese family, the Settannis. It perched high on a cliff dropping away to the sheltered cove of the Marina Piccola below and overlooked the stupendous Gardens of Augustus, on the grounds of which nestled Capri's finest hotel and spa, the Quisisana. The house had five bedrooms and Lenin was delighted not only to discover that Gorky had an excellent library, but also to be given the room next to his study, with a magnificent view over the sea. But Villa Blaesus had become a magnet to every Russian exile on Capri, and Lenin's stay was punctuated by endless comings and goings. Gorky's rising celebrity in the international literary world (his acclaimed novel *Mother* had been published the previous year), coupled with his legendary generosity, meant that he now attracted a constant stream of Russian friends and visitors—some of them rich émigrés but the majority impoverished exiles and hangers-on, whom he entertained and accommodated at his own expense. He often paid off their debts to the local hotels and taverns. The solitary police officer on the island, Cavaliere Tiseo, who had been tasked with supervising the itinerant Russians, paid little attention, so long as they didn't cause any trouble.

During Lenin's stay he played the occasional game of chess with Bogdanov on the veranda overlooking the sea (but, predictably, was a bad loser when Bogdanov beat him), or went for a walk with Gorky over the volcanic cliff paths thick with spiky, golden broom to view the ruins of Tiberius's Villa Jovis. There were impromptu musical performances with songs sung by the servants in the local Neapolitan dialect as well as the old Russian favorites. While he appreciated the beauty of the location, the translucency of the sea, and the good local wine, in general Lenin found the scenery rather too "theatrical." It seemed unreal somehow and prompted nostalgia for the open expanses of his much-loved River Volga back home.

Theoretical clashes with Bogdanov and Lunacharsky were inevitable and often went on late into the night. Lenin later joked to Gorky that it was only with his arrival that things "got out of hand." Before that everyone had gone to bed at the right time. Gorky was dismayed by what he saw: Lenin seemed "even more firm and more inflexible" than at the London congress the previous spring. Gorky disliked the cold, contemptuous manner in which his friend took constant swipes at Bogdanov, a man who, in Gorky's estimation, was "an extremely attractive person, of a very mild character" undeserving of such verbal savagery.

Away from polemics and politics, Lenin revealed another side when he relaxed among the local Caprese fishermen. He was lighthearted, with an engaging laugh, and sometimes showed a "lively, inexhaustible interest in everything in the world." He could also be "strikingly gentle." Gorky sensed Lenin's peculiar magnetism that drew ordinary people to him. For Lenin the Caprese were the "simple in heart" and he wanted to know all about them: what they earned, their schools, their attitude toward the Catholic clergy—and they in turn warmed to the almost childlike interest he took in them. His happiest time on Capri was spent with fisherman Giovanni Spadaro and his brother Francesco, Mariya Andreeva joining them as interpreter. The two men taught him to fish without a rod, using only the line and his finger to sense for the vibration when a fish took the bait. "Cosi, drin-drin," they gesticulated. "Capisce?" (Like this, drin-drin. Understand?) When Lenin landed his first mullet by this method, he delightedly repeated the phrase "drin-drin." It stuck, and for the rest of his time on Capri the Italian locals referred to him as "Signor Drin Drin."

Lenin's visit lasted about six days. When he left, Gorky accompanied him across to Naples, and they booked into a pension so that Gorky could take him on a whistle-stop tour of the local sights: a climb up Vesuvius (the robust Lenin had plenty of energy but worried about Gorky's stamina), a visit to the ruins of Pompeii, and a tour of the National Museum. When Lenin headed back to Geneva, Gorky was disconsolate. The local fishermen never forgot him or his jovial laughter. "Only a good man could laugh like that," remarked old Giovanni Spadaro. For years he would ask after Signor Drin Drin and how he was getting on. "The Tsar hasn't caught him yet?" he would remark with a grin.

⸙

FROM CAPRI, after a brief return to Geneva and lectures in Brussels and Paris on the 1905 Revolution, Lenin, now fired up for his confrontation with Bogdanov and the "god builders," headed for London on May 16. He was intent on gathering essential source material at the British Museum on physics, economics, and philosophy that was not available in the libraries in Geneva. During this, his fourth visit, he stayed in a cheap room at 21 Tavistock Place in his old Kings Cross stomping ground, a short walk from the reading room of the British Museum. He knew the library's matchless facilities would not let him down. "It's a wonderful institution," he declared; it was the best library in the world to work in. Paris, Berlin, Vienna, even Geneva did not equal it. He felt comfortable working there and liked having his own separate seat rather than working at the same long table with others, as in other libraries. He particularly commended the library's help desk, which always answered inquiries promptly, and the speedy response to book requests. The British Museum boasted a rich Russian section—with rare Russian-published books, now banned back home. Yes, the English bourgeoisie doesn't begrudge spending money on books, he conceded.

Lenin's time in London in 1908 appears to have been particularly solitary. Sometimes, after a day in the library, he went to the Anarchists Club in the East End for cheap gefilte fish, chopped liver, and herring. Volunteer Millie Sabel remembered him sitting alone in the corner, "a small, intense man" drinking Russian tea. Readers at the British Museum also noticed him; they were fascinated by the highly focused Russian who sat at his desk day in and day out with his nose in a pile of books. The poet John Masefield often saw Lenin there and wondered who that "extraordinary man" was. He seemed like someone "certain to make a mark in the world," Masefield later wrote, although he did not know the man's identity at the time. Lenin was unfailingly polite to the staff as well as fellow readers. Many years later, when Lenin had come to power, one of the old library curators recalled "Mr. Ulianov" to reader Miles Malleson as a "very nicely-spoken gentleman." "Can you tell me, sir, what became of him?" he inquired.

After a month's hard study, Lenin left London on June 10, having powered his way through some two hundred books and articles in French, German, and English. He returned to Nadya supremely confident that he had sorted out all the "inexpressible vulgarities" of Bogdanov and his group; a split with them was now inevitable. But so much work accomplished in such a short period had, as usual, eroded his health. Despite suffering from bouts of "abdominal catarrh" he continued to push himself hard, turning out articles and working on a book to counter Bogdanov's arguments, entitled *Materialism and Empirio-criticism*, before taking a few days' break alone in July in the mountains near Diablerets in the western part of the Bernese Alps. At the end of November with much trepidation he sent off his precious manuscript to his sister Anna in Moscow so that she could place it with a publisher. But even Anna, for all her loyalty to her brother, was alarmed by the book's vitriolic tone. She wrote to Lenin advising him to reduce the hyperbole, vulgar expressions, and abuse or at least tone the language down a little. Lenin agreed to a few changes but resolutely refused to allow Anna to modify any of the personal elements of his attack on Bogdanov.

Back in Geneva the political situation had changed. The Swiss police had been coming under increasing pressure from the Russian authorities to tighten up on the activities of political exiles, making it difficult for Russian émigrés to obtain residence permits. Landlords were becoming reluctant to rent to the volatile and unpredictable Russians, and signs began to appear in windows: "We rent only to people who have no dogs, no cats and no Russians."

Lurid stories about the bank robberies and expropriations by Georgian revolutionaries in the Caucasus had filtered through to the Geneva papers. One day when a Caucasian colleague, Mikhail Tskhakaya, knocked at Lenin's door in full Georgian costume looking "the picture of a brigand," his landlady had screamed and slammed the door in his face. The Mensheviks in Switzerland were using the bad press over expropriations to discredit the Bolsheviks further, calling for the end of underground work in Russia and a focus on legal party work via the trade unions. Even the rather restrained Swiss social democrats were discomfited by the presence of the Russians in their midst.

Lenin was coming under intense pressure from Bogdanov and his colleagues on *Proletarii*, who were tired of the constraints of bourgeois Geneva, to move the editorial office to Paris, where many Swiss-based Mensheviks and Socialist Revolutionaries were already decamping. He hesitated over the expense of living in Paris and losing the research facilities of the Société de Lecture. But activists Martyn Lyadov and Yakov Zhitomirsky arrived from Paris and persuaded him to transfer there, arguing that the operation would be less likely to be spied on in a bigger city. Paris was clearly becoming the new center of Russian activism abroad. Unfortunately, it was also home to the Okhrana headquarters, and Zhitomirsky, unknown to Lenin, was one of its key double agents.

On December 14, 1908, Lenin left Geneva with Nadya and her mother, having sent their possessions on ahead to Paris by slow train. He attempted to put a robust face on things: "We hope that a big city will put some life into us all; we are tired of staying in this provincial backwater." After a few days at the Hôtel des Gobelins on the boulevard Saint-Marcel they rented a four-room flat on rue Beaunier in the 14th arrondissement near the English-style Parc Montsouris, a favorite haunt of émigrés. Lenin's close colleagues Kamenev and Zinoviev both lived nearby and frequented the park with their wives and children. Lunacharsky pushed his son around the park in his pram, its innocent blankets covering a stash of illegal literature. Rue Beaunier was, for impoverished socialists such as the Ulyanovs, inappropriately elegant—and expensive at 840 francs a year, plus 60 francs tax, plus another 60 for the services of the concierge. The light, airy rooms had mirrors on the walls and marble fireplaces, and the few pathetic sticks of furniture that Nadya and Lenin had brought from Geneva looked decidedly out of place. What little they had was, nevertheless, arranged with the same obsessive neatness that Lenin demanded wherever he and Nadya lived, unlike the untidy apartments of other Russian émigrés. But their French concierge made no attempt to disguise her contempt for the cheap white table and "common chairs and stools" that her tenants brought with them. And the apartment was cold—very cold; it took three weeks of endless bureaucratic effort by Nadya to get the gas connected. Despite their hopes for a better life in Paris, Lenin and Nadya were now embarking on what she would later describe as their "most trying years of exile."

The Ulyanov family in 1879. Back row from left: Olga, Aleksandr and Anna; seated Mariya Aleksandrovna with Mariya on her knee, Ilyan Nikolaevich Ulyanov; front Dmitri, left, and on the right, Vladimir, aged nine.

Lenin's elder brother, Aleksandr, hanged in 1887 for his involvement in an assassination plot against Tsar Alexander III.

Lenin in 1897, aged 27, at the time of his exile to Shushenskoe, already bald and before he adopted the shorter, neater beard.

Holford Square, London. Lenin and Nadya lodged happily with the Yeo family at no. 30 during 1902–1903. The house was destroyed by bombing during World War II. *(Photo by Hans Wild/Time & Life Pictures/Getty Images)*

Nadya in 1903.

Nadya and her mother Elizaveta Vasil'evna in 1898, around the time they joined Lenin at Shushenskoe.

Inessa Armand, the French-born activist who wore herself out in service to Lenin, the Party, and the Revolution, dying in 1920 aged forty-six.

Inessa with her daughter Inna, born 1898; after Inessa's death in 1920, Nadya developed a particularly close relationship with Inna. *(RIA Novosti)*

Feodosiya Drabkina, the fearless bomb carrier from the St. Petersburg Fighting Technical Group, who carried weapons hidden under her coat. *(Courtesy of The Lenin Museum, Tampere)*

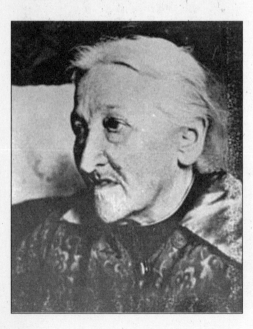

Vera Zasulich shortly before her death in 1919. An iconic figure in the Russian revolutionary movement and collaborator with Lenin on *Iskra*, she was bitterly disillusioned with Lenin's Bolshevik takeover. *(Central State Archive of Documentary Films, Photographs, and Sound Recordings of St. Petersburg)*

The Café Landolt, Geneva, a favorite haunt of the Bolshevik and Menshevik émigré Russian factions during the 1900s and the scene of many heated political arguments.

The Villa Wasa, deep in the Finnish countryside at Kuokkala. Lenin and his Bolshevik entourage used this wooden dacha as a safe house during 1905–1907. It has since been demolished. *(Courtesy of The Lenin Museum, Tampere)*

(Top) Lenin's police mug shot
from his first arrest in 1895.

(Center) Leo Trotsky's police mug shot
of 1900 at the age of 20; in 1902 he
escaped from Siberian exile and joined
Lenin in London but rapidly became
disenchanted with his extremist views.

(Left) Georgy Plekhanov, the "father"
of Russian Marxism whom Lenin initially
revered but with whom he later bitterly
quarrelled. *(RIA Novosti)*

Karl Radek, the rising star of the Bolshevik Left at the Zimmerwald Conference of 1915 and a member of Lenin's party on the sealed train in April 1917. *(Getty Images)*

Roman Malinovsky: A trusted member of Lenin's inner sanctum, he turned out to be an Okhrana double agent and was shot on his return to Russia in 1918.

Maksim Litvinov, code-named Papasha, the wily gun runner; in 1917 he became the Soviet Union's first diplomatic representative in Britain.

Yuli Martov, Lenin's closest colleague during his early revolutionary days. Alienated
from him after the 2nd Congress in 1903,
Martov led the Menshevik faction during
the years in exile.

Grigory Zinoviev, a key figure in Lenin's Bolshevik
faction and a loyal yes-man. He later became a
victim of the Stalinist purges and was shot in
August 1936.

Nikolay Burenin, a key figure in the St. Petersburg
underground involved in the dissemination of illegal literature and bomb-making. *(Courtesy of The
Lenin Museum, Tampere)*

Detective Herbert Fitch of London's Special Branch who doggedly tailed Lenin in London during the 1905 and 1907 RSDLP congresses.

The Crown & Woolpack pub on St. John Street, Islington, where Lenin often held political meetings when in London. Detective Fitch hid in a cupboard in order to eavesdrop at a meeting here in 1905.

Lenin's application, in the name of Jacob Richter, for a reader's pass to the British Museum Reading Room, April 29, 1902. *(© The Trustees of the British Museum)*

Lenin yawns during a game of chess with Aleksandr Bogdanov at the Villa Blaesus on Capri in 1908. An amused Maxim Gorky is seated between them.

Giovanni Spadaro, the old boatman who took Lenin out sea fishing on Capri during his visits in 1908 and 1910.

Joseph Fels, the American-born soap magnate who came to the financial rescue of the 1907 RSDLP congress with a loan of £1,700. The Soviet Government finally repaid the loan in 1922.

The Brotherhood Church, Southgate Road, Islington. Home to a fringe Christian Socialist Group, it was the venue for the RSDLP's 1907 Congress. The church became a centre of pacifist protest during World War I and was demolished in the 1930s. *(Courtesy of The Lenin Museum, Tampere)*

Gaston Montéhus, star of the Parisian *caféchantants*, whose socialist songs such as "Gloire au 17ème" were great favorites with Lenin.

Giovanni Spadaro, the old boatman who took Lenin out sea fishing on Capri during his visits in 1908 and 1910.

Joseph Fels, the American-born soap magnate who came to the financial rescue of the 1907 RSDLP congress with a loan of £1,700. The Soviet Government finally repaid the loan in 1922.

The Brotherhood Church, Southgate Road, Islington. Home to a fringe Christian Socialist Group, it was the venue for the RSDLP's 1907 Congress. The church became a centre of pacifist protest during World War I and was demolished in the 1930s. *(Courtesy of The Lenin Museum, Tampere)*

Gaston Montéhus, star of the Parisian *caféchantants*, whose socialist songs such as "Gloire au 17ème" were great favorites with Lenin.

Lenin out hiking in the Tatra Mountains of southern Poland c.1913–1914. *(RIA Novosti)*

The Sukiennice, Krakow's Old Cloth Market. Nadya like to shop in the open market in the square outside, whilst Lenin often had political meetings in the Noworolski Café in the arcade.

Mendel Singer (seated right) the Jewish shopkeeper of Poronin, who lent Lenin the money to get out of Galicia in 1914. Only three sons of the family, including Alojsy (second left back), who had sat on Lenin's knee as a child, survived the Holocaust. *(Courtesy of Stephanie Weiner)*

Titus Kammerer, the shoemaker, outside his shop at no. 12 Speigelgasse, Zurich. Lenin and Nadya lodged with Kammerer and his family at no. 14 next door.

A rather solemn Nadya, still plagued by her thyroid problem, photographed in Switzerland about 1915–1916.

Poronin railway station in Galicia, in southern Poland, where Lenin walked twice daily to pick up his mail.

One of the few photographs taken of Lenin in exile—this one in Poronin in 1914 before his departure for Switzerland.

Lenin deep in conversation with Swedish socialist Ture Nerman, Nadya (behind in large hat) and other members of the Sealed Train in Stockholm en route back to Petrograd, April 13, 1917. *(Courtesy of The Lenin Museum, Tampere)*

A discarded bronze bust of Lenin. Once so dominant throughout the countries of the Eastern bloc, his image has now been consigned, along with other communist statuary, to the dustbin of history. *(Courtesy of Hayley Millar/http://coffee-helps.com)*

CHAPTER TWELVE

"Why the Hell Did We Go to Paris?"

PARIS: JANUARY 1909–DECEMBER 1910

<hr />

T HE START OF A NEW YEAR in Paris marked a bleak and lonely time for Lenin and Nadya. The Russian émigré community lacked the unity and dynamism that had prevailed in Switzerland. Over time, life in Geneva had become stultifying, but even though Paris had seen revolutions in 1789 and 1848 and the Commune of 1871, "there was none of that pulse-beat of Russian revolutionary life so clearly felt in Geneva," as activist Lidiya Fotieva observed.

London, never a political center of the party in the best of times, was now "locked in silence," with the Russian enclave there decimated and disconnected from the movement. Maxim Litvinov did his best to hold together the bare bones of a Bolshevik group in a succession of damp and cramped rooms, but the gloom and the fog and British insularity had a deadening effect on the Russian spirit.

Meanwhile, back in Russia itself, underground life was crippled by a lack of funds, personnel, and morale. Early that year, Nadya, not normally one to give way to discouragement, had written despairingly, "We have no people at all. All are scattered in prison and places of exile." Lenin too was acutely dispirited by declining morale and talent: "There are few forces in Russia. Ah, if only we could send from here a good Party worker to the CC or for convening a conference! But here everyone is a 'has-been.'" He was reduced to corresponding with a shrinking network of activists; by the beginning of 1909 the RSDLP had ceased to exist. The party *was* Lenin, and by a sheer act of will he fought to keep the uncompromising flame of Bolshevism alive, as those around him left the party, conciliated with other groups, and shifted political position.

In 1909 Paris was a vibrant city embracing the modern age, with a rapidly expanding Metro, electric lighting, steam trams, the finest fashion houses in the world, and glittering new department stores. It had also by now begun to attract a new Russian exile community—the cultural elite that had left after the 1905 revolution: poets and writers such as Zinaida Gippius, Andrey Bely, Dmitri Merezhkovsky; millionaire patrons of the arts the Shchukin brothers; the painters Aleksandr Benois and Marc Chagall; and Sergey Diaghilev, who had brought his Ballets Russes to Paris that year. The cream of Russian creative talent was heading for the French capital and taking its place at the center of bohemian circles and the literary salons.

The Mensheviks were gaining strength—Plekhanov, Dan, Martov, and others now holding court in their favorite cafés, La Rotonde and d'Harcourt. Plekhanov, despite suffering poor health (he later left for Italy), still occupied the émigré higher ground as elder statesman. The Socialist Revolutionaries had found their way to Paris too; even legendary nihilist Vera Figner, finally released from her twenty-year incarceration in Shlisselburg fortress, had arrived. But Lenin remained largely detached from the cultural life of the city, its people, and the other Russian enclaves. Nor could Nadya tolerate the bourgeois profligacy of the French. They survived well enough on Lenin's party salary (in the region of 350 Swiss francs a month, a rate fixed for the Bolshevik leaders) topped up with a trickle of royalties. There were also occasional injections of money from Lenin's mother, who was preternaturally thrifty with the family fund of annuities and helped all her children financially.

As well as watching his own money, Lenin always kept careful, discreet control of party funds, be they legal or illicit. One of the most dubious sources of income, along with the bank robberies and expropriations, had been the clever purloining of the Shmit inheritance. Nikolay Shmit, nephew of Savva Morozov, the socialist sympathizer and millionaire, had committed suicide in prison in 1907 (to which he had been condemned after supporting the Moscow uprising of 1905). Two Bolsheviks were instructed, with Lenin's connivance, to ensure that Shmit's considerable fortune, devolving to his two sisters, should come to the party, for Shmit had previously intimated as much to Maxim Gorky. In order to ensure this, the two volunteers, Nikolay Andrikanis and Viktor Taratuta, each contrived marriage to the sisters. The sisters proved easy dupes in the affair, although Andrikanis later reneged on the deal and handed over only a small amount to the party. But in Paris in 1909 a substantial amount—275,984 francs—from the second sister Elizaveta (who had married Taratuta) made its way into party funds and came under Lenin's direct control as chief controller of party finances.

After the revolution Soviet hagiographers tried to portray Lenin living in abject poverty and self-denial during his years in exile. Although they were both naturally frugal, Nadya always denied that they had ever gone without, unlike many other Russian exiles. They had endured hardship, but they had never suffered like some Russian émigrés who emerged penniless from the Gare du Nord after the long train ride from Russia to crowd into the drafty, damp garrets of the Gobelin district, three or four to a room. Many never found proper paid work, nor did they receive financial help from relatives in Russia. They eked out their lives on borscht and kasha in the cheap Russian canteen on rue Pascal, where the waiters were all former Siberian exiles, or sat aimlessly reading the papers all day in the Russian library on the avenue des Gobelins for want of anything better to do. Some of the comrades with skills managed to find employment, but French factory owners often refused to hire the Russians, fearing that they would breed discontent among the workers. It was hardest of all for the intellectuals, many of whom were reduced to washing cars, cleaning, delivering milk, moving furniture, or getting up at 2:00 AM to wash the windows of restaurants and small shops. This latter work paid one franc a night, not even enough for a basic meal in the cheapest of eating places.

In contrast Lenin and Nadya always had money to buy bread, though the only meat they ever saw apart from some ham and sausage sent by Anna in Moscow was horsemeat. Occasional food parcels also arrived from Lenin's mother containing treats such as caviar and smoked sturgeon. Eating them reminded Lenin of home and provoked nostalgic thoughts of the Volga, but he generally took little interest in food and ate what he was given.

Lenin unfailingly showed concern for the welfare of new arrivals, particularly those who were ailing, many of them suffering from tuberculosis contracted in prison or exile. One such colleague, Innokenty Dubrovinsky, had arrived in Paris with suppurating open wounds on his legs caused by the chafing of heavy chains in exile, and Lenin saw to it that he had medical attention. A hardship fund was set up jointly by the various Russian groups in Paris to help impoverished exiles, but it was woefully inadequate. Lenin often added the names of those he knew to be in the blackest of misery but were too proud to ask for help. He also raised money through paid lectures. When newcomers arrived, Nadya rooted through her store of basic necessities—lamps, cutlery, and other domestic items abandoned by colleagues who had left Paris—and handed them out.

But sometimes their best efforts came to nothing. They witnessed several distressing cases of mental breakdown. Comrade Shulyatikov was an alcoholic who suffered attacks of DTs that included visions of his sister, who had been hanged in Russia for revolutionary activities. Lenin sat up all night with him ensuring he did not harm himself. Comrade Prigara, who had fought on the barricades in Moscow in 1905, went mad from hunger and privation. Lenin tried to talk him around after a suicide attempt, but a couple of years later Prigara threw himself into the Seine.

As Lenin surveyed his shrinking Bolshevik entourage of thirty or so who came and went over the next three years in Paris, he was forced to face up to the possible demise of his own faction. At such a low point, consolidation with other political émigrés would seem the most logical option, yet aside from nursing hopes of a reunion with Plekhanov's followers, Lenin remained at war with his other detractors. His former colleagues Bogdanov and Lunacharsky—even Gorky—seemed irredeemably wedded to finding non-Marxist ways of coming to terms with the disillusion and emptiness of the failure of 1905. They might have little visible support back in Russia, but intellectually they were his peers in the Bolshevist faction. Unfortunately Lenin could not see this, adhering to his own interpretation of Marxism—as any religious fanatic might—as the one true gospel. He viewed any variations to his own dogmatic view as a threat to his vision for the party and consequently sought to alienate detractors from the movement.

The women in his life—his wife, sisters, mother, and mother-in-law—remained devoted, unshakeable constants in a life forever disrupted by seething and frequently overblown political rivalries. In Lenin's surviving letters it is only his mother, Mariya Aleksandrovna, to whom he sent expressions of love and "many kisses" in brief moments of tenderness. Her failing health was a constant worry and he was excessively solicitous about her well-being. He also showed considerable tolerance and respect toward Elizaveta Vasil'evna, for whom he often brought back gifts of fresh flowers picked on his many bicycle rides out of town. He would often sit and play cards or chess with her and even tolerated her occasional cigarette. In return Elizaveta, while constantly complaining that both he and Nadya worked too hard, tried to be helpful, cooking meals, tidying, and helping dispose of piles of old letters and papers by sitting for hours meticulously tearing them into minute pieces.

Time weighed heavily on Lenin in Paris; factional quarrels filled the empty days but made the atmosphere even heavier than it was already. He looked worn and gray and wasn't eating properly. When his sister Anna visited from Russia, she noticed how shabby his clothes were and insisted on taking him out to buy a new overcoat; he complied with the greatest reluctance. He was plagued with insomnia and headaches but nevertheless dragged himself off daily on his bicycle to Paris's preeminent repository of knowledge, the Bibliothèque Nationale. Negotiating the cabs and horse trams all the way up Paris's broad boulevards and across the Seine to the Rive Gauche was a dangerous and exhausting exercise. In order to maximize his time at the library, he left at eight every morning to arrive for opening time at nine, but he would have to cycle all the way back again when the library closed for lunch at twelve till two and it was hardly worth returning afterward, as the library closed for the day at four.

The Bibliothèque disappointed and frustrated Lenin: it was drafty, badly organized, and bureaucratic, and he found the staff unhelpful. He missed the intimacy of the Société de Lecture in Geneva and the calm efficiency of the British Museum. In Paris the books he requested took an age to arrive and he was always in an impossible hurry to see them. He frequently cursed the Bibliothèque's inefficiency to Nadya and was further frustrated when he found he could not borrow books from other libraries without a character witness from his landlord, who hesitated to cooperate, given the Ulyanovs' obvious poverty. He changed his mind when Lenin produced proof of his party bank account with the Crédit Lyonnais.

Lenin's great pride and joy at this time was his bicycle. During the cold winter months he carefully greased both his and Nadya's bicycles and stored them away in the cellar. When spring came, he brought them out in anticipation of recreational rides into the countryside, such as out to Fontainebleu, Fontenay-aux-Roses, or Nadya's favorite, the Bois de Meudon. Lenin would wheel both bikes out on to the pavement, roll up his sleeves, and take off his jacket. There, surrounded by curious children from the nearby apartment block (for whom he always had a sweet in his pocket), he would happily strip, polish, and oil every part of each bicycle and pump up the tires. He thought nothing of cycling fifty miles out of Paris to admire the view from a river bank where he could swim and walk, or go to a particular place to gather lilies of the valley. His misery was therefore profound when his finely tuned vehicle was stolen from under the staircase at an apartment block on rue Richelieu near the Bibliothèque. He paid a daily charge of ten centimes to the concierge and had expected her to keep an eye on it. In defense she claimed that Lenin was merely paying for the privilege of parking the bike there. Lenin replaced the bicycle but later gave up cycling across the city. The traffic, he said, was "infernal," but with his usual restlessness he resented the half hour tram ride in each direction to get there by other means.

When he was not at the library, Lenin spent his time writing articles for Russian political journals, including a new weekly, *Zvezda* (The Star), that he had founded in St. Petersburg to help keep the underground movement alive (in direct response to the "liquidators" in the party who wanted to abandon all illegal work). He invited a broad base of social democrats, including Plekhanov, to contribute. Dissent inevitably followed, and by the autumn of 1911 *Zvezda*'s main contributors were himself and the two men who were to be his two closest allies during the years leading up to World War I, Zinoviev and Kamenev. Lenin also contributed regularly to *Proletarii* (until it was shut down in January 1910) and its replacement émigré newspaper, *Sotsial-Demokrat*, sharing control of the editorial board of the latter with Zinoviev and two Mensheviks.

In the evenings he sometimes met up with members of his group at the Café du Lion near the famous lion statue on Place-Denfert Rochereau to play chess and read the free papers. But in general the Bolshevik group favored two cafés on the avenue d'Orléans—the Aux Manilleurs at no. 11 and the Au Puits Rouge on the corner of avenue de Chatillon opposite the Saint-Pierre de Montrouge church. Here, for the price of a beer or a coffee, Lenin and his friends would sit and talk in an upstairs room. Some of them had taken to drinking sticky red grenadine and soda water, which was cheaper than alcohol. But not Lenin, who stuck to beer. Tempers sometimes ran high and meetings, particularly when gate-crashed by Mensheviks, sometimes degenerated into fisticuffs. Such conflicts served to depress the usually combative Lenin. On one such occasion he spent hours walking the streets of Paris in the dark, returning to Nadya pale and exhausted with stress. He was approaching forty, his political career was at its nadir, and the battles were never-ending.

In May 1909, after weeks of obsessive worrying over proofs and possible distortions of his meaning caused by misprints, Lenin finally published his riposte to Bogdanov, *Materialism and Empirio-criticism*, under the pseudonym "Vladimir Ilyin." His letters in the run-up to publication had been full of endless exhortations to the beleaguered Anna about how "hellishly important" it was to hurry things up. Unfortunately the print run of two thousand copies at the high price of two rubles and sixty kopeks did not bode well for sales. Nor did the withering, authoritarian tone of some of the writing.

Lenin had forbidden Anna to soften his attack on Bogdanov. The resulting three-hundred-page polemic stubbornly defended the objective truth of orthodox Marxism in the face of the new philosophical challenges posited by Bogdanov and his circle. In typically strident and often insulting language, Lenin also condemned various other detractors. He took swipes at the Mensheviks who were now working with trade unionists within the narrow legal limitations then allowed in Russia. In Lenin's eyes such work would emasculate the party—if not "liquidate" it entirely—through decentralization. People would no longer have the stomach for underground work. He also continued his war on the "recallists" in the party led by Bogdanov, who demanded that Bolshevik deputies withdraw from the third Duma, and denigrated Lenin's support of cooperation with it, insisting that the party refocus its energy on an armed insurrection. Lenin expended great nervous energy throughout the book in attacking a range of political and philosophical thinking that failed to adhere to his own inflexible view of objective reality, demonizing a host of now long-forgotten isms—empirio-monism, recallism, idealism, machism, fideism, agnosticism, liquidationism, relativism, collectivism—all of them anathema to his own monomaniacal version of Marxism. Citing Marx and Engels, he accused Bogdanov and his associates of undermining materialist Marxist orthodoxy with their metaphysical and philosophical speculations. Their attempts, as "god builders," to create a new religion of the people would divert the masses from the real-life urgencies of the class struggle.

Cynical, ironic, lambasting, and dismissive by turn, *Materialism and Empirio-criticism* was a labored polemic that attacked not only the Bogdanovites but also twenty or more distinguished European philosophers, including Hume and Kant, for failing to ground their ideas in what in Lenin's terms was material and knowable. The book found few readers, being characterized as "a deployment of heavy artillery to a part of the battlefield that had largely been vacated." It had drained his energy, as did all his verbal and written battles, filling the long, futile months of exile with yet more thousands of words of frenetic theory.

Lenin had deliberately timed publication of *Materialism and Empirio-criticism* to precede a meeting of the editorial board of *Proletarii* in Paris that June. It was effectively a meeting of the Bolshevik center as it then stood—Lenin, Zinoviev, Kamenev, and Bogdanov, plus representatives from Russian regional centers. For nine days on end, at the rather appropriately named Café Caput, Lenin fought hard to win the majority over to his inflexible point of view: "Bolshevism must now be strictly Marxist" he insisted, and must distance itself from Bogdanov and his leftists, who were corrupting the party with their "theoretical revisionism." When the meeting, which conformed to Lenin's carefully prepared plans, condemned Bogdanov, he was expelled from the Bolshevik faction (and later reformed his own group around the journal *Vpered*). Having rid himself of the "vile scoundrels" and "swindlers" in the party, Lenin had also ejected the best minds in the Bolshevik faction, unwittingly creating an imbalance within his own ranks. Many of his remaining followers, far from supporting his extremist and exclusivist line, now favored reconciliation with the Mensheviks.

Intense political squabbles, on top of long hours in the library and at his desk, reduced Lenin once more to physical collapse. The ever vigilant Nadya was quick to suggest a holiday. Nice, the playground of rich Russian émigrés, was a surprising choice of venue, given Lenin's limited means, but nevertheless he joined his brother-in-law Mark Elizarov there for an eleven-day holiday at the Hotel l'Oasis on rue Gounod at the end of February. The surroundings were luxurious, as Lenin admitted with no hint of socialist shame, and the weather sunny, warm, and dry.

Despite this holiday, by summer Lenin was again craving rest and recreation, scouring the papers for somewhere cheap to stay. Although he was fortunate that his means could stretch to such self-indulgence when so many of the Parisian colleagues were totally destitute, Lenin did not see things that way. As he observed to Gorky when reprimanding him for not taking sufficient care of his own health, "to squander official property, i.e. to go on being ill and undermining your working capacity, is something quite intolerable in every respect." Lenin considered his body a machine for revolution; keeping it in tip-top condition was only logical.

He fixed on a modest boardinghouse at Bombon, thirty miles east of Paris in the *département* of Seine-et-Marne. The concierge, Madame Lecreux, charged ten francs a day for him, Nadya, Elizaveta Vasil'evna, and his sister Mariya, meals included. Mariya needed the rest as much as he did. She had suffered a bout of typhus before leaving Russia and then had succumbed to exhaustion, trying to hold down her work for the party with studies for a teaching diploma at the Sorbonne. When she became seriously ill with appendicitis, Lenin obtained the best surgeon and a week's stay in a first-class surgical hospital. Lenin took good care of Mariya at Bombon, ensuring she had plenty of restorative food such as milk, curds, and whey, though perhaps her recuperative reading—the protocols of the fifth party congress and her brother's *Materialism and Empirio-criticism*—left something to be desired. Despite this, the family tried not to talk politics during their stay and went out walking and cycling in the Clamart forest nine miles away. Madame Lecreux, who gathered her guests together for meals at 5 rue Grande each day from their various billets in the village, was accommodating enough, but Nadya was bored and found the location dull. Additionally, she found the petty bourgeois mentality of the other guests at dinner somewhat grating. For all this, their kindly hostess later remembered her Russian guests respectfully. M. Oulianoff had been so affable and content with everything, she recalled, and he had been kind enough to teach one of the little girls how to ride his bicycle.

On September 14, Lenin and Nadya returned to Paris and the new apartment they had moved to before going on holiday. Life at rue Beaunier had become difficult; the flat was too large and expensive and their landlady had complained repeatedly about the number of scruffy *anarchistes russes*, who clumped up and down the stairs in their dirty boots to visit them. Lenin and Nadya had found a flat at 4 rue Marie Rose, a quiet side street four blocks farther north near the boulevard Montparnasse. As usual, Lenin left the domestic arrangements and the logistics of the move to the women, Nadya conceding that he "had more important things to think about." By their standards the second-floor flat was very comfortable, with central heating, a private lavatory, and a kitchen with a proper range for cooking. Lenin worked at a kitchen table covered with black oilcloth in the front room overlooking the street, his books and papers carefully stacked around him and neatly arranged on shelves. His only luxury was a chess set. Set into an alcove of this room and separated by a glass door stood his and Nadya's two plain iron bedsteads with their pristine white bedspreads. Elizaveta Vasil'evna had the better bedroom at their insistence, and Nadya did her party work in there. As she was perpetually overloaded with such work, they hired a domestic helper, Louisa Faroche, to come in for two to three hours in the morning to tidy the flat and wash dishes. All in all, as one visitor observed, rue Marie Rose presented a picture of "extreme poverty and ideal cleanliness." Maxim Gorky thought it had the air of a student lodging but without the chaos. The kitchen, as in Geneva, was the hub. You could barely get four people around the table, but nevertheless it served as dining room and sitting room where Lenin eagerly interrogated visitors from Russia, wanting to know absolutely all that was going on. "There are no superfluous details—everything has significance," he insisted. They all noticed how "Ilych" fell on news from Russia "like a hungry man on food."

Their concierge at rue Marie Rose, the venerable Madame Roux, was struck by the couple's abstemiousness—there seemed to be no personal indulgences. "Monsieur Oulianoff" neither drank or smoked, only ever went out to meetings or the library, and always kept to a very regular schedule. That in itself seemed dangerously abnormal behavior to her. Colleague Alexey Alin felt concerned over Lenin's daily trip to the Gare du

Nord to personally ensure that his articles for *Zvezda* got the mail train to Russia on time, refusing to delegate this task to one of the comrades.

In the rich cultural heartland of Paris Lenin had a range of art, music, and theater on his doorstep. But his strictly regimented lifestyle allowed little or no time for anything other than bicycle rides into the country; these at least were sacrosanct. In general, he turned his back on the cultural life of this great European city and resisted colleagues' urgings to go out and enjoy himself more. He rarely ventured into the Louvre and made only one or two trips to the conventional theater, such as to see Bourget's play about the class struggle, *La Barricade*. Paris was too ostentatious and bourgeois for his and Nadya's tastes and he remained unimpressed with highbrow culture, preferring the music halls and café concerts of Montmartre, Port St. Martin, and Montparnasse, where, as in London, he could see and hear the music of the people. The year 1909 had been a turbulent one in France: an election year marked by a month-long postal strike during which Paris—and Lenin—had been cut off from the rest of France and the world. The proofs for *Materialism and Empirio-criticism* had been held up in the backlog. The Parisian *café-chantant* artists had made much of reviling the double dealing of politicians that year, while extolling the militancy of the French proletariat. And none more so than Gaston Montéhus, whom Lenin passionately admired.

Montéhus, with his working-class message of rebellion, produced the kind of gritty poetry that appealed to Lenin. He first heard Montéhus perform at an unglamorous suburban theater on the outskirts of Paris. Subsequently he scoured the papers for announcements of his concerts, and he and Nadya often went off on their bicycles, map of Paris in hand, to seek out Montéhus's performances. They saw him often at the workers theater cum music hall on the rue Gaieté in the 14th *arrondissement*. Popularly known as Bobino, it had opened in 1812 and was located between Montparnasse station and the walls of the cemetery, not far from rue Marie Rose. Montéhus, wearing his signature ragged workman's dungarees, red foulard around his neck, and cloth cap, was a proven man of the people, singing as he did about the hardships of the worker's life and the virtues of solidarity. For Lenin he came with the best possible revolutionary credentials: his father and grandfather had both taken part in the Paris Commune. He wrote the lyrics and much of the music for his own songs, which were a mix of sentiment, patriotism, and revolutionary fervor. His most popular song, "Gloire au 17ème," was a tribute to French troops of the 17th regiment. On June 21, 1907, during a series of large demonstrations against government controls in the wine-growing Languedoc region, five hundred men of the 17th had refused to move against protesters in the town of Beziers and had taken their side instead. The song celebrated this mutiny against government oppression; for Lenin it had many echoes of the situation in Russia. He would often burst into the words of the chorus: "Salut, salut à vous, braves soldats du Dix-septième." Not surprisingly, this song became the anthem for French antimilitarist rallies during this period, along with Montéhus's hugely popular "La Grève des mères" and "Le Chant de la jeune garde."

Eventually Lenin invited Montéhus to sing at a fund-raising Russian musical evening. It was staged at the Sociétés Savants at rue Danton in the Latin Quarter, along with a buffet and lottery, to raise money for party printing costs. After the performance Lenin engaged Montéhus in an animated conversation about the future of world revolution that went on until four in the morning. Nadya and his other colleagues had rarely seen him so animated and happy. The two men became so friendly that on one occasion Lenin visited Montéhus backstage to ask him for a loan. He had never been immodest in making such requests of friends. Maxim Gorky had been another source of regular injections of cash. But that day he was out of luck. "You should have come to the matinee, my friend," Montéhus told him, for others had already visited him that day with the same thought in mind and he hadn't a sou. All he could offer Lenin was his pocket watch to take and pawn. Lenin accepted his offer; years later Montéhus received a gift from the Soviet government of a magnificent gold watch to replace the one he had given Lenin.

For all the fleeting pleasures of the *café-chantants*, visits to the sea, and bicycle rides into the countryside, Nadya was weary that year. On top of all her party work she was still doggedly pursuing the French lessons she had started in Geneva. She found little to say about their lives in the dutiful letters she wrote to Lenin's mother and sisters. In a postscript to a letter to Anna she admitted that throughout the winter of 1909–1910 she had been "in a state of utter melancholy" and had "frittered away" her time. She hadn't been able to concentrate and, suffering from bouts of depression as she did, "was in no fit state to write." Indeed, she added, there was nothing to write about. "We are just jogging along." With Volodya so wrapped up in his work, their life, she said, differed only from the previous year at rue Beaunier in that the apartment at rue Marie Rose was, mercifully, "very warm," and Volodya had become "a stick-at-home." Occasionally he would venture forth on his bicycle in pursuit of a new pastime—watching air displays.

In the summer of 1909 Frenchman Louis Blériot had become the first man to fly the English Channel, and the whole of France was captivated by this landmark achievement. Lenin would cycle to the aerodromes at Issy-les-Moulineaux and Juvisy-sur-Orge outside Paris to watch the displays. One summer day, as he was riding back from Issy, another cyclist struck him from behind, buckling his wheel and throwing him into a ditch. He fixed his bike the next day. But in December, as he was returning from another air show at Juvisy, a car hit Lenin and knocked him to the ground, leaving his bicycle a complete write-off. The driver of the vehicle turned out to be a French viscount, and Lenin, having trained as a lawyer, sought compensation in court. He won his case and the following January was able to buy a new bicycle.

—∾—

LENIN'S BRIEF WINTER hibernation at rue Marie Rose was interrupted early the following year by more frenetic political squabbles. In January a plenary of the RSDLP was called in Paris. It lasted three long and bitter weeks: "three weeks of agony" as Lenin described it, when "all nerves were on edge, the devil to pay!" The atmosphere was tense as conciliators among Lenin's Bolsheviks made a last-ditch attempt to bring the various party factions to a degree of unity. Although Lenin was determined to remain at the head of a mainstream Bolshevik party, he now lost control of the party machinery and with it all-important control of Bolshevik funds (including the Shmid inheritance, which was transferred to the neutral control of German social democrats). Worse, demands were made to close down the factional newspaper *Proletarii* and with it the Bolshevik center in Paris, and transfer operations back to the Central Committee in Russia. The plenary left him bitter and disenchanted and worse—feeling out of touch. "Paris is a rotten hole in many respects," he wrote to Mariya in Russia. "I am still unable to adapt myself *fully* to it (after living *here* for a year!)." Nevertheless, he admitted that "only extraordinary circumstances could drive me back to Geneva!"

During March and April 1910 Lenin attempted a rapprochement with Plekhanov and the Mensheviks but failed. His disillusion was extreme: "Life in exile is now a hundred times harder than it was before the revolution." With it came nothing but endless "squabbling." Yet he could not resist returning to the lion's den of theoretical conflict by accepting another invitation from Gorky to join him on Capri that summer. Perhaps the sunshine and sea air seduced him at a time when he felt weary and discouraged. He spent two weeks on Capri during June–July, traveling south by train to Marseilles where he picked up the steamer for Naples. The sea journey was cheap and evoked memories of home. It was, so he told his brother, "like travelling on the Volga." By this time Gorky had moved to a larger property—the Villa Spinola near the square on Via Lorgano. Lenin's visit inevitably provoked endless arguments with Bogdanov and Lunacharsky, who were already on Capri, and much talk of Russia on the terrace every evening after dinner. But there were nevertheless moments of relaxation: games of chess, evenings listening to Russian songs played on Gorky's phonograph, fishing trips with the old Caprese boatmen, and the diversion provided by the famous Sorrento tenor Giovannino, who came to supper and sang for them, though in error singing the czarist anthem "Bozhe tsarya khrani" (God Save the Czar).

The main reason for the move to the Villa Spinola was that Gorky, Bogdanov, and their colleagues wanted suitable premises for a party school to train young workers as activists. Capri seemed a good location, relatively safe from police surveillance and official scrutiny. The facilities for undertaking such training in Russia had evaporated. With so many arrests, new activists were needed who were trained in the underground skills of writing and disseminating propaganda and indoctrinating workers. Discussions about the inauguration of party schools for this purpose had been going on since the fifth party congress in London in 1907. Gorky's First Higher Social-Democratic Propagandist-Agitator School for Workers opened that August, funded by the income from Gorky's royalties as well as donations from admirers of his work. The school was run by Gorky in close collaboration with Bogdanov, Lunacharsky, and two additional colleagues, Gregory Aleksinsky and Nikifor Vilonov. In November a similar party school opened in Bologna, funded by money from expropriations.

Gorky had hoped to persuade Lenin to take a role in the party school, but Lenin refused. If there were going to be party schools, then he would run his own. Inevitably he would see the Capri and later Bologna schools as a direct factional threat to his own struggle to regain supremacy in the party. The Capri school further underlined the split between himself and Bogdanov that had occurred during the June 1909 meeting of the *Proletarii* board. Lenin retaliated by inviting the students in Capri to come to Paris for lectures from him, and most of them did so at the end of the year before returning to Russia to take up active work. He also tried to discredit the Bologna school and lure its students to Paris. By now, physically revived, he was already plotting to call a new party congress at which he intended to bury his opponents.

While Lenin was in Capri, Nadya and her mother had fled the scorching July heat of Paris for the Vendée, in the Bay of Biscay. Initially they stayed at a summer colony run by French socialists in hopes of getting to know them better. But the French kept their distance from the Russians and to Nadya seemed more petty bourgeois than socialist. Consequently she and Elizaveta decamped to nearby Pornic, a picturesque little seaside resort. Here they rented two first-floor rooms with a balcony at the picturesque-sounding Villa les Roses. Located on rue Mon Désir, it was a two-story Breton-style house with shutters, its garden filled with the sweet-smelling roses that inspired its name. Their hostess, a washerwoman, was very friendly and outspoken toward Nadya. She told of her run-ins with Catholic priests who tried to pressure her son into studying for the priesthood and how she had seen them off, a fact that impressed Lenin when he joined Nadya and Elizaveta on July 22. Having already enjoyed two weeks of sun on Capri, he indulged in three more weeks of complete rest—days full of swimming and cycling, soaking up the sea air and sunshine, and watching the waves roll in off the Atlantic. He seemed to have no other desire than to sit and chat with his landlord, the local coast guard, and eat the crabs that he had caught. But sometimes he could be seen sitting on the steps that led down from the balcony, hunched over a book or with a notebook in his lap.

From Pornic, Lenin traveled to an international socialist congress in Copenhagen, staying in a modest back room on Vesterbrogade arranged for him by a colleague. On August 28 the inaugural meeting of the congress was held at the Concert Palace, its walls adorned with socialist slogans and posters. Nine hundred delegates and one hundred reporters arrived to find themselves greeted by a huge rally of workers outside (it was a Sunday). At the end of the day they marched with bands, red flags, and banners through the streets of Copenhagen. Inside, the proceedings were inaugurated by a five-hundred-strong Danish workers choir. All the leading socialists from the Second International were there: Karl Kautsky, Rosa Luxembourg, and Klara Zetkin from Germany; Viktor Adler from Austria; Jean Jaurès from France; Camille Huysmans, secretary of the Second International, from Belgium; and a strong British contingent featuring Keir Hardie, Ramsay MacDonald, and Lenin's old friend Harry Quelch.

Many at the congress were preoccupied with talk of an approaching war in Europe, but this most serious issue was displaced by a great deal of discussion about unity in the trade union movement, particularly within the Austro-Hungarian Empire, and the work of the cooperative movement. Lenin, one of twenty Russian delegates at the congress representing the various social democrat groups, spoke on the role of cooperatives in disseminating propaganda and spent much of the time working hard at winning new friends in the international movement. Ivan Maisky remembered seeing him "sitting in a corner and gesticulating energetically, or with his thumbs stuck into the armholes of his waistcoat, eagerly trying to convince some European left-winger on some point." He listened carefully to other speakers, even putting his hand to his ear to catch every word of a speech that interested him and making rapid notes when he thought he had caught a political opponent out on a certain point.

By the end of the congress he had won support from Polish social democrats, but others such as the Menshevik Fedor Dan resented his relentless assaults: "There is no other man who thinks and dreams of nothing but revolution—twenty-four hours a day," he famously observed.

After the congress Lenin spent several days in the Royal Library at Copenhagen, registering under his real name Ulyanov in order to study statistical material on Danish agriculture and the cooperative movement before traveling to Stockholm on September 13 to meet up with his mother.

Throughout 1910 his nostalgia for home and his concern for his mother, whom he had not seen since 1906, grew acute. Mariya Aleksandrovna was now seventy-five and ailing. Sensing that time was running out, Lenin had persuaded her to travel from Russia with Mariya so that they could spend some precious time together. He sent detailed instructions ahead of their meeting in Stockholm with strong warnings that his mother should not exert herself in any way. When she saw him, Mariya Aleksandrovna was shocked at how thin and changed her son looked, but she took great pride in attending a speech about the Copenhagen congress that he gave to an audience of sixty while they were in Stockholm. During her stay they spent time walking in the parks and sitting talking. When the time came for them to leave, Lenin was not allowed to board his sister and mother's Russian steamship to say good-bye, for he might have been arrested: "I still remember the expression on his face as he stood there looking at mother," Mariya wrote later. "How much pain there was on his face! He seemed to feel that this was the last time he would see her and treasured the plaid travelling rug she bought for him in Stockholm, solicitous to the last about his health."

It was a sad return to Paris for Lenin that September. He didn't enjoy the city and for years afterward repeatedly asked Nadya why they had ever gone there. But his spirits lifted unexpectedly as his political fortunes began to turn. Early that month, not long after the Copenhagen congress, a new activist arrived in Paris. She would quickly come to take a leading role in organizational work for the party, with Lenin growing to rely on her for key assignments both in Europe and in Russia. "She was a very ardent Bolshevik," Nadya recalled, and with her natural charisma she "soon gathered our Paris crowd around her." Her presence and personality would, however, have their most profound effect on Lenin himself—not just in his official life but in the two most rigorously suppressed sides of his personality—his sexuality and his emotions.

CHAPTER THIRTEEN

Inessa

PARIS–PRAGUE–PARIS:
JANUARY 1911–JUNE 1912

⟨⟩

I NESSA ARMAND WAS FRENCH, as her romantic-sounding name suggests. She came, nevertheless, to embrace the revolutionary movement in her adopted country—Russia—with all the idealism and steadfastness of a true patriot, while retaining her inherent French identity. In the years leading up to the Russian Revolution she would become one of the Bolshevik faction's foremost women activists.

She was born Elizabeth d'Herbenville to a theatrical couple in Paris in 1874, the first of three daughters. Her father, who went by the stage name Théodore Stéphane, had a reasonably successful career, touring in comic opera and operetta. Her mother, Natalie Wild, had Anglo-Scottish roots and was a sometime singing teacher and actress. Inessa's parents separated during her mother's third pregnancy. Natalie's mother and her sister Sophie, who both worked as private tutors in Russia, came to Paris to persuade her to ease her burdens by allowing them to take the eldest, five-year-old Inessa, to live with them in Moscow. They taught her at home in all the social graces of a young lady of the day. Inès, as she was known in the family, became fluent in Russian, German, and English as well as her native French and played the piano beautifully. One of the families Sophie worked for, the Armands, were Russified French textile manufacturers who owned an estate at Pushkino about twenty miles from the city. Inessa often visited them. The liberal minded Armands, several of whom had been actively involved in the revolutionary movement from the 1890s, welcomed her into their extended family and provided additional tuition. It was not long before the eldest son, Aleksandr, succumbed to

Inessa's undeniable charm and beauty, and they fell in love. She was only eighteen when the Armand family accepted this fact with astonishingly good grace and allowed the couple to marry. Four children, two boys and two girls, followed in quick succession between 1894 and 1901.

During this time Inessa, pricked by a growing social conscience and increasingly bored by domesticity, became interested in Tolstoyanism and joined the Moscow Society for the Improvement of the Lot of Women, its main work being the rescue and rehabilitation of prostitutes. But within a year or two, concluding that philanthropic work would never effect radical change, she moved away from religious-based social reform to more overtly political interests.

Much as she loved her children, Inessa was a restless soul whose emotional and maternal sides frequently found themselves at odds with her commitment to social justice and revolutionary change in Russia. In the early 1900s she became embroiled in an affair with her husband Aleksandr's younger brother Vladimir, and in 1903 she left Aleksandr to live with Vladimir in Switzerland, giving birth to a son later that year. Aleksandr accepted the situation with extraordinary dignity and continued to support Inessa financially and take care of the children, particularly after 1905.

Through Vladimir, who had been politicized as a student at Moscow University, Inessa became involved in the revolutionary movement. She embraced Marxism and became a social democrat in 1903, after vacillating over which political faction to join. She would retain her passionate interest in feminist politics and women's health issues throughout her life. In 1904 she returned to Russia by train from Switzerland, her trunk full of illegal literature, which she and Vladimir distributed from their Moscow apartment.

In January 1905, during the political backlash to Bloody Sunday, Inessa came under police surveillance and was arrested. She was held in jail for four months until Aleksandr bailed her out with family money to the tune of 6,500 rubles. While she was imprisoned, Vladimir contracted tuberculosis. As soon as Inessa was released, the couple left Russia so that he could take a rest cure in the south of France, leaving the children with Aleksandr.

Returning to Russia in 1906, and despite the risks, Inessa became heavily involved in the underground once more, taking charge of propaganda work in Lefortovo, a heavily industrialized district of Moscow. In July 1907 she was arrested again. This time she was summarily exiled for two years to the town of Mezen in Archangelsk province, just outside the Arctic Circle. Vladimir followed her to this inhospitable spot, where the temperature could drop as low as minus 40 and winter lasted six long, dark months. But the harsh climate aggravated his tuberculosis and he was forced to leave. Inessa managed to get away from Mezen two months before the end of her term and headed for the south of France. Vladimir was gravely ill and died two weeks after her arrival in January 1909.

Unable to return to Russia for fear of arrest and distraught and adrift at the loss of Vladimir, Inessa remained undecided for some time about where to live. There was, as ever, the terrible pull between her children back in Russia and her passionate desire to work for the revolution. In the end, Inessa went to Paris where she met up with an émigré friend, Elena Vlasova. Here she encountered Lenin for the first time when she heard him speak at a political meeting in the Bolshevik café on the rue d'Orléans in May.

Inessa already knew the political Lenin from his written work, having been greatly impressed by *Development of Capitalism in Russia* and *What Is to Be Done?* As a clever and highly politicized woman, she was attracted to his challenging manner, dynamism, and intellect. But on this first encounter, she also was deeply in awe of him if not a little afraid. One reason might have been Lenin's disconcerting habit, in conversation, of leaning toward his interlocutors and engaging with them eyeball to eyeball.

In October Inessa decided to move to Brussels to study at the Université Nouvelle for her baccalaureate in history and political economy, as well as to further her understanding of Marxist theory. Such was her diligence that she completed her two-year course in ten months. Lenin, already impressed by her, personally arranged tickets for her to attend the eighth Socialist International in Copenhagen in September. As Inessa later recalled, her admiration for him was equaled only by her extreme sense of self-consciousness in his presence.

The International may in part have been a catalyst in their developing relationship, for soon afterwards Inessa moved to Paris with her two youngest children, Varvara and Andrey. By now a convinced Leninist, she joined the Bolsheviks and was elected to their Paris section and made Bolshevik representative to the French Socialist Party. With her fluent French and her obvious dedication to the cause, she became an integral part of the Lenin circle based at rue Marie Rose and a valuable party worker. At her own request she would now be known within the party simply as Inessa.

———

For Lenin, Inessa Armand was everything that Nadezhda Krupskaya was not. She was beautiful, sophisticated, and multilingual, as well as elegant and feminine in an instinctively French way. She was passionate and could be emotionally manipulative, where Nadya was straightforward, self-effacing, and circumspect. Inessa had strong feminist instincts and placed great value on personal happiness; Nadya never spoke of her own needs and had long since learned to give in to Lenin's irascibility. Inessa enjoyed cooking for people, a skill that Nadya had never mastered, and was a wonderful pianist, music being Lenin's one vulnerable point and a way into his closely protected emotions. Inessa was sexually unconventional, where Nadya was physically and emotionally reticent.

True, like Nadya she was sickly—imprisonment brought with it tuberculosis and a weakened constitution—but Inessa had beautiful green eyes, fine features, and wavy chestnut hair, while Nadya's as yet undiagnosed thyroid condition was rapidly destroying her looks. By the autumn of 1910, Nadya was forty-one and had long since succumbed to a self-inflicted dowdiness; Inessa was in her prime at thirty-seven. Nadya had never taken care of herself. Her once tall, slim figure was becoming increasingly shapeless, compounded by the fact that she had no interest in fashion and wore the most functional, unfeminine clothes: "Always the same black frock in winter, a light one in summer; always the same simple hat without the least trimming." The Okhrana spooks who tailed her described her appearance ungenerously as "slovenly." Clara Zetkin in later years pitied Nadya's plain dress and worn-out appearance as resembling "a tired-out wife of a worker forever worrying whether she would manage to get everything done." Alexey Alin in Paris noted only one sartorial concession in her: at the beginning of each summer Nadya took her old straw hat out from its box and gave it a fresh coat of varnish—so that as time went on the accumulating layers of varnish acquired the contours of a geological cross-section.

Lenin had spent the best part of the last eleven years with Nadya and his mother-in-law. He had female colleagues in the Bolshevik circles in London, Geneva, Munich, and even now in Paris, but none ever aroused a flicker of interest bar the enigmatic Elizaveta de K, whom he met in St. Petersburg in 1905. Whilst his marriage to Nadya had, according to her later claims, not been without love and a physical side, the couple had met and married as "fully-formed Marxists," their union's fundamental purpose being to support *his* political life. Yet Lenin was not incapable of demonstrating affection, as is clear from his letters to his mother and sisters and his concerns over their health and well-being. But in his public life he never showed overt affection for his wife. His sexuality, seemingly, had long been subordinated—along with his emotional needs—to the urgent and consuming life of politics. Sex, like music, exposed the revolutionary's emotional vulnerabilities. And that was a dangerous thing. But in Paris, with Inessa, and perhaps with others, Lenin's sexuality was finally unlocked.

Inessa Armand fascinated Lenin from the first, and he admired her political intuition. Her key role in his inner circle was endorsed when he invited her to organize a Bolshevik party school in France that ran from May 11 to September 21, 1911. It was rare indeed for Bolshevik women, aside perhaps from Nadya or Elena Stasova in St. Petersburg, to play a leading role in major party matters. Lenin's unequivocal favoritism toward Inessa was reinforced that autumn when he asked her to run the Central Committee's Foreign Bureau. With her proven linguistic skills, Inessa would play a crucial role in liaising with emigrant groups, eventually across thirty-seven European cities, a function previously fulfilled in the main by Nadya.

With his hostility toward Bogdanov and other political heretics undimmed, Lenin refused to form an association between his party school and Gorky's schools on Capri and in Bologna. He was determined to create his own school as the training ground for a new generation of loyal, hand-picked Leninist party workers, who would work to rebuild a tight-knit Bolshevik group both inside and outside Russia. The party school, for which he released 10,000 francs from party funds, also signaled his final and irrevocable break with the Mensheviks.

Lenin had already found what he thought to be the perfect location on one of his many bicycle rides with Nadya—the village of Longjumeau, about nine miles south of Paris on the Toulouse road. Lenin was convinced that locating the school outside Paris in an undistinguished location would free it from Okhrana surveillance. In a faint attempt at maintaining *konspiratsiya,* the alarmed residents of Longjumeau were informed that the Russian *anarchistes* who arrived that summer were village schoolteachers taking a refresher course.

In the 1900s Longjumeau was little more than a narrow, cobbled street—the rue Grande—of old houses with red-tiled, gabled roofs, surrounded by gardens and orchards. It was a typically sleepy French town where time appeared to stand still, with a small central square and town hall and a café at either end. The major industry was tanning, which employed many of its men; its other inhabitants tilled the soil or worked as gardeners, the women as laundresses. By day it might appear somnolent but at night the cobbled road through Longjumeau reverberated with rattling carts of milk, poultry, and fresh vegetables being sent to the central market at Les Halles in Paris. Lenin and Nadya sublet their Paris apartment for the duration, as usual bringing her mother with them, and rented two rather dark and unappealing rooms on the first floor of a house at 91 rue Grande owned by a mustard dealer. Their fellow tenants on the ground floor were a tanner and his family. Zinoviev and his wife were better accommodated nearby and hired a maid to take care of their three-year-old son.

The town was linked to Paris by a local tramline, but some of the tutors cycled out daily from the city, under strict instructions from Lenin to watch out for any spooks on their tail. Lenin and Nadya's accommodation had a courtyard and a well in back that supplied their water, but they did not cook here, instead taking their meals a half mile up the road where the school was based. These premises, at 17 rue Grande, had an attached, disused metalworker's shop in the back. Here commune members, who were farmed out to billets around the village, studied and ate their meals—good plain Russian food prepared by former Siberian exile

Katya Mazonova. She slept in the kitchen with her two children. Inessa, who had gone on ahead to set up the school with a long table, lectern, and wicker chairs for the students, had installed herself at 17 rue Grande with her seven-year-old son, Andrey. Three of the older students had come with her to help clean the place, wash the large windows, and scrub the floors.

In May the students, all specially selected by Lenin's envoys in Russia, began arriving in Paris—eighteen industrial workers inexperienced in party work—among them tanners, textile workers, and metalworkers, from St. Petersburg, Moscow, Ekaterinoslav, Nikopol, Baku, and Tiflis. They were predominantly Bolsheviks but included three Mensheviks— and two Okhrana spies. Contrary to Lenin's hopes of maintaining secrecy, the school was closely watched from its opening in June, and the two Okhrana spies among the pupils duly reported back to its Paris agency on all the participants when school was over.

Inessa, Lenin, Kamenev, and Zinoviev were the main tutors during the three-month course, backed up by a team of other lecturers and auditors. Lenin was in his element, adopting the mantle of headmaster for the duration, intent on drumming ideological conformity into the heads of his students like the good pedagogue that he was. He opened the proceedings with an analysis of the Communist Manifesto and worked his pupils hard, beginning at eight in the morning, insisting on absolute concentration from the students and meticulous preparation from the tutors. He himself gave fifty-six lectures on political economy, agrarian reform, materialism, and the theory of socialism, often first thing in the morning before cycling into Paris to take care of party matters.

The remaining subjects were split among the other tutors. Zinoviev and Kamenev taught the history of the party, Lunacharsky lectured on literature and art, and David Ryazanov presented the history of the workers movement in Europe. Nadya took a generally low-key role, although she gave some classes on how to set up an underground newspaper, and Charles Rappoport came from Paris to speak on the French socialist movement. Lenin made a point of attending all four of Inessa's lectures on political economy and the history of the workers movement in Belgium, although much to her disappointment he vetoed her request to lecture on feminist issues such as the role of women workers. (Lenin might have been impressed with her performance, but one of the two Okhrana spies reported back that she was a "weak" lecturer.)

Inessa later wrote to Lenin that it was only at Longjumeau that she finally began to get used to him and her affections grew. Sometimes the two slipped away to share a coffee in one of the village cafés; on another occasion they went into Paris with Lunacharsky and Ordzhonikidze to see a proletarian play. That the two were drawing closer must have been apparent, but to most of those gathered at Longjumeau it seemed a mutually respectful comradeship. Their animated conversation at lunch, however, was not lost on Elizaveta Vasil'evna, who, unwell for most of that year and suffering from fits of depression, grumbled about the amount of attention Inessa was getting from her son-in-law.

The weather that summer was infernally hot and Nadya found the small, airless rooms at Longjumeau oppressive, especially with no garden to sit in. She found herself taking pity on their fellow tenant, a tanner who worked long hours and would sit outside in the evening air, exhausted, when he returned from work. His wife, who worked as a charwoman, seemed equally cowed; their daughter, left at home to look after the younger children all day, seemed to Nadya to live a life of drudgery. The family's only consolation was going to church on Sunday. What a difference, Nadya thought, between these exploited French workers, who unquestioningly accepted the social system, and men like one of their students, a tanner called Prisyagin, who was already a fully fledged "class conscious fighter."

In the late afternoon when classes were over many of the commune members sought relief from the intense heat and walked barefoot out into the surrounding fields or took a swim in the nearby River Yvette. After this they would sit on the river bank or lounge on haystacks, singing Russian songs as the sun went down. Sometimes things got uproarious. The Okhrana spies in their midst noted that rather too much party money was spent on wine.

Sundays were free for recreation. The commune had four bicycles, including those of Lenin and Nadya, and on one or two occasions the students cycled into Paris under Lunacharsky's supervision to visit the Louvre. Lenin enjoyed being away from the city and the "commotion" of the Russian colony. He and Nadya, so she wrote to his mother, "cycled their heads off," going out for long excursions of forty or fifty miles at a time, leaving at six in the morning, cycling through forests, and returning late in the evening. At other times Lenin cycled around the village with a student perched precariously on the crossbars due to the shortage of bicycles.

When the course ended on August 30, the students were sent back into Russia with two hundred francs each as part of a "Russian organizing commission for calling an all-party-conference" with instructions to get themselves elected to the commission, with the help of three of the school auditors. The loyal and impressionable Inessa was now given the important role of helping arrange this conference.

If any indicator were needed of the close relationship now established between her, and Lenin, it came on their return to Paris in September 1911, when Inessa took an apartment next door to them at 2 rue Marie Rose, bringing three of her children, Andrey, Inna, and Varvara, to live with her. Although their relationship had by no means been a *coup de foudre*, it began—and ultimately ended—as a close political one. By now Inessa was deeply in love with Lenin, having overcome her initial sense of awe. He had become attracted to her warm and ardent personality, for she had two essential qualities that Nadya lacked: youth and vitality. People liked being around her; even Nadya observed how their home "grew brighter when Inessa entered it."

Living in such close proximity over the next ten months would provide Lenin and Inessa with an opportunity to have an affair, but they would have to conduct it under Nadya's nose and probably with her full knowledge, for they clearly spent a great deal of time together. As Bolshevik colleagues this would have been perfectly natural. But how Nadya felt about her growing displacement as Lenin's right-hand woman or how she dealt with her husband's obvious attraction to Inessa remains unexplained. She developed a deep affection for Inessa's three children, especially the two girls, Inna and Varvara, that continued long after Inessa's death. In later life, in the few circumspect comments she made about Inessa, Nadya was warm and generous toward her, writing that during their last year in Paris "Inessa became a person close to us" and demonstrated great affection for Nadya's mother, Elizaveta Vasil'evna.

But in the end, Nadezhda Krupskaya, scrupulous as she was about her husband's reputation and memory, would say frustratingly little about this triangular relationship, even after Inessa's death in 1920 and Lenin's in 1924. Criticism of Inessa would have reflected badly on her husband's obvious affection and respect for her. As a fellow feminist and collaborator on the first Soviet women's journal, *Rabotnitsa*, with Inessa, Nadya shared a sense of female solidarity and mutual respect in a highly chauvinistic party dominated by men. Like most of the *bolshevichki*, Nadya had never believed in the constraints of conventional marriage. It is said that she even offered to leave Lenin—either in 1911 or later in Galicia in 1913—so that he could set up house with Inessa, but he refused. He was far too dependent on her; it was Nadya's support and unfailing loyalty that had kept him sane all these years and perhaps, for that, he loved her—in his own way.

Whatever the quality of his passion for Inessa may have been, Lenin had a turbulent relationship with her, in contrast to his solid and dependable relationship with Nadya. Charles Rappoport, who had become one of Lenin's closest French colleagues, often saw him and Inessa together in a Bolshevik café on the avenue d'Orléans. He had no doubts: Lenin, "*avec ses petits yeux mongols*" (with his little Mongolian eyes), was mesmerized by Inessa.

Perhaps Nadya tolerated the affair because her untreated thyroid condition, now known as Graves' disease, reduced her sex drive. It caused her eyes to bulge and her neck and legs to swell, and brought on a general weakening of her health. The hormonal imbalance precipitated by the condition also provoked mood swings, anxiety attacks, heart palpitations, and rapid speech. Graves' disease likely denied Nadya the one thing she most longed for and which Inessa had in abundance—children. Nadya's condition had possibly made her infertile. During their time in Shushenskoe, she had coyly remarked to Lenin's mother that as far as the arrival of "a little bird" was concerned, none "wanted to come," her first and only mention of the subject in her letters. Evidence suggests that during their time in Paris Nadya ceased having sexual relations with her husband—perhaps because of her declining libido or his growing closeness to Armand. The only evidence of Lenin's feelings remains in a few letter fragments in which he addresses Inessa as *ty*—the Russian equivalent to the French *tu*—an attribution he reserved for his mother, wife, and sisters and one or two close male associates, such as Martov.

Nadya's apparently graceful acceptance of her husband's love for Inessa would have been the ultimate socialist gesture. It was reminiscent of the idealized free love relationships in Chernyshevsky's revolutionary commune in *What Is to be Done?* the socialist novel that all three of them admired. If her husband's sexual needs were to be fulfilled elsewhere, then at least it was with a fellow Bolshevik and a woman she liked. To her way of thinking nothing should ever come before the health, well-being, and needs of Ilyich in his predestined role as leader of the revolution. Although she must have felt deeply depressed, she never played the role of betrayed wife. She did not look on Inessa as a rival; in this as in all things in her life with Lenin, Nadya managed to rise above her own personal feelings.

There remain, however, many unanswered questions about the longest and most urban period of Lenin's life in exile. Living in Paris for four years with an ailing wife, if he were going to kick over the traces of his highly circumscribed sex life (inhibited since 1900 by the almost constant presence of his mother-in-law), then Paris provided every possible temptation, including a thriving sex industry. Where did Lenin really go during those many long bike rides around Paris? Did he really spend his every waking moment in the library as the Soviet record and his loyal acolytes would have everyone believe? And were his only ports of call the politically correct Bolshevik cafés of the rue d'Orléans?

Lenin's official hagiographers consistently denied that he ever went near the more bohemian haunts of Paris, but this is not so. He lived in the heart of Montparnasse, and avoiding them would have been difficult. He was certainly seen at the Rotonde—a small café favored by Russian artists, thick with the fug of Gauloises, where impoverished émigrés sat talking with empty glasses well into the night and paid the owner, Père Libion, in kind, with their paintings. Modigliani, Léger, Chagall, Soutine, and others from the Russian modernist school, as well as Picasso later, were all regulars. On one particular occasion, in a playful mood, Modigliani set fire to the Russian newspaper in which Lenin was engrossed. The English painter Christopher Nevinson remembered that many of the Russian artists at the Rotonde considered Lenin "a cranky extremist." For entertainment they sometimes went to Russian meetings held around the corner and listened to Lenin "in a spirit of irreverence" and "amused toleration." There was no doubt he was in deadly earnest: he would froth at the mouth with excitement when speaking. But according to Nevinson, "that only made him the more amusing to the Russians."

Lenin was also seen at another famous venue, the Closerie de Lilas on the corner of boulevards Montparnasse and Saint Michel, a café dominated by French writers and critics. He liked to go there to find chess partners and was often seen playing with the poet Apollinaire, always winning in spite of his best efforts to cede the occasional game to the French poet. Occasionally he went across the road to the Café du Dôme, the preserve mainly of German painters and cartoonists of the Munich-based journal *Simplicissimus*, where he was remembered for his good humor and was seen playing chess outside on its terrace. Needless to say, these watering holes were also frequented by Parisian prostitutes, and rumors later circulated in Paris that Lenin had a preference for a brothel conveniently situated near the Bibliothèque Nationale.

The French-born American writer Julien Green, who lived in this community during the war years, made a tantalizing observation in his journal that overturns the sober, asexual image of the revolutionary leader. He noted meeting a Russian émigré painter, Evichev (or Ivichev), who had known Lenin in the Latin Quarter in 1912. Evichev recalled that they never talked about politics: "We shared our women. Lenin was very gay and very good-natured, but, in matters of love, he was absolutely voracious" (Nous partagions nos poules. Lénine était très gai, très bon, et en amour, très cochon), said Evichev, claiming to have a letter from Lenin in which he expressed his interest in a certain pretty young Parisienne.

Further clues to this unofficial side to Lenin's personality are found in another French account published by writer and Orientalist Franz Toussaint in 1952. He describes making a trip to hear Lenin lecture at the party school at Longjumeau in the summer of 1911 through an introduction by the French socialist Jean Jaurès. He saw Lenin again in Paris shortly afterward, this time through mutual friend Pierre Vabre, who met Lenin regularly in the Jardin de Luxembourg. Here the three men sat near the Medici Fountain one summer afternoon and chatted about an attractive young chair attendant in the gardens called Jeanette, in whom Lenin was interested. And then there was Elizaveta de K, the young Russian activist Lenin met in 1905 in St. Petersburg and with whom he apparently had a brief affair. They met again in Paris in May 1908, when he came to give a lecture. Although the affair had ended, Elizaveta felt compelled to see him. There was something about Lenin this time, she remembered, that both attracted and repulsed her, something in his mobile, malicious little eyes, something ruthless and predatory that she did not like. They talked of the past, of 1905, Lenin's sardonic laugh punctuating the conversation as he expressed his regrets that he had failed to indoctrinate Elizaveta in his militant political beliefs. They separated as friends, on Elizaveta's condition that he would not send her any more letters full of Marxist lectures. She couldn't stand them: "I'm a woman," she told him, "and I love life."

AFTER LONGJUMEAU Lenin was called to an International Socialist Bureau meeting in Zurich in September and decided to take advantage of being back in Switzerland to give political lectures in Geneva and Berne as part of his drive to raise support for a party conference. His major topic was Stolypin and the revolution. The reactionary Russian prime minister had recently been assassinated in the Kiev opera house by a Socialist Revolutionary. He gave the speech to socialist groups in Antwerp, Brussels, and Liège before crossing to London for an appearance at the New King's Hall on November 11.

He was in the city for only three days, but he could not leave without doing some work at the British Museum, where he bumped into émigré German social democrat Max Beer. They enjoyed a sixpenny lunch afterward at a popular local restaurant. Not having seen Lenin since 1903, Beer noted that he had lost weight, his "ascetic face" and "burning eyes" giving him the look of "a monk, a missionary and a crusader." Lenin had gained considerably in "fervour, self confidence and authority." After lunch the two men repaired to the nearby German Working Men's Club on Charlotte Street for a long talk about the future of the international socialist movement and the rumblings of war associated with a growing naval rivalry between Germany and Britain. Lenin was convinced that a European war would be "the prologue of a tremendous revolutionary drama." And he was determined that the revolution, when it came, should be a socialist one and not "as the Mensheviks desire, a liberal-democratic one." Beer perceived, in the dispassionate and simple manner in which Lenin hammered home his beliefs that day, something relentlessly logical, like "an accountant explaining the various items on a balance sheet."

The same unshakeable, pedantic rationale was behind Lenin's drive to call a new party conference. He had no intention of running the risk of the three-week squabble that had prevailed in London in 1907. Having laid the ground work at Longjumeau by indoctrinating his own key party workers, he was now bent on an effective coup by his Bolshevik faction at their own carefully stage-managed conference. It did not matter to him that his Bolshevik delegates would be second-rate and inexperienced compared to the leading lights of the Mensheviks. As new blood and loyal Leninists, they would rubber-stamp his effort to regain overall control of the party, and with it a Bolshevik Central Committee. After eight years of fighting to gain ascendancy in the party after the low point of 1904, Lenin had no intention of giving his rivals any opportunity to best him. Martov, Plekhanov, Axelrod, and the nonaligned Trotsky were now dismissed as being "outside the party," even though Lenin had made the token gesture of inviting them. He knew full well that they would decline to take part.

Next came a prime example of Lenin's ruthlessness. He called for the conference to take place in Prague in the heart of the Austro-Hungarian Empire, a location with no Russian colony. Stringent passport controls prevailed, and delegates from Russia might have difficulty traveling there (a couple of them were indeed arrested en route). This was part of his plan.

On January 19, 1912, eighteen delegates—eight of them students from Longjumeau, including the promising Sergo Ordzhonikidze, who had hand-picked most of the rest in Russia—gathered in strict secrecy in Prague; two Mensheviks were also admitted. The delegates were billeted with sympathetic Czech workers in the neighborhood. There were no special concessions for Lenin, who arrived without Nadya and shared a room with delegate Stepan Onufriev—two beds, a commode, a table and chairs—in the home of a worker's family who gave up the better of their two rooms for them.

The conference—or rather cabal, for that is effectively what it was— took place in a second-floor room of the People's House, a rather grand, former palace on Hybernská Street, arranged by Czech social democrats. Contrary to Lenin's expectations, the proceedings turned into a "stormy affair." Some delegates protested the exclusion of figures such as Plekhanov and Trotsky and representatives of the other émigré groups. Delegate Suren Spandaryan from Baku condemned the "cavalier attitude" of Lenin and the émigrés for exposing workers groups back in Russia to risk and discovery: "How many comrades are in prison because of that émigré squabbling?" He and Ordzhonikidze were not the only delegates to voice concerns that the émigrés were out of touch—Lenin included—and that the social democrats would do better to build their own Russian-based organization.

Lenin fought back with his usual bullying tactics and eventually got his way, thanks to the crucial support of his yes-men Zinoviev, Kamenev, and others. His motions were carried unanimously. The Prague meeting had, in Lenin's words, "constituted itself as the supreme and legitimate assembly of the entire RSDLP," but there was no disguising his shameless usurpation of the protocols of a proper party conference. At Prague Lenin was elected as a representative to the International Socialist Bureau and member of a new Central Committee that included only one non-Bolshevik (and, despite all the warnings he stubbornly chose to ignore, a suspected double agent, Roman Malinovsky). In his usual underhanded manner he later installed on the Central Committee his rising new protégé—Stalin—currently languishing in Siberian exile at Solvychegodsk.

Bolshevik participation in elections to the fourth Duma was approved, and *Zvezda* was replaced by a legal party newspaper that the Bolsheviks could use to galvanize the vacillating and disaffected membership in Russia. Lenin had no qualms about hijacking the title of a journal that Trotsky had established in Vienna. The first issue of *Pravda* (The Truth) appeared in a print run of 60,000 copies in St. Petersburg that May, with Stalin contributing the first editorial. On May 9 Lenin met with his Bolshevik colleagues in their café on the avenue d'Orléans brandishing a copy of the first issue: "Here's our mighty agitator, our propagandist and organizer," he announced with a flourish. "It will rouse the nation, and call it to victory."

Lenin's effective coup d'état against the party in Prague elicited protest among social democrats back in Paris, and the backbiting became worse than ever, as those excluded from Prague eventually set up a rival conference. In Prague Ordzhonikidze had rightly pointed up the debilitating and destructive effect on party work, even in Russia, of this "damned emigration" with its constant rivalries and "polemical antics." "We know that the emigration has failed all along to give us anything of value," he asserted. "The emigration is nothing." Lenin understood this and was already planning to move on. Having finally achieved the party split that he had initiated in 1903, he saw no reason to remain in Paris; quite apart from the constant political infighting, Paris was too expensive and their rent had just gone up. Initially he had intended to move south to the countryside around Fontenay, which he had explored by bike with Nadya. But soon he realized a more decisive break was needed. It was time to finally detach himself from the émigré centers of Western Europe. He felt an increasing need to be closer to Russia, worried as he was about his mother's frail health. His sisters had both been arrested in Saratov and could not take care of her. Perhaps this added to a growing sense of guilt that all these years he had never been there for her.

In April events in Russia played into his hands: striking miners in the Lena goldfields in southeastern Siberia were fired on indiscriminately by troops. As a result, two hundred miners were killed and many more wounded. Echoes of Bloody Sunday reverberated across Russia in an ensuing wave of strikes and rallies that culminated on May Day in a mass protest and demands for an eight-hour workday. Russia was on the move toward militancy once more. Only the previous autumn Lenin had been so discouraged that he wondered whether he would live to see the rising of the tide once more in Russia, as he confided to his sister Anna. In 1912, writing of the second wave of revolution that was developing "before our very eyes," he began to believe that he just might. His fanatical belief in the eventual victory of the proletariat was as strong as ever. He wanted to ensure that his consolidated Bolshevik Party, as it now effectively was, would be in the vanguard. Events in Prague had clearly indicated to Lenin that the Bolshevik movement in Russia was gaining strength—and credibility—without him. Realizing he might be losing control, he decided to move his operation farther east, nearer to Russia. He chose Galicia, once part of Poland, at that time part of Austria-Hungary. His two primary collaborators, Zinoviev and Kamenev, would go with him.

On June 17, 1912, Lenin, Nadya, and Elizaveta Vasil'evna left Paris suddenly, without even notifying their relatives in Russia. They sublet their apartment to a Pole and left all their furniture behind. Lenin traveled incognito as usual, wearing his bowler hat, with a bath towel under his arm containing three shirts and two toothbrushes. Nadezhda carried some parcels of books and Elizaveta brought their paltry possessions, cards, and chess set. Many in their circle could not understand why Lenin had not opted for Finland again—or even Sweden. Elizaveta de K, who was now living in Paris, thought him mad to choose Galicia, where Russians were thought badly of. But at least the border with Russia (or rather the Polish lands that were then part of the Russian empire) was only a couple of miles to the north and St. Petersburg, twenty-four hours away on an express train. The local Galician police would have no truck with the Okhrana; communications with Russia were better and their letters would be safe from interception.

Nadya was clear in her own mind that a change was a good thing: "Another year or two of life in this atmosphere of squabbling and emigrant tragedy would have meant heading for a breakdown." Life abroad had "frayed everyone's nerves considerably." Naturally she made no mention of Inessa, but her husband's affair must have added to her desire to leave Paris. In any event, Lenin and Inessa appear to have broken off their relationship at around this time, perhaps because Lenin insisted that the revolution was once more demanding their overriding attention. As dedicated revolutionists all three would have been reluctant to allow passion, sexual jealousy, or rivalry to undermine their shared political goals. We shall never know the details, but that summer, they clearly resolved their problems by a combination of accommodation, dissimulation, and discretion, sufficient to ensure that as comrades they could continue working together.

As her tenants M. and Mme. Oulianoff departed from rue Marie Rose, their concierge, like Mrs. Yeo in London before her, was sad to see them go. Never, in three years, did she have the slightest cause for complaint: "They always paid their 700 francs yearly rent most punctually."

CHAPTER FOURTEEN

"Almost Russia"

KRAKÓW–BIAŁY DUNAJEC–PORONIN: JUNE 1912–AUGUST 1914

———— ⚬⚬⚬ ————

RAIN 13 FROM VIENNA'S NORDBAHNHOF made its way slowly through the night across the Habsburg empire to Kraków. But the family was strapped for cash and could not afford the luxury of a sleeping car. They did their best to get some rest on their uncomfortable seats as the train headed north, crossing the Moravian border at Lundenburg and then turning northeast into the Polish territory of Galicia, past the city of Oświęcim (later notorious for the nearby German concentration camp Auschwitz).

After such slow and uncomfortable progress from Vienna they were glad to see the sunshine of Kraków when they emerged from the main station at 9:30 on that Saturday morning, June 22. They could sense the nearness of their homeland. Galicia seemed familiar to Lenin; it was "almost Russia!" As far as they all were concerned, their life here would be a "semiexile," for the border with the Russian empire was only a few miles away.

Leaving their luggage at the station, they headed off to meet their contact, Sergiusz Bagocki, a Russian-born Pole and former exile who was now a medical student at the university. Bagocki was secretary of the Kraków-based Committee of Aid to Political Prisoners and had plenty of contacts in the city. The rendezvous point was a short walk from the station at the city's Jagiellonian University. It was a pleasant summer day and they were not unduly anxious as they sat and waited on a bench in the Planty gardens that circled the university's medieval perimeter, watching as people promenaded past and children played on the grass.

But after half an hour, as no one appeared, Lenin's nerves began to become jangled. *They* had arrived on time. Where was their escort?

In fact Bagocki was sitting not far away from them wondering the same thing. He had never met Lenin and did not realize that the rather inconsequential-looking man sitting nearby with his dowdy wife was the political leader he revered above all others. It was only after he began pacing about nervously that Nadya plucked up the courage to inquire if he was Comrade Bagocki.

Kraków was a beautiful medieval city that until the end of the six-teenth century had been the capital of a great Polish–Lithuanian state, the seat of the Jagiellon dynasty. For centuries it had been a center of Pol-ish and Jewish culture and was resplendent still with the architecture of its past heyday, including its fourteenth-century university and medieval castle and one of the oldest Jewish quarters in Europe. In 1772, when Austria annexed territories during the partition of Poland, it became part of the kingdom of Galicia and Lodomeria. In 1815 the Congress of Vi-enna (which ended the Napoleonic Wars) gave it the status of an inde-pendent city-state, but it was formally annexed by Austria after a failed uprising in 1846. Under the aging Habsburg emperor, Franz Joseph, Gali-cia had become that empire's most densely populated, northernmost province, bordering the Polish territories of the Russian empire to the north and east, with a population mix of Jews, Poles, and Germans. It was also a hotbed of patriotic resistance to Habsburg domination.

The arrival of Mr. and Mrs. "Włodzimierz Ulianoff" from Paris at the Hotel Victoria was noted the next day in the local paper, *Czas*, but they didn't stay long. Lenin and Nadya had already decided against living in the center of Kraków, which at that time of year was hot, stuffy, and over-crowded. They both preferred woodlands and open spaces, and Bagocki booked them into the Hotel Victoria west of the city in the working-class suburb of Zwierzyniec. Eventually they decided on Salvator, the more salu-brious, newly developed end of Zwierzyniec that was home to civil ser-vants and professionals. The streets might still be unpaved and muddy, but at the end of the city tramline, at 218 Ulica Zwierzyniec, they found a pleasant first-floor apartment in a large, unfurnished detached house that they shared with Zinoviev, his wife Zina, and, much to Lenin's pleasure, their young son Stepa. Permission for Lenin to live and work in Kraków had been arranged with the Austrian interior minister Jakub Hanecki, a prominent Polish social democrat who lived just along the road.

Nadya enjoyed Zina's company on their daily trips into Kraków's vast central square with its busy market of Jewish traders inside the shopping arcade known as the Sukiennice, once a medieval cloth hall. Outside, the square was alive with the vibrant costumes of barefoot peasant women in gaudy headscarves and picturesque national dress, selling milk, cheese, vegetables, and poultry, as well as carved wooden toys and long strings of dried mushrooms. It all reminded Nadya of Russia. Lenin felt the same; to his mind, even the Jews of Galicia were like those in Russia.

Compared to the smelly and populous heart of old Kraków, where the impoverished Jews who labored in its metalworks and cigarette factories lived crowded into dilapidated old tenements and cobbled courtyards, Zwierzyniec was a paradise. Located near a lovely open stretch of parkland known as the Błonie, it was free from the disease and squalor of the working-class districts of Kraków and did not suffer from the intense heat of the city center in summer. The mighty Wisła River was a couple of miles away, where Lenin and Nadya could swim in sight of the bell towers of the sixteenth-century Bielany monastery on a nearby hilltop. And they had the pleasures too, on their doorstep, of the Las Wolski—a vestige of the vast primordial forest that had once covered much of Central Europe and for centuries had been a royal hunting forest. This last became a great favorite, where, after Lenin had finished his daily quota of work, he and Nadya could indulge in bicycle rides, as well as one of their favorite leisure pursuits—mushroom picking. In the winter, for the first time since leaving Munich, Lenin took up skating at the ice rink down the hill from the botanical gardens, often taking young Stepa Zinoviev with him. Back at the house in Zwierzyniec he regularly enjoyed games of rough-and-tumble with Stepa. What a pity he and Nadya didn't have a boy like him, he told Zina; they were both so very fond of him.

Although he openly used his real name, Ulyanov, Lenin registered with the Austro-Hungarian police as a correspondent of the newspapers *Pravda* (St. Petersburg) and *Sotsial-demokrat* (Paris).

The political atmosphere for Lenin in Kraków was a great deal more relaxed; the Austrian political system, unlike its Russian counterpart, allowed freedom of the press and democratic elections. The police kept

Lenin under discreet surveillance but observed a Ruritanian laxity that did not trouble him and his circle. Despite their chronic shortage of money, he and Nadya lived a fairly untrammeled, petty bourgeois existence that would have been the envy of many an exile elsewhere in Europe. Newspapers arrived from Russia within three days and their mail was not tampered with, although for safety's sake Lenin had many letters to him sent in care of a professor at the university. Members of Bagocki's committee acted as couriers, taking letters, journals, and parcels across the border into Russia, seven miles away. This avoided the use of foreign postage marks, which alerted the Okhrana. Local workers and peasants also acted as couriers in the border area, since the Austro-Hungarian and Russian authorities allowed them to travel back and forth across the frontier on a *polupaska* (semipassport) to their places of work or to sell goods at market.

Lenin and Nadya nevertheless drilled all activists visiting from Russia in the arts of disguise and *konspiratsiya*. A man named Shumkin took it all very seriously, walking the streets of Kraków at several paces behind them with his cap pulled down over his eyes. Nadya recalled with amusement that he looked so patently conspiratorial that he immediately attracted the attention of the Kraków police. Bizarrely, an officer called on Lenin—of all people—asking whether he knew this man and could vouch for him.

Unlike the other European cities in which Lenin and Nadya had lived, Kraków had no Russian political community, although it did have four thousand voluntary exiles—mainly Poles born in territories controlled by the Russian empire who had moved to the less repressive territories of Austria-Hungary. As Poles who followed Marx, Bagocki, Hanecki, and their fellow activists were natural allies of the vehemently anti-czarist Russians. But the Polish social democrats, like the Russians, had undergone a split. The original Polish Socialist Party was founded in Paris in 1892 with Polish nationalism and independence as its primary objectives. In 1906 it split between a Marxist faction, the PPS-Left, which adopted an internationalist program, and a right-wing group of non-Marxist nationalists under Józef Piłsudski, who dreamed first and foremost of violent insurrection and a unified and independent Poland. With many Polish socialists putting their patriotism before their socialism,

Lenin dismissed them as being of little interest except in their anti-imperialist sentiments.

Lenin felt a sense of relief at being in Kraków and liked the place, even though he considered it a backwater: "No matter how provincial and barbarous this town of ours may be, by and large I am better off here than I was in Paris," he told his family. He made no effort to learn Polish, resorting to German and sign language with the locals. He liked Polish food, especially the traditional hearty soup *żurek* and *kwaśne mleko* (sour milk), but when it came to Polish culture he remained resolutely philistine. Nadya could not persuade him to look at Polish art "at any price." Lenin's forays into the city included the occasional meeting with colleagues in the Noworolski café at the Sukiennice, although he preferred the Jama Michalika café on Floriańska. With its dark art nouveau interior it reeked of Mitteleuropa, and he and his colleagues could sit for hours in a corner and hardly be noticed.

Nadya, for her part, did at least have some rudimentary knowledge of Polish, sufficient to decipher the newspapers when needed. Her father, Konstantin Krupsky, had served in the Russian military in Poland and later returned as a government official to Warsaw, where she had lived from age two to five. But she found Polish society very Catholic, if not feudal, and was sensitive to the marginalization of Jews and the wretched poverty she saw in Kraków. Otherwise, she went about her party and domestic duties as usual, without complaint. Despite a steady stream of visitors from Russia, however, she felt lonely and isolated; by January 1913 she was complaining in letters to Lenin's family that her life was very monotonous and she had "scarcely any acquaintances here." After twelve years on the move, nothing could mitigate the increasing sense of homesickness both she and Lenin were by now suffering. In their heart of hearts, they and Elizaveta Vasil'evna longed to return to Russia, as did many of their long-term émigré friends. "We avoided speaking of this subject," wrote Nadya, "but all of us secretly thought about it."

Part of the reason Nadya was depressed was that she was far from well, experiencing palpitations, dizzy spells, and an increasing sense of exhaustion. Problems with her bulging eyes made it increasingly difficult for her to code and decode letters. To make matters worse, her elderly mother was becoming senile and was more of a burden than a help around the house. Nadya had long since trained herself to internalize her physical problems; she did not have time to be ill and did her best to hide how she felt. And Lenin, as usual, was too busy to notice. After they settled in to their new home, he reverted to the familiar routine of locking himself away for strictly regulated, uninterrupted periods of work— writing for the various Russian and émigré journals, corresponding with the editorial board of *Pravda,* which he was bombarding with articles on an almost daily basis, meeting with activists, firing off endless instructions to his Duma deputies and party workers in Russia. This was followed by periods of recreation—cycling, walking, and swimming.

But for the most part Lenin stayed at home, churning out three hundred articles and other political tracts during his time in Galicia, peppering his letters with the usual complaints: the Kraków libraries weren't up to scratch and he wished he had the resources of Geneva or London; there weren't enough connections with and news of party workers in Russia; the editorial board of *Pravda* sent him "stupid and impudent letters"; they were "pitiful dish rags" who were ruining the cause and he wanted to kick them out.

His daily life alternated between bouts of the familiar rage, stress, and impatience. He fumed when the newspapers arrived late and obsessed over his favorite bogeymen, the "liquidators" back in Russia—anyone who talked of conciliation and party reunification or, worse still, liberal reform. It was one thing to have fought in person for, and won domination over the Bolshevik faction at close quarters in Prague. But after twelve years of exile, with his energy constantly being diverted into often futile émigré squabbles, he was beginning to sense the tenuousness of his hold on the party back home. Much to his dismay, Lenin's six Bolshevik delegates to the fourth Duma elections were working closely and peacefully with the seven Mensheviks. The final split he initiated in Prague had not yet taken effect among them. By far the most pressing preoccupation, however, was his lack of money. His regular articles for *Pravda* brought him one hundred rubles a month contributor's fee, but these were now his primary source of income in the absence of literary work, which had all but dried up.

Inessa soon arrived in Kraków but stayed with Lenin and Nadya only long enough to take instructions from him on a risky new mission. He needed her to go back into Russia undercover to pass on the resolutions of the Prague conference, keep an eye on the election of his Bolshevik candidates to the fourth Duma, and find out what was going on at *Pravda*. Stalin and its other editors had been exhibiting a worryingly conciliatory line with the Mensheviks in its pages and had also turned down forty-seven of his articles and amended many others. He was fed up with writing for "the waste-paper basket" without the courtesy of being told why.

Lenin must have understood the risks Inessa took as a former political prisoner and escapee wanted by the Okhrana. Her return would invite immediate arrest, yet he made light of it. Where party work was concerned he totally disengaged from any feelings he had for her, even as the mother of five children. She and her inexperienced traveling companion Georgy Safarov (one of the newly trained Longjumeau party workers) were dispensable: "If they are not arrested, this will be useful," he wrote to Kamenev as Inessa headed for the border, disguised as a Polish peasant under the improbable false passport of Frantsiska Kazimirovna Yankevich. The mission was doomed; Okhrana agents were watching Inessa from the moment she entered Russia. Ailing and short of money, she nevertheless tramped the streets of St. Petersburg disguised in dirty boots and an old shawl, visiting underground cells. Soon she sent back word confirming that the party was in disarray. The police had greatly improved their techniques for infiltrating underground groups, and the cells had been decimated by a big wave of arrests that May. Those who survived were increasingly isolated from each other and from the party organization abroad. Many of the secret addresses used by Nadya for correspondence had been uncovered by the Okhrana or lost, and with them her network of contacts.

Within a couple of months of settling in at Zwierzyniec, Lenin became impatient with its distance from Kraków's main station and post office. In addition, the house had no gas or electricity, which was also an inconvenience. Finally, on September 2, the family moved to the city center. Their new home was on the first floor of a two-story apartment block on Ulica Lubomirskiego, a new development built in 1911 in the Wesoła district. Although it was in the city, it had an open view of the road through fields to the border with Russia in the north. Much to her pleasure, Nadya could still hear the nightingales sing. It was conveniently located for Lenin's purposes just behind the railway station, with many of his Polish socialist contacts living in the nearby streets, whose addresses were used as safe houses for party correspondence and visiting comrades from Russia.

In November Lenin decided it was time to meet with his Bolshevik six from the new Central Committee he had established at Prague, and he summoned his colleagues to his apartment in Kraków. As Duma delegates, most of them could leave Russia on legal passports, but Stalin, who only a few months previously had absconded yet again from exile in Siberia, was obliged to made his way undercover from Russia and risk rearrest. He was smuggled out of St. Petersburg in a covered cart, then crossed Finland by train on a fake Russian passport to Åbo. There he was provided with a Finnish passport and took the ferry to Germany and a train to Kraków. He went straight to Lenin's flat and received a warm welcome. But the food, thanks to Nadya's poor culinary abilities—particularly when put under pressure to feed a roomful of party workers—left a lot to be desired. Stalin was dismayed at being fed Polish sausage when he craved his favorite Georgian shashlik.

During the meeting, he found Lenin's hard-line tactics out of touch with the growing mood of conciliation within the party in Russia. After ten days Stalin returned to Russia by a smuggler's route but was back again in December after Lenin demanded a visit to discuss the nationalities question. This was one of the most pressing issues that any postrevolutionary regime in Russia would have to address. Non-Russians composed over 56 percent of the population of the czarist empire, and imposing a new socialist system across such a vast range of religious and ethnic groups would be a major task. After another long journey, Stalin arrived ravenous but took the precaution of dining out at the Hawelka on Market Square. Lenin did his best to be solicitous, even getting in bottles of beer for him, but the two men were nervous and watchful with each other. Nevertheless, Lenin saw in Stalin a loyal party worker who, as an ethnic Georgian, seemed well equipped for the role of developing Bolshevik policy on this issue.

During his second visit to Poland, Lenin invited Stalin to stay on in Kraków and write an important Leninist party paper on the nationalities question, aimed at garnering support for the Bolsheviks from minority groups in the Duma. Galicia, with its mix of nationalities, was good raw material. Stalin had little experience in writing political literature, but working under Lenin's watchful eye, he produced a document that suited his requirements. At Lenin's diktat it underlined the loyalty of all nationalities to a future federalist, socialist state, while offering token ideals of autonomy for national groups as smaller republics with the right of secession. Lenin was very pleased with the end result, and his "wonderful Georgian" headed back to St. Petersburg, where was arrested in February and sentenced to another four years in exile.

~

BY EARLY 1913 Nadya's health was in serious decline; her sense of loneliness also continued to provoke bouts of depression. Although she had seen "doctor-comrades" in the exile community who were trained physicians, no one had as yet correctly diagnosed her condition. After much persuasion by Lenin she took up Bagocki's recommendation to go to one of the best neurologists in Kraków, Dr. Jan Landau, at the neurological clinic at the university where Bagocki was finishing his medical studies. Nadya was soon writing to inform her mother-in-law that "on top of all that, it has been discovered that I have thyroid trouble." The doctor had "frightened" her by giving her three-hour sessions of "electrical treatment," electro-convulsive therapy to help counter her erratic behavior, and feeding her bromides to slow her rapid speech. But these treatments only made her feel sick and dizzy, so that "after it I wander about half the day like a lunatic." The doctor also recommended she take several months' rest in the mountains. After much discussion, in early May Lenin and Nadya traveled to the Podhale region, eighty-five miles south of Kraków, where she could enjoy the clean air of the Tatra Mountains. The cost of living there was cheap, and the quiet location would allow Lenin to get on with his writing. But he refused to make a decision until Bagocki could assure him that the postal communications by rail from there were good and would not disrupt his contact with St. Petersburg.

They settled in Biały Dunajec, a small hamlet north of the larger village of Poronin—a row of thatched cottages strung out along the road, with a couple of shops and a post office. They rented a large, chalet-style house with a veranda from a local Góral woman, Teresa Skupień, with Lenin, Nadya, and her mother taking the downstairs rooms. The upstairs, reserved for visitors from Russia, was constantly in use. Lenin made full use of the daylight, working hard until 7:00 PM. There was no electricity in the area, and reading after dark by the light of a kerosene lamp was difficult. The Zinovievs came with them, renting a house along the road in Poronin. It would have been preferable to live a little farther south on the railway line at the spa and health resort of Zakopane that nestled so picturesquely in the foothills of the Tatra Mountains, but with its exclusive sanatoriums for TB patients it was too crowded and far too expensive.

Nadya loved the Tatra Mountains, the tranquility, and the breathtaking views. The air was wonderful; the surrounding scenery ravishing, with waterfalls, fast-flowing mountain streams, lush meadows, and a backdrop of snow-capped mountains. When the weather was fine, Lenin got up early for a swim in the nearby Dunajec mountain stream. But these lovely sights were often obliterated by the rain that descended almost daily from the Tatras and swathed the entire area in a heavy mist. The weather did not, of course, deter Lenin, who was at his happiest out in the wilds on arduous hikes that were well off the tourist trail, always ensuring he had with him both straw hat, hanging on a string from his jacket, and umbrella-cum-walking stick, against either climatic contingency.

Although the mountain air was thought to help Nadya's condition, being seven hundred meters above sea level may well have stressed her weak heart. On clear days she was able to walk the incline to a vantage point at the back of their house to take in the view, but her health prevented her from taking the kind of arduous walks the couple had done in Switzerland. Yet still she put Lenin first: his nerves were "playing up" and the unimproved roads and constant rain made the area unsuitable for cycling, which frustrated him. Privately, she was relieved. It meant that Volodya couldn't "overtire himself."

Lenin always had been one for a physical challenge. He once toiled for twenty-five miles on his bicycle out of Biały Dunajec on the terrible Galician roads in order to join Bagocki for a hike up Babia Góra, one of the highest and most famous peaks in the Western Range of the Tatra Mountains. The two men nearly got lost as night descended, but luckily found a hiker's hut to shelter in. Much to Lenin's disappointment heavy rain the next morning prevented them from continuing to the top. Having got back down the mountain, he and Bagocki then had to struggle all the way home through thick mud on their bikes. Lenin remained bullish; the mountain was not going to defeat him. The first free day he had he would come back and do the job properly. Two weeks later he kept his word, this time wisely opting to travel to Zakopane on the train and bringing a lantern. Leaving the hikers hut at 4:00 AM on Lenin's insistence, he and Bagocki clambered to the top of Babia Góra in heavy mist and couldn't see a thing. Lenin patiently sat down to wait in the early morning light; suddenly the skies cleared, revealing a magnificent view of the Tatras. "There you are," he laughed. "Our efforts were not wasted." Persistence in mountain climbing, as in politics, always paid off for him.

The quiet life he led at Biały Dunajec calmed Lenin's nerves, but sometimes the remoteness made it feel like Shushenskoe, where life was reduced to counting the hours until the next mail delivery. Every day, if it was too muddy to cycle, Lenin would walk along the railway track from Biały Dunajec to the station at Poronin to collect his letters. The post office was located in a large house with wood carvings that also served as the local hotel. The postmaster, Tadeusz Radkiewicz, recalled that Lenin often used to stay for awhile, talking to the locals and visitors. His wife was amazed at the great pile of letters and newspapers Lenin carried back each time. Nobody, she said, "subscribed to so many newspapers in so many foreign languages." Then he would be off again, down the track, reading his letters as he walked.

To break the monotony of life at Biały Dunajec, Lenin often cycled down into Zakopane to use the library of the Society of the Tatras, which housed a collection of socialist writings. His main contact in town was Boris Vigilev, a Russian who had been expelled from Moscow University in 1902 for revolutionary activities. As a TB sufferer he had gone to Zakopane for his health and now worked at the local meteorological station. Vigilev introduced many of the local Polish intelligentsia to Lenin, who sometimes stayed the night with him and his wife at their little house near Zakopane station.

For some years a thriving intellectual and artistic community had been growing at Zakopane. Its members had a strong national awareness as Poles rather than Austro-Hungarian subjects and naturally gravitated to Galicia, which had increasingly become a propaganda base for Polish socialists campaigning against the Austrian government. There the Polish left had greeted revolutionary events in the Russian empire in 1905 with great enthusiasm. Galicia was a region with strong nationalist sentiments, much like those that had created the state of Piedmont, which from 1859 to 1861 had been the springboard for Italy's unification. The vibrant Góral culture of the region's free peasants, who were not answerable to landlords, was an inspiration to politicians and writers alike. In the summer months Zakopane became the unofficial regional capital of Polish intellectual life. It was no accident that the nationalist leader Józef Piłsudski, who had joined the assassination plot against Alexander III for which Lenin's brother Aleksandr Ulyanov was hanged in 1887, had a house not far from where Lenin was staying in Biały Dunajec. The Podhale region provided him with the best political and intellectual network in Galicia, and soon he would be very glad of it.

On fine days in Zakopane—which were few as the rain was persistent—Lenin liked nothing better than to sit in front of the post office on the main street, Krupówki, reading the papers. Sometimes he and Vigilev met and played chess over coffee with the local intelligentsia at their popular haunts—the Morskie Oko or the Café Trzaski. Nobody in Zakopane took much notice of the Russian-looking intellectual. Many sick ones came regularly for treatment at the sanatoriums, so it was a useful cover. In time Lenin met some of the leading Polish intellectuals of the day: the novelists Władysław Reymont and Stefan Żeromski; the poet and dean of the University of Lwów, Jan Kasprowicz, and Władysław Orkan, one of the great descriptive novelists of peasant life in the Podhale.

Meanwhile, Nadya's condition, which she had suffered so stoically for so long, was becoming acute. Lenin's doctor brother Dmitri had advised against surgery, but Lenin meanwhile had done his own research. Bagocki suggested he take Nadya to see the top expert on the condition in Berne, Switzerland. Professor Emil Theodor Kocher was no run-of-the-mill surgeon. He was a specialist in endocrinology and in 1909 had been awarded the Nobel Prize for his work on the thyroid gland; in 1912 he had donated a large sum to the founding of the Research Institute in Biology at the University of Berne. When it came to matters of personal health, Lenin never hesitated to seek the very best doctors, no matter the expense, and this applied to Nadya too. But in order to raise the money for her treatment, he had to send urgent begging letters to the editors of *Pravda* to hurry up payment for articles that had been published.

Through Russian contacts in Berne, Professor Kocher was approached and agreed to undertake the operation. Nadya was now too ill to travel alone and so in early June 1913 Lenin, reluctant as ever to leave his work, accompanied her on the seven-hundred-mile train journey to Berne, where Nadya was to undergo thyroidectomy, a relatively new procedure. Bagocki moved into their apartment for the duration to look after Elizaveta Vasil'evna, who had become, in his estimation, increasingly "helpless." Nadya was deeply apprehensive about the procedure but was in the best possible hands. By 1912 Kocher had performed two thousand thyroidec-tomies with a high success rate. The operation, although traumatic, was the only option at a time before drugs had been developed to treat the condition. Arriving in Berne on June 25, Lenin was furious to discover that Professor Kocher was in great demand, and they would have to take their turn in line. The good doctor was difficult. "He's a celebrity and likes to be begged," Lenin remarked. But worse, in such straitened circum-stances, he found himself haggling over the cost of the operation with the "tight-fisted Frau Professor."

As Nadya waited for her operation, Lenin filled the days reading med-ical books on her condition, sitting with her for a while and then disap-pearing off to the nearest library. His stress levels rose during the two weeks they spent waiting while Nadya underwent tests. On July 10 she finally underwent a thyroidectomy—without a general anesthetic. Her ir-regular heartbeat (due to a defect known as atrial fibrillation) made anes-thesia dangerous. The following day she was prostrated by a high temperature and delirium but soon began to recover.

While Nadya was hospitalized, Lenin made up for lost time, traveling to Lausanne, Berne, Geneva, and Zurich to give a series of lectures. Soon Nadya was anxious to get back to her party work and Lenin was not in-clined to dissuade her. They left Berne before she was fully recovered, al-though Dr. Kocher, oblivious to the couple's financial difficulties, ordered Nadya to rest and recuperate in the Alps for two weeks. The medical and travel costs had left them desperately short of money. Nadya fiercely re-sisted all requests to cut back on her party work and go to the doctor for regular checks. She made only one concession to her impaired health: after their return to Biały Dunajec on August 4 there would be no more long hikes for her in the mountains.

———

NO SOONER were they back from Switzerland than Lenin called a conference of party functionaries that ran from September 21 to October 1 at their house, with Lenin enlisting the owner of the Poronin inn to accommodate the twenty-two delegates. During the conference it was resolved to formally split the social democratic delegation in the Duma into Bolsheviks and Mensheviks so that the Bolsheviks could capitalize politically on a new wave of strikes and protests taking place in Russia. Despite all the efforts to observe *konspiratisya*, details of the conference were later passed back to the Okhrana by two spies in their midst.

When the conference was in full swing, Inessa arrived from Russia, much to everyone's surprise. In September the previous year the Okhrana, having gleaned what it wanted by tailing her across St. Petersburg, raided a political meeting and arrested her. She had been held in solitary confinement for six months, where the first telltale signs of tuberculosis had manifested themselves. Once more, her husband Aleksandr gallantly bailed her out. She managed to spend some time with her children at Pushkino and on holiday in the Caucasus. Then, with Aleksandr's blessing, she fled Russia for Finland, leaving the children in his care. From there she took a boat from Sweden to mainland Europe and headed straight for Galicia to join Lenin's Bolshevik circle.

Inessa was sick and exhausted, yet, as Nadya noted with admiration, "flung herself into party work with her usual ardour." After the conference, some of the delegates enjoyed mountain walks together, including a visit to the spectacular Czarny Staw, the "black lake," so called because its waters reflect the dark colors of the mountains that tower around it. Located high in the Tatras, it leads on, in a magical double concentric circle, to another even larger lake, Morskie Oko, "eye of the sea," set deep in a valley like an eyeball in a socket. As most of the group collapsed, exhausted, for lunch and a cigarette, Lenin agitated to press on to the nearest peak and did so with Bagocki in tow. Even though Bagocki was ten years younger than Lenin, he had a hard time following him as he scrambled up and down the steepest paths.

The emotional closeness between Lenin and Inessa may have peaked in Galicia during the last months of 1913, although, considering the close proximity of their colleagues, it is unlikely that they found much time alone. Paris had been different, with Lenin so often out and about across the city providing plenty of opportunities. The happy mood continued when the group returned to Kraków in October. Inessa took a room at the Kamenevs' house. Her lively presence lifted everyone's plummeting spirits, for life in Galicia was becoming very dull. Lenin and Nadya had run out of good Russian literature, having left the best of their books behind in Paris, and were yet again reading their dog-eared copy of *Anna Karenina*. Inessa played the piano for them and encouraged them to accompany her to a series of Beethoven concerts. Much as he loved hearing Inessa play the odd Beethoven sonata, Lenin's patience that year did not stretch to a full-blown concert, and he stayed for only part of one or two of them. Nadya later recalled in her memoirs that "that autumn all of us—our entire Kraków group, were drawn very close to Inessa . . . we lived together in a small, close and friendly circle." But in Kraków, what else was there to do but hang on each other's company and go out walking, rejecting as they did the more philistine pursuits of the cinema enjoyed by some of their colleagues? And so, this strange, politically united yet emotionally disjointed trio took strolls together across the Błonie.

Nadya appears to have welcomed Inessa's companionship, taking an interest in her children and often talking about them with her. Lenin worked well when Inessa was near; even mundane meetings with her brought light and happiness into his life. But before long the emotional strain, for Inessa at least, precipitated a crisis.

Planning to stay in Kraków, Inessa had written to Aleksandr asking him to send the children to her in time for Christmas. Nadya even went out flat hunting with her. But on December 18, without warning, Inessa suddenly left for Paris. Nadya tactfully suggested in her later memoirs that she had become bored with the cultural limitations of Kraków. But it is more likely that a resurgence of feeling between her and Lenin, or most certainly for her part, had led to difficulties in Lenin's marriage, at a time when Nadya had barely recovered from her thyroid operation and was feeling particularly vulnerable. Any demonstration of renewed affection between Lenin and Inessa at this time would have been very painful for her. It also would have aroused the demon of divided loyalties in Lenin—the pull of his feelings for Inessa versus their deleterious effect not just on his relationship with Nadya but also on the overriding demands of the party, which always came first.

Nadya of course could afford to be magnanimous in her toleration, even though it hurt. She had devoted her life to Lenin and he valued her selflessness; Ilyich would never leave her. But clearly Inessa had found the strain too much. A letter she wrote to Lenin in early January 1914 (but never posted) clearly conveys an end to the affair and her pain at parting from him. For once the Parisian in her did not enjoy being back in her native city; she now found Paris and all its bourgeois splendour "repugnant." It evoked too many memories of past feelings and no doubt their time together at rue Marie Rose after Longjumeau in the autumn of 1911. Being back in Paris was, for a clearly heartbroken Inessa, "somehow so final": "We have parted, you and I have parted my darling, and it is so painful. I know you won't come back here again! I feel it!" Never afraid of expressing her emotions, Inessa was candid as she had never been before: "I know only too well, as I never did before, what a big place you occupied, here, in my life in Paris." Yet even here, in a city from which she now felt alienated, she added, "I could get by without your kisses if only just to see you." But she accepted that her plaintive hopes of just seeing Lenin sometime were now dashed.

There could be no idealized ménage à trois, Chernyshevsky-style, of herself, Lenin, and Nadya, even though she might have been prepared to accept it on whatever modified terms he dictated. She dreaded being deprived of his company, but as a good and loyal Bolshevik accepted that Lenin had "carried through" their separation for reasons other than "his own sake." The fact that in her letter she immediately went on to talk of her affection for Nadya, whom she had loved "almost from the first meeting," makes the reason for their separation absolutely implicit—to avoid further wounding a vulnerable and sick woman.

For by early 1914, Nadya was suffering a recurrence of her physical problems. Her neck was swelling again and she was having bouts of heart palpitations. She wrote to Professor Kocher, who asked to see her, but she resisted the thought of another traumatic operation, not to mention the expense. The despair of her weakened physical state was compounded by her growing sense of isolation, not helped by the fact that Lenin went to Paris in the second half of January—ostensibly to "work in a library," as Nadya informed his mother, but almost certainly to try and patch things up with a wounded Inessa. The man who had previously despised Paris as "a nasty hole" now headed straight for the boardinghouse where Inessa was living. He stayed there a week, but he was accompanied by one of his Bolshevik Duma deputies, Roman Malinovsky. Nevertheless, soon after, he was telling his mother that there was "no better and more lively town to stay in for a short time" than Paris. One can only conclude, in the absence of any documentary proof, that Inessa's gracious acceptance of their untenable situation had brought about this dramatic change of opinion and a readjustment in their relationship to that of a warm friendship, for soon Lenin was sending his "very, very, very best regards" to her. Inessa was back on side once more.

We have no way of knowing how deep the wounds of her thwarted love for Lenin went or how profoundly Inessa suffered the loneliness and despair of life back in Paris that year. In the end, throwing herself back into party work was the only abiding consolation.

Lenin, having regained her affection, adjusted quickly. Work had always been a surrogate for the things missing in his life—the very things that give balance to most ordinary lives—and he had a ruthless ability to compartmentalize any emotional pain he might have felt. Soon after his return from Paris he was back in dictatorial, bureaucratic mode, writing more letters to Inessa than to anyone else in the party, relying on her loyalty and good judgment. The usual instructive missives on a wide range of party matters flowed from his businesslike pen, in which all too often he indulged his rage and bad language against his political adversaries, for which Inessa was an acquiescent sounding board. She was, after all, a good and unquestioning functionary; he trusted her and did not want to lose her. In Paris she could keep her ear to the ground on the work of conciliators and liquidators within the émigré community and ensure that Lenin's Bolsheviks toed the line. In time the Okhrana would consider Inessa to be "the right hand of Lenin," but it would become an increasingly onerous burden for her.

The peremptory commands came thick and fast that year in a torrent of letters, relieved only by the occasional placatory opening or closing allusion (where it has survived) to Inessa as his "dear friend." Inquire about this, Lenin commanded. Get hold of that. Who wrote this? Why had he not been sent the proofs of some article or other? Send me copies of this, that, and the other. When Inessa failed to respond promptly, barbed comments followed about her tardiness. "Is it the post again?" Lenin's histrionic demands for the "strict execution" of his instructions were draining Inessa dry while he continued to enjoy the unchallenging, "narrow, quiet, sleepy" life of Kraków, equally unchallenged by the other loyal female lieutenant in his life—Nadya.

Only occasionally has a passing observation of the pain he caused Inessa survived in Lenin's letters, which clearly have been tampered with and parts destroyed, either by himself or perhaps by Inessa. "If possible do not be angry against me," he implored in June 1914. Nadya, no doubt aware of what Lenin's trip to Paris had entailed, was keeping her distance from Inessa, answering her letters in an uncharacteristically perfunctory manner, despite the fact that the two women were now collaborating on a new journal, *Rabotnitsa* [The Woman Worker], launched that February. In May 1914, as Lenin and Nadya returned to the house at Biały Dunajec for a second summer, Inessa quietly disappeared from Paris for a much needed reunion and holiday with her children at a resort near Trieste on the Adriatic coast. She had not seen them for a year; Lenin must have been aware of that, yet still she was not allowed to escape his demands for long. In July he called on her to take on a difficult, if not controversial leading role, representing his interests at a forthcoming unity conference of Russian political groups called by the International Socialist Bureau in Brussels for July 16–18. While it was clear that he trusted her—as a woman—where he distrusted most of the men in his orbit, and relied on her fluent French, it was the most self-serving of demands at a time when even a loyal party worker such as Inessa was entitled to some respite. He seems to have conveniently forgotten how he himself always ensured that he had holidays when he needed them.

Sending Inessa to Brussels was an act of cowardice, a ploy to defuse a reprimand in front of the gathered members of the Socialist International on his aggressive and divisive behavior that he knew was coming. The Belgian and German socialists were after his blood, but he could rely on Inessa to be his sacrificial lamb by bearing the brunt of it. Flattering, cajoling, bullying in letter after letter, he worked hard at persuading her to attend on his behalf. If she refused to go, it would "place us in an *absolutely impossible* position." "You will manage splendidly!" he assured her. "I am positive you will carry off your important role with flying colours." Inessa was exhausted, but Lenin insisted. All she had to do, after all, was "fix up the children for 6–7 days." Besides it was essential that she, with her impeccable French, present his position at a conference where that would be the dominant language. He would work out her tactics down to the "minutest detail," even down to instructions on how to deflect Plekhanov, who enjoyed disconcerting women in the party. "Consent, do!" he urged her. "It will make a good change for you and you will help the cause!!"

Ah, the cause—always the cause! A change of scene was the last thing Inessa needed. But how could she refuse, faced with the moral blackmail of her Duty to the Party, which in Lenin's eyes transcended duty to children and family? Once again she capitulated to his demands.

Lenin wrote a speech for her, defending his Bolshevik Central Committee as representing the entire party, confident now that Bolshevik gains in the Duma had strengthened his position. Inessa was instructed to fight off suggestions of "idiotic conciliationism" and supplied with obsessively detailed notes. The International was shocked by Lenin's "impudence" when a nervous Inessa read out his report in a low voice on July 17. In it he enumerated fourteen conditions that had to be adopted before there could be unity on policy, such as closing Menshevik newspapers that opposed the Bolsheviks. Lenin's demands were arrogant and monstrous. Inessa had struggled and not been able to read the whole report in the time allotted her, but Lenin was content. "You handled things better than I could have done," he congratulated her. "Your task was heavy and . . . you have rendered a very great service to our Party." She certainly had, for he knew full well that he would have lost his temper and made matters worse. And then, having been told by another delegate that Inessa had seemed unwell, he asked if she was very tired, if she was angry with him. Inessa for once was unimpressed by Lenin's empty words and flattery. She resisted his demand to traipse all the way to Biały Dunajec and report to him on the conference in person. All she wanted to do was go back to the Adriatic to her children, and then return with them to Russia. In time this latest bout of disillusion in Lenin would fade, as party work once more took over; but for now Inessa retreated from him emotionally.

CHAPTER FIFTEEN

A Russian Spy in Galicia

BIAŁY DUNAJEC–NOWY TARG: AUGUST 1914

⊶⊷

O N AUGUST 1, 1914, Inessa's hopes for a reunion with her children, whom she had recently sent back to Russia from Italy, were dashed when Germany declared war on Russia, throwing Europe into turmoil, disrupting the railway system, and leaving her stranded a long way from home. In remote Galicia Lenin had not paid much attention to the crisis in Europe that had been escalating since Archduke Franz Ferdinand, heir to the Habsburg thrones, was assassinated on June 28 in Sarajevo. Although he had long argued that a European war would be a useful stepping-stone to revolution and civil war in Russia, he had confided to Gorky that he doubted that "Franz Jozef and Nicky will give us this pleasure." Disregarding rumors of impending war when they began circulating in Galicia at the end of 1912, he was caught napping by the rapid chain of events in the summer of 1914, as he had been in January 1905.

The Austro-Hungarians issued an ultimatum demanding a full investigation into the assassination. When the Serbs failed to supply an adequate response, the Austro-Hungarians declared war on Serbia on July 28. The government of Nicholas II immediately declared war on Austria in Serbia's defense and mobilized Russian troops on the border with Austro-Hungarian Galicia in preparation for an invasion. Soon the Russians were joined by France and Britain, under the terms of their Triple Entente of 1907. Germany joined the fray as well, already spoiling for a fight with Britain after a decade-long naval race between the two nations. In addition, it had been allied with Austria-Hungary since 1882 under the Triple Alliance with Italy.

An inevitable clash of interests—between socialist conscience and patriotic duty—now confronted the socialists of Europe. War precipitated the collapse of the European socialist movement—the Second International—as the various groups within it turned their attention to their own national war effort. Soon after war was declared in August, the German social democrats voted in the Reichstag in favor of issuing government war credits. British and French socialists, despite pockets of opposition in their ranks, similarly capitulated.

Lenin was disgusted by his fellow leftists, and his Bolshevik deputies in the Duma refused to support the czar's war. But with the German social democrats who had long dominated international socialism siding with the government, the death knell of the International had sounded. It was the beginning of the end of a European-wide socialist movement established by Karl Marx in London with the First International back in 1864, in which Lenin had regularly participated since 1905.

On August 5, when he opened the papers and saw that the German social democrats had capitulated, Lenin declared to Bagocki: "From today I cease to be a social democrat and have become a communist." It was a prophetic comment, marking Lenin's future emphasis on the militant, traditional origins of the Marxist movement. After the disastrous 1913 meeting of the Socialist International in Brussels, where Inessa had done Lenin's dirty work, it was unlikely they would miss him. For fourteen years the International had tolerated the Russians' factional quarrels and their deleterious effect on the movement in Europe. It had tired of Lenin's relentless invective and his doctrinaire pronouncements. The president of the International, Emile Vandervelde, had never liked Lenin, observing, from his headquarters in Brussels, that no one had ever paid much attention to "this little man with the narrow eyes, rusty beard and monotone voice, for ever explaining with exact and glacial politeness the traditional Marxist formulas."

When rumors of war first began to circulate, Lenin foresaw a possible move to Vienna or Stockholm, but for the time being he preferred to stay in Galicia and "take advantage of the desperate hatred of the Poles towards tsarism." He realized that the conflict between Russia and Austria-Hungary could undermine the Russian government further, now that renewed strikes and unrest were hitting St. Petersburg. *Pravda*, the victim of repeated closures, confiscations, and prosecutions, was shut down by the government in July for taking a stand against the war. Kamenev, whom Lenin had sent to Petersburg early in 1914 to edit the newspaper, had been arrested. Lenin's protégé Stalin had also had been lost to him: he had been moved to a remote settlement at Kureika in the Arctic Circle from which there was no escape, the authorities having gotten wind of his plans to flee from exile in Turukhansk.

As a resident alien in a country that was at war with Russia, Lenin could not afford to be complacent. Arriving in Galicia, he had been confident that the Austro-Hungarian authorities would not molest him; for their part the Austro-Hungarians had seen him as a useful anti-czarist weapon in their running disputes with Russia. The war changed everything, but Lenin didn't have the wherewithal to leave, with no more money coming from *Pravda* and his party salary from Russia also interrupted by the war. He hurriedly began devising a retreat to neutral Switzerland or Sweden. If the local Austro-Hungarian police did not swoop soon and inter him as an enemy alien, the Russian Southwestern Army might do far worse when it invaded Galicia.

Within days, xenophobia and spy mania spread across Europe and reached Poronin, and conservative local peasants began eying Lenin's colony nervously. The Catholic priest instructed his flock to keep an eye on the "Muscovite" group, muttering darkly about Russians "putting poison into the wells." The servant girl Nadya had hired to help around the house after Elizaveta Vasil'evna became incapacitated had been spreading gossip about them and was promptly put on the train back to Kraków. But it was not long before a vigilant Góral peasant informed the local Austro-Hungarian gendarme that he had seen the mysterious Russian gentleman who often came to Poronin sitting on a hill, writing in a notebook. Perhaps he was making strategic observations to send back to his Russian paymasters?

On August 7 the officer came and undertook a fairly inept search of Lenin's house at Biały Dunajec and found an old, unloaded Browning pistol and several notebooks full of figures and statistics—Lenin's notes for a paper on agrarian reform. Thinking them to be some kind of secret code, the gendarme confiscated them, while overlooking the lists of revolutionary activists in Galicia that Nadya kept. He ordered Lenin to accompany him to the local police station at the nearby town of Nowy Targ for questioning. The last train that day had gone, so Lenin would have to appear at Poronin station for the 6:00 AM train the following morning.

The minute the policeman left, Lenin hurtled into Poronin on his bike to consult with Bagocki, who turned to his network of Polish socialists and intellectuals in Zakopane. He and Lenin cycled ten miles to see Dr. Kazimierz Dłuski, who in 1902 had opened a pioneering TB sanatorium where Bagocki had been treated for the tuberculosis he contracted in exile in Siberia. Dłuski, who was also lobbied by Zinoviev, offered to stand as a character witness for Lenin. Back at Poronin, Hanecki was primed to enlist his local connections. If Lenin did not return from Nowy Targ the next day, having convinced the police of his innocence, then Hanecki would lobby the *starosta*—the Galician provincial administrator in Nowy Targ—as well as government bureaucrats in Kraków. Later that afternoon Lenin went to the post office, where, using his real name, he wired the chief of the Kraków city police:

> The local police suspect me of espionage. I lived in Kraków for two years, in Zwiezsynice [sic] and 51 Ul. Lubomirskiego [sic]. I personally gave information about myself to the commissary of police in Zwiezsyniec. I am an emigrant, a Social-Democrat. Please wire Poronin and mayor of Nowy Targ to avoid misunderstanding. *Ulyanov.*

That night, Lenin and Nadya were unable to sleep. In time of war "misunderstandings" such as this could be blown out of all proportion. Nothing could dispel the anxiety they both felt about the danger he was in.

The next day, on arriving in Nowy Targ, nine miles north of Poronin, Lenin was escorted to the old jail in the southwest corner of the main market square. His newfound notoriety had preceded him. Word had reached the town from Poronin and spread like wildfire, from window to window and street to street, that the authorities had arrested "a Russian spy" and were bringing him to the jail. Ten-year-old Leopold Trepper, who had friends in Poronin, was one of a gang of Jewish children who ran to the railway station to see the prisoner arrive. "A short, stocky man got out, flanked by two policemen," he later recalled. "He had a little red beard and a big cap tilted over his forehead." They followed the prisoner to the jail, which happened to be located opposite the synagogue. It was Saturday and observant members of the two and a half thousand strong Jewish community of Nowy Targ were at worship inside, but news of the "spy's" arrival did not deter the worshipers from leaving their prayers inside the synagogue to come out and take a look at him.

At the jail Lenin was incarcerated in a collective cell along with some local peasants, mainly noisy drunks, who had not paid their taxes or had let their identity papers expire. His formal interrogation was conducted by the county commissioner of police, Kazimierz Głowiński, who carefully noted the prisoner's personal effects: ninety-one kroners and ninety-nine halers (about $6.50 in today's money), a black watch, and a penknife. They took him to the photographer's studio nearby for a mug shot. It was his fourth time in prison but Lenin tried to keep his spirits up, convinced that this "silly" accusation would soon be rectified. The Kraków police, he knew, were "well aware" of his anti-czsarist sentiments and had no reason to hold him.

But while the authorities in Kraków might be sympathetic, the obtuse and bureaucratic *starosta*, when Hanecki visited him, played things stubbornly by the book. Austria and Russia were at war; this Russian had been caught with some kind of secret ciphers in his possession. Clearly he was a spy and had to be tried by a military tribunal. There was nothing he could do. The reality was deeply disturbing: held under suspicion of spying, his case, if the intercession of his influential patrons failed, would be handed over to the military court of the Kraków garrison. And there was only one possible end result: the firing squad. Back in Russia the Okhrana had been informed of Lenin's arrest and had passed on secret instructions to General Mikhail Alekseev in command of the Russian forces on the southwestern front with Galicia to arrest him at the first opportunity and send him back to Petrograd (as St. Petersburg had recently been renamed).

Although they might not have known much about Lenin before his arrest, the local intelligentsia in Zakopane started to rally to Lenin's defense. Władysław Orkan wrote to the *starosta* at Nowy Targ saying he knew Lenin personally as a respected man of letters who had been "compelled to live abroad because of his implacable opposition to the Russian authorities." Stefan Żeromski drew up a petition to the Austro-Hungarian authorities seeking Lenin's release and circulated it in Zakopane (even as his son Adam was organizing the local Polish scouts in setting up ammunition dumps in the mountains in anticipation of a Polish uprising under freedom fighter Piłsudski). The literary celebrity Jan Kasprowicz would have liked to do more, but having a Russian wife, he was under suspicion himself. Now that war in Europe was facilitating their hoped-for armed struggle for an independent Poland, these patriots sympathized with Lenin's revolutionary objectives in Russia, even though he may have cared little for their Polish nationalist dreams. Within days the jail at Nowy Targ was being bombarded with an endless stream of letters and telegrams demanding Lenin's release.

Having warned local officials that mistreatment of a distinguished international socialist could have serious repercussions, Hanecki widened his appeal to more influential contacts. He wrote to the noted Polish social democrat and lawyer, Dr. Zygmunt Marek, as well as Ignacy Daszyński, a Polish socialist and leader of the Austrian social democrat party at the Austrian parliament, both of whom had supported Lenin's move to Kraków. Marek knew how to work the legal system and insisted to the Nowy Targ police that Lenin was "blameless and trustworthy." The next step was to mobilize social democrats in the Austro-Hungarian government in Vienna to intercede on Lenin's behalf. On August 11 Marek helped Nadya compose a letter to Viktor Adler, a member of the International Socialist Bureau and leader of the Austrian social democrats, followed by another on August 14 to a prominent international socialist in Lwów, Herman Diamand. Adler was a moderate socialist who had backed the Austrian government's decision to go to war. In normal circumstances Lenin would have had no truck with him as a conciliator and "opportunist." Privately he had no more respect for Adler than he did for many of the Polish socialists now helping him, but now was not the time for political scruples. Nor was it for Adler and Diamand, who both overlooked their own ideological differences with Lenin, feeling morally bound to defend a fellow socialist who had been wrongfully arrested and whose life was now at stake.

Back in Nowy Targ, Hanecki had wangled special privileges for Nadya so that she could visit Lenin daily by train from Poronin, bringing food parcels. In between visits she struggled to pack up their things in anticipation of his release. As she did so, she had to face the hostility of locals who despite the protestations of Lenin's innocence were now gripped with war fever. Shades of the lynch mob loomed; Nadya heard the peasants coming out of church discuss what they would do to Russian spies if they got their hands on them. She and Hanecki feared that even if Lenin was released, the Góral peasants might come and finish him off. To add to the strain, her mother was sick and had become increasingly bewildered and confused. "What has happened to Volodya?" she asked repeatedly. Had he been drafted into the Russian army? She became so agitated when Nadya left the house for Nowy Targ that one of the comrades had to come and watch over her.

Practical support was to come from another and most unexpected quarter. During his twice-daily trips into Poronin Lenin had befriended the local Jewish shopkeeper, as had the other Russians staying with him at Biały Dunajec. As Yiddish speakers the Galician Jews could easily converse with Lenin for he spoke excellent German, whereas Polish remained for him largely impenetrable. All he could manage with the non–Yiddish speaking local peasants was a kind of "distorted Russian." The Galician Jews would have shared Lenin's political sympathies as a man of violently anti-czarist sentiments, since the Jews of the Russian empire had suffered greatly over the last twenty years in a wave of savage pogroms. During his time in the mountains, Lenin developed the habit of stopping off at the general store owned by Mendel (Emanuel) Singer, sometimes for supplies but more often than not simply for a chat. The shop, which had been established by Mendel's father Salomon, sold both retail and wholesale goods (to smaller stores in the region): everything from hardware to building materials, to farming equipment, household goods, and food— local favorites such as sheep's cheese, sour cherries, and freshly baked rye bread. Lenin would often sit talking to Mendel, dandling the shopkeeper's young son Alojzy on his knee. Such was their cordial relationship and the Russians' unremitting penury that Singer had long been extending credit to Lenin and his colleagues down the road.

The Jews in Poronin advised Lenin to seek the help of Dr. Bernard Cohen, a noted Jewish lawyer in Nowy Targ, to defend him if his case went to trial. Dr. Cohen had added his voice to those lobbying his friend and fellow lawyer Dr. Zygmont Marek, who by then had also been approached by the Polish socialists. Even in Poronin, the Jews came to his defense, with Mendel Singer organizing a committee of "respectable citizens" to petition for his release and collect money toward his defense.

While all this was going on, Herman Diamand traveled to Vienna, where, with Adler, he petitioned for an interview with the Austro-Hungarian interior minister, Dr. Karl Baron Heinold. Ulyanov, they assured him, was no threat but a fanatical enemy of czardom. His imprisonment would only arouse the anger of Russian workers against Austria-Hungary, while his release would encourage them to take an anti-czarist stand, which would advantage Austria by undermining the Russian war effort. After Adler and Diamand guaranteed that Lenin was no spy, Heinold wisely resolved that they were right and that Ulyanov "may render great services under the present conditions," as events in April 1917 were to show. On August 17 he telegraphed the police in Kraków ordering Lenin's release.

Lenin left Nowy Targ on August 19 after twelve days in jail; Nadya was waiting for him at the gate. Not wishing to wait around for the train, they hired a horse and cart to return to Biały Dunajec to finish packing. Lenin later made light of it all, claiming that the time he did in Nowy Targ was "very easy" and he was well treated. He had spent his days drawing on his old legal training, doing the proper socialist thing and giving fellow prisoners legal advice. At night, sitting on his iron bedsted, as Nadya later wrote, he pondered the "further course of the Party" at length and dreamed of the current imperialist war being transformed into a heroic class war of proletariat versus bourgeoisie. On his release he found that there was now an acute shortage of currency throughout Galicia. Once more out of funds, Lenin paid a visit to Mendel Singer in Poronin. The good shopkeeper needed no persuasion to lend him several hundred kroners to pay for the family's fare out of Galicia. On August 27, having sent thank-you letters to Adler and Diamand, as well as to Kasprowicz and the community in Zakopane who had campaigned for him, Lenin left Biały Dunajec.

Even after the war was over, the Jews of Nowy Targ (where Mendel and his family had opened a new store) still talked behind Mendel's back of his folly in lending money to the "Russian spy" and his wife. But Lenin did not forget the favor, any more than he did the loan from Montéhus in 1909. In 1918 Mendel Singer received a letter from the Soviet leader: "Please accept my apologies for leaving without paying you in 1914, owing to difficult circumstances. The money is enclosed. Vladimir Ilyich Lenin." Two years later, a Soviet official came to the area to retrieve the many books and papers that Lenin and Nadya had been forced to leave behind—in safekeeping in Mendel's attic.

⸺

SHORTLY BEFORE LENIN was arrested in August 1914, Józef Korzien-owski, an émigré Polish writer who had been visiting Kraków with his family when war broke out, took the last civilian train out of the city, seeking refuge in Zakopane. As a British subject he was liable for arrest and joined many other refugees heading for the Tatras, where he remained trapped until October.

By an uncanny coincidence, Joseph Conrad, the man who later immortalized the world of the Russian revolutionary in exile in his novels, passed by Lenin's door on the railway line south from Kraków on August 2. It raises the tantalizing possibility that during those five days preceding Lenin's arrest the two men may have encountered each other in one of the cafés in Zakopane, for they moved in the same intellectual circles. It was Conrad's first visit to his native Poland in forty years—and it would be his last.

This necessary but painful pilgrimage into his Polish past had been a reminder of the tragic early deaths of his parents, imprisoned by the Russians for their part in the Polish uprising of 1863. His native land held few happy memories for him and he was glad to return as soon as he could to his untrammeled exile in a farmhouse on the south downs of Kent. In contrast, Lenin, now longing to return to his homeland, had three more years of exile yet to endure. As their paths metaphorically crossed in Galicia, these two self-imposed exiles headed off along very different trajectories in history, as the Russian and Austro-Hungarian guns boomed across the eastern front one hundred miles away.

⸺

THAT SUMMER OF 1914, as the Galician authorities were becoming increasingly paranoid about the presence of Russian spies in their midst, Lenin was finally forced to confront the presence of one particularly damaging spy—or rather *agent provocateur*—among his own. All those years of coded letters, disguises, false passports, dead letter boxes, and endless complicated subterfuge—all the paraphernalia of Lenin's obsessive world of *konspiratisya*—had failed to protect his innermost circle from penetration by a double agent. Worse, it was a man Lenin had come to admire and trust.

By 1910 Roman Malinovsky, a St. Petersburg activist and secretary of the Metalworkers Union, had become a key party worker in Russia, despite heavy drinking and convictions for theft and rape. That May, when arrested by the Okhrana, he succumbed to bribery and blackmail, agreeing to become their double agent in the Bolshevik faction, code-named "Portnoy" (the Tailor). His starting salary of one hundred rubles a month rapidly rose to five thousand and later to seven thousand rubles a year, with bonuses for particularly valuable information. Over the next four years, although he was by no means the only spy in the Bolshevik ranks, Malinovsky would reveal the party names and aliases of a string of key activists in some fifty-seven reports to the Okhrana, as well as passing on details of safe houses for meetings and hiding places for party propaganda. He was soon reporting on a weekly basis, under the new but unoriginal code name of "Iks" (X) with his own personal telephone hotline to the Okhrana installed in his apartment.

Meanwhile, by 1912 he had so ingratiated himself with Lenin, impressing him with his hard work, his oratory, and his trade union connections, that at the Prague conference Malinovsky was elected to the Central Committee, delegated to the International Socialist Bureau, given a trusted position on the *Pravda* board, and leadership, that autumn, of Lenin's six Bolshevik delegates to the fourth Duma. Once he was inside the Duma, the Okhrana instructed Malinovsky to do his utmost to accelerate a Bolshevik–Menshevik split in the RSDLP. In Galicia Lenin was equally anxious to do so. For once the two sides concurred, though for different reasons: the Okhrana wishing to dilute the power of a united RSDLP front against the government and Lenin wishing to establish the authority of his Bolshevik group over all the others.

Despite Malinovsky's trusted position, not everyone in the party was taken in by his good looks and swaggering manner. He performed well on the podium and was a natural leader, but several in the RSDLP had become suspicious of him, and in 1913 the Menshevik Martov openly denounced him as a spy. Lenin refused to listen to the growing chorus of doubt, even in the face of suspicious arrests in Russia—notably of Ordzhonikidze in April 1912 and two of Lenin's best lieutenants, Yakov Sverdlov in February and Stalin in March 1913. In each case Malinovsky had been one of the few people privy to the details of their movements in the underground.

In early May 1914 Malinovsky's nerve finally broke. Trying to juggle the two roles and fearing exposure, he had begun drinking heavily. The Okhrana had become uneasy about the success of his militant speeches in the Duma. They began to undermine his value as a double agent by "pour[ing] water on the millwheel of revolution." If Malinovsky were revealed as a government agent, the Duma would be deeply compromised. They ordered him to resign.

Much to Lenin's consternation, Malinovsky left the Bolshevik Duma faction in disarray before heading for the frontier, the Okhrana having paid him off with six thousand rubles, a passport, a revolver, and a ticket out of Russia. (The remaining five Bolshevik deputies were later arrested for opposing the war.) In the meantime, Vienna-based Nikolay Bukharin, another up-and-coming Bolshevik theorist, had added to the voices questioning Malinovsky's loyalty, convinced that his own arrest in Tula in 1911 had been engineered by him. He came to Biały Dunajec to persuade Lenin of the fact and recalled how unsettled he was by it all. Matters were brought to a head when Malinovsky himself turned up soon after. As Malinovsky hung around in Poronin lonely and alienated from the rest of Lenin's circle, Lenin pondered his options. Bukharin heard him pacing the floor in the room below his at night. The next morning Lenin greeted him as though there was nothing wrong, but he looked haggard. He had, as Bukharin concluded, "simply put on the armour of his iron will" and refused to believe the allegations. "Nothing," as most in Lenin's entourage had long since discovered, "could ever break through it." Lenin's continuing state of denial was deflected into one of his characteristically shrill newspaper pieces denouncing it all as a dirty, malicious slander and a Menshevik plot. He was backed up in his conclusions by Zinoviev and Hanecki, who likewise toed the line, vouching for Malinovsky's "political honesty."

In the end Lenin was forced to hold a summary tribunal and made the token gesture of expelling Malinovsky from the Bolshevik Party, not on suspicion of being an *agent provocateur* but for abandoning his colleagues in the Duma. To admit that he had been such a bad judge of Malinovsky's character would have been damning for the leader of the Bolsheviks. Ejecting Malinovsky, however, was not sufficient to dispel the bad atmosphere created by the affair. Malinovsky's suspected betrayal had been allowed to go on too long; he had caused too much damage, poisoning the atmosphere surrounding Lenin and his entourage at a crucial time of political crisis in Europe. Preoccupied with this, the "fetid back parlour of revolutionary politics," Lenin had allowed himself to be hoodwinked. His political acumen had let him down at one of the most important turning points in history.

CHAPTER SIXTEEN

"This Damned Switzerland"

BERNE: SEPTEMBER 1914–FEBRUARY 1916

⸻

Lenin and Nadya stayed on in Kraków only long enough to witness with horror the arrival of the first batches of wounded from the front. By late August Viktor Adler managed to arrange military papers for Lenin, Nadya, and Elizaveta Vasil'evna to travel to Vienna, where they could obtain the relevant documentation for a return to Switzerland. Before leaving Kraków, they hastily packed up the manuscripts, Central Committee archives, and other party papers that they had been able to bring back with them from Biały Dunajec and left them for safekeeping with their Polish comrades. On August 29, with an overwhelming sense of weariness, they boarded yet another train, heading for yet another modest apartment, somewhere in yet another European city. Neutral Switzerland was the closest and only option. During their brief stopover in Vienna, Lenin went in person to thank Viktor Adler for his intercession, and Adler recounted his visit to the interior minister. "Was he absolutely convinced," Heinold had asked him, "that this Ulyanov was an enemy of the tsarist government?" Oh yes, replied Adler, "a more implacable enemy even than your excellency."

The rail journey to Switzerland was unbearably slow, with the train constantly being shunted aside to make way for military convoys. On September 5 the family at last arrived in Zurich. This, however, was not their final destination; Zurich was too expensive and was filling up with Russian exiles from war-torn Europe. With their income from Russia cut off by the war and finding it difficult to sell articles or translations, the family faced serious financial problems. Lenin wasn't able to get his hands on the Shmit money being held by the German social democrats, which might have helped defray his party expenses. The only thing that saved them from destitution was a four thousand ruble legacy—the life savings of Elizaveta Vasil'evna's recently deceased sister, a frugal teacher in Novocherkassk. A clever banker in Vienna managed to transfer the money out of Galicia for them—while retaining half of it for his services.

The thought of being back in bourgeois Switzerland was discouraging. The couple decided to go to Berne, "a dull little town," wrote a resigned Lenin to Inessa in late September, "but . . . better than Galicia and the best there is." At least he would have access to good libraries again. He had missed them.

On October 16 the family moved into two furnished rooms on the Distelweg, "a tidy, quiet street" in the Längasse quarter near the Bremgarten forest; the Zinovievs found a place nearby. They rented their rooms from a woman who took in ironing, but they were so small that for a while they ate in a nearby subsidized student canteen, which charged only sixty-five centimes for dinner. In return for the discount they took turns washing dishes twice a month and performing other menial duties, from which Lenin, despite the comrades insisting otherwise, refused to be exempted.

Inessa too was living in Switzerland, still on the run from the Russian police. Her tuberculosis had taken her to a mountain resort at Les Avants at the eastern end of Lake Geneva. Hearing of Lenin's departure from Galicia, she moved to Berne when he and Nadya arrived, taking an apartment about ten minutes' walk away on Drosselweg. Lenin ostensibly enlisted her to work on projects relating to socialist women as well as putting her linguistic skills to good use in the international socialist movement. Whatever her party skills, there was by now an inevitability about Inessa and Lenin's constantly fluctuating relationship and their enjoyment of each other's company that Nadya accepted and was drawn into. That autumn, the trio who had enjoyed walks on the Blonia together in Galicia kicked the yellowing leaves across the forest roads of Berne in comradely fashion, so Nadya later wrote, while Lenin expounded on his plans for the international struggle ahead.

With his long-standing female backup team of Nadya, Inessa, and the now declining Elizaveta Vasil'evna in place, and to temper his frustration at the lack of news from Russia Lenin once more retreated into his research, taking little interest in the ongoing war. Although impoverished, his life, now back in this "damned Switzerland," actually became cozy, bourgeois, and dull. "Sleepy Berne" was conducive to work, particularly with the first-class facilities of the Swiss National Library on his doorstep. The libraries were welcome surrogates now that the mail and newspapers from Russia were becoming increasingly intermittent. The past, as always, held far more interest for him than the present, as he threw himself into a renewed interest in the philosophy of Hegel and Aristotle, Shakespeare and the poetry of Goethe, Byron, and Schiller. He even studied aesthetics—John Ruskin's writings on painters. To generate some income through journalism, in November he revived the émigré newspaper *Sotsial-demokrat* (discontinued in 1913) and managed to get a major article on Karl Marx placed with the Russian *Granat* encyclopedia, urging his brother-in-law Mark Elizarov to press for prompt payment on his behalf.

Politically, Lenin now turned to a series of pamphlets and letters condemning the "bourgeois chauvinism" of the war. *The Tasks of Revolutionary Social Democracy in the European War* and *The War and Russian Social Democracy* were the first of many condemnations of the German social democratic sellout. Lenin called for the czarist monarchy to be defeated and the imperialist war turned into a European civil war. These and other "defeatist" propaganda tracts were smuggled into Russia via the Bolshevik underground, which had been relocated under Aleksandr Shlyapnikov to Stockholm. But as the war continued, maintaining this network in the face of the increasingly vigilant Swedish police became more difficult.

To Lenin, the war raging in Europe was a clear manifestation of the final, imperialist stage of capitalism long predicted by Karl Marx. Russian socialists had a duty to propel this imperialist war from the trenches to the final stage in his longed-for scenario: nothing less than an all-out civil war across Europe between the proletariat and the bourgeoisie. The troops in the front lines must turn their guns on their officers.

From his base in Berne Lenin took his message to the exile groups of Switzerland—Lausanne, Geneva, Zurich—arguing against the "bourgeois reformism" in Russia that threatened to obstruct the path of revolution by settling for parliamentarianism and legality. If he nursed a fear, it was only that the war would not last long enough to develop into a European revolution. But as the war continued, the Russian émigré camps began lining up against each other as so often before.

The antiwar camp was led by Lenin and his circle of Bolsheviks in Switzerland, while the social patriots—Plekhanov and Lenin's erstwhile colleague (that "swine") Potresov—were supporting the monarchy's military campaign. Plekhanov would have been only too glad to join the army, he declared, if he were not "too old and sick." Plenty of eager Russian exiles in Paris were even now signing up for the French army. Knowing this, Lenin made sure he was in the audience at a crowded political meeting at the Maison du Peuple in Lausanne when Plekhanov gave a keynote speech defending the governments of France, Belgium, and Britain deciding to take up arms against German aggression. White with intensity, his screwed-up eyes glittering with fury, Lenin took the floor in response. Clutching a glass of beer in his hand, he vehemently defended his belief that it was the duty of all social democrats to turn the war into a conflict between the proletariat and the ruling classes. Events in Europe were moving inexorably toward his goal, or so he now believed. Soon afterward, therefore, he drafted a program under which a future Bolshevik government would immediately withdraw Russia from the war, nationalize the banks and the land, and introduce an eight-hour working day. The Germans, by now au fait with the circumstances of Lenin's release at Nowy Targ, were already receiving intelligence from agents in Switzerland of Lenin's potential usefulness to them in sabotaging the Russian military campaign, and they were looking at ways of secretly funding Bolshevik subversion. Russia was the weakest link in the Triple Alliance. As for Lenin himself, capitulation to Germany was perfectly acceptable in his book if it precipitated the end of czarism in Russia, which he believed was "a hundred times worse than kaiserism."

With such thoughts increasingly preoccupying him, early in 1915 Lenin unexpectedly found himself drawn into a quite different debate with Inessa Armand. Prompted by a discussion of love and marriage with her daughters Inna and Varvara the previous autumn, in late 1914 Inessa had begun work on her own feminist-socialist discussion of the family, free love, and women's rights in marriage. She had long wanted to write a doctoral thesis on the subject and the first opinion she sought on the draft was, naturally enough, Lenin's. She anticipated a sympathetic response but the one she received was harsh and tactless in its demolition of what for her was an important discussion of sexual intimacy.

Even in a socialist tract, such a subject would have had uncomfortable personal overtones for Lenin. Sexuality was *not* a Marxist subject and he responded in the only way he could—with dry and dispassionate theory, dismissing Inessa's arguments out of hand in typically doctrinaire, even puritanical fashion. She was politically incorrect in her interpretation of "free love"; it was a bourgeois concept, not a proletarian one. Such an immoral, self-interested pursuit all too often brought with it promiscuity and adultery, in his opinion.

Inessa's angry defense exposed her Achilles' heel—a romantic psyche not attuned to the self-denying rigors of party life. Surely even fleeting passion was "more poetic and pure than the loveless kisses exchanged as a matter of habit between husband and wife," she argued. Lenin's response was to nitpick, pointing out that she made no real distinction between the "loveless kisses" of marriage and the "loveless kisses of a fleeting passion." Weren't both equally reprehensible? But his main cavil was political—that Inessa had overlooked the class angle in her argument. The only logical and objective solution to the question of "free love," based on strictly Marxist class principles, was civilian marriage—with love—between true proletarians devoted to a shared cause. In other words, the relationship he had with Nadya.

Lenin's rejection of Inessa's fundamental belief in the honesty of love above all must have cut to the quick, for it had prompted her to leave her husband Aleksandr in 1905, driven by a consuming passion for his brother Vladimir. Lenin's response revealed a side of him she had not seen before and brought home to Inessa how little the need for love figured in Lenin's life. For all-too-brief a time he had succumbed sexually and emotionally to his attraction to her; from now on she would have to come to terms with inhabiting only a corner of his affections. He alluded to this in a rare admission that his "experience of the *most complete* friendship and *absolute* trust was limited to only two or three women," she no doubt being one of them. That was as far as it would ever go with him.

Meanwhile, Inessa had work to do. On March 26–28 she was to represent the Bolsheviks at an International Conference of Socialist Women held in the Volkshaus in Berne. Although as a man he was excluded, Lenin made sure he controlled what his female delegates—Nadya, Inessa, and Zina Zinovieva—did by sitting the conference out in the café downstairs, firing off instructions at every juncture and ensuring that though they lost the vote, his trusty delegates split the conference, overriding the largely pacifist sentiments of the women gathered there by propounding Lenin's highly inflammatory calls for revolution and civil war.

Lenin was short of Bolshevik delegates at the Socialist Youth Conference, held in the same venue a week later, but he again commandeered Inessa to speak for him, although at forty-one she was hardly a "youth." Once again, Lenin hovered in the café below and sent Inessa in on the third day with a tough counterresolution to the conference calls for peace in Europe. The Bolsheviks again lost the vote, but their opposition was published in the official record. As with the women's conference, the public restatement of Lenin's leftist position enhanced his growing political profile.

In the spring of 1915 Lenin, Nadya, and Elizaveta Vasil'evna all went down with influenza, from which the latter never fully recovered. Nadya's mother was now chronically sick and shrunken and showing the unmistakable signs of senility. For some time she had longed to go back to Russia, but Lenin and Nadya had refused to allow it as there was no one there to look after her. And so she had resolved to sit it out and go back with them when the time finally came. But on the night of March 20 she died in her sleep at the age of seventy-five, having diligently served the cause by coding and decoding letters, sewing special skirts and waistcoats for carrying illegal literature, scrupulously shredding mountains of party documents, cooking and cleaning as loyal helpmate and comrade.

A rather different version of the story circulated in Russia for many years after the revolution. During her mother's last illness Nadya had sat up with her night after night. She was exhausted and asked Lenin to relieve her so that she could get some rest, insisting, however, "Don't fail to wake me up when mother needs me." Lenin promised to do so, drew his chair alongside Elizaveta's bed, and settled down with his books. During the night, as he sat there engrossed, Elizaveta quietly died. When Nadya emerged the following morning to take over once more, Lenin told her that her mother had died in the night. Nadya was heartbroken: "Why didn't you wake me up?"

"But I acted strictly in accordance with your instructions," he responded. "You wanted to be awakened in case your mother needed you." Elizaveta Vasil'evna had died and, quite simply and logically, "did not need her any more."

Lenin's coldly pragmatic response hid a genuine sorrow at his mother-in-law's death, even though she had constantly complained that Lenin would kill both "Nadyusha" and himself with the hard life they led. Elizaveta Vasil'evna had often quarreled with Lenin over religion, but the long years in exile had changed all that. "I was religious in my youth," she told Nadya, "but as I lived on and learned life, I saw it was all nonsense." With this in mind, she requested that she be cremated after her death, a practice only legalized at the turn of the century and still frowned on, particularly in bourgeois Switzerland. On March 23, Nadya and Lenin sat and waited at the crematorium. Two hours later they were handed a "tin can" full of her mother's still warm ashes, which they buried in the Bremgarten cemetery. Another tie with Mother Russia was lost to them.

Lenin and Nadya returned to their lodgings at Distelweg to discover they were now persona non grata with their landlady, who was horrified that Elizaveta Vasil'evna had not been given a decent Christian burial. She asked her tenants to leave; she wished to rent the room to "believers." They found a small apartment not far away on Waldheimstrasse. It was sunny and pleasant and they got on well with their new landlady. But it didn't last long; Nadya was very sick again, experiencing a lot of heart pain, her condition no doubt aggravated by grief over her mother's death. She consulted another distinguished specialist—Professor Hermann Sahli in Berne—but, much to her relief, he did not favor surgery. He looked upon her condition as being partly psychosomatic, preferring to treat the condition as stress-related, requiring sedatives and a good rest in the mountains. Lenin therefore sought out a suitably cheap retreat away from the tourist resorts, settling on the Hotel Marienthal at Sörenberg in sight of Mount Rothorn. It wasn't a particularly scenic location, just a few houses scattered along one long street, and the fifty-mile journey there at the beginning of June was tortuous to say the least—by post coach to Flühli and then by hired carriage, courtesy of the restaurant owner in Flühli, to their hotel. With money so short, the five francs a day full board had been the cheapest they could find. Inessa soon joined them, loaded with Lenin's special requests—French novels, dozens of a particular kind of large envelope, citric acid crystals (*zitronensaüre*), and details of the overnight huts in the mountains for hikers run by the Swiss Alpine Club.

Inessa stayed on with them until autumn. The residents did not know what to make of this strange Russian with his trio of women (Inessa's colleague Lyudmila Stal' joined them from Paris for a visit) and the fact that he was spotted bathing nude in the nearby Emme River. But the group kept to themselves, rising early and going to bed "with the roosters." They never undertook any of Lenin's long overnight hikes but did walk up on to the Rothorn on several occasions. Nadya must have been feeling better, for even this hike, modest by Lenin's standards, took eight hours. It was worth it for the views of the Bernese Oberland and Lake Lucerne. They also spent time picking berries and mushrooms in the forest. In the mornings Inessa played the piano, wrote letters to her children, and in the privacy of her room continued her work on love and the family. Lenin did not appear to do much party work; he read novels by Victor Hugo and often borrowed a bike and went off on his own.

Six months of rest and recreation in the mountains—even for the sake of his wife's health—did not go down well later with Lenin's hagiographers. With a war in Europe and Russia once more sliding into crisis, they had to convince the communist faithful that Lenin did more at Sörenburg than just pick mushrooms and enjoy the view. The truth was that he was far more preoccupied with abstract theory than the terrible slaughter going on daily at the front. He never was able to identify with human suffering in all its brutal reality but only with the collective masses in an abstract way. There was only one thing about the war that interested him: what would follow in its aftermath. From Sörenburg he supposedly pursued party work, correspondence, and political study, having books sent by post from libraries in Berne and Zurich. But he did not produce anything significant, publishing only four articles, although during the war he crammed twenty-three notebooks full of his political and economic musings.

On around September 2 Lenin and Inessa left Nadya at the hotel to travel to a major conference called by Swiss and Italian social democrats at Zimmerwald. Lenin wanted to get there early to lobby Karl Kautsky's delegates as they arrived. Kautsky was a Marxist intellectual whom Lenin had venerated in the *Iskra* years and for whose German publications he had written articles. But Kautsky's group had now joined its leader in putting their patriotism before their socialism. To Lenin, these cowardly "Kautskyite shitheads" were heading down the road of "bourgeois pacifism."

The dislocations of war inevitably affected attendance numbers at the congress. Only thirty-eight delegates were able eventually to gather on September 5 at the Volkshaus in Berne; the British, American, and French contingents had been refused permission to travel by their governments. Those who did get to Switzerland were taken by horse-drawn carriage to the Calvinist village of Zimmerwald six miles away, which comprised a few farms and a hotel-pension, the Bon Séjour. Here they were booked in, unconvincingly, as members of an "ornithological society" and would be cut off from letters from the outside for the duration. The parochial aspects of it prompted Trotsky, who was there as an independent, to observe that "half a century after the founding of the First International, it was still possible to seat all of the internationalists in four coaches."

Lenin arrived, suitably dressed with rucksack on his back, looking like "a Swiss mountaineer." He was determined to use the first major wartime conference of the Socialist International as a forum for his Marxist position on the war, irrespective of the pacifist voice rising within the movement. However, he and Zinoviev (Inessa was there only as interpreter) had to share the eight Russian votes with the Mensheviks Axelrod and Martov, two Socialist Revolutionaries, the unaligned Trotsky, and a Latvian representative. The first couple of days followed the usual pattern of endless procedural bickering. Karl Radek, the Polish representative now making his mark alongside Lenin on the left, fired the first volley in the opening address. Revolution, not peace, should be the objective of the present war, he said, for only a socialist revolution could bring a genuine and lasting peace. Angelica Balabanoff was impressed once more with Lenin's verbal and polemical skills, demonstrated in his persistent interruptions and attempts to introduce his own counterresolutions at every twist and turn of the agenda. But she found such political tactics primitive in their stubborn single-mindedness, and his use of his subordinate Zinoviev to perform "unfair factional manoeuvres" distasteful. As the meeting moved toward the final vote, Balabanoff remembered how tense the atmosphere had become in that "small, dark, enclosed, smoke filled room, on a drear, cloudy autumn night." The delegates were exhausted, she recalled, "scraps of paper lay about on the tables—the work was completed, but the weariness was so great that almost no joy could be taken in its realization."

Lenin failed to win a majority on his uncompromising resolution to turn the imperialist war to a civil war, with delegates unwilling to appear as traitors back home by voting against their national war effort. But the resulting manifesto issued by the conference (Lenin's militant draft having been rejected), while not satisfying his lofty demands, did at least uphold the ongoing struggle. "The war-makers lie when they assert that the war would liberate oppressed nations and serve democracy," it declared. "The real struggle is the struggle for freedom, for the reconciliation among peoples, for socialism."

As the delegates dispersed after this, the third conference that year during which Lenin's extreme left position had bulldozed its way into the agenda, it was now clear that he was the undisputed leader of a small but determined faction in the International that would henceforth be referred to as the "Zimmerwald Left." The conference had been initiated with every good intention of creating unity among socialists in time of war. But instead, Lenin's faction of eight had broadened the growing schism between the moderates and the left, driving a controversial political wedge between them, underlining the failure of international socialism to find a common voice and setting the political tone in Europe for a century to come. He left as he had arrived, stick in hand and rucksack on his back, to rejoin Nadya at Sörenburg. He was as exhausted as he had been after the 1907 congress in London. The next day they went for a walk up Mount Rothorn where, having reached the top, Lenin promptly lay down and fell fast asleep. Nadya sat there for an hour watching the clouds break over the Alps as her husband slept "like the dead."

BY SEPTEMBER Nadya's thyroid trouble was better. She and Lenin had intended to stay at Sörenburg until autumn, but bad weather appeared early in October. Back in Berne, they were forced to confront their old demon: money. They were so hard up that life had become "devilishly difficult" and they were forced to move to even cheaper accommodation: a sparsely furnished single room with electricity and bath on the third floor of a house at 4a Seidenweg. While Lenin went off to give fee-paying lectures in Lausanne, Geneva, and Zurich, Nadya tried to get work tutoring or writing. She produced a pamphlet on the elementary school and democracy and asked her sister-in-law Mariya in Russia to try to get it published. Lenin also suggested they try to obtain a commission to jointly write a pedagogical dictionary. In January 1916 their circumstances were so straitened that they were not required to pay the two hundred franc fee when they applied to extend their residence permit.

Early that year Inessa, once more under pressure from Lenin, returned to her party work in Paris, having already more than served the party at four contentious socialist conferences in 1915. Her task now was to liaise with antiwar French socialists on Lenin's behalf in hopes of building his Zimmerwald Left. As far as the French Sureté agents who tailed Inessa were concerned, Inessa was *la maîtresse de Lénine*. She had a difficult time in Paris trying to raise support for Lenin's antiwar stance. He meanwhile grew impatient for results and was annoyed by her silences. Inessa resolutely ignored his letters demanding news, his expressions of faux "surprise" when he heard nothing from her, and his halfhearted queries about whether he had "offended" her or whether she was ill. In fact she was fed up with being constantly placed under enormous pressure to produce results. Ultimately she was able to report some limited success with socialist youth groups and a couple of trade unions.

Lenin's response was dismissive. He had expected Inessa to achieve nothing less than a split among French socialists for and against the war. For Inessa this must have been the final insult, particularly in view of the risks she had taken in returning to Paris during wartime—a city not known for pacifist sentiment. An angry postcard to Lenin prompted nothing but a scolding for her "fit of temper" (ironically, he was a far worse hostage to rage). Coming so soon after his profoundly wounding criticisms of her pamphlet on love and the family, it provoked in Inessa a deep depression which clearly transmitted itself to Lenin—if only by her silence. He continued to express genuine enough concern for her health in the letters that followed, but once her mission in Paris was over Inessa retreated from him, just as she had in December 1913.

CHAPTER SEVENTEEN

"One Fighting Campaign After Another"

ZURICH: FEBRUARY 1916–APRIL 1917

———— ⊸∞⊶ ————

B
Y EARLY FEBRUARY 1916 life for Lenin and Nadya at Seidenweg was becoming difficult. They didn't get on with their landlady, who exasperated them with all kinds of demands, so they decided to spend a few weeks in Zurich where Lenin could use the libraries. Moisey Kharitonov, secretary of the Zurich Bolshevik section, met them at the train and invited them to live with him and his wife but Lenin and Nadya refused. One of the reasons was Lenin's concern that the postman would have to cart their considerable amounts of mail up four flights of stairs several times a day.

Instead, they rented a room in a boardinghouse in the city center, taking their meals nearby on Geigerstrasse at a small eating house on the second floor of a dilapidated old house near the Limmatquai run by a buxom blond, Frau Prelog. The dining room was little more than a dimly lit corridor with bare walls and rough wooden tables, and it smelled "more like a mouldy cellar than a restaurant." Lenin, however, seemed to like its plebeian qualities and the fact that his coffee was served in a cup with a broken handle.

He and Nadya soon discovered that aside from the unappetizing thin soups and dried roasts, they shared their dining room with a prostitute and other undesirables, what Nadya described as "the lower depths of Zurich." Red Maria, so named for her long, golden red hair, regularly regaled them both with stories of how she had turned to prostitution to support her old mother and younger siblings. The war, she complained, had taken her soldier lover from her; it was "nothing but a robbery of men, a dirty trick invented by the rich," at which Frau Prelog would chime in, saying she couldn't understand why the soldiers didn't shoot their officers and go home. Such forthright comments were music to Lenin's ears, as young Romanian socialist Valeriu Marcu noted on sharing a meal with him there. Lenin's face shone with pleasure; Frau Prelog was, in his opinion, quite "magnificent."

An advertisement for a cheap room on the notice board at the Zur Eintracht—a workers club set up by Swiss social democrats where they also went for cheap lunches—took Lenin and Nadya to new accommodation on Spiegelgasse. Within a couple of weeks they had decided to stay in Zurich. They enjoyed the buzz of the city after the unchallenging peace and charm of Berne. The lakeside and nearby Zürichberg—a wooded hillside overlooking the city—were great favorites for walks. The city was even better served by libraries than Berne, with a fine public library, the Center for Socialist Literature, and the cantonal archives in the neo-Gothic choir of the Predigerkirche, a seventeenth-century church. There were also plenty of cheap eating places and lively political discussion clubs in the vicinity.

In this, the last year of his exile, Lenin's peregrinations came fittingly full circle. Zurich, a great cultural center at the heart of the Protestant Reformation of the 1520s, was now a busy financial and commercial center, as well as the de facto cultural capital of Europe during the war years. In the 1870s it had seen an influx of Russian student exiles with the arrival of two revolutionary heroes—the anarchist Mikhail Bakunin in 1872 and the revolutionary socialist Petr Lavrov soon after. It had been the first foreign university city to welcome young Russian women, many of whom came to study medicine at a time when university education in Russia was closed to them. The Russians congregated together in a particular part of Zurich—the Oberstrasse near the Polytechnic, living in the same extreme poverty as their fellow exiles in Geneva. The outbreak of war in 1914 had seen a sudden influx of Russian immigrants from other exile communities in Europe. And such now was their impoverishment that a Committee of Social Salvation had been set up to rescue many of them from starvation. Lenin and Nadya too were struggling; the cost of living "makes one despair," Lenin wrote to his sister Mariya. The inheritance money from Nadya's aunt had almost run out and war had brought rising prices and higher exchange rates. Shortage of money therefore brought them to a small, dark room overlooking an equally dark courtyard up a dingy staircase at 14 Spiegelgasse.

The five-story house, with its low ceilings and green wooden shutters, was sixteenth-century in origin and had a restaurant, the Jakobsbrunnen, on the ground floor. It was located on a narrow, cobbled alley lit by old cast iron lanterns. They shared the building with an assortment of tenants, their room sublet by the tenants of a flat on the second floor—a shoemaker named Titus Kammerer, who ran his business from number 12 next door. Barely six feet across the alley were a cabinetmaker, a laundry, and a secondhand book shop. Here, in the heart of the old medieval city with its winding alleys, the closely packed, gabled houses with top floors overhanging the walkways were perpetually dark and dank. The winter was bitter when Lenin and Nadya moved in, and they had no heating. Their room was perpetually dark, which meant they either had to go to the expense of burning kerosene lamps during the day or seek shelter in the nearby library. They had a single table to eat and work on, a sofa, and a couple of chairs, so when visitors arrived they had to sit on the beds. They couldn't open their windows even if they wanted to, for on the other side of the courtyard at the back was a sausage maker, and the stink of boiling bratwurst pervaded the street during the day.

The smell might have been terrible, but Spiegelgasse had its compensations. It was only a few minutes' walk from the libraries, where Lenin now spent his days from nine until twelve, returning home for lunch and then promptly reclaiming his seat at two to make the most of the afternoon sessions. Their landlords the Kammerers were wonderful: kindhearted and down-to-earth. They and their three sons happily watched out for the postman and took in the mail at their shop next door when Lenin and Nadya were out at the library. They also proved to be as vocal in their socialist and anti-imperialist sentiments as Frau Prelog and Red Maria. As soon as he had heard Frau Kammerer declare that "the soldiers ought to turn their weapons against their governments," nothing would induce Lenin to leave. He had wanted all along to live with a "Swiss working-class family," ignoring the fact that the Kammerers, as shopkeepers, were decidedly petty bourgeois. And even though they could have found someplace better for the same twenty-eight francs a month (they'd managed to haggle the price down from thirty), here they were among friends.

Titus Kammerer, while concerned at how "very plain" the Ulyanovs' lifestyle was, considered Lenin "a good fellow"—strong and stocky with "a neck like a bull." One of his sons remarked that if Lenin's thick neck was a sign of willpower, then he "must possess an iron will." Kammerer and his wife had been apprehensive when Nadya had inquired about the room because she was "of the Russian type" and rather unprepossessing. But they soon discovered she was "a good soul" and felt sorry for her. She was sick a lot of the time and didn't take care of herself. "Mrs. Lenin would have been a good *Hausfrau*," they concluded, "but she had her mind always on her other work." She still managed to burn even the simple pan of oatmeal they were reduced to eating for lunch. "There!" remarked Lenin with a chuckle to his landlord. "You see, we live in grand style. We have roasts every day." All the "Lenins" ever seemed to have at lunchtime was oatmeal or boiled potatoes; in the evening it was "tea and buttered bread." Meat was a special luxury reserved for Sundays.

The family took pity. Frau Kammerer taught Nadya how to cook cheap and satisfying meals in her own kitchen, "a narrow intestine of a room" where there was barely space for the two of them. Noticing how worn out Lenin's boots were, Titus made him a pair of "very coarse, solid shoes," reinforced with thick nails for hiking. Lenin wore them all winter; whenever he went out in his boots and his worker's cap "one would have taken him for a mechanic," observed Herr Kammerer. That winter, as Nadya later recalled, they were so short of money that their sole indulgence—which they enjoyed on Thursdays when the Predigerkirche was closed—was the two bars of nut chocolate they bought before heading off for a walk on the Zürichberg. Such, now, was the "doubly rigid economy in our personal life."

<hr>

AT THE END OF APRIL 1915 Lenin attended a follow-up conference to Zimmerwald held at the Hotel Bären in Kienthal, a resort on the shores of Lake Thun in the Bernese Oberland. As usual he arrived early, at the head of a contingent of twelve that included Inessa and Zinoviev. He was well primed for his campaign to win delegates—with sheaves of draft res-

olutions and notebooks "full of calculations on the likely affiliation of each and every delegate on every conceivable issue."

He worked hard to win support and was in a stronger position than at Zimmerwald. Yet he remained in the minority, again losing the vote on his call for all-out civil war in Europe. However, he came away feeling that in general his position had strengthened since Zimmerwald. The majority opposed his position, but the conference did at least condemn pacifism and allude to the eventual overthrow of the capitalist class. And there was no doubt that his increasingly commanding presence was noted in the Second International.

Returning to Spiegelgasse in early July, Lenin finished what was to become his best-known theoretical work, *Imperialism: The Highest Stage of Capitalism*, although it would not be published in Russia until after the revolution. As with all his other work at this time, his incentive to write was as much financial as political. But it served as a timely restatement of his militant Marxism, loaded with statistics and charts showing how between them Britain, Germany, France, and the United States had carved up the exploitable world between them, now owning nearly 80 percent of the world's finance capital. Western capitalism had reached an inevitable stage in its historical development—the point at which rival imperialist empires were now approaching cataclysm over their rival markets and colonies. Capitalism in its highest stage, which it had now reached, bred war by its competitive nature. In the end an assiduous Marxist undermining of imperial rule would prompt the proletariat to rebel in search of peace and self-determination; of that he was convinced.

Political work had to be interrupted at the end of July when Nadya's health collapsed. She refused to spend precious money on doctors and had struggled to keep up with a paid job she had taken as secretary of the Bureau for Political Emigrant Relief. But clearly she had to take time off and recuperate. Lenin too was keen to get away somewhere quiet "to think his ideas out to the end," away from the stifling Spiegelgasse at the height of summer. This time they opted for a rest home, forty-six miles southeast of Zurich in the canton of St. Gallen. Their hotel, the Pension Tschudiwiese, was situated on Mount Flums high in the Alps near the Austrian frontier. It was so inaccessible that they had to walk five miles up a steep, narrow path to get to it, their bags following by donkey. Lenin considered the climb worth the effort. The pension was half the cost of Sörenburg, although it operated a strict regime involving copious doses of its "milk cure" four times a day. Here they were cut off from everything. The postal service consisted of a decrepit donkey that toiled up and down the mountain once a day. With no Russian comrades to break the boredom, all they did was walk and gather mushrooms and berries, the wild raspberries and blackberries they picked being a guilty supplement to the tedious, sugarless milk diet. Lenin capitulated to the remoteness of Flums and did little other than read the papers and clean his and Nadya's walking boots daily with military precision. Their only entertainment was the occasional accordion playing of their host's son in the evening. Some of the guests would get up and dance, but not Lenin. Nor could he abide the hotel's custom of serenading departing guests off at 6:00 A.M. with a rousing chorus of "Good-bye Cuckoo."

Not long after the couple arrived at Flums, terrible news came from home. Lenin's mother had died in Petrograd on July 25. She had been unwell when she went to visit Mariya not long before, and Mariya insisted that she remain with the family in their flat on Shirokaya Street. The end came shortly after, on holiday at a village outside the city. Lenin had not seen his mother since Stockholm in 1910. His letters to his sisters in Russia expressing his grief have not survived, and Nadya, careful always to avoid the personal in her later memoir, only noted that Volodya went off for long walks alone in the mountains. He eventually received a small share of what was left of his mother's estate, but aside from the personal loss, he and Nadya had both lost the crucial financial support they had intermittently received from their mothers. With his mother gone, Lenin rarely wrote to his sisters; nor did Nadya, who had largely done so out of duty on her husband's behalf. Her relationship with Mariya and Anna had been uneasy at the best of times.

With their emotional links to Russia now broken, life in Zurich that winter became even more cheerless and impoverished. Lenin did not enjoy hanging around in cafés full of "revolutionary windbags" any more than he had elsewhere. He avoided the emigrant clubs and stuck to a small circle of a dozen or so people. But he felt fettered. His circle seemed to be growing smaller by the day, the political life around him less and less intense with his Bolshevik group scattered in small pockets across Europe.

Sometimes he ventured forth from the library to take part in the discussions held at the Zur Eintracht, where he could read the free newspapers and hold meetings in its lecture room. The Café Adler was another haunt where his group used a back room for meetings. But perhaps the most famous venue favored by the eclectic mix of bohemians, exiles, and émigrés who haunted Zurich during the war years was the Café Odéon on Limmatquai. Here James Joyce, Albert Einstein, the young Benito Mussolini, and even the legendary Mata Hari had savored the coffee and cake. Lenin went there to catch the latest of the six daily editions of the *Neue Zürcher Zeitung* and the international magazines. It is tempting to imagine him drinking coffee in sight of James Joyce, as the Irish writer wrestled with his new novel *Ulysses* at another table.

On returning from the mountains in September, Lenin and Nadya changed rooms at 14 Spiegelgasse, moving to the front of the building overlooking the alleyway and the shops opposite. From here they could not have failed to notice the Cabaret Voltaire on the corner, home since February to a new and anarchic form of art and entertainment, Dada. While he had no truck with futurism and cubism and other isms currently considered to be "the highest revelations of the artistic genius," the subversive nature of Dada as performance might well have aroused Lenin's curiosity, sufficient to cross the road and take a look, in the same way that the London music hall and the *cafés-chantants* had done in Paris. The avant-garde theater director and founder of the Cabaret Voltaire, Hugo Ball, wrote that Lenin "must have heard our music and tirades every evening" from across the street. Another member, Richard Huelsenbeck, recalled a visit by Lenin and Romanian painter Marcel Janko. The Dadaists associated with the Russian community in Zurich and held evenings at the Café Meierei for their "Russian friends," perhaps as fundraisers to bail them out of poverty. In later years the movement's leading light, Tristan Zara, claimed to have "exchanged ideas" and played chess with Lenin in Zurich, but it's more likely Lenin would have had little interest in artistic eccentricity at such a difficult time. Hans Richter, another Dadaist, saw him often in the central library on Zähringerplatz and heard him speak at a political meeting in Berne. He remembered being impressed by Lenin's good German. The Swiss authorities, he noted, seemed "much more suspicious of the Dadaists" than they were of "these quiet, studious Russians." The Dadaists, with their anarchic principles, "were capable of perpetrating some new enormity at any moment," whereas the Russians, in their own unostentatious little way, were merely "planning a world revolution."

It was hard for the Swiss police to keep tabs on them all, for Switzerland in 1917 was swarming with artists, revolutionaries, bohemians, and spies—from professionals based at the embassies of the belligerent nations to waiters, serving maids, and domestic staff in the hotels. They were bribed to watch, look, and listen. Everything was reported, everything was supervised as agents circulated their daily reports, telephones were tapped, and "wastepaper baskets and blotting pad correspondence was sedulously reconstructed." No one, however, was taking much notice of Lenin at the time; his deliberately inconspicuous lifestyle near a sausage maker on Spiegelgasse was part of his tried and trusted conspiratorial method of blending into the background. The Austrian playwright Stefan Zweig, who had fled to Zurich because of his pacifist sympathies and saw Lenin from time to time at the Café Odéon, later recalled wondering how this obstinate little man ever became so important.

One young American on the bohemian circuit in Zurich certainly remembered Lenin—the sixteen-year-old modernist composer Otto Leuning, who had come to study at the Zurich Conservatory of Music. Short of money, he was taken by fellow student Otto Strauss to eat at the cheap Tivoli restaurant near the university—it was where all the poor émigrés ate because you could get credit for up to three months. One day Strauss leaned over to Leuning and hissed, "Ssh, sshh. Revolutionaries . . . over there," pointing to three men making their way to a table at the rear. "That's Ulyanov, a Russian revolutionary, also known as Lenin," he whispered. The men came almost every day at lunchtime, as unobtrusively as possible, and sat in a corner and talked. Lenin, he said, was a well-known figure in the city libraries. Leuning took a long, hard look. Lenin's "clean, sculpted features" were fascinating—there was something of a "workingman's Cardinal Richelieu" about his pale face and marble-like forehead, and his eyes transmitted "a sense of great concentration and power." All in all Lenin "gave out the vibrations of a completely coordinated human being, charged with electricity, in total command of the moment."

But in reality he was far from being in command of events, living out his days in the libraries, churning out more articles, "steeping himself in theoretical work" as Nadya loyally recalled, using work as a way of assuaging his grief over the loss of his mother, once more too engrossed intellectually to take note of what was going on in Russia.

There was, however, one other person to whom Lenin continued to pour out his general and growing sense of frustration, depression, and utter weariness—Inessa Armand, who was now living at Clarens near Montreux. He hadn't seen her since Kienthal the previous year and knew that she was now lonely and unwell. She had gone back to Les Avants in November, had drifted on to Sörenberg and from there to Clarens, perhaps in hopes of continuing her own work, for there was a good Russian library nearby. At the end of December Lenin had told her that her latest letters "so full of sadness" had "evoked such gloomy thoughts in me and aroused such feelings of guilt, that I can't come to my senses." With Inessa still punishing him with her silence, he finally had to admit, in a crushing understatement, that this indicated a "certain changed mood" on her part.

The fragments of evidence that remain in Lenin's letters to Inessa expressing his concern for her health all point to her suffering from depression or perhaps mental breakdown. She was tired of being a party factotum and Lenin's "Girl Friday," and longed to find expression for her socialist-feminist interests. But she also knew full well that the only way she could resist his bullying and the hurt she felt at his savage criticism of her political thinking was to deny him news of herself. Lenin's endless letters, phone calls, and telegrams followed her wherever she went, still complaining about her failure to respond. While simultaneously harassing her with endless instructions and queries, he urged her to take trips, go on a lecture tour, meet new people, move somewhere more conducive, get back into her stride with work that would "engross her." For Inessa as a woman, however, the solution was perfectly simple. The romantic idealist in her craved the one thing Lenin couldn't and wouldn't give her—his unqualified love. Having wished he could "press her cold hands and warm them" in November, by January 1917 he was telling her in no uncertain terms that when she finally chose a place of residence she was "*not* to take into account whether I will come there. It would be quite absurd, reckless and ridiculous if I were to restrict you in your choice of a city by the notion that it 'may' turn out in the *future* that I, too, will *come there*!!!"

There may well have been a degree of that most *un*socialist thing in all this—emotional manipulation on Inessa's part, as well as a degree of dependency on Lenin's. He might be insensitive to many things but he had always been able to judge Inessa's mood swings, even from a distance, and he valued her company and approbation. But now Inessa wished to reconfigure the boundaries in her working relationship with him and assert her political and intellectual equality, and he found that unsettling. With this in mind she resisted his calls to return to Russia as an agent of the Central Committee or to work for it in Norway. Instead, she merely agreed to translate some of his political brochures—only to have Lenin nitpick over them. Such demands deflected Inessa from her desire to write her own material and improve her understanding of Marxist theory.

As always, Lenin refused to be drawn into an emotional response to her behavior that could potentially impinge on his political life. Her female irrationality was a trial; she was too mercurial, too erratic. Or perhaps it was hormonal—menopausal even? "You must be in an excessively nervous state," he wrote to her; it was, he said, the only explanation his infallible Marxist logic could find "for the number of theoretical oddities in your letters." Even though she remained, with Nadya, an essential sounding board, Lenin's letters to her now took on a perceptible frostiness. She had barely written to him at all that year, and then only to challenge an inconsistency in his political writing. Lenin had responded predictably with a theoretical lecture and accused her of being "one-sided and formalistic." The dispute between them rumbled on, with his responses becoming ever stiffer, as he retreated in his closing salutations from the "friend" of earlier letters to simply "Lenin," offering nothing but a "firm handshake." The kisses of the past might still be dear to Inessa, but he had long suppressed all thought of them. Nevertheless, the unfinished business between them lingered on.

That final winter in Switzerland Lenin felt increasingly out of touch with events in Russia as he battled against the "socialist chauvinists" and pacifists in Europe intent on prematurely ending the war. Nor could he even rouse the socialist conscience of émigré Russian workers and other groups in Zurich as he had hoped. Nadya had never seen her husband in a more "irreconcilable mood." He was quarrelling with everyone, even his closest ally Zinoviev, and he dreaded giving lectures in case they aroused further political conflict. All his strength and energies were draining away. After sixteen homeless years of crisscrossing Europe, of which he had spent barely two in regular paid work, he was still living the peripatetic life of a "café conspirator" whose name was little known in Russia beyond the political groups. "There it is, my fate," he shrugged in a letter to Inessa in late December 1916. It all seemed so hopeless; nothing but "one fighting campaign after another—against political stupidities, philistinism, opportunism and so forth." He seemed to have no inkling that back home, the political tide was turning in his favor once again.

⸻

EARLY RUSSIAN SUCCESSES against the Austro-Hungarians in Galicia in 1914 had been followed by a succession of crushing defeats, as the ill-equipped and largely conscript army of peasants was pushed back from East Prussia by the well-oiled might of the German military machine. Defeat had brought disaffection and desertion in the army, which escalated in September 1915 when Nicholas II sacked his uncle, Grand-Duke Nikolay, as commander in chief and assumed command of the troops.

Voices were raised in the Duma to protest the czar's military incompetence as morale plummeted in the Russian army. The countryside was crippled by a labor shortage as 18 million men were called up and peasants abandoned the land to seek work in munitions factories in the city. Taxation no longer covered rocketing war debts as the cities ran short of food and fuel. The relentless spiral of hunger and demoralization led to renewed militancy among the peasantry and the urban working class. A wave of strikes brought factories to a standstill, and the railway system descended into chaos. National unity was further undermined by a rapid hiring and firing of key ministers: four prime ministers, six interior ministers, and four agriculture ministers, as Czarina Alexandra browbeat her husband into sacking voices of moderation in his government. The monarchy's reputation descended to an all-time low in the wake of Alexandra's relationship with the religious charismatic and healer Rasputin, the only person who seemed able to control her son Alexey's life-threatening hemophilia. Liberals in the government and even among the officer class and the aristocracy were now openly talking of Nicholas and Alexandra as a danger to the country and advocating their overthrow. Otherwise, sooner or later a revolution would bring them down.

From the confines of democratic, bourgeois Switzerland—a "country of health resorts" with no perceptible revolutionary working class—Lenin and Nadya began to get some sense that "a revolutionary struggle was mounting." "Life was astir," she recalled later, "but it was all so far away." On January 22 Lenin gave a lecture on the 1905 revolution to young socialists at the People's House in Zurich. In it he observed that Europe was "pregnant with revolution" but had no idea whether his generation would live to see it. When pressed on the subject by Valeriu Marcu, he was unable to predict exactly when revolution in Russia might finally break. "Perhaps in two, perhaps in five, at the latest in ten years," he offered. Despite the fact that this had been his constant, waking thought for the last twenty years or more he was totally unprepared when revolution was finally unleashed in Russia in March 1917.

With few letters getting through from Russia, Lenin was unable to gauge the resurgence of popular antipathy toward the czarist regime that broke on the anniversary of Bloody Sunday on January 9, 1917, when 150,000 workers struck in Petrograd. In response, Lenin concluded that the "mood of the masses" was "a good one." Shortly afterward, revolution came sooner than he had expected.

As the temperature in Petrograd plummeted to 35 degrees below, longer and longer queues of people stood waiting for bread deliveries and then, desperate with cold and hunger, began breaking into the bakeries. Bread rationing followed as queues lengthened for every basic commodity: meat, sugar, tea, potatoes. On International Women's Day, February 23, women left their factories to protest food shortages. *Khleb*—bread—was the only word on their lips as they marched the streets of the city. By the end of February much of Petrograd was at a standstill, a large proportion of its population on the streets protesting. Crowds marched with banners proclaiming their virulent hatred of Nicholas and his German-born wife Alexandra: "Down with the German woman," "Down with the czar." Rioting was followed by looting and anarchy.

The force of history had finally carried discontent in Russia to the brink—against the mismanaged war, the collapsing economy, the recklessly squandered Russian lives on the eastern front, and an incompetent government dominated by a German-born czarina whose political loyalties were doubted by many. Socialist propaganda among the troops and the peasants had eroded confidence further. When the government called in the military, the Petrograd garrison refused to fire on strikers and mutinied. By March 12 the mob had broken into the Tauride Palace, the seat of the Duma. On March 15, 1917, Czar Nicholas II abdicated and the Winter Palace was taken.

Inside a week the Romanov empire had fallen in an almost bloodless people's revolution. Where the revolution went from here was fundamentally a matter of who was best placed to seize political power. For even as Russia ceased to be a monarchy it failed to become a republic, entering a period of chaos and uncertainty as the inexperienced, ad hoc Petrograd Soviet of Workers and Soldiers Deputies—an amalgam of these groups with unaligned socialists and Mensheviks—vied with Alexander Kerensky's Provisional Government for political control. Lenin's core of a thousand seasoned Bolsheviks in Petrograd struggled to make their mark under the inexperienced leadership of thirty-three-year-old worker Aleksandr Shlyapnikov and the even younger Vyacheslav Molotov (playing a secondary role) in the absence of their leaders still in Europe—compared to the greater numbers of Mensheviks and Socialist Revolutionaries. The Petrograd Bolsheviks now anxiously awaited Lenin's return.

CHAPTER EIGHTEEN

From the Spiegelgasse to the Finland Station

ZURICH–PETROGRAD: MARCH–APRIL 1917

———∞∞∞———

O N THE MORNING OF MARCH 15 the first news of the revolution reached Zurich. Lenin was about to return to the library after lunch when a Polish colleague, Mieczysław Bronski, rushed through the door: "Haven't you heard the news?" he said. "There's a revolution in Russia!" Telegrams announcing the turmoil in Petrograd had been published in the day's paper. Lenin and Nadya hurried down to the windy lakeshore to read the *Neue Zürcher Zeitung* and other newspapers displayed on billboards along Bellevueplatz. They weren't sure what to believe, as Nadya told a friend, but the Russians in Zurich were excited. "Perhaps it is another hoax, but perhaps the truth." They did not dare hope it was true.

Titus Kammerer remembered that day clearly as the only time his otherwise quiet tenants were rowdy. Lenin and Nadya's tiny room was invaded by twenty or so Russians who sat wherever they could "on the bedside table, on the chest, on the washstand, on the beds" excitedly discussing events back home. Frau Kammerer became anxious about Nadya when told they would be returning to "this insecure land," Russia. But she had to go, Nadya assured her—that was where her work was. "Here I have nothing to do."

Lenin's return to Russia was now imperative. His entire circle in Zurich and Berne was "dreaming of leaving," and he had no intention of lingering in Switzerland for months as he had done in 1905. History in Russia was suddenly moving too fast for him.

Zinoviev arrived from Berne the following day to find Lenin sending a stream of directives to his Bolshevik colleague Aleksandra Kollontai in

Stockholm to step up revolutionary propaganda and intensify the struggle for an international proletarian revolution in advance of his return. For this the masses had to be armed, and proletarian organization was the key. The Bolsheviks had to wrest control of the Petrograd Soviet from the bourgeoisie in the Provisional Government, as well as all other political factions. Visions of the heroism of the Paris Commune, which had long been his revolutionary template, blended effortlessly in Lenin's mind with plans for storming the seat of government in Petrograd. The scenario might be heroic, but the undemocratic means he intended to use to seize power were cynical. In his mind, the seizure of power should be followed by an armistice with Germany. But Lenin, at a distance, was out of touch with popular feeling. In the current wave of patriotic, revolutionary fervor against an oppressive regime, the people would not countenance immediate capitulation to Germany and an end to the war. Nor was Lenin right in his misguided fears of a czarist counterrevolution.

He spent the days in Switzerland in a state of consuming agitation, his nervous energy in overdrive. Knowing that the British and French would never allow him a transit visa to Russia through Allied territory in Europe, he first thought of returning via England under a false passport. But that was too risky: he would likely be arrested and interned for the duration of the war. Other plans for getting back verged on craziness—disguised in a wig via England to Holland and then on through Scandinavia; by plane perhaps; or even smuggled through Germany.

On March 19, 1917, Russian émigrés met at the Zur Eintracht Club to discuss ways of getting home. The German socialist Willi Münzenberg was there; it was the first time he had ever seen Lenin "so excited and so furious." He paced up and down the room, declaring, "We must go at all costs, even if we go through hell." The Menshevik Martov, equally eager to return to Russia (arriving a month after Lenin), suggested that the best chance would be to advise the Petrograd Soviet to offer to repatriate German and Austrian prisoners of war in exchange for the group's safe conduct home via Germany.

For once Lenin confirmed Martov's idea as "excellent": "We ought to get busy with it." But he was too impatient to wait for agreement from Petrograd, knowing that such a trade-off from the Russian side would be a protracted affair. Mindful of his personal security and political reputation, he insisted on negotiating with the Germans through an intermediary: "I cannot personally make any move unless very 'special' measures have been taken," he wrote to Inessa. The Swiss socialist Robert Grimm—a "detestable centrist" in Lenin's eyes after the experience of Zimmerwald but like many who came and went according to political expediency, useful to him now—was recruited to negotiate.

Since Lenin's arrest in Galicia in 1914, the Germans had been aware of his potential usefulness to them in subverting the Russian war effort and bringing it toward a speedy conclusion. They had been pumping German marks into revolutionary antiwar propaganda in Russia since 1915, in hopes of engineering a defeatist peace in Russia so that German troops on the eastern front could be diverted to the deadlocked Western campaign against Britain and France. Robert Grimm now approached Count Gisbert von Romberg, the German ambassador in Berne, who was coming under pressure even from the kaiser himself to accede to the Russian radicals' request for safe conduct through Germany. Lenin's Polish colleague Yakub Hanecki was already in Stockholm raising money for his return and had been appointed as his foreign representative to the Bolshevik Central Committee, when another player and an associate of Hanecki's entered the game.

Alexander Helphand (code-named "Parvus"), the enigmatic German social democrat who had provided valuable assistance to Lenin during his *Iskra* days in Munich, arrived in Switzerland. Having grown fat, sexually corrupt, and wealthy on business concerns in Turkey, the opportunistic Helphand had gone over to the German government, operating as an arms contractor and recruiting for the war effort with an import-export business based in Copenhagen as the front. He was profiteering on the illegal trade in medicines, drugs, and smuggled goods to the Russians. In addition, he was heavily involved in the German propaganda drive directed at czarist troops and intended to destabilize the czarist regime, thanks to millions of marks in seed money from the German government. In order to effect Lenin's return to Russia, Helphand used his influence in high places, notably with General Eric Ludendorff, who became convinced that "from a military point of view" Lenin's journey under German protection was justified, "for it was imperative that Russia should fall." Ultimately the German Foreign Office brokered the deal through its minister Richard von Kühlmann, Ludendorff being responsible for the transportation side of things.

Unlike Lenin, many of those in Zurich now so desperate to return to Russia were tormented by doubts. Going home with German help would be extremely compromising, both politically and morally. Lenin had no such qualms; in order to keep his hands clean he seconded Karl Radek to deal directly with Helphand. He didn't care where the money came from to get him back to Russia, any more than he ever had any scruples about using money from bank robberies and other expropriations to fund the cause. What *did* keep him awake at night was the thought that events in Russia might leave him behind.

Day after day Lenin scoured the papers for scraps of news—the London *Times*, Paris *Le Temps*, the *Berliner Tageblatt*, the *Frankfurter Zeitung*—and constantly checked the billboards for the latest editions of the *Zürcher Post* and *Neue Zürcher Zeitung*. He had to get back and make the Russian revolution his own, the one he had envisaged all these long, hard years, before it became someone else's. "What torture it is for all of us," he wrote to Hanecki, "to be sitting here at such a time." By March 23 his rising hysteria was infecting all of his letters: "What if *no passage whatever* is allowed *either* by England *or* by Germany!!!" he wailed to Inessa. "And this is possible!"

———∞∞∞———

LENIN WAS SO DESPERATE to get himself and Zinoviev to Petrograd that he came up with ludicrous schemes. On March 30 he asked Hanecki to find two deaf-mutes in Sweden vaguely resembling them both so that they could have false passports made and impersonate them to get into Russia, an idea Nadya quickly scotched for its absurdity, by reminding Volodya that he often talked in his sleep and would soon give himself away. His unease about what might await him in Russia rose when he read in the *Petit Parisien* that Pavel Milyukov, minister of foreign affairs in the Provisional Government, had threatened to prosecute anybody who returned to Russia with German assistance.

Meanwhile, Grimm's cautious inquiries were not moving fast enough for Lenin. On April 3, Fritz Platten, the secretary of the Swiss social democrats, took over negotiations with Romberg in Berne at Lenin's request. Finally the German high command communicated its agreement to the transit of Russian revolutionaries to the Foreign Ministry in Berlin "if effected in a special train with reliable escort."

At a meeting at the Volkshaus in Berne, Platten, as a neutral observer officially taking responsibility for the revolutionaries about to travel, outlined the procedure. He helped compose the statement they must all sign before leaving, acknowledging they were aware that the Provisional Government might put them on trial for high treason on their return and that they therefore took full responsibility for their own journey. It was one thing for moderates such as Plekhanov to return to the bosom of Russia (which he had done a week previously), but quite another for radicals such as Lenin. He accepted the terms in full knowledge that he could not predict what awaited him in Petrograd, demanding that their train carriage be guaranteed extraterritorial immunity and that there would be no passport inspections. The train would thus be metaphorically "sealed" from outside intrusion, giving rise to the long perpetuated misconception that the Bolsheviks had literally been locked into their train carriages, like a malevolent genie in a bottle.

During Lenin and Nadya's final days in Zurich the Kammerers moved to a bigger apartment on Culmannstrasse and offered to rent them a large and airy room. But they had only been there a couple of days when word came from Platten on April 5 that the protocol for Lenin's travel had come through and he and his colleagues were to gather at Berne to finalize the arrangements for the journey with Romberg. The couple had two hours to liquidate their household in Zurich, choose what few possessions they wanted to take, and destroy many of their papers. They would leave for Berne on the next available train that afternoon. Much to her dismay, there was no time for Nadya to retrieve her mother's ashes from the crematorium and take them, as Elizaveta Vasil'evna would have wished, back to Russia.

The war in Europe meanwhile had now entered a new and dramatic phase with the U.S. declaration of war against Germany on April 6. From now on, any new government in Russia would be closely scrutinized by the Americans, and with this in mind, only the day before his departure, Lenin put a call through to the American embassy in Berne. It was Easter Sunday and the embassy was closed for business. Lenin's call was taken by a young U.S. diplomat newly arrived in the city, twenty-four-year-old Allen Dulles. Passing through his office en route to a tennis match with a girlfriend, he was asked to take a telephone call from a disreputable-sounding Russian émigré demanding to speak to someone in authority. At that particular moment Dulles was less interested in the game of nations than in his game of tennis and he told the agitated caller to ring back on Monday, as the office was closed. The voice insisted he had something important to negotiate with the embassy. Dulles equally insisted he should call back the following day. "Pity," said the voice, "tomorrow will be too late." It was a classic diplomatic blunder and one that Dulles dined out on across America in later life as head of the CIA. He had missed his own personal historic moment; the moral of the tale was that a good diplomat should never refuse to listen to anyone about anything, however improbable.

As word seeped out to news correspondents about Lenin's return to Russia on a special train provided by the Germans, it also spread across the émigré cafés, where socialists, writers, and reporters gathered to discuss this dramatic turn of events. Ernst Nobs, editor of the *Zürcher Volksrecht,* had broken the story to his colleagues on the French paper *l'Humanité* and the Viennese *Arbeiterzeitung.* They were all "beside themselves with anger" at Lenin's treachery in accepting help from the Germans. "Pandemonium broke out" at the Pfauen Café, which many of them haunted and where the German novelist Stefan Zweig and the "habitually remote and dignified" Romain Rolland joined in the spontaneous discussions. Rolland, a high-profile pacifist and socialist, showed Zweig a telegram he had received from Lenin, imploring him to join his journey to Russia. Rolland, however, would not be used to add moral authority to Lenin's cause. Lunching with Austrian friends the next day, journalist J. Ley was introduced to James Joyce, who remarked that Lenin's return on a "sealed train" seemed "just like the Trojan Horse" to him. Ludendorff must, he thought, be "pretty desperate."

The right-wing German militarist and the Bolshevik arch-revolutionary going in hand in hand seemed like an absurd joke. But Lenin was in deadly earnest about the historic role now before him. Spanish socialist Julio Alvarez del Vayo was one of many foreign observers and journalists who saw him address a gathering of the Russian colony of Berne on the

Lengenstrasse the night before he left. "We have before us a struggle of exceptional gravity and harshness," he declaimed, as he paced up and down, clutching at his lapels. "Let us go into that battle fully conscious of the responsibility we are taking. We know what we want to do. The law of history imposes our leadership, because it is through us that the proletariat speaks."

On April 8 those departing for Russia with Lenin gathered at the Volkshaus in Berne, including the Zinovievs and their nine-year-old son Stepa; Radek; up-and-coming activist Georgy Safarov and his wife Valentina; the Kharitonovs; and another child—Robert, the four-year-old son of Jewish Bundists in the group, who kept everyone entertained with his ingenuous remarks en route. Inessa was there at Lenin's request, but she kept a strangely low profile throughout the journey. The next day, Easter Monday, Lenin's party took an ordinary scheduled train back to Zurich. On arrival, he and Nadya stopped off at the Kammerers to say good-bye, pick up their belongings, and leave some possessions in their safekeeping. Then they joined the others for a farewell lunch at the Zahringerhof Hotel. Fritz Platten had arranged for as many as sixty people to travel but in the event there were thirty-two, including himself. Nineteen were Bolsheviks, including Lenin's inner circle of a dozen or so. During the lunch, Lenin read a "Farewell Address to the Swiss Workers," in which he expressed his reservations about events taking place in Russia. He was leaving in hopes that the revolution in a country as backward and unprepared as his homeland "*may*, to judge from the experience of 1905, give tremendous sweep to the bourgeois-democratic revolution in Russia and *may* make our revolution the *prologue* to the world socialist revolution. It was, at the least, "a *step* toward it."

The scene at Zurich's central train station that afternoon was chaotic, with a "swarm of people around Lenin and Zinoviev, who were both being stormed with thousands of questions." It looked, remembered Platten, "more like a disturbed ant colony than anything else." The passengers had been given special numbered passes (no passports were used), and Lenin was entrusted with three thousand Swiss francs for the tickets. This had been raised by the Committee for the Return of Russian Political Exiles hastily set up by Grimm, to complement the thousand francs Lenin had already raised by other means in Zurich. The Russians were insistent on accepting no help from the Germans other than transport. Lenin insisted that they pay for their tickets and bring their own food— bread, sausage, cheese, chocolate, and so on.

There were no newspaper reporters or photographers to mark this historic event, but word spread like wildfire around the émigré student community that Lenin was leaving. The young American composer Otto Leuning and his friend Otto Strauss went to take a look, arriving at 10:30 AM on that cold and drizzly Easter Monday. There was an air of great expectancy at the station as Lenin arrived, the knapsack on his back crammed full of books and papers. He was followed by a small group of shabby Russians carrying the few possessions they were able to take with them in a few battered suitcases plus an assortment of baskets and packages containing provisions for the journey as well as pillows and blankets. Lenin and Nadya had little to show for their sixteen years in exile, their baggage amounting to "a basket of household items, a basket with prized books, a box full of newspaper cuttings, and another of archival material, a basket of newspapers and a Swedish kerosene stove" (for making the all-essential tea en route). Standing there on the platform, constantly checking his watch as the departure time approached, Lenin seemed anxious but energized at the prospect of what lay ahead. Anatoly Lunacharsky couldn't help thinking as he observed him that privately Lenin knew this much: "At last, at last the thing for which I was created is happening."

Young medical student Angelika Rohr, who lived up on the Zürichberg, was also one of the students who had rushed to the station to see Lenin leave, slipping and falling as she hurried down the winding paths of the hillside to get to the Hauptbahnhof in time. When she arrived, a crowd had gathered at the far end of the platform and was "swarming around a man who stood in the open window of the car." Lenin was leaning out, gesticulating to those outside, answering a deluge of questions in fluent German. One of the Swiss comrades seeing him off said he hoped they would see him back again soon. Oh no, Lenin responded, "that would be a bad political sign."

Lenin's send-off from Zurich was not entirely warm. Some were there to protest his journey home, supposedly in the pay of the Germans. International socialists had already voiced their disapproval, claiming that

Lenin was betraying the Zimmerwald Left like "a German child." A scuffle broke out when German socialist Oscar Blum tried to get on the train but was thrown off by Lenin, who feared he was a police spy. Right up to the last minute some of Lenin's friends begged him to abandon his mad journey through Germany. Willi Münzenberg recalled how sanguine Lenin was about the risk they were all taking. As the train doors closed, Lenin leaned from the window, shook his hand, and said, "Either we'll be swinging from the gallows in three months or we shall be in power."

When the bell sounded to signal the train's departure, a crush of people pressed forward trying to shake Lenin's hand: one hand after another stretched high to meet his at the window. Angelika Rohr was one of those who ran alongside the train when at 3:10 PM precisely it slowly pulled out of the station. As it gathered speed, she desperately tried to grasp Lenin's hand. A loyal chorus of the *Internationale* sung badly by Swiss socialists echoed after the train. But it was matched by shouts of "German spies!" "Traitors!" "Pigs!" and other catcalls, with some demonstrators running alongside the train and hitting it with sticks as it passed out of view into the smoke and fog. Excited but also disturbed by what they had witnessed, the two Ottos repaired to the Café Odeon for an espresso and a long discussion of events.

At Thengen on the Swiss border, much to the Russians' dismay, petty-minded Swiss customs officials confiscated a large part of their food parcels. At the tiny frontier station of Gottmadingen they were to transfer to their special "sealed train." Here they were herded into a customs shed in two groups—male and female—and made to wait. Under the gaze of uniformed and jackbooted German officers, they all feared imminent arrest. After a nervous wait huddled protectively around Lenin, who had retreated as far out of sight as he could, the group expected the worst. But finally they were escorted to their own specially commandeered military train—a locomotive, plus a green-painted coach comprised of three second-class compartments (mainly for the couples and children) and five third-class compartments, where the single men and women would have to endure the hard wooden seats. The two German officers escorting them took a compartment at the rear, beyond which was a baggage wagon. No sleeping cars were provided, though there was a toilet at each end. A chalk mark drawn along the corridor indicated where the German section of the train began. Once three of the car's four doors at the Russian end were closed shut, Platten marked them with chalk in German as "sealed."

⸺⸺

ONCE INSIDE THE TRAIN Lenin and Nadya were assigned their own second-class compartment at the end of the carriage where he could work hopefully uninterrupted on revising his "theses" on revolution in Russia. For now, at the eleventh hour, Lenin the archetypal pragmatist, was frantically reappraising and reconfiguring his take on the classic, Marxist two stages of revolution to which he had till now held so rigidly. Russia, he had always felt, was too backward to avoid the crucial first stage of a bourgeois revolution, which in its turn would be overthrown in the second stage by a triumphant proletariat after a period of politicization and indoctrination by his elite Bolshevik shock troops. But such was the volatile situation now prevailing in Russia that an immediate and dramatic transition straight to the second stage could and ought to be achieved, led by an armed and militant Petrograd Soviet. The key to it all would be the massive Bolshevik propaganda campaign being funded by German money.

Soon after their departure from Gottmadingen, as Lenin wrestled with this major revision of his political thinking, he became irritated by laughter and joking coming from the compartment next door. Inessa and others were being entertained by the irrepressible, impish Radek, with his Rabelaisian sense of humor. Lenin thought Radek, with his round-rimmed spectacles and tobacco-stained teeth, "an insufferable fool." Olga Ravich was delighted by Radek's jokes, delivered in a thick Polish accent. But her raucous cackle so irritated Lenin that he walked in and summarily marched her off to another compartment. Nor could he stand the thick fug of smoke that had rapidly enveloped the entire carriage. Radek's stinking pipe, a permanent fixture in his mouth, was the worst offender. Lenin therefore limited smoking to the lavatory. Realizing this would create a queue, he found a suitably socialist solution. Taking some paper he cut it up as tickets, issuing the group with one ticket for lavatory use and the other for smoking in order to prevent queues and uncomradely disgruntlement.

Occasional sporadic bouts of singing followed during the next few days of the journey, but as the deadeningly long train ride through Germany progressed most of those on board, in the absence of sleeping cars, succumbed to extreme exhaustion. Nor were they in the mood for huge plates of pork and potato salad brought to them when the train halted in an empty station on the third night by pale, skinny girls, visibly shaking from the hunger now gripping the whole of Germany. The Russians refused the food and told the girls to eat it.

As they traversed Germany, the travelers remarked on how few German men they saw at the stations; the countryside too seemed empty, abandoned. Berlin, where their train was forced to wait an interminable twenty hours, struck them as particularly silent and desolate. Indeed people everywhere in Germany had seemed to the Russians thin and cowed; they were all clearly tired of the war. During the long stopover in Berlin some German social democrats got on the train and tried to speak to them, but the Russians refused. Lenin stayed in his compartment writing and thinking, hardly noticing the grimness of Germany at war.

The journey north to the Baltic took four days. Thinking ahead against every possible contingency, the German high command had agreed that in the event of difficulty getting the Russians across neutral Sweden, the army would see them into Russia across its own front lines. Crossing Germany was not without hitches. Troop movements caused missed connections in Frankfurt, which meant that the party arrived at the German port of Sassnitz too late to take the boat that night. The Germans unceremoniously locked the group into a room overnight. The next morning the Russians had to endure a rough four-hour crossing to Trelleborg. On arrival they provided the Swedish authorities with a list of false names when asked for a passenger list. Old conspiratorial habits died hard. Many of the group had become violently ill during the crossing, but not Lenin; he had paced around on deck as though trying to hurry the boat across. On the Swedish side Hanecki was waiting for them. They had only fifteen minutes to transfer to a train for Malmö, where Swedish social democrats laid on a traditional smorgasbord for them, their first proper meal since Berlin, which the Russians "annihilated . . . with incredible speed." The restaurant employees took them "for a band of barbarians." Then after intense discussion of the latest news from Russia the party traveled on to Stockholm with tickets provided by Hanecki. Meanwhile Platten—the only one allowed to leave the train at stations en route—brought them newspapers and beer.

As the train headed off on the long haul to Stockholm, the exhausted travelers tried to sleep. But Lenin sat up half the night talking and planning with colleagues. He refused to speak to the newspaper correspondents who boarded the train at 9:00 AM the next morning, having seen Lenin's photograph in the Swedish daily *Politiken*—the first time his photograph had ever appeared in this way. An hour later the train reached the Swedish capital. Fredrik Ström and Ture Nerman, two of Lenin's Swedish supporters on the Zimmerwald Left, greeted them along with the mayor, Carl Lindhagen, and escorted them on foot to the Hotel Regina where they were given a grand reception.

Lenin would not hear of resting in Stockholm. He crammed a lot into one brief day in the city, his relentless energy like that of a locomotive, as Ström recalled. First he composed a press release on the terms under which the group had traveled across Germany, followed by hurried consultations with Swedish comrades and visits to bookshops. On that day the first flickering film images were captured of him. Lenin wisely refused a meeting with Helphand, who had made his way to Stockholm, wishing to retain an alibi of supposed innocence in regard to Helphand's nefarious dealings with the Germans. Finally, and much to his annoyance, he was prevailed upon to go shopping.

The two years of penury in Switzerland had left his clothes in an extremely shabby state. His overcoat was threadbare around the hem, his trousers baggy at the knees from constant wear. As for the hob-nailed boots so kindly made for him by Herr Kammerer, they simply were not appropriate for a political leader returning in triumph to his homeland. Under pressure from Radek, Lenin ventured into Bergstrom's department store, courtesy of funds provided by the Vera Figner Society for Assistance to Emigrés and Returning Exiles. "After considerable strife," as Radek recalled, Lenin agreed to a new pair of trousers and a decent pair of shoes. But he refused a new overcoat or extra underwear. He was "not going back to Russia to open a gentleman's outfitters," he grumbled, but he did agree also to a new bowler hat. In a famous photograph taken of Lenin in Stockholm crossing the Wasagaten locked in conversation with Ture Nerman, he can be seen in a derby hat and carrying an umbrella, still an unlikely looking revolutionary figure. Fredrik Ström thought he looked "like a workman on a Sunday excursion in unsettled weather." Another colleague thought that Lenin looked more like a provincial schoolteacher. Behind him, her shapeless figure engulfed in a baggy coat and voluminous hat, walked Nadya, and behind her Inessa in a rather more svelte outfit and jaunty hat.

In Stockholm, Lenin appealed to the Swedes for money to help with the costs of the journey. Even the Swedish foreign minister made a donation, saying he would gladly contribute "so long as Lenin leaves today." Lenin was equally glad to move on; "every minute was precious" to him. At 6:37 PM one hundred people gathered to see Lenin's party off on the evening train to Finland, armed with bouquets of flowers. Lenin "was the centre of attention," according to Swedish socialist Hugo Sillen, smiling and laughing from the window of his carriage. The mood was highly charged. With the *Internationale* playing and red flags waving from the windows, the train headed off for the Finnish border. It was a long haul, the party not taking the usual and quicker route by boat across from Stockholm to Åbo, for fear of arrest the minute they set foot in Finland. So they took the circuitous route by train, a very slow way of getting on with the job for Lenin, the eternal man in a hurry. But at least they had bunks to sleep in. That first night Lenin and Nadya crammed into a sleeping compartment with Inessa and a Georgian Bolshevik, David Suliashvili. Lenin sat up reading the first Russian newspapers he'd been able to get hold of, muttering curses at what he read in them and ignoring Nadya's entreaties not to catch cold and get some sleep. A slow and frustrating three days around the Gulf of Bothnia followed. Lenin had plenty of time to ponder the next possible hurdle—a British refusal to allow them all entry into Finland. The British might view them as subversives intent on undermining the Russian war effort on the Allied side.

Early on a very frosty April 15 the train pulled into the Swedish border station of Haparanda. From here the party had to go by horse-drawn sledge, two at a time downhill and across the frozen river to the railway depot at Torneo, a bleak and swampy area on the Finnish side, where they could pick up the main rail line to Helsingfors. They could see red flags flying from buildings in the town beyond and many shed tears knowing they were at last on Russian soil. But Lenin's apprehensions about arrest grew.

Torneo had been a sleepy garrison town prior to the war, but since then it had became an important border crossing for supplies and people.

Crucially, it was the only rail link by which the Russians could reach their Western allies. Such a strategic crossing point was haunted by spies, and Lenin was alarmed to see that the soldiers on the Russian side of the border were backed up by British officers, who had taken control since the revolution.

The British immediately dispatched a telegram to Kerensky's Provisional Government in Petrograd asking whether "a mistake had not been made in permitting Lenin to return." The reply had come back that "the new Russian government rested on a democratic foundation"; Lenin's group should be allowed to enter. Even so, the British were not inclined to let the Russians through without subjecting them to considerable humiliation. One by one the travelers were taken off to be strip-searched—even the women and children—and interrogated. Their luggage was opened and they were made to fill out questionnaires. On his, Lenin stated he was "Russian Orthodox" by religion and that he was a political refugee who had gone abroad illegally. He had no intention of remaining in Finland, and gave his sister Mariya's address in Petrograd. British military control officer Harold Gruner was one of the MI5 intelligence officers on duty that night. Affectionately known as "the Spy" among his friends, he spent many years later trying to live down his role in strip-searching the "arch-revolutionary" Lenin and allowing him into Russian territory, even though the British ambassador in Stockholm had by now conceded that "it appeared wiser to let things take their course" in Russia and allow the revolutionaries to enter. Gruner was teased unmercifully by his colleagues for "locking the stable door when the horse was out, or rather, in." It had felt as though he alone held responsibility for having brought about the Soviet revolution, remarked his colleague William Gerhardie. "Were he a Japanese, he would have committed hari-kari."

── ∞ ──

ONCE THE TRAVELERS got past the British border guards, the townspeople of Torneo were waiting with a much warmer welcome. Lenin stopped to give a short speech and take a look at the Russian papers, especially *Pravda,* but he didn't like what he read. Stalin and Molotov were taking too soft a line with the Provisional Government, and Malinovsky's betrayal as a double agent had been confirmed. Lenin was appalled: shooting was too good for him. At Torneo he had been forced to say good-bye to Fritz Platten, who was refused permission to enter Finland, as was Karl Radek. His disguise as a Russian did not fool anyone. With enormous relief Lenin sent a historic telegram ahead to Mariya in Petrograd:

TELEGRAM NO. 148, FORM NO. 71,
RECEIVED APRIL 2, 1917 AT 20 HRS 8 M.

ULYANOVA, SHIROKAYA, 48/9, APT. 24, PETROGRAD,
FROM TORNEO, 2. 18 HRS 12 M.
ARRIVING MONDAY 11 P.M. INFORM *PRAVDA. ULYANOV*

The stress of the long journey now turned to visible excitement; Lenin's face lit up with laughter as the group crammed into the "wretched" third-class compartments so familiar to them. Even Nadya found their rickety carriage strangely comforting: "We are on home territory now," Lenin said, brandishing his fist, "and we'll show them we are the worthy masters of the future!"

All the way to Petrograd, the Finland State Railways train was crammed full of Russian soldiers. Lenin spent time talking with them about the war, the land, and the new Russia to come, as the train headed south along the coast before turning inland to complete the six hundred miles to the border through great expanses of dense forest deep in snow, past dramatic outcrops of the pink granite so characteristic of Finland. Eventually the train emerged at the network of lakes surrounding Tammerfors, then headed across to the major rail junction at Riihimaiki north of Helsingfors where they changed trains for the final leg on the Riihimaiki–St. Petersburg railroad. The travelers crowded at the windows for their first glimpses of familiar Russian territory as the train rumbled on through the birch trees, passing the little railway halts at Åggleby, Lahti, Terijoki, Kuokkala—places familiar to Lenin, Nadya, and their associates from their days spent hiding in Finland. At last the locomotive steamed into the Karelian isthmus and arrived at Beloostrov, the border post between Finland and Russia. Lenin's sister Mariya was waiting in the drizzling rain along with a large crowd of local workers and other comrades, including Kamenev, Aleksandr Shlyapnikov, and Alexandra Kollontai. Kollontai had been scheduled to give a speech but lost her nerve and simply kissed Lenin's cheek and thrust a bouquet into his hands. While a half-hour customs check ensued, Lenin, growing increasingly apprehensive that he and the others might be arrested by the Provisional Government on their arrival, spent much of the time preparing their legal defense in such an eventuality.

Locomotive 293 of the Finnish State Railways, now decorated with red revolutionary bunting, was hours late, never getting above forty miles an hour before, its bell clanging, it finally came in sight of Petrograd's Finland Station. The crowd, subjected to a long wait, was growing volatile and restive as the train finally pulled in at 11:10 PM, its three front lights blinding everyone as it ground to a halt in a great hiss of steam.

The impending arrest Lenin had dreaded turned out to be a triumphant hero's return. A surprise welcome planned ahead by the comrades in Petrograd had been kept from him—Ilyich, as they knew, "so hating every kind of ceremony." The Finland Station was far from majestic—small and very provincial in look and size—but Shlyapnikov had ensured the choreographing of a proliferation of banners emblazoned with socialist slogans and greetings and a sequence of triumphal arches of red and gold which filled the station, as worker and soldier bands played a rousing chorus of the *Marseillaise* (not yet having been taught the more appropriate melody of the socialist *Internationale*).

As the steam subsided, a small, stocky man in a shabby overcoat and a bowler hat descended from the train, still clutching the now forlorn bouquet given him by Kollontai. At age forty-seven Lenin epitomized the "old man" image attached to him in the party. Feodosiya Drabkina, the intrepid bomb carrier from 1905, noted how bewildered and awkward he seemed to feel at this unexpected welcome, particularly when he was escorted past an honor guard composed of sailors from the 2nd Baltic Fleet based at Kronstadt, who saluted him in their familiar navy blue uniforms, striped shirts, and caps with red pompoms. Nadya followed at two paces, completely overlooked as always.

Holding back the crowds, the official greeting party ushered Lenin, bouquet still awkwardly in hand, into what used to be the imperial waiting room. He looked strained as he was forced to stand and listen to a pedestrian welcome speech by Nikolay Chkheidze—the Menshevik president of the Petrograd Soviet and a man he disdained. Lenin looked around distractedly and seemed to be "watching events which do not concern him in the least," as one observer noted. However, he could not have failed to notice Chkheidze's pointed remark that the principal task ahead for the "revolutionary democracy" was to "defend our revolution both from within and from without." Clearly there were already doubts in the Petrograd Soviet about Lenin's true intentions as a returning political hero.

After briefly acknowledging Chkheidze's welcome, Lenin vigorously reiterated the principles he had mouthed all along, promising that the present "predatory imperialist war" was but the beginning of a civil war all over Europe and that the people should not trust the Provisional Government. The official delegation was alarmed by his uncompromisingly militant tone. There was no talk now of the textbook two-stage road to socialism Lenin had long propagated in the illegal literature. Russia, to Lenin's mind, was ripe for an immediate transition to a socialist state, although no one in the revolutionary leadership in Petrograd was prepared for it. Lenin's new perspective was a direct threat to the already precarious position of the Provisional Government.

The crowd outside the station shivering in the cold wind from off the nearby River Neva was, by now, increasingly vocal in its demand to see Lenin, and a group of soldiers and sailors entered the waiting room and carried him out on their shoulders. It was Easter weekend and there had been no newspapers, so word of Lenin's arrival had been spread across the workers tenements of Vyborg and the military barracks of the city by leaflet and billboard. "Lenin arrives today. Meet him," they exhorted, and thousands of people had turned out, holding aloft their banners, their faces lit by flaming torches, waiting patiently to see a man about whom they had heard so much but who was, to all intents and purposes, a stranger to them—and they to him. On that cold night in April 1917, on the huge square outside the Finland station, Lenin finally saw the Russian masses as they really were and witnessed what Nadya called "the grand and solemn beauty of the Revolution" in all its visceral power and immediacy—an experience he had missed in 1905. "Yes," he whispered under his breath, as he emerged out onto the square packed with thousands of eager faces: "Yes, *this* is the revolution."

Izvestiya, the official organ of the Soviets, later described the scene. As Lenin appeared on the square outside the station, the sea of faces surged and swayed in its effort to see him as it greeted him with deafening cheers. Searchlights from the Peter and Paul Fortress nearby had been trained along the front of the station, eerily penetrating the late night fog descending on the city and illuminating the waving banners with their words of welcome.

By now, having exchanged his bowler hat for the worker's peaked cap that would become his hallmark, his coat open to the cold of the spring night, and with his shiny new shoes reflecting the flickering light all around, Lenin was lifted onto an armored car provided for the occasion. The atmosphere was electric; the sense of euphoria palpable. "Just think," recalled an exhilarated Feodosiya Drabkina of that memorable night, "in the course of only a few days Russia had made the transition from the most brutal and cruel arbitrary rule to the freest country in the world." The same armored car on which Lenin, leader of the new socialist order, now stood had only a week earlier been sent in against protesters on the Nevsky Prospekt.

Exhausted though he was, Lenin launched into a short speech full of implacable rage against the old order and illuminated by breathtaking revolutionary certainty. Nikolay Sukhanov from the Petrograd Soviet captured the mood when he later noted that Lenin's voice had seemed like "a voice from the outside," a voice that had not witnessed the events in Russia through which so many of those gathered there had suffered. Lenin's words seemed "*new* and brusque and rather deafening." The man who had for the most part led the revolution from exile was clearly someone to be reckoned with, but they didn't yet know what to make of him.

As the crowd rumbled in excitement, with sailors and soldiers hurling their caps in the air for joy, only a few fractured words of Lenin's speech penetrated the crowd. The people needed three things—peace, bread, and land. They must "fight for the social revolution, fight to the end, till the complete victory of the proletariat." And then, amid the clamor, one distinctive Leninist phrase was hurled at the crowd—a phrase that would echo down through the dislocations of a century molded and ultimately haunted by the ruthless enshrinement of Lenin's communist dream— "Long live the worldwide socialist revolution!"

After sixteen years of exile and seven long days on this, the last of so many interminable train rides across Europe, Lenin was finally home.

Good-bye Lenin

⸺◦❦◦⸺

I N THE END, LENIN'S WORLDWIDE socialist revolution never happened. Soon after arriving in Petrograd, he outlined his blueprint for Russia in his April Theses. But the proletariat wasn't ready to do things his way, any more than the masses in Germany were ready to rise up in the socialist revolution he had predicted there. Throughout the summer Lenin relentlessly hammered his argument home at rallies and conferences, but unrest continued, as the Provisional Government entered a period of experimental democracy and came into increasing conflict with the Petrograd Soviet. Chaos in the cities led to a resurgence of violence. When the Provisional Government released details of Lenin's secret deal with the Germans over his return to Russia, the public mood turned against the Bolsheviks. In July he was forced back into hiding in Finland, until he was able to return once more, a slightly lower-profile conquering hero, in October 1917.

He came back on the same train to the Finland Station after the Bolsheviks, with the support of the Petrograd Soviet, staged a final, decisive coup d'état against the Provisional Government. But there was no quick-fix transition to the new socialist state Lenin had theorized about for so long. By 1918 his attitude had hardened as he and the Bolsheviks struggled to hold on to power against counterrevolutionary groups, and civil war loomed. It would rage across Russia for the next four years, leaving 11 million people dead.

As for the major players in Lenin's life in exile, they were all destroyed or worn out by the revolution they had worked so hard to create. Plekhanov was the first casualty. Now very sick, and unable to come to terms with Lenin's takeover in October, he expected to be arrested or assassinated at any time. Terminally ill, he once more went into exile—to a sanatorium in nearby Finland, where he died of tuberculosis in May

1918. Martov continued to lead the Menshevik opposition to Lenin's new government, but in 1920 he was forced back into exile, this time in Germany. Tuberculosis claimed him too, after he steadfastly refused to give up smoking. A quiet, sad man, cruelly consigned by Trotsky in 1917 to the "dustbin of history," his lonely life in exile went out, forgotten, like a guttering candle in 1923. Trotsky survived as a political renegade in the Soviet Union until driven out by Stalin in 1928. A Spanish communist assassin caught up with him in Mexico City in 1940, by which time Stalin had systematically seen off most of the Old Bolsheviks of Lenin's émigré circle. Zinoviev and Kamenev were shot after a terrifying show trial in August 1936. Even Stepa Zinoviev perished in the roundup of sons, wives, and daughters of those purged, shot in 1937. The eternal optimist, Radek, went to Germany in 1919 and doggedly tried to incite Lenin's great socialist revolution. Returning to Russia in 1922 and feeling politically insecure after Lenin's death, he managed to ingratiate himself with Stalin for a while before falling out of favor. The knock on his door came in 1937. He escaped execution and died forgotten, somewhere in the Gulag in 1939.

As for the women in Lenin's life, Vera Zasulich, his first comrade during the difficult early years in exile in London and Munich, and one he had so greatly respected, returned to Russia after the 1905 revolution. Now fifty-seven and weary of underground life, she retired to a small cottage and her garden. Like Martov and Plekhanov, she was appalled by Lenin's Bolshevik takeover and despaired at seeing the Russia she had loved so much disappear before her eyes. Still revered by those who had known her as a pioneering radical intellectual, she lived out her days in increasing poverty and slovenliness in a Writers Home in Petrograd, dying at the age of seventy-one in 1919, having confided to her sister that "everything that was dear to me for my entire, long life has crumbled and died."

Lenin's sisters Anna and Mariya remained loyal Leninists and party workers until their dying day, in 1935 and 1937 respectively, their many arrests and periods of exile in service to the party marginalized in the history books, as were the roles of most other female Bolsheviks. The exception was Elena Stasova, who lived on into her nineties, the last of the old guard to die, in 1967. Inessa, despite her despair at the failure of her relationship with Lenin, remained under his spell to the end, rising to become one of the most outstanding Bolshevik women of her generation and using her elite position to fight tirelessly for women's equality in the Communist Party. But her exhausting duties to Lenin, the party, and the state wore her out. She became increasingly lonely, reflecting morbidly on her past, never coming to terms with her unfulfilled love for Lenin. By 1920 she admitted in her diary to feeling "dead inside." All the joy had long gone out of her life; the only people she had warm feelings for were her children—and Vladimir Ilyich. Sick, depressed, and disillusioned, she took Lenin's advice and went away to the Caucasus to rest and wallow in her loneliness. There she contracted cholera and, with no will to go on living, died on September 24, 1920. Her body was brought back to Moscow for burial; Feodosiya Drabkina's daughter Liza saw the sad little funeral cortege of two bony black horses drawing Inessa's zinc coffin on a bier from the Kazan station, followed by a distraught Lenin, "propped up" by Nadya, his face swathed in a thick scarf to hide his grief.

Nadezhda Krupskaya outlived her husband by fifteen years, becoming a respected educationist during the Stalin era and keeper of the official Leninist flame as propagated by Stalin's cult of the personality. She was appalled by Lenin's embalming and enshrinement on Red Square, knowing he would have hated it and privately wishing he could be cremated and laid to rest in the Kremlin Wall alongside Inessa's ashes. Although she had been one of the outstanding female Bolsheviks of her generation she was never allowed any public political voice by Stalin, who feared the respect she enjoyed among the people. By the late 1930s she had become a thorn in his side as a constant reminder of the old guard of the party that he was now systematically and brutally eliminating. Nadya lived on, under constant surveillance and increasingly isolated, a powerless witness to the liquidation of her generation. She collapsed in 1938 after being denounced by Stalin's hatchet man, Nikolay Ezhov, head of the NKVD. She died the following year, supposedly of appendicitis. Some say she was poisoned.

Lenin effectively enjoyed only five years in power before entering a terminal decline in December 1922. Inessa's death in 1920 had a profound effect on him. He seemed visibly destroyed by grief at her funeral, but of course never spoke publicly about her and the Soviet record remained stonily silent on the subject of their relationship. Her premature death no doubt contributed to his final decline. He died on January 21, 1924, supposedly the victim of a series of seizures, but, as now seems likely, having succumbed to syphilis contracted sometime in the 1900s.

The syphilis diagnosis has been supported as well as vigorously contested by historians and physicians inside and outside Russia, with the Soviets insisting that Lenin died of a stroke, as did his father before him. Concealment of the truth about the private lives of Soviet political heroes, particularly every aspect of Lenin's private life, was raised to an art form under Stalin by legions of official historiographers. It could not really be otherwise: The puritanical Lenin, fountainhead of a cult of revolutionary sainthood, had no time for sex, or so the Soviet people were led to believe. But the clues are there about Lenin's sexuality and the sexual deprivation he probably suffered, as a result of Nadya's thyroid condition and consequent loss of libido. Lenin's illness was well-known among his doctors in the Kremlin and syphilis specialists in Germany and Switzerland, such as Professor Max Nonne, had been treating him with arsenic since the war years. In his final months Lenin also received doses of Salvarsan, a pioneering treatment for syphilis first marketed in 1910. One of the reasons he survived an assassination attempt in August 1918 was that the bullets coated in arsenic intended to finish him off failed to work. By then he was so overdosed on arsenic that he had developed a high tolerance to it. In the end the brilliant brain that had turned out 10 million words of political argumentation published across fifty-five volumes of collected essays, pamphlets, and letters burned out. The final photographs taken of him show a confused and helpless cripple, deprived of the power of speech and with an insane, fixed stare.

———

BETWEEN 1918 AND 1968, 350 million copies of Lenin's works were published in sixty-three languages of the Soviet republics and thirty-five foreign ones. His collected works ran through five editions, the fifty-five-volume edition, published between 1958 and 1965, running to around 14 million copies alone. At the height of the Leninist cult and during the still friendly Allied relations of the 1940s, the great leader's every step across Europe was memorialized. In London no one was ever certain of precisely which had been Lenin's favorite seat in the British Museum reading room in order to commemorate it, but the Marx Memorial Library, which took over the building at Clerkenwell Green where Lenin had edited *Iskra*, still preserves his tiny editorial office as it was when he used it. The house he lived in at Percy Circus was redeveloped in 1970, but a blue plaque was mounted on its surviving back wall, where it remains today. The monument erected to commemorate Lenin's stay in Holford Square (1902–1903) had a more turbulent fate. The house itself, along with much of Holford Square, was destroyed by bombing during the war, but in March 1942 during Aid for Russia Week the Soviet ambassador Ivan Maisky was invited to unveil a Lenin memorial featuring a bust designed by Russian-born sculptor Berthold Lubetkin erected near the site of number 30. It was a mark of respect for a wartime ally, but during the Cold War the memorial was regularly vandalized by right-wing Mosleyites. Eventually the bust was moved to the Islington Museum at the Finsbury Library on St. John Street, a short walk from Lenin's old London haunts.

Across the Channel in Paris, the apartment at 4 rue Marie Rose was acquired by the French Communist Party in 1945 and opened as the Musée Lénine, recreating the modest ambiance of the rooms occupied by Lenin, though not with the original furniture. But with interest in Lenin declining, the museum closed its doors in November 2007 and the French Communist Party sublet the premises to a literary magazine. The plaque mounted outside has recently been removed to discourage the curious.

Today, an experienced walker armed with a good map can still follow the route of Lenin and Nadya's long Swiss hike of 1904. But there are few traces of Lenin's presence in Switzerland, apart from the plaque that remains at 14 Spiegelgasse. When Lenin and Nadya departed from Zurich, they left a pile of letters and manuscripts for Titus Kammerer to destroy and entrusted a box of belongings to him. Lenin said he would reclaim the items if he returned; otherwise Titus should do what he wanted with them. Titus had taken the furniture from their room on Spiegelgasse with him to Culmannstrasse. Many subsequent lodgers might have been shocked to know that they had slept in a bed once occupied by Lenin, the leader of the Russian Revolution, and his wife. After Lenin died in 1924, Titus opened the box to discover that moths had destroyed everything except an old gray overcoat of Lenin's, which he gave to his son. The tea kettle, strainer, tea glasses, and butter knives that had been everyday essentials in Lenin and Nadya's life, he also gave to his son. When Kammerer died in 1951, Dr. Johannes Itten, director of Zurich's Kunstgewerbemuseum, struck a bargain with Kammerer's son for this Lenin memorabilia to go into his museum. Soon after, however, he was pressured into handing these priceless communist relics over to the Soviets in East Berlin, in trade for the return of valuable sculptures stolen from the Kunstgewerbemuseum by the Nazis.

At two crucial points in his exile, Lenin was forced to rely on locals for help: in Finland in 1907 and Galicia in 1914. Thanks to the intercession of the Finns and the Poles, Lenin evaded either being handed over to the Okhrana, being imprisoned or worse, executed. After the revolution the Soviet hagiographers consistently and persistently played down the contribution of these national groups in the story, particularly that of the Poles; the role of the Jews in assisting Lenin's departure from Galicia was totally ignored. In the years of the postwar Soviet domination of Eastern Europe, plaques and museums commemorating Lenin's life and sometimes presence in their countries appeared all over the Eastern Bloc. But with the rise of Gorbachev and glasnost in the 1980s and the destruction of the Berlin Wall at the end of 1989, they just as quickly began to disappear. The death knell of the Lenin memorabilia industry was sounded in 1991 with the collapse of the Soviet regime. A year later the major focus of the Lenin cult, the Lenin Museum in Moscow, was closed, its vast array of exhibits dismantled. Many Lenin statues and memorials have since disappeared from Russian cities, but two notable ones remain: his mausoleum on Red Square and the great statue of Lenin that dominates Lenin Square outside the Finland station. However, during the early morning hours of April Fool's Day 2009, someone planted TNT inside the statue and blew a gaping hole in Lenin's rear.

Today the only museum permanently dedicated to the story of Lenin in exile and revolution is in Tampere, Finland. Despite their uneasy relationship with both the czars and the Soviets, the Finns take a more tolerant view. Like him or loathe him, Lenin and to a lesser extent the Russian underground that made such good use of safe houses in Finland are part of their history. Since opening their own Lenin Museum in 1946, the Finnish authorities have allowed a number of memorials to be installed, including a plaque at the station at Littoinen where Lenin jumped from the train, a statue in Kotka, and a commemorative bust in Turku (formerly Åbo). There is still a small Lenin museum at Parainen in the southwest archipelago, located in the Fredriksson house where he sought refuge during his escape from Finland during Christmas 1907. A Lenin Park in Helsinki still bears his name, despite numerous calls for it to be changed. The Finns preserve this link with their past not out of a veneration for Lenin but out of respect for their own history and the part that socialism played in their struggle for independence from Russia.

⸺∞⸺

IT IS RATHER a different story with the Poles. When Lenin arrived in Kraków as a political exile in the summer of 1912, he was welcomed by Polish socialists as a loyal Russian patriot and a man after their own heart. They gave him refuge and an introduction into Polish intellectual and political circles. They applauded his anti-czarism and his vehement anti-imperialism, for Poland had suffered centuries of depredation at the hands of the Russian and other voracious empires, with vast tracts of territory at the time of war's outbreak in 1914 carved up between Austria-Hungary and Russia.

Eight years later, during the civil war that followed the 1917 revolution, the Poles encountered the full horror of the new regime when their former political ally and sympathizer Lenin reneged on his promises of support for Polish independence and sent in the Red Army to push revolution west through Poland, and on into Germany. In 1920, against all odds, the Poles, led, ironically, by Józef Piłsudski, repulsed the Russians from the gates of Warsaw in a humiliating defeat at the River Vistula. Polish resistance to Soviet domination during the ensuing century continued, but it did not survive the juggernaut of Stalinism. Under the German–Soviet Nonaggression Pact of 1939, the Soviets put paid to Poland's brief period of independence (of a kind) under Piłsudski. In 1944, as the German Wehrmacht retreated from Poland, one million Red Army troops replaced it, reducing Poland to a buffer state, as it had been so many times in the past.

The subsequent Sovietization of Poland was one of Stalin's spoils of war. It was a territory over which he exercised the closest control and the most assertive campaign of indoctrination. Polish culture and autonomy was buried in the gray postwar years as its people descended into drabness, Stalinist drudgery, and resignation. Soon after the end of the war the NKVD arrived to retrace Lenin's footsteps in Poland in order to create the official hagiography of his time there. As elsewhere in Eastern Europe, the Lenin plaques and statues, museums and memorabilia sprang up at five major centers, even though the places concerned retained no visible trace of Lenin's sojourn there between 1912 and 1914. The houses in Kraków at Zwierzyniec and Ulica Lubomirskiego were given commemorative plaques; the summer house at Biały Dunajec was made into a museum with a carefully reconstructed interior of suitably appropriate ethnic Polish furniture; the guest house along the road in Poronin where the Central Committee had stayed in 1913 became a Lenin museum in 1947. The prison at Nowy Targ was turned into the Lenin Scout House—an important local center for the indoctrination of the young—and his cell there lovingly recreated for their edification. By the time Lenin museums were set up in Kraków in 1954 and Warsaw in 1955, 617 people were employed in maintaining the Lenin industry in Poland. But the Soviet state did not pay the operating costs: these were raised from "voluntary" donations made by Polish workers.

It now became a civic duty for all good Polish communists to make at least one visit to Poronin. Every time they did so, their party card or trade union card was punched with a red stamp bearing Stalin's profile and a number. By May 1955, 9 million Poles had visited Poronin. The more red stamps you had on your party card, the better communist you were. By this time diligent party hacks were turning out paeans of praise to Lenin as an ardent champion of Poland's "right to self-determination and national independence." Lenin's views on the subject were "consistently democratic and imbued with proletarian internationalism and a profound and sympathetic understanding of the Polish people's aspirations."

Stalin's more visible and enduring parting gift to the Polish people, however, was a sprawling communist utopia—the model industrial suburb of Nowa Huta—completed after his death in 1953 in an area of green fields and marshes on the eastern outskirts of Kraków. This vast socialist-realist workers paradise was built supposedly to "counter the class imbalance" of old bourgeois Kraków by creating a working-class satellite town that would lead the way in the new Soviet era. The reality was a soulless and architecturally uniform travesty of the Polish architectural heritage—a carbuncle of steel and concrete in dramatic contrast to the colorful, meandering streets of medieval Kraków.

Nowa Huta was intended to serve as a dormitory for the 40,000 or so workers who labored in its vast new Lenin steelworks that covered an area of twenty square kilometers, its sulphurous air attacking the lungs of its 200,000 inhabitants and eating away at the fabric of Kraków's historic buildings. At the end of the long, straight Alley of Roses that intersected the town, its focal point was a hulking, seven-ton statue of Lenin, erected in 1973 in its central square. From here, neat, straight roads radiated out, Renaissance style, from the Great Leader's looming presence, in a perfect and orderly grid, to Nova Huta's uniformly gray and dehumanizing A, B, C, and D districts and their ranks of concrete, utilitarian apartment blocks. The town had everything—theaters, parks, cultural and political centers; kindergartens, health centers, and hospital facilities; schools and libraries; and an efficient tram system. But it had no soul, nothing but the stink of heavy industry, and no heart either; the Soviet planners had forbidden the erection of a single church. Nor did the Lenin statue come free. Workers from the Nowa Huta steelworks were induced to sacrifice their three-month bonuses to pay for it.

The ominous communist ambiance of Nowa Huta may have cowed the ordinary working Poles who toiled in its leviathan steelworks, but the flame of Polish nationalism and with it a violent hatred of Lenin and the Soviet legacy never died down. It might have flickered and dimmed during the early years after the Soviet backlash to the Hungarian uprising in the 1950s, but with the rise to international prominence of Karol Wojtyła as archbishop of Krakow (later Pope John Paul II) in the 1960s, it became a focal point for resistance to communist domination. Though the Soviets denied this devoutly Catholic nation churches, religious activism in Poland never ceased to have a vigorous underground life. In 1967, in a courageous assertion of nationhood and religious identity, the foundations were laid in Nowa Huta for a huge new Catholic church—The Ark of the Lord—consecrated by Wojtyła in 1977. It rose like a great defiant battleship in Nova Huta, its high stone walls and jutting presence creating a seemingly impregnable spiritual fortress for the Catholic faithful and dwarfing the statue of Lenin just along the road. Polish resistance to communism escalated rapidly with the rise of the Solidarity movement in the 1980s in Nova Huta and in the shipyards of Gdansk. Nowa Huta's Lenin Avenue became Solidarity Avenue; the name change marked the beginning of the end of communist dominion. During the 1980s someone left a bicycle propped up against Lenin's statue in Nowa Huta with a message that he should get on his bike and leave.

On the night of November 24, 1989, the eve of a state visit to Moscow by Polish Prime Minister Tadeusz Mazowiecki, the statue of Lenin at Nowa Huta was doused in paint and an attempt made to damage it by fire. It was the third time militant young members of the anticommunist Federation of Fighting Youth had tried to rid Nowa Huta of Lenin's presence, clashing with the militia in the process. A couple of weeks later, several thousand Nowa Hutans gathered in the heavy frost of early morning to watch the statue being dismantled by a massive crane. The local council had decided to remove it in order to avert further violence, assuring the invisible communist faithful that it was being taken away for "necessary repairs."

Down in the Podhale region of southern Poland, where Lenin and Nadya escaped the summer heat and claustrophobia of overcrowded Kraków, the house where they lodged at 9 Piłsudska Ulica in Biały Dunajec still stands. A helpful local man will point it out to you for the price of a beer. But it isn't a Lenin museum anymore. It was renovated nine years ago by its enterprising new owner and transformed into the Lenin Guesthouse. Lenin sightseers are discouraged; the new owner caters to paying guests only, largely from Japan and Russia.

The people of Biały Dunajec and nearby Poronin, where Lenin walked daily to collect his mail from the post office and meet visitors at the train, have always been uncomfortable with the imposition of a cosmetic Leninist connection. They hated the phony local history that had him talking in the fields with indigenous Góral peasants, like Jesus preaching to the faithful (which overlooked the fact that Lenin had no knowledge whatsoever of their dialect). The Lenin Museum in Poronin became the rallying point for enforced indoctrination under the Soviets; the Lenin statue erected outside in 1950 was a gift from the workers of Leningrad. From Poronin, you could take the Lenin trail to the Tatras and Morskie Oko. But the Poles in Galicia paid minimal lip service to the "celebration" of

Lenin's presence in their midst. During the communist years every train coming south from Krakow to Zakopane in the Tatras was obliged to stop at Poronin to allow communist tourists to worship at the Lenin Museum. Coach loads of children were brought on school trips. Everyone was obliged to attend the various Lenin ceremonials at the museum but felt ashamed at having to do so. As time went on, authorities found it increasingly difficult to drum up crowds for such occasions and had to import loyal communists from Leningrad to swell their numbers. In the end they were forced to manipulate events, ensuring that the big Lenin Day held in July in Poronin coincided with the public holiday and Saint's Day of St. Mary Magdalene. Russian communists visiting Poronin on that day would be misled into thinking that the crowds pouring from the local churches in national costume were there to celebrate Lenin.

Privately, Lenin's time in Poland became the butt of endless jokes and apocryphal stories. The local scouts took to singing rude songs around the campfire. One of them went: "In Poronin, on the stove, hang the underpants of Lenin." One of the most popular tales was told by local Tatra guide Stanisław Gąsienica-Byrcyn, who sometimes accompanied Lenin on hikes into the mountains. On one occasion in the autumn they were 7,200 feet up and coming back down the wet and slippery slope of a deep chasm. Lenin at that time was accompanied by three colleagues, including two women, when he slipped and fell into a gully between the snow and the rock face. They struggled in vain to get him out; in the end it was Stanisław who managed to haul Lenin clear on a rope. For years afterward, whenever he had a drink too many, Stanisław would bore everyone with the story of how there had been a moment when had had held the fate of the entire world on a "little piece of string." Word got back to the communist authorities and Stanisław suddenly stopped talking.

Regular acts of protest against Lenin's posthumous presence in Poland continued, however, even in the Tatra Mountains, where the Lenin memorials did not survive unscathed. Loyal communists on the Czechoslovakian side of the nearby border erected signs commemorating Lenin's hikes in the northwestern peaks of Rysy and Babia Góra. Communist excursion groups toiled up there on pilgrimages on Lenin Day, but that didn't stop the Poles on the other side from repeatedly vandalizing the memorials. The Czech communists fixed the signs in place every summer with concrete, and every winter the Poles would come and hack them down again. In the heyday of Solidarity a local man, Piotr Bąk, carved the word *Solidarność* across the brow of Lenin's bronze plaque on its mountain shrine, and he remains proud to this day for having done so. When members of Ruch—an organization dedicated to overthrowing communism and establishing a truly free Polish state—tried to burn down the Lenin Museum at Poronin on the Lenin centenary in 1970, they were sentenced to seven years in jail. But such savage sentences did not deter others from pouring red paint over the statue every time a communist delegation from Russia was due. Eventually the authorities had to mount a twenty-four-hour armed guard of plainclothes policemen and informers. After 1989, vociferous demands to liquidate the Poronin museum increased, with petitions being sent to the Polish culture minister.

The Poronin museum witnessed its last big propaganda exercise in 1988, when Soviet president Mikhail Gorbachev visited. The final decisive act of protest came on January 30, 1990, when at 6:00 AM one of the guards was awakened by a tremendous crash. Outside he discovered Lenin's three-ton bronze statue toppled over in the snow. The chains used to pull it down were lying on the ground nearby and a steel wire was still wrapped round its neck. People in Poronin had a good idea who the culprit was, but they were unwilling to talk, and a wall of silence greeted official investigators from the Criminal Justice Department. Ten years later, a local Góral man and well-known activist, Józef Kaspruś, "confessed" to the crime, although he never named his accomplices. Soon after the statue was pulled down, and despite the authorities' fear of Soviet reprisals, the museum was closed for "renovation," its artifacts carted off to the Museum of Communism in Kozłówka. Eventually it was turned into a library. The statue's concrete foundations are still there, only they are now hidden by overgrown bushes; the ornamental lake that once graced the front of the museum is today a play area for the local kindergarten.

If you venture to the small town of Nowy Targ today, you can still find the prison where Lenin was held in August 1914, but you would hardly recognize it as such. Its unprepossessing, newly painted exterior announces that it is now a youth center. Although it ceased to be a jail in 1948 its life as an obligatory place of pilgrimage for good Polish communists was not a long one. All the plaques indicating Lenin's presence here were removed in 1989. Inside on the ground floor Lenin's supposed cell, so carefully preserved for sixty years or more, has been dismantled and its artifacts destroyed or dispersed. The plaque outside, so frequently daubed with paint by protesters, was taken down. But in the building's damp, dark basement you can still see the cobwebbed iron bars of the original cell windows of the old prison and, randomly propped against a wall, the last remaining scratched and dusty prison door with its rusty inspection hatch and lock. But Lenin's ghost no longer walks in Nowy Targ. If you ask locals to direct you to the old prison they are more likely nowadays to point you to the other one, where the Gestapo tortured members of the Polish resistance during World War II.

In the meantime, a new home has been found for the Lenin statue removed from Nowa Huta. After lying in storage at Wróblowice for three years, it was bought in the 1990s by Swedish millionaire and businessman "Big Bengt" Erlandsson for 100,000 Swedish crowns. It now graces his High Chaparral theme park outside Stockholm with a cigarette in its mouth and an earring in one ear. After only seventy-three years of Leninism, capitalism is rapidly debasing the last of the legacy of a communist icon. Meanwhile, in Nowa Huta plans were announced in 2008 for the Museum of the History of Poland to be constructed in the town's now decaying but architecturally important Kino Światowid, built in high Stalinist, socialist-realist style.

The final subversive act for Poles seeking to bury their Leninist past is taking a Crazy Guides communist tour of Nowa Huta in an old East German Trabant or staying at one of the "Good-bye Lenin" hostels. Cheap, cheerful, and friendly, the hostels offer a convivial environment where weary backpackers can lounge as scruffily and lazily as they like for as long as they wish, doing absolutely nothing. In the stairwell outside, Lenin and his fellow communist icons, Trotsky, Marx, and Ché, are transmuted into punk rockers and hippies. They gaze down on visitors from psychedelic frescoes that, in the irreverent postcommunist world, wave two Polish fingers at the good old Leninist principles of tidiness, order, and self-discipline.

ACKNOWLEDGMENTS

Chasing Lenin's footsteps across Europe during a seventeen-year period in which he did a great deal of traveling is a tall order and I was faced with invidious choices during the writing of this book as to which of the many places he lived in I could afford to get to. In the end I decided on visiting those countries for which I had no knowledge of the language—Finland and Poland—where I had particular need of the help of others in accessing the source material. In September 2008 my dear friend Christina Zaba accompanied me on a trip to Poland, traveling south with me from Kraków to Nowy Targ, Biały Dunajec, Poronin, Zakopane, and the Tatra Mountains. By a stroke of good fortune this is an area she knows well, and Christina was a tireless and generous guide and interpreter as well as a good walking companion on a memorable hike into the mountains. Our wonderful driver, Jerczy, waited patiently on many occasions, as we stopped and looked and took photographs along the way. During that trip I met and talked with many Poles about Lenin's time in the Podhale region. I am particularly indebted to Piotr Bąk, former mayor of Zakopane, and his wife Joanna for entertaining us with wonderful homemade pierogi and talking at length, and with considerable insight and humor, about Lenin's legacy in Poland.

In Finland in October 2008, I was given the warmest of welcomes by Leena Kakko, curator, and Aimo Minkkinen, director, of the Lenin Museum in Tampere. In this, the last surviving full-time museum dedicated to his life, I was given the free run of the museum's wonderful collection of books on Lenin and provided with photographs for this book, for which

I am most grateful. Aimo most generously gave up his time to drive Leena and I all the way down the southwestern peninsula of Finland in pursuit of the story of Lenin's escape from Finland at Christmas 1907. Anne Bergström, who runs the small Lenin Museum in the Fredrikssen House, originally located at Norrgården but which has now been moved to Parainen, opened up specially out of season so that I could see this lovely house and the room in which Lenin stayed. After completing my research in Finland, Leena was a good-natured traveling companion on a memorable train ride from Helsinki to St. Petersburg's Finland Station and arranged private views at the Museum of Political History and the Lenin rooms at the Smolny. My thanks go to Evgeny Artemov and Lora Buday at the former and Ol'ga Evstaf'eva and Natalya Dolgorukova at the latter.

In the UK I was once again assisted in my research by Phil Tomaselli, an expert PRO searcher who hunted out what Lenin material there is, sadly none of it pre-1917. Sir Ian Blair put me in touch with Andrew Brown in the Directorate of Information at the Metropolitan Police, who also confirmed that, much to my historian's regret, no early police files on Lenin's time in London between 1902 and 1911, if they ever existed, have survived. John Callow at the Marx Memorial Library on Clerkenwell Green offered welcome advice and the use of this wonderful repository. Martin Banham and Lorraine Lees at the Islington Local History Centre in the Finsbury Library in London were most helpful in searching for Lenin material and to my delight produced a wonderful box of cuttings from the local press and other material relating to Lenin's time in London. Professor Bill Fishman, an expert in the history of Russian and Jewish East End radicals, offered valuable insights and provided me with some of his articles. My friend and fellow Russianist Melanie Ilic, Reader in History at the University of Gloucestershire, was once again supportive and helpful, pointing me to the valuable section on Lenin and Bolshevik Russia at the University of Birmingham's European Resource Centre. Ana Siljak at Queen's University, Kingston, Ontario, offered valuable information on the last days of Vera Zasulich. Bob Henderson provided copies of his articles on Lenin's time at the British Library reading room.

Thanks to the wonders of the internet I was able to track down information on the European rail system in the 1900s, aided by the expert knowledge of Richard Putley, Janusz Lukasiak, and Peter Northover. In

Oxford, Reija Fanous very kindly translated material for me from Finnish and Dag Martinsen did likewise from Swedish. I am also particularly indebted here at Oxford to my friend Linora Lawrence for putting me in touch with Professor Ronald Chaplain, who offered not only a fascinating and extraordinary personal story behind the Iron Curtain but valuable evidence on both Lenin's final illness and Nadezhda Krupskaya's physical condition. Professor John Wass offered additional information on thyroidism. During my research I drew on the opinions of Professor R. Carter Elwood and Michael Pearson, who have both written books on Inessa Armand. In a late breakthrough on Lenin's time in Paris, Ross King passed on information about the bohemian life of the city in the 1900s. Richard Davies at the Leeds Russian Archive kindly checked through my bibliography, and Professor Harry Shukman at St. Antony's College, Oxford, once again offered advice and moral support in the writing of this book.

A special word of thanks must go to the generosity of Stephanie Weiner in California, whom I found, in a moment of researcher's serendipity, on the internet, and who provided me with information from an unpublished family memoir as well as a wonderful photograph of Mendel Singer, the Jewish storekeeper in Poronin, and his family; I am indebted to her for permission to reproduce it in this book. Hayley Millar kindly allowed me to use her photograph of Lenin's discarded statue. I could not end these acknowledgments without commending the work of the Marxist Internet Archive, which is making available online the entire forty-three-volume English language edition of Lenin's *Collected Works*, an invaluable aid in the writing of this book. See www.marxists.org/archive/lenin.

In *Conspirator* I provide an alternative view of Lenin the man during his long exile in Europe, a part of his life that standard biographies often neglect in favor of the years in power. It was something of a challenge to approach my subject, as a woman, a feminist, and a nonacademic, against the grain of traditional biographies of major male political figures. During my research I made a point of seeking out lost, forgotten, or undiscovered accounts of Lenin in exile between 1900 and 1917, many of them in foreign languages. There is still more material out there waiting to be discovered, I am sure of that. For this reason I would greatly welcome any new information readers might like to share, as well as comments and suggestions, to the contact page at my website, www.helenrappaport.com.

Throughout this project my brothers Peter and Christopher were once again an enormous support to me, as too my agent and friend, Charlie Viney, who continues to guide and encourage me in everything I do. Fellow writer Susan Hill has been a wise and valued mentor; my commissioning editor at Basic Books, Lara Heimert, showed enthusiastic support for this book and for my writing from the outset, which is greatly appreciated, as did her assistant, Brandon Proia, and copy editor Chrisona Schmidt, both of whom provided a meticulous edit of the text.

I should, in closing, point out that the Russian transliteration system used in this book is that by Oxford Slavonic Papers. Finally, for the sanity of the reader and to avoid confusion, because Lenin spent most of the years 1900–1917 in Europe—outside the events going on in Russia—all dates given are according to the European Gregorian calendar and not the Russian Orthodox Julian one.

HELEN RAPPAPORT
October 2009, Oxford

NOTES

∞∞∞

Introduction: Shlisselburg Fortress, 1887

3   *poorly lit first and second floors:* For a fascinating account of life as a prisoner in Shlisselburg, see Vera Figner, *Memoirs of a Revolutionist,* vol. 2, *When the Clock of Life Stopped.* Figner was held here for twenty years and released in 1904. Mikhail Novorussky, a co-conspirator of Aleksandr's who pleaded for mercy and was reprieved, wrote an account of his incarceration; see *Zapiski Shlisselburzhtsa.* For fuller details of the regime at Shlisselburg, including internal photographs and diagrams, see Gernet, *Istoriya Tsarskoi t'yurmi,* vol. 3, chap. 4, "Shlisselburgskaya krepost." For a compelling Western account of the prison written by émigré anarchist Prince Petr Kropotkin, see "A Russian State Prison," *Times,* August 21, 1903, p. 6.

5   *fulfilled their duty:* Ivansky, *Comet in the* Night, p. 292. The story of Aleksandr Ulyanov's brief life and involvement in the plot to assassinate Alexander III is contained in Ivansky, *Comet,* which includes accounts of the trial and Aleksandr's testimony. See also Trotsky, *Young Lenin;* and Deutscher, *Lenin's Childhood.*

6   *"the study of worms":* Krupskaya, *Memories of Lenin,* p. 18.

7   *iron-clad, remorseless will:* The rise of revolutionary Marxism has been discussed at length in many books, but see, for example, Leszek Kolawkowski, *Main Currents of Marxism: Its Rise, Growth, and Dissolution,* 3 vols. (Oxford: Clarendon, 1978); and George Lichtheim, *Marxism: A Historical and Critical Study* (London: Routledge & Kegan Paul, 1964). For an eloquent summary of Russian populism, see Isaiah Berlin, introduction to Venturi, *Roots of Revolution.* Berlin's essay on Plekhanov, "The father of Russian Marxism," in *The Power of Ideas* (London: Chatto & Windus, 2000) encapsulates the man, his thinking, and his legacy with clarity and brevity, as too does Lunacharsky, *Revolutionary Silhouettes.*

Chapter 1: Leaving Shushenskoe

9   *"the very edge of the world itself":* N. P. Silkova, *Ocherk istorii krasnoyarskoy kraevoy organizatsii KPSS 1895–1980* (Krasnoyarsk: Knizhnoe Isdatel'stvo, 1982), p. 34. The saying went: "Net mesta glushe Shushi, dal'she Shushi Sayany, za Sayanami krai svet."

321

9   *Siberian Italy:* CW 37: 111.

10 *first to leave the examination hall:* Deutscher, *Lenin's Childhood*, p. 60. For overviews of Lenin's childhood and education, see Deutscher, *Lenin's Childhood*; Trotsky, *Young Lenin*; Theen, *Lenin*; and Service, *Lenin: A Biography*, chaps. 1–6.

10 *"a certain unsociability":* Deutscher, *Lenin's Childhood*, pp. 66–67. Ironically, Ulyanov's headmaster was the father of Aleksandr Kerensky, who in 1917 was briefly head of the Provisional Government after the czar abdicated in March. Kerensky would be ousted by Lenin after the October Revolution. Trotsky, *Young Lenin*, pp. 112–113.

11 *Strict, authoritarian, and frugal:* The memoirs of Lenin's sisters Anna and Mariya are the most valuable source; see *VoVIL*, vol. 1. These have been expanded on by Service from newly available archival sources in *Lenin: A Biography*; see especially chapters 1–2. Wolfe, *Three Who Made a Revolution*, chaps. 2–5, remains a valuable source, as do Deutscher, *Lenin's Childhood*; Trotsky, *Young Lenin*; and Valentinov *Early Years of Lenin*.

13 *"dangerous addictions":* Deutscher, *Lenin's Childhood*, p. 30; Krupskaya, *Memories*, pp. 39–40.

13 *"grimly restrained":* Dmitri Ulyanov, quoted in Beryl Williams, *Lenin*, p. 19.

14 *"plodding genius":* Isaiah Berlin, introduction to Franco Venturi, *The Roots of Revolution* (London: Phoenix, 2001), p. xx.

14 *revolutionary struggle to come:* N. G. Chernyshevsky, *What Is to Be Done?* (New York: Vintage, 1961), pp. 229–233.

14 *self-denying precepts:* Valentinov, *Encounters*, p. 67; Volkogonov, *Lenin*, pp. 20–21. For a discussion of Chernyshevsky's influence on Lenin, see Valentinov, *Early Years*, chap. 6; Chernyshevski, *What Is to Be Done?* and Chernyshevski, "Rebirth of V. Ulyanov."

14 *"a charge for a whole life":* Valentinov, *Early Years*, p. 136.

15 *the knack of making complex political ideas simple:* Krupskaya, *Memories*, pp. 15–18. To Lenin she was "Nadya" throughout their life together. In exile Nadya often signed herself as "Ulyanova"; the later attribution of "Krupskaya," her maiden name, is anachronistic to this story; Nadya adopted it after they returned to Russia.

16 *Evasion and subterfuge:* Daly, *Autocracy*, pp. 77, 102.

16 *only young according to his identity papers:* Potresov, "Lenin," p. 293.

16 *"big brains . . . pushed his hair out":* A. I. Ivansky, *Petersburgskie gody*, pp. 88–90.

16 *"nothing of the 'radical' intellectual":* Weber, *Lenin*, p. 7.

16 *"Ulyanov occupies himself with Social Democratic propaganda":* Possony, *Lenin*, pp. 61–62.

17 *to evade any police who might be tailing him:* Payne, *Life and Death of Lenin*, p. 37.

17 *"one of the best of our Russian friends":* Weber, *Lenin*, p. 9.

17 *"temperament of a fighting flame":* Perepiska G. V. Plekhanova i P. B. Akselroda (Moscow: Redaktsiya Berlina, 1925), 2:269–270; Rice, *Lenin*, p. 45.

18 *had to eat six ink pots:* Clark, *Lenin*, p. 42; CW 37: 327; Krupskaya, *Memories*, p. 29.

18 *books being delivered to prisoner Ulyanov:* Krzhizhanovsky, in Tamara Deutscher, *Not by Politics Alone*, p. 50.

19 *dreamed whole chapters of the book in progress:* CW 37: 85.

19 *"monotonous, bare and desolate steppe":* CW 37: 91–92.

20 a *"hearty welcome" from Yudin:* See letter to sister Mariya, March 10, CW 37: 94. In December 1906 the Yudin collection was acquired by the Library of Congress in Washington.

20 *"everything is as it should be":* CW 37: 98.

21 *couldn't get used to such old "news":* CW 37: 95.

21 *"Shu-shu-shu is not a bad village":* CW 37: 107.

22 *letters . . . "from every corner of Russia and Siberia":* CW 37: 160.

22 *systematically arranged in date order:* Fellow exile Gleb Krzhizhanovsky testified that Ulyanov would become incensed if anyone tried to read him news from papers out of the meticulous date sequence in which he had arranged them. See Tamara Deutscher, *Not by Politics Alone*, p. 53.

22 *wiping his pen on his jacket lapel:* See letters for February 7 and February 24 in CW 37: 150–154, 160–162.

22 *"literary manifestations" of every kind:* CW 37: 117.

22 *"today you write one article, tomorrow another":* CW 37: 124.

23 *"like a real Siberian":* CW 37: 129.

23 *skating far better than shooting:* CW 37: 227.

23 *"my sedentary life":* CW 37: 253.

24 *"I am in no hurry for books":* CW 37: 138.

26 *"unbelievably weak" and "opportunistic":* CW 37: 281.

Chapter 2: Igniting the Spark

27 *Mecca for revolutionaries:* Valentinov, *Early Years*, p. 158.

28 *Nadya was the sick one:* She was probably suffering from a prolapsed womb, which may also explain her inability to conceive. Information from Dr. Ronald Chaplain.

28 *perpetually driven, racing:* Lepeshinsky, *Na povorote*, p. 104.

29 *planned launch of the journal:* On the surveillance of Ulanov in Pskov, organized by Colonel Piramidov of the St. Petersburg Okhrana, see Erokhin, *Shushenskii arsenal*, p. 191.

30 *"directly sensing Russia":* Krupskaya, *Memories*, p. 55.

30 *"The charged atmosphere burst into a storm":* "How the 'Spark' Was Nearly Extinguished," CW 4: 340.

31 *voluminous and often ponderous writings:* Payne, *Life and Death*, pp. 144–147.

31 *growing domination over the party:* "How the Spark," CW 4: 331–349; Wolfe, *Three*, p. 174; Service, *Lenin: A Biography*, pp. 132–133.

31 *"keep a stone in one's sling":* "How the Spark," CW 4: 342

31 *provoked a recurrence of his stomach problem:* Many Lenin sources labor Bernstein's theories at excessive length. For concise appraisals, see Read, *Lenin*, pp. 40–41; Payne, *Life and Death*, pp. 134–138; Wolfe, *Three*, pp. 164–169.

31 *"trip down the Rhine":* CW 37: 298.

32 *kept the Russians under close surveillance:* Johnson, "Zagranichnaia Agentura"; Zuckerman, *Tsarist Secret Police Abroad*, chap. 2.

32 *intent on subversive activities:* Possony, *Lenin*, p. 74.

32 *active and vocal movement for social democracy:* Williams, "Russians in Germany," pp. 122–123.

33 *advice on smuggling literature:* Zuckerman, *Tsarist Secret Police Abroad*, pp. 38–39.

33   *"artist had to appear un-bourgeois"*: Robert E. Norton, *Secret Germany: Stefan George and His Circle* (Ithaca: Cornell University Press, 2002).

34   *fifty-three, overweight, and disheveled*: Payne, *Life and Death*, p. 140; Dann, *Lenin and Nadya*, pp. 72–74.

34   *"true to the core"*: Bergman, *Vera Zasulich*, p. 164. For an interesting contemporary portrait of Zasulich, see Stepniak, *Underground Russia*, pp. 106–114; Payne, *Life and Death*, p. 144; Muraveva, *Lenin v Myunkhene*, p. 104.

34   *first issue of Iskra*: For details see Brachmann, *Russische Sozialdemokraten* (Berlin: Akademie-Verlag, 1962), pp. 1–52.

35   *"settle down to work"*: CW 37: 307.

35   *"a rotten autumn"*: CW 37: 310.

36   *how Russians managed to stay alive*: CW 37: 313–316.

36   *"did not like it very much"*: CW 37: 323.

36   *"looking purposely like an innocent provincial"*: Krupskaya, *Memories*, p. 49.

37   *Jordan K. Jordanov, a doctor of law*: Hitzer, *Lenin in München*, p. 206.

37   *slovenly habits of Vera Zasulich*: Krupskaya, *Memories*, p. 53.

38   *meals in cheap eating houses*: For an amusing account of the Lenins' diet, see Elwood, "What Lenin Ate."

38   *Zur Frankenburg snack bar*: Muraveva, *Lenin v Myunkhene*, pp. 48–49. Kaiser's original interview about the Ulyanovs as tenants appeared in *Süddeutsche Zeitung*, April 22, 1960.

38   *disturb his train of thought*: Krupskaya, "Iz Otvetov na Ankety," in *VoVIL* 1: 586.

39   *"perpetually arguing"*: Lunacharsky, *Revolutionary Silhouettes*, pp. 131–132.

39   *crockery that could be thrown away after use*: Aline, *Lénine à Paris*, p. 21.

39   *places like the Café Luitpold*: Krupskaya, *Memories*, p. 59; for a portrait of Martov, see Lunacharsky, *Revolutionary Silhouettes*, pp. 131–140.

39   *sitting in the Café Luitpold*: Haimson, *Making of Three Russian Revolutionaries*, p. 109.

40   *stern and bad-tempered*: Haimson, *Making*, p. 125; Getzler, *Martov*, p. 64.

40   *a golden time*: Haimson, *Making*, pp. 34–36.

40   *"go there when you are young"*: Quoted in McNeal, *Bride of the Revolution*, p. 91.

41   *"tense as a scene from Dostoievsky"*: Krupskaya, *Memories*, p. 58.

41   *Ulyanov's love of power*: Struve, "My Contacts and Conflicts with Lenin," pp. 591–592.

41   *"an impudent boor"*: Quoted in Pipes, *Struve*, p. 264.

42   *seized at Polangen*: CW 34: 63; see also Hill, *Letters of Lenin*, footnotes on pp. 129, 137, 139, 141.

42   *"prisons crammed full"*: CW 34: 59.

42   *"delay, carelessness, loss"*: CW 34: 65–66.

43   *1,599 German marks per month*: McNeal, *Bride*, p. 98.

Chapter 3: *Konspiratsiya*

46   *list of 1,896 political and social issues*: Marcu, *Lenin*, p. 89; McNight, "Lenin," p. 18.

46   *"science of destruction"*: There are many published versions, for example, www.uoregon.edu/~kimball/Nqv.catechism.thm.htm.

47   *effective system of distribution:* Wildman, "*Iskra* Organization in Russia," p. 485.

47   *"highest level of perfection":* Lenin, quoted in Daly, *Autocracy Under Siege*, p. 102; "Nasushchnyi vopros," in *PSS* 4:194.

47   *Ulyanov's guiding principle:* Possony, *Lenin Reader*, p. 322; Lenin, *Selected Works*, 2:151.

47   *"things you need to talk about":* Lyadov, in OVIL 1900–1922, p. 45.

48   *"The Horse":* Deich, *Rasskazy o Lenine*, pp. 155–156.

48   *comic book spies:* Deich, *Rasskazy o Lenine*, p. 177; Bobrovskaya, *Twenty Years*, p. 59.

48   *a sympathetic doctor:* Elwood, *Russian Social Democracy*, p. 94; Krupskaya, *Memories*, pp. 70–71.

48   *Russian painter Ilya Repin:* Stasova, *Vospominaniya;* for interesting insights into life in the underground, see pp. 39–45.

48   *How to Conduct Oneself Under Interrogation:* Written by Vladimir Makhnovets and published in 1900 by the League of Russian Social Democrats Abroad.

49   *leaflets . . . pasted on walls:* Shub, *Lenin*, pp. 62–65.

49   *equal risks with the men:* Ulam, *Lenin and the Bolsheviks*, pp. 214–215.

49   *learned how to make bombs and shoot guns:* Clements, *Bolshevik Women*, pp. 10–13.

49   *treated them as equals:* Krupskaya, *Memoirs*, p. 60.

50   *instructions from Ulyanov:* Turton, *Forgotten Lives*, pp. 34–35, and especially chapter 2, "The Underground." Turton illustrates the heretofore undervalued contribution of Anna and Mariya and the extent to which they lived full and independent lives within the movement rather than being "worshipful devotees" of their brother's work.

50   *"hotbed of provocation":* Haimson, *Three Russian Revolutionaries*, p. 134.

50   *police raids and arrests:* Haimson, *Three*, pp. 135–136.

51   *Her socialist conscience:* Haimson, *Three*, p. 137.

51   *names, aliases, and addresses:* Clements, *Bolshevik Women*, pp. 79–81.

52   *"flesh of my flesh":* Clements, *Bolshevik Women*, p. 85.

52   *printing and distributing political broadsides:* Clements, *Bolshevik Women*, pp. 68–74.

52   *"righting the emotional wrongs":* Wolfe, *Three Who Made a Revolution*, p. 247.

53   *next train out of Kiev:* Burenin, *Pamyatnye gody*, pp. 157–160.

54   *most dependable route:* Muraveva, *Lenin v Myunkhene*, pp. 87–88; Wildman, "*Iskra* Organisation in Russia," p. 489.

54   *six thousand tiny skerries:* Futrell, *Northern Underground*, pp. 41–48.

55   *St. Petersburg children's nurse:* Burenin, *Pamyatnye gody*, p. 28.

55   *Finnish opera star:* Dashkov, *Po Leninskim mestam Skandinavii*, p. 21.

55   *way station for illegal literature:* Burenin, *Pamyatnye gody*, p. 29.

55   *knock at the door:* Burenin, *Pamyatnye gody*, p. 38.

56   *"Nina":* O'Connor, *Engineer of Revolution*, pp. 42–45.

56   *Okhrana "spooks":* Elwood, *Russian Social Democracy*, p. 53.

56   *careless and naive:* See, for example, Daly, *Autocracy Under Siege*, p. 42.

57   *Stasova became so adept:* Deich, *Rasskazy o Lenine*, pp. 158–159.

57   *police raids and arrests:* Kahn, *Codebreakers*, p. 343; Williams, *Other Bolsheviks*, pp. 8–14.

57   *a "fly" (mukha):* Lauchlan, *Russian Hide and Seek*, p. 120.

57   *"letters about handkerchiefs (passports)":* Krupskaya, *Memories*, p. 69.

58   *demonstrations and strikes:* Piatnitsky, *Memoirs*, p. 41.
59   *"not enough revolutionaries":* Lyadov, *Iz zhizni partii*, p. 10.

Chapter 4: Becoming Lenin

61   *Friends of Russian Freedom:* Deich, *Rasskazy o Lenine*, p. 164.
61   *decided to return home:* Prokhorov, in OVIL *1900–1922*, pp. 22–23.
61   *"a dozen dawdlers":* CW 34: 136.
62   *revolutionary committees:* CW 34: 93, 100–101.
63   *"cog[s] in the revolutionary machine":* Krupskaya, *Memories*, p. 60.
63   *romantic idealism:* Payne, *Life and Death*, p. 151.
63   *Ulyanov was there to lead the way:* For discussions of *What Is to Be Done?* see Ulam, *Lenin and the Bolsheviks*, p. 228–236; Read, *Lenin*, pp. 52–59; Service, *Lenin: A Biography*, pp. 139–142.
64   *"useless and harmful":* Lenin, "What Is to Be Done?" in *Selected Works* (Moscow: Foreign Languages Publishing House, 1960), 1:212.
65   *extraordinarily penetrating:* Meshcheryakov, in *VoVIL* 1:220.
65   *battle for ideological leadership:* CW 34: 103.
66   *succession of pseudonyms:* Read, *Lenin*, p. 44.
66   *pleasing congruence:* For an interesting discussion of the Lenin pseudonym, see Shtein, *Ul'yanovy i Leniny*, chap. 11.
67   *"overturn the whole of Russia":* David Footman, *Red Prelude* (London: Barrie & Rockliff, 1968), p. 87; Wiliams, *Lenin*, p. 32; "What Is to Be Done?" CW 5: 467.
67   *revolutionary elite:* Wildman, "*Iskra* Organization," p. 493.
67   *"leading organ of the party":* Wildman, "*Iskra* Organization," p. 497.
67   *"stronghold of capitalism":* Krupskaya, *Memories*, p. 64.
67   *the man to watch:* Volner, *Psevdonimy V I Lenina*, p. 52.

Chapter 5: Dr. and Mrs. Richter

70   *"most comfortable place":* Thompson, *Guard from the Yard*, p. 34.
70   *tiny house in Highgate:* Henry Brailsford, "When Lenin and Trotsky Were in London," p. 86.
70   *take lemon with their tea:* Madame Olga Novikoff, *Russian Memories* (London: Herbert Jenkins, 1917), p. 201.
70   *they didn't cause trouble:* Woodhall, *Secrets of Scotland Yard*, p. 74; Slatter, *From the Other Shore*, pp. 13, 35.
71   *"attached not the slightest importance":* Brust, quoted in Aldred, *No Traitor's Gait*, 1:278.
71   *"fervour of the Apostles":* Armfelt, "Russia in East London," p. 25.
71   *"conspiratorial point of view":* Krupskaya, *Memories*, p. 69.
71   *"his self-effacing wife":* Alekseev, "V. I. Lenin v Londone," in Golikov, *VoVIL* 2:216.
72   *"makes a foul impression":* CW 43: 80.
72   *printer compositors":* 1901 Census, RG13, piece 145, folio 77, p. 13. The children were Louisa Mary, Leonard, Robert, Alfred, and Harry. The Yeo family's side of the story was told by eldest son Leonard and his sister Louisa in 1939 at a press conference called by the Finsbury Communist Party after newspaper reports denied Lenin had ever lived at 30 Holford Square. "Lenin's Clerkenwell Home: Recollections of His Landlady," *Guardian*, July 20, 1939, p. 15.

72 *she fainted:* "Lenin's Clerkenwell Home."
72 *but no pictures or decorations:* Atkins, "Lenin Was Their Lodger," p. 14; Muravyova, *Lenin in London,* p. 23.
72 *they paid their rent:* "The Londoner's Diary," *Evening Standard,* August 30, 1941, p. 2.
73 *always willing to learn:* See Maisky, *Journey into the Past,* pp. 83–87, for Rothstein's account of Lenin at Holford Square. Atkins, "Lenin Was Their Lodger," p. 14.
73 *"unused to English ways":* Letters to the editor, *Islington Gazette,* October 15, 1963, p. 4.
73 *"most ordinary little man":* Atkins, "Lenin Was Their Lodger," p. 14.
74 *words ... were sufficient food:* Maisky, *Journey into the Past,* p. 86.
74 *"the Russian intellectual is always dirty":* Krupskaya, *Memories,* p. 74.
74 *lodgings on Holford Square:* Karachan, *Lenin in London,* p. 15. The second commune address, at Percy Circus, was discovered by Bob Henderson in the British Museum's list of ticket holders under Martov's name; www.bobhenderson.co.uk/libhist.html.
75 *Harry Quelch:* The building now houses the Marx Memorial Library, an outstanding collection of socialist books and literature, established in 1933 in response to the book burning then taking place in Hitler's Germany.
75 *only enough room:* Beer, *Fifty Years of International Socialism,* p. 14; Lenin, obituary for Harry Quelch, *CW* 19: 369–371.
75 *"ginger-haired young man":* "Londoner's Diary," *Evening Standard,* August 30, 1941, p. 2.
75 *considerable financial difficulty:* Pyatnitsky, *Memoirs,* p. 53.
75 *domed reading room:* Krupskaya, *Memories,* p. 65.
76 *"a holiday!":* Alekseev, in Golikov, *VoVIL* 1:218.
76 *day-to-day editorial work:* Golikov, *VoVIL* 1:216; Trotsky, *On Lenin,* pp. 40, 43.
76 *escapees from Kiev prison:* *CW* 36: 123.
76 *"simply swallows books":* Maisky, *Journey into the Past,* p. 84.
76 *"nor could anybody understand us":* Krupskaya, *Memories,* p. 65.
76 *"exchange Russian lessons for English":* *Athenaeum,* May 10, 1902, p. 577.
77 *particular friendship with Rayment:* Henry Rayment obituary, *The Times,* October 11, 1921, p. 13.
77 *British socialist thinking:* Semenov, *Po leninskim mestam,* pp. 18–20, whose 1960 account appears to have been based on a conversation with Zelda Kahan (1886–1969). In 1913 Kahan married English communist William Peyton Coates, under which surname she was later known. Zelda Coates's short but valuable "Memories of Lenin in London in 1902–3 and 1907" was published in *Labour Monthly,* November 1968, pp. 506–508.
77 *paid more attention to the crowds:* Aldred, *No Traitor's Gate,* 1:278; Karachan, *Lenin in London,* p. 18; Semenov, *Po leninskim mestam,* p. 24; Coates, "Memories of Lenin," p. 507.
77 *Britain's "two nations":* Krupskaya, *Memories,* p. 65.
78 *Adam's Chop House:* Semenov, *Po leninskim mestam,* p. 27.
78 *mold it to his own purpose:* Lenin, "Interview with Arthur Ransome," *CW* 33: 400.
78 *"illogicality of the everyday":* Gorky, quoted in Francis Sheppard, *London: A History* (Oxford: Oxford University Press, 2000), p. 301. The Pindar of Wakefield is still there. It is now a popular music venue known as The Water Rats. The music

events are held in the old music hall at the back. The Crown & Woolpack on St. John Street still has its original exterior but is now a smart hairdressing salon.

79   *"smoke wreathed city"*: Krupskaya, *Memories*, p. 68.

79   *"studying the country"*: CW 37: 358.

79   *frequented by Russian émigrés*: Maisky, *Journey into the Past*, p. 36.

79   *Marxist revolutionary socialism*: Pimlott, *Toynbee Hall*, pp. 151–153.

80   *he was convinced*: Bowman, "Lenin in London," pp. 336–338.

81   *"essence of Capitalist Society"*: Krupskaya, *Memories*, p. 66.

81   *"playing at bears"*: Coates, "Memories of Lenin," p. 507.

81   *"worn to shreds"*: CW 34: 105.

82   *"to rush about"*: CW 34: 111.

83   *wealth of statistical evidence*: Trotsky, *My Life*, p. 126.

83   *temporal and the spiritual camps*: Trotsky, *On Lenin*, pp. 30, 45; Elizabeth Hill in her pseudonymous *For Readers Only* (London: Chapman & Hall, 1936) identifies one of Lenin's favorite venues for listening to socialist oratory as the "Southwell Place Labour Church," but no information on it has been found.

84   *copious amounts of mustard*: Trotsky, *On Lenin*, p. 37.

84   *hard-edged party*: Trotsky, *On Lenin*, p. 35.

84   *Russian Social Democratic Labor Party*: Alekseev, "V. I. Lenin v Londone," in Golikov, *VoVIL* 1:217.

84   *anniversary of the Paris Commune*: The building was taken over in 1906 by the East End Jewish Anarchists Club founded by Rudolf Rocker, and thereafter was known as the Worker's Friend Club. In 1907 it would be a popular haunt of Russian delegates to the RSDLP congress in London.

85   *"everything is crowded out"*: CW 37: 354.

85   *visit to the German theater*: CW 37: 355. Possibly an allusion to a German language performance at the Communist Club in Charlotte Street. The club had a stage and was used at weekends for concerts and other theatrical performances.

85   *Lenin's increasing stranglehold*: Getzler, *Martov*, p. 65; Zasulich remained at Sidmouth Street until 1905, when she returned to Russia and dropped out of political life. She later opposed Lenin's Bolshevik takeover and died in 1919.

85   *"like cats"*: Weber, *Lenin*, p. 30.

86   *"far better to deal with"*: Letters to the editor, *Islington Gazette*, October 15, 1963, p. 4. The house at 30 Holford Square was badly damaged by bombing in 1940 and was demolished as part of the major redevelopment of Holford Square after the war. The flat occupied by Zasulich and colleagues at Sidmouth Street also disappeared during redevelopment.

86   *"such a world shaker"*: "Lenin's Clerkenwell Home," *Guardian*, July 20, 1923, p. 15; Atkins, "Lenin Was Their Lodger," pp. 14–15; Krupskaya, *Memories*, p. 67.

Chapter 6: "The Dirty Squabble Abroad"

87   *confined to bed*: Krupskaya, *Memories*, p. 79; Kudryavtsev, *Lenin's Geneva Addresses*, p. 38. For a possible alternative diagnosis of this rash, see page 355.

87   *Lenin insisted*: Kulyabko, in *VoVIL* 1:231–232.

87   *factored in time*: Kulyabko, in *VoVIL* 1:230.

88   *"already in my inkwell"*: Kudryavtsev, *Lenin's Geneva Addresses*, p. 47.

88   *lived in a state of transit*: Bobrovskaya, *Twenty-Five Years*, pp. 93–96; Stasova, *Stranitsy*, p. 49; Kudryavtsev, *Lenin's Geneva Addresses*, pp. 42–43; Krupskaya, *Memories*, pp. 80–81.

89   *warehouse attached to the Maison du Peuple:* Trotsky, *My Life*, p. 138; Shotman, *Zapiski*, pp. 83–84.

89   *appearance of conspirators:* Marcu, *Lenin*, p. 102; Shotman, *Zapiski*, pp. 83–84.

90   *bales of wool:* Shotman, *Zapiski*, pp. 83–84.

90   *Each speaker was allowed half an hour:* Lepeshinsky, *Protokoly*, 2:9–10.

90   *gathering he had dreamed of:* Krupskaya, *Memories*, p. 83.

91   *"whatever the cost":* CW 34: 153.

91   *vigilant control of the party:* Deutscher, *Prophet*, p. 63.

91   *searched the baggage:* Wolfe, *Three*, p. 274.

91   *giving the police the slip:* Shotman, *Zapiski*, p. 85.

91   *went away satisfied:* Shotman, *Zapiski*, pp. 85–86.

91   *paced the deck watching the storm:* Zemlyachka, in *VoVIL* 1:235.

92   *a "small square" near Kings Cross:* "Our London Correspondence," *Guardian,* July 12, 1939, p. 10, says Alekseev moved to Holford Square from 22 Ampton Street in October 1902; Muravyeva, *Lenin in London*, p. 76.

92   *their landladies:* Semenov, "Lenin in London," *Soviet Weekly,* April 21, 1960; Semenov, *Po leninskim mestam*, p. 48; Shotman, *Zapiski*, p. 87.

92   *Communist Club:* The club was regularly used as a venue by the British Social Democratic Federation, later becoming notorious for "red agitation." It came under increasing surveillance when war broke out in 1914 because of its German connections. Suspected of being a hotbed of anti-British sedition, it was closed down.

92   *alternative venues:* Rothstein, "Lenin in Britain," p. 18. There have been some claims that the Brotherhood Church on Southgate Road in Islington was a venue for the 1903 congress, but no evidence has been found to support this. It is much more likely that the delegates, of whom there were far fewer than at the 1907 congress, stuck to smaller venues in the area of the Communist Club off Tottenham Court Road.

92   *British police presence:* Shotman, *Zapiski*, p. 87.

93   *party should remain narrow:* Weber, *Lenin*, p. 33.

93   *extent of his ambition:* Payne, *Lenin*, p. 172.

93   *Lenin was a bulldog:* Trotsky, *On Lenin*, p. 61.

93   *strength and intellectual passion:* Shub, *Lenin*, p. 78.

93   *"hardness" in contrast to the "softness":* Service, *Lenin: A Biography*, p. 155.

93   *fought like "a madman":* Kochan, "Lenin in London," p. 232; Wolfe, *Three*, p. 276.

94   *subsequent attempts:* Deutscher, *Prophet*, p. 67.

94   *endless wrangling:* CW 34: 168–170.

94   *Party unity came first:* Bergman, *Martov*, pp. 193–194; Krupskaya, *Memories*, p. 57.

95   *Lenin's "majoritarians" . . . Martov's "minoritarians":* Although the terms *bolshevik* (maximalist/majoritarian) and *menshevik* (minimalist/minoritarian) originate from the split at the 1903 congress, it was some time before they became common currency for defining the two factions. For a while the two groups were known within the movement as the "hards" and "softs," with Lenin also favoring the disparaging term "Martovites." Martov did not resist the *menshevik* attribution, although his group were for some time to come the majority. After the 1905 Bolshevik-only congress in Finland, the two terms rapidly came into use.

95   *product of the atmosphere:* CW 34: 164.

95   *Karl Marx's grave:* Semenov, *Po Leninskim mestam*, p. 49.

96   *"discordant tone":* Deutscher, *Prophet*, p. 50.

96   *ride roughshod:* Trotsky, *My Life,* p. 142; Trotsky, *On Lenin,* pp. 60–61.

96   *"iron fist":* Deutscher, *Prophet,* pp. 67–68.

96   *"cruel conflicts and countless victims":* Trotsky, *My Life,* p. 143.

97   *narrow-minded sectarianism:* Potresov, *Posmertnyi sbornik,* pp. 294, 299.

97   *"battle of recriminations":* Krupskaya, *Memories,* p. 91.

97   *his new bicycle:* Ulam, *Lenin,* p. 239.

97   *head swathed in bandages:* Krupskaya, *Memories,* pp. 93–94.

97   *pushing and shoving:* Bonch Bruevich, *Vospominaniya,* pp. 24–25.

98   *"no worse a blind alley than to leave work":* Krupskaya, *Memories,* p. 94.

98   *unbridgeable gulf:* Krupskaya, *Memories,* pp. 92–93.

98   *"War has been declared":* CW 36: 128.

98   *Martov and his hysterical scandalmongers:* CW 34: 187.

98   *brought onto the Central Committee:* Service, *Lenin: A Biography,* p. 157.

98   *"with our own people":* CW 36: 128.

99   *chosen path toward revolution:* Service, *Lenin: A Biography,* pp. 158–159; Kulyabko, in *VoVIL* 1:232.

99   *laughed more heartily:* Bonch-Bruevich, *Vospominaniya,* pp. 300–301.

99   *his own table . . . near the window:* "Lenin's table," with numerous names carved on it, as well as stains from generations of beer mugs, apparently remained at the Café Landolt for many years, but disappeared when the café was refurbished. An amusing account from the *Tribune de Geneve,* August 3, 2006, p. 28, can be found at www.lescommunistes.org/lenine/table.html.

100 *emergency exit onto a narrow lane:* Bonch-Bruevich, *Vospominaniya,* pp. 30–32; Kudryavtsev, *Lenin's Geneva Addresses,* pp. 51–53, 56.

100 *practical work of the underground:* Lunacharsky, *Revolutionary Silhouettes,* pp. 36–37.

Chapter 7: "Strong Talk and Weak Tea"

101 *Krzhizhanovsky's secret letter:* Valentinov, *Encounters,* pp. 9–10.

102 *"we must learn to smash mugs":* Valentinov, *Encounters,* pp. 19–21.

102 *cheaper at only twenty kopeks:* Fotieva, *Pages from Lenin's Life,* p. 5.

102 *La Petite Russie:* Deborah Hardy, "The Lonely Émigré: Petr Tkachev and the Russian Colony in Switzerland," *Russian Review* 35 (1969): 401.

103 *father of Russian Marxism:* Ulam, *Lenin and the Bolsheviks,* p. 239.

103 *different types of Russian political exiles:* Kudryavtsev, *Lenin's Geneva Addresses,* p. 7.

103 *"orgies of strong talk and weak tea":* Margherita Sarfatti, *The Life of Benito Mussolini* (London: Thornton Butterworth, 1925), pp. 104, 108, 112.

103 *"the shadow of autocracy":* Joseph Conrad, *Under Western Eyes* (Harmondsworth, UK: Penguin, 2007), p. 91; Balabanoff, *My Life as a Rebel,* p. 83.

104 *banality of the city:* For an interesting discussion of the Russian colony of *Karuzhka* as described in Joseph Conrad's *Under Western Eyes,* see Paul Kirshner, "Topodialogic Narrative in *Under Western Eyes* and the Rasoumoffs of 'La Petite Russie,'" in Gene M. Moore, ed., *Conrad's Cities* (Amsterdam: Rodopi, 1992), pp. 223–254. See also Kudryavtsev, *Lenin's Geneva Addresses,* pp. 65–68.

104 *rowdy singsongs:* Moore, ed., *Conrad's Cities,* p. 244.

104 *victory parades along the rue de Carouge:* Moore, ed., *Conrad's Cities,* p. 253.

104 *"inert memories and hopes"*: Alexander Herzen, *My Past and Thoughts* (Berkeley: University of California Press, 1973), p. 358. For an interesting overview of Russian exiles in Geneva, see Balabanoff, *My Life as a Rebel*, pp. 81–84.

105 *"hypnotic influence"*: Valentinov, *Encounters*, p. 42.

105 *her hero enjoyed so few creature comforts*: Bobrovskaya, *Twenty Years*, chap. 6; Kudryavtsev, *Lenin's Geneva Addresses*, p. 51.

105 *Lenin enjoyed . . . Tchaikovsky's Barcarolle*: Essen, in Golikov, *VoVIL* 2:114–115.

105 *"Lenin's corner"*: Valentinov, *Encounters*, p. 43.

106 *the cartoons*: Fotieva, *Pages from Lenin's Life*, pp. 15–16; Spiridovich, *Istoriya bol'shevizma v Rossii*, pp. 151–160; Getzler, *Martov*, pp. 90–95.

106 *"in such a depressed state"*: Lepeshinsky, *Na povorote*, p. 198.

107 *"the conductor's baton"*: Valentinov, *Encounters*, p. 113.

107 *extreme form of centralism*: Valentinov, *Encounters*, pp. 121–125.

107 *true social democrat*: Valentinov, *Encounters*, pp. 127–129.

108 *"constant turmoil"*: CW 37: 361–362.

108 *"greetings from the tramps"*: CW 37: 363.

108 *took a few books with them*: CW 37: 361–362; Krupskaya, *Memories*, p. 98.

108 *Nadya with her weak constitution*: For details of the route of this two and a half month walking tour, see Elwood, "Lenin on Holiday," pp. 121–123.

109 *"Mensheviks are making a fine mess"*: Essen, in Golikov, *VoVIL* 2:118.

109 *arrested again*: Essen was sentenced to five years of exile at Archangel but escaped and made her way back to St. Petersburg in September 1905 to work once more for the revolution.

109 *the magnificent Jungfrau*: Elwood, "Lenin on Holiday," p. 122.

110 *in the back room of a small hotel*: The venue was arranged by Bonch-Bruevich; see *Vospominaniya*, pp. 44–45.

110 *"cobwebs of petty intrigue"*: Krupskaya, *Memories*, p. 98.

111 *it "did not make much difference to him what he ate"*: Fotieva, *Pages from Lenin's Life*, p. 11.

111 *library was quiet and underused*: Bingley, *Lenin, Krupskaya, and Libraries*, p. 61.

111 *"bury his nose"*: Krupskaya, *Memories*, p. 99.

112 *"height of folly"*: Kudryavtsev, *Lenin's Geneva Addresses*, p. 77.

112 *Cryptic messages*: Fotieva, *Pages from Lenin's Life*, pp. 8–9.

113 *"nothing of her own"*: Valentinov, *Encounters*, p. 142.

113 *"hanging people like you from the lampposts"*: Tyrkova-Williams, *Na putyakh k svobode*, pp. 188–190.

114 *constant interruptions*: Lepeshinsky, *Na povorote*, pp. 221–224; Lepeshinskaya, *Vstrechi s Ilichem*, pp. 40–48; Fotieva, *Pages from Lenin's Life*, pp. 11–12; Kudryavtsev, *Lenin's Geneva Addresses*, pp. 85–88.

114 *"We must get that money"*: CW 43: 132–133.

115 *a library, a restaurant, and a small publishing house*: Williams, *Other Bolsheviks*, p. 26.

115 *"claptrap"*: Valentinov, *Encounters with Lenin*, pp. 211–215.

116 *"social-revolutionary movement"*: Kochan, "Lenin in London," p. 232.

116 *"banging on the door"*: Andrei Maylunas and Sergei Mironenko, eds., *A Lifelong Passion: Nicholas and Alexandra in Their Own Words* (New York: Doubleday, 1997), p. 251.

Chapter 8: "On the Eve of Barricades"

117   *January 22, 1905:* By the Gregorian, Russian Orthodox calendar the old style date was January 9.

117   *Palace Square: Times,* January 23, 1905, p. 5.

117   *125,000 workers were on strike:* Gerald D. Surh, *1905 in St. Petersburg* (Stanford: Stanford University Press, 1989), p. 165.

117   *"We workers and people of St. Petersburg":* Payne, *Life and Death of Lenin,* p. 184.

119   *several volleys from the troops:* For his eyewitness account of Bloody Sunday, see Father Gapon, *The Story of My Life* (London: Chapman & Hall, 1905), pp. 174–185. Salisbury, *Black Night,* pp. 116–128, contains a vivid account. See also Shukman, ed., *Encyclopedia of the Russian Revolution,* pp. 104–109; Figes, *People's Tragedy,* pp. 173–179; Pipes, *Russian Revolution,* pp. 21–27.

119   *"no longer a workman's question": Times,* January 23, 1905, p. 5.

120   *a thousand casualties:* Surh, *1905 in St. Petersburg.*

120   *"there is no czar":* Pipes, *Russian Revolution,* p. 25; Gapon, *Story,* p. 185.

121   *reprimanded for disturbing the peace:* Khanin, in OVIL 1900–1922, pp. 25–26.

121   *"the eve of barricades":* As Lenin described events in February 1905, "The First Lessons," CW 8: 140.

122   *"the disgusting 'beyond-the-frontier' existence of the émigré":* Read, *Lenin,* 226–227; Wolfe, *Three Who Made a Revolution,* p. 360.

122   *Mensheviks had a broader base of support:* Salisbury, *Black Night,* pp. 118, 646.

123   *"rickety and precarious":* Salisbury, *Black Night,* p. 117.

123   *"chief of the general staff":* Valentinov, *Encounters,* p. 21.

124   *"like a war council":* Wolfe, *Three,* p. 347.

124   *piles of English and Russian newspapers:* Losev, in VoVIL 1:298.

124   *time for a cheap lunch:* Muraveva, *Lenin in London,* pp. 150–152.

125   *levels of* konspiratsiya *were high:* Muraveva, *Lenin in London,* p. 151.

125   *infiltrate it:* Fitch, *Traitors Within,* pp. 20–21.

125   *"bloodshed on a colossal scale":* Fitch, *Traitors Within,* p. 23.

125   *"passionate magnetism":* Fitch, *Traitors Within,* p. 24. See also "Memories of a Meeting with Lenin," *Islington Gazette,* January 31, 1964. Harry Moring, who took over the Crown & Woolpack in 1941, said the cupboard was still there when he retired in 1955.

125   *drafting resolutions:* Salisbury, *Black Night,* p. 161.

126   *"cut-throat ideas of revolt":* Fitch, *Traitors Within,* pp. 25–26. Extensive checks by the archivist of the Metropolitan Police at the request of the author have confirmed that sadly none of the Special Branch reports by Fitch and his colleagues have survived for this or the 1907 congress.

127   *"squabbling, gossip and tittle-tattle":* CW 34: 43.

127   *"talking about bombs":* Payne, *Lenin,* p. 189.

128   *his clarion calls:* Wolfe, *Three,* pp. 421–423.

128   *they were unable to bend:* Futrell, *Northern Underground,* p. 60.

128   *change shape and size from fat to thin:* Drabkina, *Chernye sukhari,* pp. 27–28. Drabkina was married to party man Sergey Gusev, Lenin's favorite singer from Geneva days, whose real name was Yakov Drabkin. In December 1904 Gusev had been sent back to St. Petersburg undercover to work as secretary to the Petersburg Committee of the RSDLP and was instrumental in setting up the fighting technical group with Burenin, to which his wife gave such dedicated support. See also Kalmykov, *Boevaya tekhnicheskaya gruppa.*

129 "*Alpha*" *and* "*Omega*": Kalmykov, *Boevaya tekhnicheskaya gruppa*, p. 101.
129 *breaking all the rules of* konspiratsiya: Burenin, *Pamyatnye gody*, pp. 59–60.
130 *bomb-making operation*: Burenin, *Pamyatnye gody*, pp. 57–58. For further invaluable and rare information on the many key activists in Burenin's group, see also Kalmykov, *Boevaya tekhnicheskaya gruppa pri PK i TsK RSDRP 1905–1908gg.*
130 *hid them under their clothes*: Kalmykov, *Boevaya tekhnicheskaya*, p. 103.
131 "*The time of the uprising*": CW 34: 158.
131 *strike . . . spread to every major city*: Salisbury, *Black Night*, pp. 152–155; Figes, *People's Tragedy*, p. 189; Wolfe, *Three*, pp. 363–364.
133 "*conspiracy device*": Drabkina, *Chernye sukhari*, pp. 26–30.
133 *how to prime the bombs*: Drabkina, *Chernye sukhari*, pp. 31–32. Soon after the suppression of the Moscow insurrection Gorky and Andreeva fled to Finland. From there they set off on a fund-raising tour of the United States in 1906.
133 *Presnya district was laid waste*: Figes, *People's Tragedy*, pp. 200–201; Salisbury, *Black Night*, pp. 171–173.
134 "*need for Social-Democratic unity*": CW 34: 363–364.
135 *took a train to Helsingfors*: Dashkov, *Po leninskim mestam*, pp. 54–55.

Chapter 9: Stolypin's Neckties

137 *Okhrana spooks*: Krupskaya, *Memories*, pp. 122–123.
137 "*zealous reporter*": Krupskaya, *Memories*, p. 123.
137 "*They passed like comets*": Aline, *Lénine à Paris*, p. 20.
138 *the party had expressly forbidden*: Lenin's close ally Zinoviev made this claim in his hagiography of Lenin. See Beucler, *Les amours secrètes*, p. 24.
139 "*as though about to plunge into cold water*": Beucler, *Les amours secrètes*, p. 41.
139 *let his emotional guard slip*: Beucler, *Les amours secrètes*, pp. 44–49.
139 *furious, self-flagellating energy*: Beucler and Alexinsky's 1937 book, *Les Amours secrètes de Lénine*, based on conversations with Elizaveta de K (referred to in French as Lise de K) in exile in Paris and letters she received from Lenin claimed that the couple had an intermittent affair in 1905–1906, with subsequent brief meetings in Geneva and Paris in 1908 and Galicia in 1914. Some of the letters were published simultaneously in France in 1936 in facsimile in the journals *l'Humanité* and the Russian émigré *Illyustrirovannaya Rossiya* but are now lost. *Les Amours* has inevitably been the subject of considerable debate among Lenin biographers, particularly David Shub and his detractors. See for example, Shub, "Fact or Fiction on Lenin's Role," *New International* 16, no. 2 (1958): 86–91, sec. 6. While the Beucler book makes no overt claims of a sexual relationship, the title clearly has that intention. Although the affair cannot be substantiated (the anonymity of Elizaveta de K supposedly being maintained to protect the feelings of Nadezhda Krupskaya), there is detailed observation of Lenin's personality in her account of their meetings that rings true; see Shub, *Lenin*, pp. 459–460; and Robert Payne, *Life and Death*, pp. 201–211. More recently, Volkogonov, *Lenin*, p. 31, supports the book's authenticity. It is plausibly suggested that one of the reasons Elizaveta de K's identity was never revealed and her Lenin letters were lost is that her silence was effectively bought by the Soviets in return for a pension and the withdrawal of Soviet police intimidation. For both sides of the argument, see Robert H. McNeal, "Lenin and 'Lisa de K,' a Fabrication," *Slavic Review* 28, no. 3 (1969): 471–474; and a refutation of this article by Folke Dovring, *Slavic Review* 29, no. 3 (1970): 570–573.

140 *transport into Russia:* Futrell, *Northern Underground*, pp. 68–69.

141 *Finland would be granted its independence:* There is no popular history in English of the Finnish revolutionary movement at this time. But see Futrell, *Northern Underground* and the website of the Lenin Museum in Tampere, www.lenin.fi/uusi/uk/communo5.htm. The Finns achieved independence from Russia on December 18, 1917.

141 *"mountain eagle":* Montefiore, *Young Stalin*, p. 97.

141 *Lenin's charisma:* Montefiore, *Young Stalin*, p. 124; Rappaport, *Joseph Stalin*, pp. 163–164.

142 *"tremendous tasks of a new active movement":* Krupskaya, *Memories*, p. 131.

143 *"decidedly factional":* Krupskaya, *Memories*, p. 134.

143 *keeping his Bolshevik faction alive:* Ulam, *Lenin and the Bolsheviks*, pp. 303–304.

143 *"lead us by the rope":* Shub, *Lenin*, p. 109.

144 *destroy his opponent:* Wolfe, *Three*, p. 403.

144 *"the worms in the grave of the revolution":* Payne, *Life and Death*, p. 196.

145 *"Stolypin's necktie":* "Executions in Russia," *New York Times*, March 20, 1909, p. 3.

145 *"Stolypin's carriages":* Montefiore, *Young Stalin*, p. 153; Figes, *People's Tragedy*, p. 221.

146 *door was never locked:* Krupskaya, *Memories*, p. 139.

146 *Lenin rattled off an article:* Payne, *Life and Death*, p. 168.

146 *raising thousands of rubles:* For a detailed account of Stalin and Kamo's colorful bank-robbing career, see Montefiore, *Young Stalin*, chaps, 17–18, 20.

146 *a team of bandits:* Montefiore, *Young Stalin*, pp. 138–139.

146 *common criminals and "swindlers":* Geifman, *Thou Shalt Kill*, pp. 116–117.

147 *dirty money:* Geifman, *Thou Shalt Kill*, p. 118.

147 *revolutionaries were openly dealing with armaments firms:* Zuckerman, *Tsarist Secret Police Abroad*, pp. 170–171.

147 *a succession of arms deals:* Sheinis, *Litvinov*, pp. 52–56.

148 *"Gustav Graf":* Sheinis, *Litvinov*, p. 61.

148 *a new safe haven:* For Litvinov's underground career from 1906 to 1908, see Sheinis, *Maxim Litvinov*, pt. 1, "Papasha." Litvinov lived in London for ten years from where he ran the UK wing of Bolshevik underground operations; after the revolution he was appointed Russian ambassador to Britain.

149 *"poisoned weapons":* Payne, *Life and Death*, pp. 198–199.

Chapter 10: "The Congress of Undesirables"

152 *destination was Copenhagen:* Gandurin, *Epizody podpol'ya*, pp. 12–17; Dashkov, *Po leninskim mestam*, pp. 105–107.

152 *Lenin sent a telegram:* Dashkov, *Po leninskim mestam*, pp. 108–110.

152 *provided they did nothing illegal:* Lyadov, *Iz zhizni partii*, pp. 197–198.

153 *the Russians' money ran out:* Lyadov, *Iz zhizni partii*, pp. 198–199.

153 *motley crew of Russians:* Gandurin, *Epizody podpol'ya*, p. 25.

153 *"grandiose fantasmagoria":* "Revolutionists in London," *Daily News*, May 1907, p. 7; Gandurin, *Epizody podpol'ya*, p. 26. See also Peter Higginbotham, "Rowton Houses," www.workhouses.org.uk/index.html?Rowton/Rowton.shtml.

153 *extraordinary assemblage of . . . revolutionaries:* Elia Levin, "The Social Democratic Party of Russia and Its Recent Congress," *Social Democrat* 11, no. 9 (1907): 540.

154   *"nameless army from Russia"*: "Nameless Army from Russia," *Daily Mail*, May 10, 1907, p. 5; "A Congress of Undesirables," *Daily Mail*, May 14, 1907, p. 6.

154   *epitome of conspiracy and intrigue*: Duden and Laue, "The RSDLP and Joseph Fels," p. 23; Balabanoff, *My Life as a Rebel*, p. 86; *Daily News*, May 10, 1907, p. 7.

154   *her essential work for the party*: Krupskaya, *Memories*, p. 142; Kiselev, in OVIL *1900–1922*, p. 85.

154   *a cheap room in Bloomsbury*: Bassalygo, in VoVIL 3:81. It is unclear exactly where Lenin stayed during the congress, but logic dictates that he would have returned to his old haunts in the Kings Cross area, as he did in 1905. Simon Sebag Montefiore asserts in *Young Stalin* (p. 146) that Lenin and Krupskaya (who did not attend the congress but stayed behind in Finland) were accommodated in relative comfort in a hotel in "Kensington Square." This would be totally out of character for both of them, even had Nadya been with him. Lenin's frugality would never have allowed him to stay in expensive West London, let alone remove himself from the other delegates in the East End, as he was anxious to maintain his influence over them. Congress delegate N. Nakoryakov mistakenly states in OVIL *1900–1922*, p. 70, that Lenin's lodgings were in "Kingston Square," which might explain the confusion with Kensington Square—except that no such square existed. Lenin is much more likely to have stayed in the region of Holford Square or Percy Circus, which he knew from previous visits.

155   *worried about their damp sheets*: Andreeva, *Perepiski*, pp. 95–96.

155   *a tiny cubicle with a horsehair mattress*: Jack London, *People of the Abyss*, 1903, chap. 20, http://london.sonoma.edu/Writings/PeopleOfTheAbyss/Tower House. Whitechapel was one of six Rowton Houses built in London by the philanthropist Montague William Lowry-Corry, 1st Lord Rowton. It was finally closed down in the late 1970s. For twenty years it lay derelict, the haunt of squatters, drunks, and drug addicts, until sold to a developer in 2004. It has now been converted into expensive apartments.

155   *abyss of human suffering*: For a vivid description of the Russian delegates' culture shock, see Gandurin, *Epizody podpol'ya*, pp. 26–28.

156   *he had ways of raising the money*: Many years later, Bacon told his story to the *Daily Express*, January 5, 1950.

156   *"world's storm-centre of anarchism"*: Fitch, *Traitors Within*, p. 33.

156   *inaugural meeting*: Fitch, *Traitors Within*, p. 29; Thomas, "History Was Made in London," p. 16.

157   *Arbeter Fraint*: Fishman, *East End Jewish Radicals*, pp. 262–264; Kendall, *Revolutionary Movement in Britain*, pp. 77, 81.

157   *There would be no trouble*: Woodhall, *Secrets of Scotland Yard*, pp. 94–95. Woodhall does not identify the year of this anecdote but the venue must make it 1907, as the Worker's Friend Club did not open until 1906 and Kropotkin's health failed shortly after and he moved to Brighton.

158   *a turbulent congress*: Fitch, *Traitors Within*, pp. 28–30.

158   *Christian socialist group*: The *Evangelical Alliance* 11 (1857): 183 lists the Southgate-Road Congregational Chapel in an area then known as De Beauvoir Town. Other evangelical publications allude to it having been newly built in 1852 as home for a Congregational community based at the eighteenth-century Pavement Chapel on nearby New North Road. When Wallace's Brotherhood Church took it over in the 1890s, the Southgate Road Chapel had been derelict for some time. For a description, see Brailsford, "When Lenin and Trotsky Were in London," p. 87; Willats, "Lenin and London," p. 4; and Maisky, *Journey into the Past*, pp. 136–137. The church was used for Pacifist meetings during World War

I, provoking a demonstration and riot in 1917. It became a target for vandals and remained derelict after the Brotherhood community left the premises. It was demolished in 1934.

158 *vegetarian meal and ongoing discussion:* The church was noted for its eccentric humanitarian pursuits, having been the venue for the fourth International Vegetarian Congress in 1897.

158 *a church offering refuge to the godless:* Gandurin, *Epizody podpol'ya*, p. 28.

158 *made over the use of the building:* Stanley Buder, *Visionaries and Planners: The Garden City Movement and the Modern Community* (Oxford: Oxford University Press, 1990), pp. 54–55. See also A. G. Higgins, *A History of the Brotherhood Church* (Stapleton, UK: Brotherhood Church, 1982). Descriptions of the 1907 congress in previously published Lenin biographies refer erroneously to Frank Swann as the resident incumbent. But Swann, a close friend of British socialist and newspaperman George Lansbury, who was also a member, did not take over as pastor until 1912.

158 *they crammed into the stuffy little church:* "Revolutionaries' Surprise," *Daily Mail*, May 13, 1907 p. 5; "In Fear of Spies," *Daily News*, May 13, 1907, p. 7; Gorky, *Days with Lenin*, p. 5.

159 *"to which faction do you belong?":* Balabanoff, *My Life as a Rebel*, p. 87.

159 *"protracted, crowded, stormy and chaotic":* Trotsky, *My Life*, p. 175; Balabanoff, *My Life as a Rebel*, p. 87.

159 *"Russian police have long ears":* "Nameless Army from Russia," *Daily Mail*, May 10, 1907, p. 5.

160 *"aiming and pulling the trigger":* "Revolutionists' Duma in London," *Daily Mail*, May 11, 1907.

160 *"arrant nonsense":* Lyadov, *Iz zhizni*, p. 204; *Times*, May 13, 1907, p. 5; *Daily News*, May 16, 1907, p. 7.

160 *"aren't here for no good":* *Daily Mirror*, May 16, 1907, p. 4.

160 *uniformed bobbies:* *Daily News*, May 18 and 22, 1907; Sebag Montefiore, *Young Stalin*, p. 150.

161 *fist fights:* Balabanoff, *Impressions of Lenin*, p. 18.

161 *"fury of the disputes":* Gorky, *Days with Lenin*, pp. 7, 11.

161 *so much was at stake:* Coates, "Memories of Lenin," p. 508.

162 *"buttoned up like a Protestant pastor":* Gorky, *Days with Lenin*, pp. 12, 15.

162 *the urban proletariat and the peasantry:* Stalin, "Notes of a Delegate," pp. 21–23.

162 *torment of the human spirit:* Nakoryakov, in *OVIL 1900–1922*, p. 70; Gandurin, *Epizody podpol'ya*, p. 39.

163 *laughed loudly at the clowns' pratfalls:* Gorky in Golikov, *VoVIL* 2:250.

163 *a man of the people:* Gorky, *Days with Lenin*, p. 17.

163 *watching the Russian agents:* Lyadov, *Iz zhizni partii*, p. 205.

164 *millionaire Savva Morozov:* Service, *Lenin: A Political Life*, p. 166.

165 *"a stupid affair":* Dudden and Laue, "The RSDLP and Joseph Fels," p. 34.

165 *"wild beasts in a zoological garden":* Lyadov, *Iz zhizni partii*, p. 203.

165 *"a set of self-righteous crooks":* Lyadov, *Iz zhizni partii*, pp. 202–204; Garnett, *Constance Garnett*, pp. 233–234; Joseph Szigeti, *With Strings Attached* (London: Cassell, 1949), pp. 69–70.

166 *pressing financial needs:* Brailsford, "When Lenin and Trotsky Were in London," p. 86.

166 *he was still on his feet:* Brailsford, "When Lenin and Trotsky Were in London," p. 87.

166   *Fels pressed one of the single-tax leaflets:* Dudden and Laue, "The RSDLP and Jospeh Fels," pp. 43–45. Fels repeatedly asked for his money back but died in 1914. After the revolution in 1917, the Bolsheviks continued to stall, but eventually repaid the money to his widow. See also Brailsford, "When Lenin and Trotsky Were in London." Angelica Balabanoff notes in *Impressions of Lenin* (p. 25) that Fels was a dedicated autograph collector, which explains why he was so keen for the members of the congress to sign the loan agreement.

167   *"not one gesture":* Balabanoff, *Impressions of Lenin,* pp. 17–18.

167   *a "lost soul":* Andreeva, *Perepiski,* p. 96.

167   *the end of his own political hopes:* Getzler, *Martov,* p. 119.

167   *bank robberies and "gangsterism":* Stalin, "Notes of a Delegate," pp. 11, 13.

167   *spectacular bank heist:* Sebag Montefiore, *Young Stalin,* pp. 154–155.

168   *protection of the British flag:* Times, May 28, 1907, p. 6; *Daily News,* June 3, 1907, p. 7.

168   *"would have a warm time on their return in Russia":* Letter from Reuter's correspondent T. Beaugard to Henry Brailsford at the *Daily News,* June 3, 1907. This and Brailsford's covering letter to MacDonald can be found in PRO 30/69/151. See also *Daily News,* May 23, 1907, p. 7.

168   *an accurate written record:* Lenin's obsessiveness as he exhaustively worked over every last detail is vividly captured by stenographer N. S. Karzhansky in "V. I. Lenin na s'ezde RSDRP," in *VoVIL* 1:356–363.

168   *to evade identification and arrest:* Krupskaya, *Memories,* p. 143.

169   *"History is now being made in London":* "Maxim Gorki at Secret Duma," *Daily Mirror,* May 15, 1907.

169   *"the most dangerous . . . of all the Revolutionary leaders":* New York Times, May 21, 1907.

Chapter 11: On Thin Ice

171   *sat by the lighthouse:* Krupskaya, *Memories,* p. 143.

172   *"reaction was going to drag on for years":* Krupskaya, *Memories,* p. 146.

172   *clean, orderly, and formidably cold:* Krupskaya, *Memories,* p. 145; Kudryavtsev, *Lenin's Geneva Addresses,* p. 113.

172   *they learned Lenin's true identity:* Lenin v vospominaniyakh finnov, p. 48.

173   *sea route to Sweden:* Lenin v vospominaniyakh finnov, p. 49.

173   *delay sailing:* Lenin v vospominaniyakh finnov, p. 50.

174   *had thrown a snowball at Borg's window:* Lenin v vospominaniyakh finnov, p. 51.

174   *"I've walked further distances in Siberia":* Lenin v vospominaniyakh finnov, p. 54.

175   *cupboard full of rifles:* Lenin v vospominaniyakh finnov, pp. 55–56.

175   *code name "Dingo":* Malmberg, "What If Lenin Had Drowned Here?"

176   *confiscated alcohol:* Lenin v vospominaniyakh finnov, pp. 61–63.

176   *would never surrender:* Lenin v vospominaniyakh finnov, p. 62.

177   *smuggling arms, illegal literature, and people:* Dashkov, Po leninskim mestam, pp. 134, 138.

177   *Lenin made the sign of the cross:* Malmberg, "What If Lenin Had Drowned Here?"

177   *"Oh, what a silly way to have to die":* Arkady Rylov's socialist-realist painting of this event, *Tyazhelyi put'* (The Hard Road), shows Lenin striding ahead of his

two Finnish guides across the ice. However, coward that he was, he most certainly would have followed, letting them test the ice first.

177 *the steamship from Åbo:* Accounts of this final stage of Lenin's journey from Prostvik are patchy and conflicting. See Dashkov, *Po leninskim mestam*, p. 138. In all, Lenin's journey out of Finland lasted five or six days, from about December 19 to 25, 1907. Ludwig Lindström was the only participant to publish a detailed account of his role in the escape, reprinted in *Lenin v vospominaniyakh Finnov*, pp. 53–64, but it aggrandizes his own role, and some of it conflicts with other evidence. The most accurate and best researched account is in Dashkov, *Po leninskim mestam*, pp. 112–138, but it is still unclear whether Lenin boarded the steamship at Kaasluoto—which was about ten miles from the farm at Västergården—or nearer, from the tiny skerry Själö. Local Finns favor the latter location.

177 *Lenin boarded the* Stella*:* There is some dispute as to which ship Lenin caught. In *Po leninskim mestam Skandinavii*, p. 130, Yuri Dashkov stated that Lenin took the *Bore I* from Åbo at 4:00 pm on December 25 that year. The Lenin Museum in Tampere is reliably informed that it was in fact the *Stella* of the same Bore Company. Lenin was already in Stockholm by December 27, when he registered that day at the State Library.

177 *Elizaveta Vasil'evna was ailing:* Service, *Lenin: A Biography*, p. 185.

178 *picked up the steamer for Sassnitz:* Hamilton-Dann, *Vladimir and Nadya*, p. 124.

178 *clearly not who they claimed to be:* Krupskaya, *Memories*, p. 147.

178 *"I feel just as if I'd come here to be buried":* Krupskaya, *Memories*, p. 148.

178 *walking around the lake in the dark:* Krupskaya, *Memories*, pp. 153–154.

179 *"There is no* live *work":* CW 43: 134.

179 *reading her French grammar primers:* Krupskaya, *Memories*, p. 162.

179 *covered the margins with scribbled notes:* Beucler, *Les amours secrètes*, pp. 105–106.

179 *Lenin's romantic friendship with Elizaveta:* The couple continued to exchange desultory letters and postcards until war broke out in 1914; Elizaveta de K's letters to Lenin have been lost, but some of the dozen or so he wrote to her, which are instructional rather than romantic, were reprinted in facsimile in *L'Intransigéant* (1936). See chapter 9. For summaries of their relationship, see Payne, *Life and Death of Lenin*, pp. 201–211; Shub, *Life and Death*, passim.

179 *double agents and spies:* CW 37: 158; Beryl Williams, *Lenin*, p. 108.

180 *demanding their extradition:* Shub, *Lenin*, pp. 123–125.

180 *further party disintegration:* Ulam, *Lenin and the Bolsheviks*, pp. 348–350.

180 *smuggle the newspaper into Russia:* Kudryavtsev, *Lenin's Geneva Addresses*, p. 114.

180 *a pitiful trickle:* Wolfe, *Three Who Made a Revolution*, p. 538.

181 *"like a fishwife":* CW 34: 387.

181 *heretical views:* Kudryavtsev, *Lenin's Geneva Addresses*, p. 115.

181 *"political decadence":* CW 34: 168.

181 *"ridiculous, harmful and philistine":* Kudryavtsev, *Lenin's Geneva Addresses*, p. 116. In his letters to Gorky between February and April 1908 he expounds at length on Bogdanov and others. CW 34: 379–390.

181 *he started teaching himself Italian:* CW 34: 165.

182 *"unity between scientific socialism and religion":* Krupskaya, *Memories*, p. 160.

182 *isolated location:* Shirley Hazzard, *Green on Capri: A Memoir* (London: Virago, 2000), pp. 119–124.

182 *perched high on a cliff:* In 1908 the villa was not called Villa Krupp, as books about Gorky's time on Capri and Lenin's visit often assert. Friedrich Krupp, the

armaments millionaire, visited the island regularly from 1898. He stayed at the Grand Hotel Quisisana on the grounds of the nearby Gardens of Augustus and indulged in homosexual escapades. In gratitude to Capri for curing his asthma and depression, he funded the construction of a road, the via Krupp, to provide access from the hotel to the marina piccolo below. Gorky lived at the Villa Blaesus from November 1906 to March 1909, moving to the larger Villa Behring, known as the Red House, to run his party school there, before moving one final time to the Villa Pierina on the south side of Capri. He left the island in 1913 to return to Russia. In later years the Villa Settanni was converted into a hotel and renamed the Villa Krupp. A bust of Lenin on a stone plinth can be found in the Gardens of Augustus.

183   *Cavaliere Tiseo:* Cerio, *Masque of Capri*, p. 68.

183   *occasional game of chess:* During this visit the first photographs of Lenin to be taken since 1900 were captured by Mariya Andreeva's son, Yura Zhelyabuzhsky. Lenin had routinely resisted being photographed, for obvious reasons. Zhelyabuzhsky was a keen photographer and recorded a sequence of photographs of Lenin playing chess with Bogdanov on the terrace of Villa Blaeus, surrounded by party activists and visitors. These photographs were later doctored under Stalin. David King, *The Commissar Vanishes* (Edinburgh: Canongate, 1997), pp. 18–21; Moskovsky, *Lenin v Italii*, p. 23.

183   *things "got out of hand":* CW 37: 83.

183   *verbal savagery:* Gorky, *Days with Lenin*, p. 25.

184   *"simple in heart":* Gorky, *Days with Lenin*, pp. 26–27; Cerio, *Masque of Capri*, pp. 95–96.

184   *Signor Drin Drin:* Gorky, *Days with Lenin*, p. 27; Cerio, *Masque of Capri*, p. 96; Vol'ner, *Psevdonimy*, p. 107. For an interesting fictionalization of the visit based on research in Capri and interviews with Gorky's Italian servants, see Zinaida Guseva, *Svidanie na Kapri* (Moscow: Sovetskaya Rossiya, 1968), pt. 2.

184   *"The Tsar hasn't caught him yet?"* Gorky, *Days with Lenin*, p. 28; Cerio, *Masque of Capri*, p. 96.

185   *spending money on books:* Simsova, *Lenin, Krupskaya, and Libraries*, p. 61; Kudryavtsev, *Lenin's Geneva Addresses*, p. 116.

185   *"a small, intense man":* Bill Fishman, "Millie Sabel, Yiddishe Anarchist," *East London Arts Magazine*, Winter 1967, p. 3.

185   *"certain to make a mark in the world":* Masefield, letter of November 15, 1964; quoted in Corliss Lamont, *Remembering John Masefield* (London: Kaye & Ward, 1972), pp. 83–84.

185   a *"very nicely-spoken gentleman":* John Strachey, "The Great Awakening," *Encounter* pamphlet 5, 1961, p. 7.

185   *"inexpressible vulgarities":* CW 37: 166.

186   *"no dogs, no cats and no Russians":* Kaganova, *Lenin vo Frantsii*, pp. 37–38.

186   *"the picture of a brigand":* Krupskaya, *Memories*, p. 152; Kaganova, *Lenin vo Frantsii*, pp. 35–38.

186   *one of its key double agents:* Krupskaya, *Memories*, p. 166; Kudryavtsev, *Lenin's Geneva Addresses*, p. 122.

186   *"provincial backwater":* CW 37: 172.

187   *stash of illegal literature:* Aline, *Lénine à Paris*, pp. 38–39.

187   *"common chairs and stools":* Grechnev, in OVIL 1900–1922, p. 94; Krupskaya, *Memories*, p. 167.

187   *"most trying years of exile":* Krupskaya, *Memories*, p. 166.

Chapter 12: "Why the Hell Did We Go to Paris?"

189 *"We have no people at all"*: Fotieva, *Pages from Lenin's Life*, p. 22; Wolfe, *Three Who Made a Revolution*, p. 543; CW 34: 415.

190 *cream of Russian creative talent*: Salisbury, *Black Night*, pp. 216–217.

190 *rate fixed for the Bolshevik leaders*: Volkogonov, *Lenin*, p. 57.

191 *Nadya always denied*: Krupskaya, "O Vladimire Il'iche," in Golikov, *VoVIL* 2:581.

191 *for want of anything better to do*: Ehrenburg, *People and Life*, pp. 75–77; Kaganova, *Lenin vo Frantsii*, p. 30.

191 *one franc a night*: Manuilsky in Petrov, in OVIL *1900–1922*, pp. 107–108.

192 *domestic items*: Kaganova, *Lenin vo Frantsii*, p. 42; Aline, *Lénine à Paris*, pp. 12–13, 29–30.

192 *Prigara threw himself into the Seine*: Krupskaya, *Memories of Lenin*, pp. 171, 185; CW 35: 144.

193 *Elizaveta . . . tried to be helpful*: Aline, *Lénine à Paris*, p. 18.

193 *noticed how shabby his clothes were*: Kaganova, *Lenin vo Frantsii*, pp. 41–42.

193 *his time at the library*: Kaganova, *Lenin vo Frantsii*, p. 47; Krupskaya, *Memories*, p. 168.

194 *recreational rides into the countryside*: Fréville, *Lénine à Paris*, p. 160.

194 *lilies of the valley*: Zinoviev, *Lenin*, pp. 68–69.

194 *his usual restlessness*: Krupskaya, *Memories*, pp. 168–189; Aline, *Lénine à Paris*, p. 16; CW 37: 456–457.

194 *Bolshevik group favored two cafés*: Fréville, *Lénine à Paris*, p. 137. Both the Au Puits Rouge and Aux Manilleurs cafés have long since disappeared. Avenue d'Orléans is now avenue du Général Leclerc.

195 *"hellishly important"*: CW 37: 426–427.

196 *monomaniacal version of Marxism*: Williams, *The Other Bolsheviks*, pp. 138–139.

196 *deployment of heavy artillery*: Payne, *Life and Death*, pp. 228–230.

196 *"Bolshevism must now be strictly Marxist"*: Read, *Lenin*, p. 91.

196 *"theoretical revisionism"*: Wolfe, *Three Who Made a Revolution*, p. 569.

196 *Bogdanov . . . was expelled*: Weber, *Lenin*, pp. 65–66.

197 *surroundings were luxurious*: Elwood, "Lenin on Holiday," p. 150.

197 *Lenin considered his body a machine*: CW 35: 112.

197 *affable and content with everything*: Krupskaya, *Memories*, p. 173; Fréville, *Lénine à Paris*, pp. 89–90.

198 *anarchistes russes*: *Quand Lénine Vivait à Paris*, p. 38.

198 *"had more important things to think about"*: Krupskaya, *Memories of Lenin*, 167.

198 *a domestic helper, Louisa Faroche*: Mel'nichenko, *Ya tebya ochen' lyubila*, p. 88.

198 *"extreme poverty and ideal cleanliness"*: Lyudvinskaya, in *VoVIL* 2:281–282.

198 *"like a hungry man on food"*: Gopner, in *VoVIL* 2:289.

198 *Lenin's daily trip to the Gare du Nord*: Kaganova, *Lenin vo Frantsii*, p. 342; Payne, *Life and Death of Lenin*, p. 232; Aline, *Lénine à Paris*, p. 44.

199 *Montéhus's performances*: Krupskaya, "O Vladimire Il'yche," p. 582; Beucler, *Les Amours secrètes*, p. 127.

199 *workers theater cum music hall*: Gaston Montéhus was a Jew, born Mardochée Brunswick in Paris in 1872. He rose to fame as a popular singer/song writer, turning out more than three thousand songs. A socialist and an ardent antimilitarist, he was hugely popular with the Parisian working class after he moved to the capital in 1900. Some of his performances were shut down for being too politically subversive. At the height of his success when war broke out in 1914, his social-

ist sympathies were called into question. He was accused of being a police spy and fell into disfavor. He never recovered his former popularity and died alone in 1952. Boulouque, "Mardochée Brunswick; Singer of Socialist Songs Sets Paris Aflame," *New York Times*, June 30, 1912; Kataev, *Malen'kaya zheleznaya dver,* pp. 54–69, a fictionalization that includes Kataev's research on Montéhus in Paris and interviews with people who knew him. Montéhus became a Freemason in 1902 and allegedly introduced Lenin to his lodge, the Union of Belleville, which Lenin joined. Cabaret Bobino still thrives on the rue de la Gaieté.

199 *revolutionary credentials:* Tat'yana Lyudvinskaya, who was in Lenin's Paris circle, remembered his enthusiasm for Montéhus in her memoir of Lenin: *Velikii, blizkii, prostoi.* Marcel Cachin, a French socialist and founder of the French Communist Party, also recalled (in conversation with Kataev) Lenin's visits to the café concerts, notably Bobino, to hear Montéhus perform. For general background, see Francois Caradec and Alain Weill, *Le café-concert* (Paris, Massin, 1980).

200 *anthem for French antimilitarist rallies:* To hear an original recording of Montéhus singing "Gloire au 17ème," go to www.chanson.udenap.org/fiches_bio/montehus.htm.

200 *future of world revolution:* Aline, *Lénine à Paris,* p. 46; Kaganova, *Lenin vo Frantsii,* pp. 320–321.

200 *magnificent gold watch:* Leo Campion, *Les Anarchistes dans la F[ranc] M[aconnerie]* (Marseilles: Culture et Liberté, 1969), p. 52.

201 *"just jogging along":* CW 37: 431.

201 *He won his case:* Fréville, *Lénine à* Paris, pp. 161–162; Aline, *Lénine à Paris,* pp. 82–83.

201 *"three weeks of agony":* CW 34: 420.

202 *"only extraordinary circumstances":* CW 37: 451.

202 *"squabbling":* CW 34: 421.

202 *"like travelling on the Volga":* CW 37: 462.

202 *"Bozhe tsarya khrani":* Caruso, *Lenin a Capri,* pp. 101–102; see also Cerio, *That Capri Air,* p. 96.

203 *split between himself and Bogdanov:* For a study of the party schools, see Elwood, "Lenin and the Social Democratic Schools."

203 *Lenin [invited] the students in Capri:* Elwood, "Lenin and the Social Democratic Schools," pp. 374–376.

203 *picturesque little seaside resort:* Fréville, *Lénine à Paris,* pp. 109–110.

204 *hunched over a book:* Shaginyan, "Retracing Lenin's Steps," p. 195.

204 *All the leading socialists:* For an account of the congress, see Maisky, *Journey into the Past,* chap. 17.

204 *listened carefully to other speakers:* Maisky, *Journey,* p. 16.

204 *"thinks and dreams of nothing but revolution":* Shub, *Lenin,* p. 137.

205 *"solicitous to the last about his health":* Dann, *Lenin and Nadya,* p. 137.

205 *repeatedly asked Nadya:* Krupskaya, *Memories,* p. 166, where the Russian "I kakoi chert pones nas v Parizh!" is more laboriously translated as "That the devil made us go to Paris?"

Chapter 13: Inessa

208 *Four children:* For details of Inessa's early life, see Pearson, *Inessa: Lenin's Mistress;* Elwood, *Inessa Armand.*

209 *in May:* This date is according to Inessa's colleague Elena Vlasova. Mel'nichenko, *Ya tebya ochen' lyubila,* p. 94. Elwood, *Inessa,* p. 69, concurs.

209 *sense of self-consciousness:* Pearson, *Inessa*, p. 90.

210 *she joined the Bolsheviks:* Elwood, *Inessa*, pp. 77–78.

210 *"slovenly":* "His Paris Concierge Pays Tribute to Lenin," *New York Times*, April 25, 1921, p. 2; McNeal, *Bride*, p. 138.

210 *"a tired-out wife":* Zetkin, "My Recollections of Lenin," in *They Knew Lenin*, p. 12.

211 *accumulating layers of varnish:* Aline, *Lénine à Paris*, p. 27.

211 *"fully-formed Marxists":* Vasilieva and Porter, *Kremlin Wives*, p. 10.

211 *liaising with emigrant groups:* Elwood, "Lenin and the Social Democratic School," pp. 86–89.

212 *irrevocable break:* Elwood, "Lenin and the Social Democratic Schools," p. 381.

212 *village schoolteachers:* Elwood, "Lenin and the Social Democratic Schools," p. 383; Payne, *Life and Death of Lenin*, p. 239.

212 *Zinoviev and his wife:* Fréville, *Lénine à Paris*, p. 195.

213 *students had come with her to help:* Elwood, "Lenin and the Social Democratic Schools," 384; Fréville, *Lénine à Paris*, 195; Krupskaya, *Memories*, p. 191; Mel'nichenko, *Ya tebya*, pp. 124–125. The house in which Lenin and Nadya stayed is now 91 rue Président Mitterand. For evocative photographs of Longjumeau, see Feld, *Quand Lénine Vivait à Paris*, pp. 154–167.

213 *predominantly Bolsheviks:* See Elwood, "Lenin and the Social Democratic Schools," pp. 384–385, for details about the students and their backgrounds. Not much is known.

214 *she was a "weak" lecturer:* Elwood, "Lenin and the Social Democratic Schools," p. 386.

214 *Elizaveta Vasil'evna grumbled:* Mel'nichenko, *Ya tebya*, p. 128; Elwood, "Lenin and the Social Democratic Schools," pp. 386–388.

214 *"class conscious fighter":* Krupskaya, *Memories*, p. 192.

214 *party money was spent on wine:* Elwood, "Lenin and the Social Democratic Schools," p. 388.

214 *"commotion" of the Russian colony:* Fréville, *Lénine à Paris*, p. 197; Elwood, "Lenin on Holiday," p. 124.

214 *"cycled their heads off":* CW 37: 610.

215 *get themselves elected to the commission:* Elwood, "Lenin and the Social Democratic Schools," pp. 289–290.

215 *deeply in love with Lenin:* Pearson, *Inessa*, p. 90.

215 *"grew brighter when Inessa entered it":* Payne, *Life and Death*, p. 235.

215 *"Inessa became a person close to us":* McNeal, *Bride*, pp. 139–140.

216 *turbulent relationship:* Lidiya Dan, who worked on *Iskra* with Lenin in Munich, suggested that Lenin also had an affair or flirtation with émigré Gregory Alexinsky's wife Alya in Paris, but, as with his alleged affair with Elizaveta de K, there is no substantiating evidence. Alexinsky fell out with Lenin politically in Paris and formed an independent left-Bolshevik group with Bogdanov and others. Dan claimed in an interview that another activist, Ekaterina Kuskova, "told me in great detail about his romance with Armand," confirming that it was "a very stormy affair." See Haimson, *Making of Three Russian Revolutionaries*, pp. 124–125. Similar rumors filtered through from another leading *bolshevichka*, Aleksandra Kollontai, who supposedly fictionalized the Lenin-Inessa-Nadya triangle in her 1927 short story "A Great Love." Whether any of Lenin's contemporaries were more candid about his relationship with Armand in their letters or memoirs is not known; if they were, such material would have been ruthlessly expunged by Stalinist historiographers in the creation of the Leninist cult of personality,

much as any personal comments in the surviving letters from Lenin to Armand were. Krupskaya, as loyal keeper of Lenin's flame, remained stonily silent on the subject. See also McNeal, *Bride*, pp. 140–141.

216 *mesmerized by Inessa:* Valentinov, *Encounters with Lenin*, p. 60.

216 *"a little bird":* CW 37: 578.

216 *ceased having sexual relations:* According to Lidiya Fotieva, Nadya moved into her mother's bedroom at rue Marie Rose. *Fotieva iz zhizni Lenina*, p. 10.

216 *evidence of Lenin's feelings:* For Lenin's use of *ty*, see Wolfe, "Lenin and Inessa," pp. 97–98; and Valentinov, *Encounters with Lenin*, pp. 60–61, Lenin wrote some 135 cards and letters to Inessa, the great majority between 1911 and 1917, but her daughter Inna, who was close to Nadya and wished to spare her feelings, did not hand them over to the Central Committee archives until after Nadya's death in 1939. The Soviet authorities, no doubt exercised by the possibly compromising nature of the letters, were reluctant to publish them for some time. But eventually, conscious that their largely political content was part of Lenin's historical legacy, they released a few in 1950. Finally in 1964 ninety-five of the Lenin–Armand letters were published in the fifth edition of Lenin's *Collected Works* and elsewhere. The first major collection of Armand's letters came in Russia in 1975, but these were mainly to her children. More of the missing Lenin letters to Armand did not appear in Russia until the 1990s. Of the Lenin letters published, many have been tampered with; pages are missing and in others the no doubt affectionate opening and closing remarks to Inessa have been torn off. For a discussion of the Lenin–Armand letters, see Elwood, "Lenin and Armand."

218 *"only made him the more amusing":* Alexey Aline, in *Lénine à Paris*, pp. 72–74, denied that Lenin ever set foot in a bohemian café in Montparnasse and claimed that he did not like La Rotonde. But see C. R. W. Nevinson, *Paint and Prejudice* (London: Methuen, 1937), pp. 65–66; Jean-Paul Crespelle, *Chagall* (New York: Coward-McCann, 1970), pp. 19–23; Noel Riley Fitch and Andrew Midgely, *The Grand Literary Cafés of Europe* (New Holland Publishers, 2006), p. 36; Piers Letcher, *Eccentric France*, Bradt Travel Guides, 2003, p. 85.

218 *playing with the poet Apollinaire:* Cecily Mackworth, *Guillaume Apollinaire and the Cubist Life* (London: John Murray, 1961), p. 5.

218 *a brothel . . . near the Bibliothèque Nationale:* It is alleged that for a book or an article published in 1960 French journalists tracked down the brothels in Paris that Lenin is said to have visited and interviewed the prostitutes who serviced him. The author has so far not been able to trace this source, alleged on p. 130 of Juri Lina, *Under the Sign of the Scorpion: The Rise and Fall of the Soviet Empire* (Stockholm: Referent, 2002). Despite its anti-Russian bias and unsavory politics, Lina's book is fully annotated and repeats allusions to Lenin's sexual activities in Paris that have filtered through other French-based sources, including the suggestion that Paris is probably where he picked up the syphilis that killed him, possibly as early as 1902–1903, when he made a couple of lecture trips over from London. Nicholas V. Feodoroff, in *Soviet Communists and Russian History* (New York: Nova Science Publishers, 1997), p. 27, suggests that Lenin's sexual encounters with prostitutes began during his student days in Kazan. See the notes in the epilogue.

218 *"he was absolutely voracious":* Julien Green, *Journal, 1928–1954* (Paris: Librairie Plon, 1938), vol. 4, entry for February 5, 1932, pp. 84–85. Green offered his own rather coy English rendition of the original French in his edited version of the journal in *Personal Record, 1928–1939* (New York: Harper, 1939), p. 76: "We were sharing our ladies. Lenin was very gay and good-natured; he was a sensualist." In

his *Lénine Dada* (p. 26), Dominique Noguez says that the French critic Philippe Vanini telephoned Green on February 16, 1989, for confirmation of this story and was told by him that the painter's name was either "Evitcheff ou Ivitcheff" (Evichev or Ivichev). So far it has not been possible to identify him further.

218 *attractive young chair attendant:* Toussaint, *Lénine inconnu,* "La Chaisière de Luxembourg," pp. 9–57. Toussaint's unverified claims have been dismissed out of hand as pure fiction by the hagiographers, notably the French communist Jean Fréville, author of the official version, *Lénine à Paris* (p. 179), and Alexey Aline in his book of the same title. But despite the perceived flippancy of this particular sequence, Toussaint's book contains a detailed, serious summation of Lenin's extensive political arguments. Both Aline and Fréville had political reasons for defending Lenin's spotless reputation as a moral puritan, yet there were times when he went away from his Russian political colleagues to unwind. Detractors unwilling to countenance a sexual side to Lenin the plaster saint similarly refuse to entertain the memoirs of Elizaveta de K in *Les Amours secrètes de Lénine.* But the sheer fact that rumors about Lenin's sexual exploits have emerged only tentatively from his Paris period suggests that there is some substance to them; either that or, as the Soviets would have it, there was a French conspiracy to discredit him. At this juncture there simply isn't enough concrete evidence to argue the case conclusively, but the clues are there in Lenin's relationship with Armand. See also the epilogue to this book.

219 *"I love life":* Beucler and Alexinsky, *Les Amours secrètes de Lénine,* pp. 95–101.

220 *like "an accountant explaining":* Beer, "Interview with Lenin," pp. 148–149, 154, 158.

220 *"outside the party":* Elwood, "Lenin and the Social Democratic Schools," p. 390.

220 *no special concessions for Lenin:* Amort, "Lenin in Prague," p. 20; Semashko, in *OVIL 1900–1922,* pp. 229–301; Onufriev, in *OVIL 1900–1922,* p. 304.

221 *the émigrés were out of touch:* Swain, "The Bolsheviks' Prague Conference Revisited," pp. 134–138.

221 *"legitimate assembly of the entire RSDLP":* Service, *Lenin: A Political Life,* 2:23.

211 *"our mighty agitator":* Lyudvinskaya, *Veliki, blizki,* p. 21.

222 *"The emigration is nothing":* Service, *Lenin: A Political Life,* 2:21.

222 *"eventual victory of the proletariat":* Krupskaya, *Memories,* p. 202; Mel'nichenko, *Ya tebya,* p. 144.

223 *safe from interception:* Krupskaya, *Memories,* p. 202; Alexinsky, *Les Amours secrètes,* pp. 200–201.

223 *"frayed everyone's nerves":* Krupskaya, *Memories,* p. 197.

223 *resolved their problems:* Bob Gould, "Lenin, Krupskaya, and Inessa Armand," http://members.optushome.com.au/spainter/Armand.html.

223 *"They always paid":* "His Paris Concierge Pays Tribute to Lenin," *New York Times,* April 25, 1921, p. 2.

Chapter 14: "Almost Russia"

225 *Saturday morning, June 22:* Adamczewski, *Lenin w Krakowie,* p. 56. I am grateful to Peter Northover for information on trains between Paris and Kraków.

225 *"semiexile":* CW 37: 479; Krupskaya, *Memories,* p. 204; Sobczak, "Two Years in Poland," p. 16.

226 *Mr. and Mrs. "Włodzimierz Ulianoff":* Adamczewksi, *Lenin w Krakowie,* p. 61; Najdus, *Lenin i Krupska,* contains much useful information, especially chapter 3: "Lenin i Krupska pod Opieka Krakowskiego Zwizku."

226 *218 Ulica Zwierzyniec:* The house, now renovated, is still there, although the street name has changed to 41 Królowej Jadwigi. The commemorative plaque to Lenin has long since been removed.

226 *Permission for Lenin to live and work in Kraków:* Hanecki is referred to as Yakov Ganetsky in Russian sources. He became well-known by the pseudonym Jakub Fürstenburg as a financial expert responsible for laundering Bolshevik funding in Germany in 1917. He became the first director of the Soviet Central Bank in 1918.

227 *reminded Nadya of Russia:* CW 37: 479.

227 *mushroom picking:* Sergiusz Bagocki's [Bagotsky] reminiscences of Lenin in Poland are useful. See Bagotsky, "V. I. Lenin v Krakove i Poronine," in *VoVIL* 1:438–456. Sobczak, "Two Years in Poland," while slavishly communist, contains valuable information. See also Krupskaya, *Memories,* p. 206. Adamczewski, *Lenin w Krakowie,* contains contemporary photographs and other ephemera linked to Lenin's residences in Poland.

227 *a boy like him:* Shub, *Lenin,* pp. 145–146.

228 *in care of a professor at the university:* Sobczak, "Two Years in Poland," p. 17; Krupskaya, *Memories,* p. 204.

228 *an officer called on Lenin:* Krupskaya, *Memories,* p. 205.

228 *non-Marxist nationalists under Józef Piłsudski:* Józef Piłsudski's elder brother, Bronisław, along with Lenin's brother Aleksandr, had been a member of the group that plotted the assassination of Alexander III. Jozef was implicated and arrested in 1887 with his brother, serving five years of hard labor in Siberia. After mobilizing his underground Polish forces during World War I, he became the first leader of an independent Poland in 1918.

229 *"I am better off here than I was in Paris":* CW 37: 519.

229 *"at any price":* CW 37: 508.

229 *without complaint:* Krupskaya, *Memories,* p. 207.

229 *"scarcely any acquaintances here":* CW 37: 614; Najdus, *Lenin i Krupska,* pp. 102–103.

229 *"secretly thought about it":* Krupskaya, *Memories,* p. 234.

230 *"pitiful dish rags":* Wolfe, *Three,* pp. 605–606.

230 *final split:* Ulam, *Lenin and the Bolsheviks,* pp. 386–387; Wolfe, *Three,* pp. 604–605.

231 *writing for "the waste-paper basket":* Krupskaya, *Memories,* p. 209; Salisbury, *Black Night,* pp. 243–244; CW 43: 293.

231 *Frantsiska Kazimirovna Yankevich:* Pearson, *Inessa,* p. 97; Krupskaya, *Memories,* pp. 298–299.

231 *secret addresses:* Pearson, *Inessa,* pp. 99–100.

231 *hear the nightingales sing:* CW 37: 494.

232 *a vast range of religious and ethnic groups:* Sebag Montefiore, *Young Stalin,* pp. 219–221.

233 *loyalty of all nationalities:* Rappaport, *Joseph Stalin,* p. 164, 189; Sebag Montefiore, *Young Stalin,* p. 227.

233 *"wonderful Georgian":* Krupskaya, *Memories,* p. 227.

233 *"like a lunatic":* Bagocki, "V. I. Lenin," p. 447; CW 37: 617. Information from Dr. Ronald Chaplain; see note in epilogue. For a discussion of Nadya's thyroid condition, see Leonhard Haas, "Lenins Frau als Patientin bei Schweizer Arzten," in *Jahrbucher für Geschichte Osteuropas* (1969), 7:420–436. Additional information from Professor Chaplain.

234 *no electricity:* Bagotsky, "V. I. Lenin," p. 449.

234 *arduous hikes:* Ganetsky, "S Leninym," p. 97.

235 *Persistence . . . always paid off:* Bagotsky, "V. I. Lenin," pp. 441–442.

235 *reading his letters as he walked:* Sobczak, "Two Years in Poland," pp. 17–18.

236 *political and intellectual network in Galicia:* Information from Piotr Bąk, former mayor of Zakopane. Bąk observed in conversation with the author that in their later memoirs, and for obvious reasons, some of these eminent Poles regretted helping Lenin in 1914. See also Bernov, *Lenin v Krakove*, p. 206; Adamczewski, *Lenin w Krakowie*, contains a wonderful collection of contemporary photographs of the Podhale and the Góral peasants.

236 *the Morskie Oko or the Café Trzaski:* Vigilev took a rare photograph of Lenin in Zakopane in 1914, one of only four taken of him prior to the revolution. See Najdus, *Lenin i Krupska*, pp. 94–102. For a selection of photographs of Lenin's Polish associates in Zakopane, see Adamczewski, *Lenin w Krakowie*, pp. 132–191. Another useful account of his time in the Tatras can be found in Bernov, *Lenin v Krakove*, chap. 10, "Poronin i Tatry."

237 *increasingly "helpless":* Bagotsky, "V. I. Lenin," p. 450.

237 *"tight-fisted Frau Professor":* CW 43:358a.

237 *Her irregular heartbeat:* Information from Professor Ronald Chaplain.

238 *no more long hikes for her:* Bagotsky, "V. I. Lenin," p. 450.

238 *she fled Russia for Finland:* Elwood, *Inessa Armand*, p. 95.

238 *"with her usual ardour":* Pearson, *Inessa*, p. 104; Krupskaya, *Memories*, p. 231.

239 *scrambled up and down the steepest paths:* Bagotsky, "V. I. Lenin," pp. 450–451.

239 *he loved hearing Inessa play:* Elwood, *Inessa Armand*, pp. 118, 99–100.

239 *"close and friendly circle":* Krupskaya, *Memories*, p. 231.

239 *light and happiness:* Mel'nichenko, *Ya tebya ochen' lyubila*, pp. 180–181.

239 *Inessa suddenly left for Paris:* Ibid., p. 106.

240 *"almost from the first meeting":* "Inessa Armand," *Svobodnaya mysl'* (1992): 80–81. This crucial and illuminating letter from Inessa is the only unequivocal statement about their relationship from either party that has so far come to light. For obvious reasons, nothing remotely candid has survived in the many published editions of Lenin's letters, although there are passing hints of his affection for her. Drafted around January 1914 in Paris, it first came to light in the post-Soviet era, when it was published in 1992 in the Russian journal *Svobodnaya mysl'* (above). For a discussion of its implications, see Elwood, "Lenin and Armand"; Pearson, *Inessa*, pp. 106–112; and Chapter 17 of this book.

241 *not to mention the expense:* McNeal, *Bride*, p. 149.

241 *"lively town to stay in":* CW 37: 514.

241 *"the right hand of Lenin":* Elwood, *Inessa Armand*, p. 125.

242 *loyal female lieutenant:* Ibid., pp. 126–128; see Lenin's letters to Inessa in CW 43 for 1913 and 1914.

242 *a new journal, Rabotnitsa:* Pipes, *Unknown Lenin*, p. 26; Pearson, *Inessa*, pp. 119–120.

243 *"with flying colours":* CW 43: 406–407, 409–410, 417–420.

243 *"Consent, do!":* CW 43: 409–410, 417–420, 423; Elwood, *Inessa Armand*, pp. 130–136; Pearson, *Inessa*, pp. 119–122.

243 *Inessa had seemed unwell:* CW 43: 425.

Chapter 15: A Russian Spy in Galicia

245 *"Franz Jozef and Nicky":* CW 35: 76.

246 *"have become a communist":* Bagotsky, "V. I. Lenin," p. 454.

246　*"traditional Marxist formulas"*: Barbara Tuchman, *The Proud Tower: A Portrait of the World Before the War, 1890–1914* (London: Papermac, 1980), p. 435.

246　*renewed strikes and unrest*: CW 35: 76.

247　*Lenin's protégé Stalin*: His removal to Kureika defeated even the wily Stalin, who was forced to sit out the rest of his sentence in exile until the revolution in 1917. See Rappaport, *Joseph Stalin*, pp. 262–263.

247　*didn't have the wherewithal to leave*: Bernov, *Lenin v Krakove*, p. 223.

247　*"putting poison into the wells"*: Kupskaya, *Memories*, p. 240.

247　*Russian paymasters*: Bagotsky, "V. I. Lenin," pp. 45–46; Krupskaya, *Memories*, pp. 240–241.

248　*"suspect me of espionage"*: Bernov, *Lenin v Krakove*, p. 225; Krupskaya, *Memories*, p. 241; CW 43: 430–431.

248　*the danger he was in*: Krupskaya, *Memories*, p. 241.

249　*news of the "spy's" arrival*: Trepper, *The Great Game*, p. 3. Trepper emphasizes the fact that the devoutly Catholic and Jewish communities of Nowy Targ co-habited happily at that time. Economic hardship, not anti-Semitism, drove out much of the Jewish population of Nowy Targ before World War I, with many Jews emigrating to the United States and Canada. For a valuable firsthand portrait of the town and a vanished world, see Trepper, *The Great Game*, pp. 5–11. The synagogue is now a cinema.

249　*Lenin was incarcerated*: Trepper, *The Great Game*, p. 3, is very clear about this. Nowy Targ jail in those days had only one collective cell for petty criminals. Yet according to all the subsequent Soviet books, and indeed the sanctified "prison cell no. 5" that was lovingly recreated as part of the Leninist cult, the prison had several cells. It would appear therefore that the interior of the building that the author saw in September 2008 was a later modification.

249　*the prisoner's personal effects*: Bernov, *Lenin v Krakove*, p. 225. Information from Christina Zaba.

249　*nothing he could do*: Ganetsky [Hanecki], "S Leninym," p. 98.

249　*firing squad*: Wolfe, *Three Who Made a Revolution*, pp. 684–686.

249　*he was under suspicion*: Information from Christina Zaba and Piotr Bąk. Kasprowicz's assertion, as recorded by Bagotsky in "V. I. Lenin," pp. 455–456, runs counter to the local story, which had it that Marisya Kasprowicz, a general's daughter from St. Petersburg, asked her husband, who played cards with the local judge at Nowy Targ, to exert his influence in the campaign for Lenin's release. The Kasprowicz house in Zakopane, Villa Harenda, is now the Kasprowicz Museum.

250　*Polish nationalist dreams*: Sobczak, "Two Years in Poland," p. 17; Bagotsky, "V. I. Lenin," pp. 455–456; Adamczewski, *Lenin w Krakowie*, pp. 248–253; information from Christina Zaba.

250　*whose life was now at stake*: McNeal, *Bride*, 153, 155. Sobczak, "Two Years in Poland," p. 16; Bernov, *Lenin v Krakove*, pp. 226–227; Golikov, *Biokhronika* 3:268.

251　*might come and finish him off*: Krupskaya, *Memories*, p. 242.

251　*come and watch over her*: Krupskaya, *Memories*, p. 243.

251　*"distorted Russian"*: CW 37: 496.

252　*committee of "respectable citizens"*: I am indebted to Stephanie Weiner in California for sharing information about her great-uncle Emanuel Singer with me from Alojzy Singer's unpublished memoir. Passing allusions to this untold story can be found in Michael Walzer-Fass, *Remembrance Book of Nowy Targ and Vicinity* (Tel Aviv, 1979), p. 17; Trepper, *The Great Game*, pp. 3–4. Fass is most easily accessed at www.jewishgen.org/Yizkor/Nowy_targ/Nowy_Targ.html#TOC.

252 *ordering Lenin's release:* Wolfe, *Three,* p. 686; Bernov, *Lenin v Krakove,* pp. 230–231.

252 *he was well treated:* CW 37: 520.

252 *"further course of the Party":* Krupskaya, *Memories,* p. 242, a key part of Leninist folklore, perpetuated by the Soviets ever after (e.g., in Bernov, *Lenin v Krakove,* p. 228).

252 *to pay for the family's fare:* By the end of August Inessa Armand in Switzerland had also raised money from "unspecified sources" to help Lenin out and had organized its transfer, presumably to him in Kraków or more probably Vienna. Elwood, *Inessa Armand,* p. 143.

253 *Mendel's attic:* Information from Stephanie Weiner. Born in Nowy Targ in 1904, Trepper became a Zionist activist in Israel and later went to Moscow to organize and coordinate Red Orchestra, an intelligence network in Nazi-occupied Europe. Not long after Lenin left Galicia, Mendel Singer's store was burned down by a disgruntled employee who had been dismissed for stealing. The family moved to Nowy Targ, where Mendel built a new store. In 1942 a ghetto was established by the Nazis at Nowy Targ and used as a holding center for the Jewish population of Podhale. Many local Jews were forced to dig mass graves where they were shot and buried. Others were gassed in mobile trucks or shipped in boxcars to the death camps, including Belzec and Auschwitz. Mendel Singer was taken away to Kraków and murdered. His wife Helena and three of his sons perished. The other three, including Alojzy, who sat on Lenin's knee, survived the Holocaust.

253 *untrammeled exile:* See Grażyna Branny, "Conrad in Krakow" in *Conrad's Europe,* 3rd International Joseph Conrad Conference, Kamień Śląski, Kraków, September 2004, www.culture.pl/en/culture/artykuly/es_conrad_2004_branny. Conrad wrote a moving account of this visit, although it says very little about Zakopane, in "Poland Revisited," in *Collected Works of Joseph Conrad* (London: Routledge, 1995), 19:141–173.

254 *particularly valuable information:* Elwood, *Life Without a Cause,* p. 18.

254 *hotline to the Okhrana:* Ibid., pp. 33, 36.

255 *his good looks and swaggering manner:* Wolfe, *Three,* p. 600.

255 *Malinovsky . . . privy to the details:* Sebag Montefiore, *Young Stalin,* pp. 228–312; Shub, *Lenin,* p. 148.

255 *deeply compromised:* Salisbury, *Black Night,* p. 246; Elwood, *Life Without a Cause,* p. 42.

255 *"could ever break through it":* Wolfe, *Three,* pp. 614–615; Shub, *Lenin,* pp. 146, 152–153.

256 *"political honesty":* Salisbury, *Black Night,* p. 245; Elwood, *Life Without a Cause,* pp. 11, 57.

256 *His political acumen had let him down:* Salisbury, *Black Night,* p. 247. After leaving Poronin, Malinovsky joined the Russian army, was wounded, and was captured by the Germans. From his prison camp he offered his services to Lenin again, disseminating antimilitary propaganda among his fellow Russian prisoners. Lenin and Nadya responded by sending food parcels, clothes, and books. In November 1918 he unwisely returned to Petrograd, where he was arrested, interrogated for nine days, and tried by a revolutionary tribunal. When told he would be taken out and shot, Malinovsky agreed that the sentence was just. See Wolfe, *Three,* chap. 31, "The Case of Roman Malinovsky"; and R. Carter Elwood, *Roman Malinovsky.*

Chapter 16: "This Damned Switzerland"

257 *for safekeeping with their Polish comrades:* Bernov, *Lenin v Krakove,* p. 23, endorses this fact, though it ignores the role of the local Poronin Jews, as do other Soviet sources. Their contribution, like Polish contributions during August 1914, was completely marginalized in the official record. It was 1924 before the first consignment of material held in Poland found its way back to the Central Committee in the Soviet Union; in 1933 another group of books and manuscripts turned up, and in 1953 a collection of documents and letters was found in a Kraków archive, deposited there for safe keeping by Bagotsky, and sent to the Soviet government. See "Vladimir Lénine dans les bibliothèques polonaises," *IFLA Annual* 1970, p. 136.

257 *"a more implacable enemy":* Krupskaya, *Memories,* p. 244.

258 *clever banker in Vienna:* Ibid.

258 *access to good libraries again:* CW 43: 432.

258 *washing dishes twice a month:* Krupskaya, *Memories,* p. 252; Kudryavtsev, *Lenin v Berne,* p. 40.

258 *the international struggle ahead:* Krupskaya, *Memories,* p. 252.

259 *"Sleepy Berne":* CW 37: 522; Kudryavtsev, *Lenin v Berne,* pp. 49–56.

259 *prompt payment:* See CW 35:173–174.

259 *"bourgeois reformism":* Read, *Lenin,* p. 113.

260 *signing up for the French army:* Ulam, *Lenin and the Bolsheviks,* pp. 395–396.

260 *duty of all social democrats:* Krupskaya, *Memories* p. 249; Read, *Lenin,* p. 131.

260 *"worse than kaiserism":* Clark, *Life and Death,* pp. 162–165; CW 35: 163.

261 *the question of "free love":* For further discussion, see Elwood, *Inessa Armand,* pp. 145–149; and Service, *Lenin: The Biography,* pp. 231–232.

261 *"two or three women":* Volkogonov, *Lenin,* p. 46. This assertion was cut from the letter Lenin sent to Inessa in its original form when published in volume 48 of Lenin's *Sobranie Sochinenii.* In the absence of names one can only surmise that the possible candidates were Nadya, Inessa, and either his first love in St. Petersburg in the early 1890s, Apollinariya Yakubova, or the elusive Elizaveta de K. Inessa never finished writing her pamphlet on free love; perhaps she felt unable to continue without Lenin's approval. Her initial draft of it has not survived.

262 *growing political profile:* Elwood, *Inessa Armand,* pp. 157–160.

262 *helpmate and comrade:* Krupskaya, *Memories,* pp. 261–262.

263 *"did not need her any more":* Levine, *The Man Lenin,* p. 164; Wilson, *To the Finland Station,* p. 461.

263 *wished to rent the room to "believers":* Krupskaya, *Memories,* p. 262.

263 *a good rest in the mountains:* McNeal, *Bride,* p. 150. Information from Professor Ronald Chaplain. See also Haas, "Lenins Frau."

264 *Lenin's special requests:* CW 43: 347.

264 *read novels by Victor Hugo:* Krupskaya, *Memories,* p. 264; Elwood, "Lenin on Holiday," p. 125.

264 *pick mushrooms and enjoy the view:* See, for example, Kudryavtsev, *Lenin v Berne i Tsyurikhe,* pp. 65–69.

264 *economic musings:* Elwood, "Lenin on Holiday," p. 126 n. 10; Krupskaya, *Memories,* p. 264; Service, *Lenin: A Political Biography,* 2:95, 99.

265 *"Kautskyite shitheads":* Nation, *War on War,* pp. 78, 81; Wilson, *To the Finland Station,* p. 450.

265 *"ornithological society"*: Elwood, *Inessa Armand*, p. 164; Senn, *Russian Revolution in Switzerland*, p. 91.

265 *"was still possible to seat all of the internationalists in four coaches"*: Trotsky, *My Life*, p. 249.

265 *"a Swiss mountaineer"*: Vasili Kolarov, "At the Zimmerwald Conference," in *They Knew Lenin*, p. 70.

265 *genuine and lasting peace*: Nation, *War on War*, pp. 86–87.

266 *"almost no joy"*: Clark, *Lenin*, p. 173; Nation, *War on War*, p. 91.

266 *"The real struggle"*: Payne, *Life and Death*, p. 251.

266 *Lenin's faction of eight*: Nation, *War on War*, pp. 88–91. The Zimmerwald eight were Lenin, Zinoviev, the Polish representative Radek, a Latvian J. Berzin, Julian Borkhat from Germany, and two Swedes—Zeth Höglund and Ture Nerman. The final member, the Swiss socialist Fritz Platten, would play a key role in Lenin's return to Russia in 1917.

266 *slept "like the dead"*: Krupskaya, *Memories*, p. 267.

266 *"devilishly difficult"*: CW 37: 530, 526–527.

267 *circumstances were so straitened*: Weber, *Lenin*, p. 115.

267 *la maîtresse de Lénine*: McNeal, *Bride*, p. 157; Elwood, *Inessa Armand*, p. 174.

267 *his halfhearted queries*: CW 43: 504–506.

267 *the final insult*: Elwood, *Inessa Armand*, pp. 167–171; Pearson *Inessa*, pp. 133–134.

Chapter 17: "One Fighting Campaign After Another"

269 *four flights of stairs*: Kudryavtsev, *Lenin v Berne*, p. 133.

269 *"the lower depths of Zurich"*: Krupskaya, *Memories*, p. 271; Marcu, "Lenin in Zurich," p. 550.

270 *Lenin's face shone with pleasure*: Marcu, "Lenin in Zurich," pp. 550–551.

270 *Committee of Social Salvation*: Meier, *Knowledge and Revolution*, p. 60.

270 *"makes one despair"*: CW 37:530.

271 *perpetually dark and dank*: Levine, *The Man Lenin*, p. 32; Kudryavtsev, *Lenin v Berne*, pp. 135–136; Kharitonova, "V. I. Lenin v Tsyurikhskoy sektsii bol'shevikov," in *OVIL 1900–1922*, p. 150. The lower end of Spiegelgasse opposite number 14 was widened later, when several houses were demolished.

272 *they were among friends*: Krupskaya, *Memories*, p. 272. Twenty-eight francs in 1917 was the equivalent of $5 or £2.50 sterling.

272 *"possess an iron will"*: Payne, *Life and Death*, p. 251; "We Rented to the Lenins," pp. 26–27.

272 *"one would have taken him for a mechanic"*: "We Rented to the Lenins," pp. 26–28; Levine, *Lenin the Man*, pp. 32–33; Kharitonova, "V. I. Lenin," in *OVIL 1900–1922*, pp. 150–151; Ybarra, "Lenin Lived Poorly," p. 5.

272 *"doubly rigid economy"*: Krupskaya, *Memories*, p. 284.

273 *notebooks "full of calculations"*: Rice, *Lenin*, p. 32.

273 *increasingly commanding presence*: Ulam, *Lenin and the Bolsheviks*, pp. 400–401.

273 *he was convinced*: Ibid., pp. 406–407.

273 *"to think his ideas out to the end"*: Krupskaya, *Memories*, pp. 277, 284.

274 *"Good-bye Cuckoo"*: Ibid., pp. 278–279; Elwood, "Lenin on Holiday," pp. 126–127.

275 *drinking coffee in sight of James Joyce*: Leuning, *Odyssey*, pp. 122–123; Solzhenitsyn, *Lenin in Zurich*, p. 210.

275 *moving to the front of the building*: Kudryavtsev, *Lenin v Berne*, p. 140.

275 *cafés-chantants*: Fischer, *Life of Lenin*, p. 489. The possibility of Lenin crossing paths with Dadaist Tristan Zara and writer Joyce was explored with considerable wit by Tom Stoppard in his 1974 play *Travesties*.

275 *recalled a visit by Lenin*: Ball, *Flight out of Time*, p. 117; Dominique Noguez, *Lénine Dada*, pp. 13–15, 147–148. Noguez argues forcefully for a closer association between Lenin and the Dadaists, but the evidence is too tenuous to hold water.

276 *"planning a world revolution"*: Richter, *Dada*, p. 16.

276 *"blotting pad correspondence"*: Zweig, *The Sealed Train*, pp. 241–242.

276 *"command of the moment"*: Leuning, *Odyssey*, p. 123.

277 *a "certain changed mood"*: Volkogonov, *Lenin*, pp. 42–43; this section appeared in the published edition of Lenin's letters.

277 *"absurd, reckless and ridiculous"*: Pipes, *Unknown Lenin*, p. 34.

278 *"theoretical oddities"*: Pearson, *Inessa*, p. 142. The issue of what exactly Inessa wrote in her letters to Lenin is frustrating, bar the unposted letter of January 1914 published in Russia in 1992 (see *"almost from the first meeting"* in Chapter 14), in which she poured out her heart to him (pp. 222–223). The Lenin–Inessa story is fundamentally one-sided, with only passing clues in his surviving letters to the emotional content of her letters. Had letters from Inessa to Lenin been contained in the archives in 1992, when the crucial letter was published, it is only logical that they would have been published as well. This suggests that Lenin destroyed Inessa's letters when he received them, as he did other correspondence from activists in the underground as a matter of security. Inessa's letters probably would have been far too candid and too private to keep. Lenin was mindful enough of his posthumous reputation to ask Inessa to return his letters to her, which suggests that he certainly would have ensured that hers to him did not fall into the wrong hands. The most likely scenario therefore is that he destroyed them or Nadya did so after his death, if he kept them out of sentiment. I am grateful to Professor R. Carter Elwood, Professor Robert Service, and Michael Pearson for their comments in this regard.

278 *kisses of the past*: See Lenin's letters to Inessa, November 25 to December 13, 1916, in *CW* 35: 248–269. For a perceptive view of Inessa's behavior at this time, see Solzhenitsyn, *Lenin in Zurich*, pp. 69–73.

279 *"irreconcilable mood"*: Ulam, *Lenin and the Bolsheviks*, p. 403; Krupskaya, *Memories*, p. 285.

279 *"café conspirator"*: Shub, *Lenin*, p. 181.

279 *"philistinism, opportunism"*: *CW* 35: 259.

280 *bring them down*: For overviews of the rapidly degenerating situation in Russia, see Salisbury, *Black Night*; Pipes, *The Russian Revolution*; and Figes, *A People's Tragedy*.

280 *"but it was all so far away"*: Krupskaya, *Memories*, pp. 268, 275.

280 *popular antipathy toward the czarist regime*: Because Lenin was living in Europe when events in Russia unfolded and in order to avoid confusion between the Julian calendar still operating in Russia at this time and the civil Gregorian one used throughout Europe, all dates are given per the Gregorian calendar. The "February revolution," as it is often referred to in Russia, actually took place in March according to today's calendar.

281 *a period of chaos and uncertainty*: Ulam, *Lenin and the Bolsheviks*, pp. 409–411.

281 *awaited Lenin's return*: Ibid., p. 420.

Chapter 18: From the Spiegelgasse to the Finland Station

283 *"Perhaps it is another hoax"*: McNeal, *Bride of the Revolution*, p. 165.

283 *"Here I have nothing to do"*: Krupskaya, *Memories*, pp. 286–287; "We Rented to the Lenins," p. 28.

284 *armistice with Germany*: CW 43: 616. For Lenin's directives, see CW 35: 295–300. Krupskaya, *Memories*, p. 287.

284 *misguided fears*: Volkogonov, *Lenin*, p. 106; Payne, *Life and Death*, pp. 274–275.

284 *plans for getting back*: Krupskaya, *Memories*, pp. 287–288; Zinoviev, *Lenin*, p. 290; CW 43: 616–618; CW 35: 300.

284 *"We ought to get busy with it"*: Willi Münzenberg, "Lenin and We," in *They Knew Lenin*, pp. 84–86.

285 *"unless very 'special' measures have been taken"*: CW 43: 617.

285 *a "detestable centrist"*: Payne, *Life and Death*, p. 279.

285 *defeatist peace in Russia*: For further discussion of the German financial investment in Lenin's revolution, see Pearson, *The Sealed Train*, pp. 104, 114, 290–291; and Volkogonov, *Lenin*, p. 116.

285 *destabilize the czarist regime*: Clark, *Life and Death*, pp. 168–169.

285 *"imperative that Russia should fall"*: Shub, *Lenin*, p. 210.

285 *brokered the deal*: Ley, "Memorable Day," p. 497.

286 *money from bank robberies and other expropriations*: Considerable debate continues on the precise extent of German financial support for Lenin's return to Russia and the October Bolshevik coup d'état. See Volkogonov, *Lenin*, 109–128, for a discussion of the murky role played by Hanecki and Helphand. Volkogonov alleges that large amounts of money were transmitted from Berlin to Hanecki via the New Bank in Stockholm and laundered through a cover account at the Bank of Siberia in Petrograd. He also observes that compromising documentary evidence relating to this money was destroyed after the revolution, Lenin being "very good at keeping secrets" (111, 121). In later years it was alleged that the Bolsheviks received up to 50 million gold marks in subsidies from the Germans. For his pains the loyal Hanecki suffered arrest and torture under Stalin and was shot, along with his wife and son, in November 1937 (Volgonov, *Lenin*, p. 128).

286 *rising hysteria*: Zinoviev, *Lenin*, p. 28; Payne, *Life and Death*, p. 276; Krupskaya, *Memories*, p. 288; CW 35: 309; 43: 620.

286 *scotched for its absurdity*: Radek, "Lenin's Sealed Train," p. 92; Krupskaya, *Memories*, p. 288.

286 *prosecute anybody who returned to Russia*: CW 43: 625.

287 *"special train with reliable escort"*: Payne, *Life and Death*, p. 285.

287 *malevolent genie*: Münzenberg, in *They Knew Lenin*, p. 86.

287 *her mother's ashes*: In 1969, in deference to Nadezhda Krupskaya's wishes, the Soviet Central Committee had Elizaveta Vasil'evna's ashes returned to Russia. See Service, *Lenin: A Biography*, pp. 509–510.

288 *diplomat should never refuse to listen*: Peter Grose, *Allen Dulles: Spymaster* (London: André Deutsch, 1995), p. 26. Dulles's appointment in Berne did not officially commence until April 23, but he spent considerable time in the city prior to his transfer from Vienna. Lenin's motive for the call is not altogether clear: clearly to hedge his bets with America but perhaps also to secure tacit approval for a visa and a refuge should his usurpation of power in Russia not go as planned.

288 *Rolland, however, would not be used:* Stefan Zweig, *The World of Yesterday* (London: Cassell, 1987), pp. 203–204. Rolland soon ran into trouble with the Swiss authorities and needed to get out of Zurich. Ironically, in view of his rejection of Lenin's invitation, it was thanks to Lenin's intervention that he was allowed to travel to Russia with Martov a month later on the second "sealed train" laid on by the Germans for a large group of Mensheviks (pp. 207–208).

288 *absurd joke:* Ley, "Memorable Day," p. 496.

289 *"Let us go into that battle":* Vayo, *Last Optimist,* p. 124; see also Aline's account in *Lénine à Paris,* pp. 119–120.

289 *"a step toward it":* CW 23: 367–374.

289 *"disturbed ant colony":* Heresch, *Blood on the Snow,* p. 86.

289 *the thousand francs Lenin had already raised:* Clarke, *Life and Death,* p. 198.

290 *small group of shabby Russians:* Leuning, *Odyssey,* pp. 124–125.

290 *sixteen years in exile:* Moskovsky, *Lenin v Shvetsii,* p. 100.

290 *"the thing for which I was created":* Salisbury, *Blood on the Snow,* p. 406.

290 *Angelika Rohr:* Heresch, *Blood on the Snow,* p. 86.

290 *"bad political sign":* Rozenthal, "Lenin in Switzerland," p. 13.

291 *mad journey through Germany:* Shub, *Lenin,* p. 21; Zinoviev, *Lenin,* p. 291.

291 *"swinging from the gallows":* Sean McMeekin, *The Red Millionaire: A Political Biography of Willi Münzenberg* (New Haven: Yale University Press, 2003), p. 45.

291 *repaired to the Café Odeon:* Heresch, *Blood on the Snow,* p. 87; Payne, *Life and Death* p. 296; Pearson, *The Sealed Train,* p. 78; Leuning, *Odyssey,* p. 125.

292 *doors at the Russian end were closed shut:* Payne, *Life and Death,* p. 297; Pearson, *The Sealed Train,* p. 82; Clarke, *Life and Death,* p. 204.

292 *uncomradely disgruntlement:* Radek, "V plombirovannom vagone," pp. 129–130; 000 Krupskaya, *Memories,* p. 294; Haupt and Marie, *Makers of the Russian Revolution,* pp. 379–381.

293 *Russians gave . . . their own food:* Usevich, "Iz vosmpominanii o V. I. Lenine," p. 149.

293 *grimness of Germany at war:* Lilina Zina, "Tov. Lenin edet v Rossiyu," p. 2.

293 *list of false names:* Radek, "V plombirovannom vagone," p. 313.

293 *Lenin . . . paced around on deck:* Pearson, *The Sealed Train,* pp. 100–101; Moskovsky, *Lenin v Shvetsii,* pp. 105–106.

293 *"band of barbarians":* Radek, "Lenin's Sealed Train," p. 92, a variant of Radek's 1924 *Pravda* article. The *New York Times* article is a translation of one published around the same time in the French communist paper *l'Humanité* entitled "How the Bolshevist Bacillus Was Discovered by the Germans and Transported to Russia by General Ludendorff."

294 *energy like that of a locomotive:* Moskovsky, *Lenin v Shvetsii,* p. 114.

294 *new bowler hat:* Radek, "V plombirovannom vagone," p. 132; Moskovsky, *Lenin v Shvetsii,* p. 118; Elwood, *Inessa Armand,* p. 203. Radek noted that when he finally was allowed into Russia in November 1917, he noticed that Lenin was still wearing the Stockholm trousers, already "respectably tattered."

295 *provincial schoolteacher:* Futrell, *Northern Underground,* p. 155.

295 *"every minute was precious":* Ibid., p. 156; Ganetsky, "Priezd tov. Lenina," pp. 139–140; Moskovsky, *Lenin v Shvetsii,* p. 115.

295 *man in a hurry:* Dann, *Lenin and Nadya,* p. 192.

295 *next possible hurdle:* Elwood, *Inessa Armand,* p. 204; Clarke, *Lenin,* p. 208.

296 *"rested on a democratic foundation":* "Calls Soviet Foe of Trade Unionism," *New York Times,* December 4, 1919, p. 7, citing testimony of Lieutenant A. W. Kliefoth,

assistant U.S. military attaché in Russia, who was the passport officer at Torneo when the Russians arrived.

296 *Mariya's address:* Zinoviev, *Lenin,* p. 291; Futrell, *Northern Underground,* pp. 98–99; Payne, *Life and Death,* pp. 305–306.

296 *"Were he a Japanese":* Lord Howard of Penrith, *Theatre of Life* (London: Hodder & Stoughton, 1936), 2:264; William Gerhardie, *Memoirs of a Polyglot* (London: MacDonald, 1973), p. 130; information from Phil Tomaselli, to whom I am grateful for alerting me to this story.

297 *"worthy masters of the future":* Moskovsky, *Lenin v Shvetsii,* p 136.

297 *expanses of dense forest:* Krupskaya, *Memories,* p. 295; Wilson, *To the Finland Station,* pp. 469–470; Zinoviev, *Lenin,* p. 292.

298 *kissed Lenin's cheek:* Kathy Porter, *Alexandra Kollontai* (London: Virago, 1980), p. 245.

298 *"hating every kind of ceremony":* F. F. Raskolnikov, *Kronstadt and Petrograd in 1917* (London: New Park, 1982), p. 68.

299 *returning political hero:* Payne, *Life and Death,* pp. 310–311; Zinoviev, *Lenin,* p. 293; Krupskaya, *Memories,* p. 296; Wilson, *To the Finland Station,* pp. 472–473.

299 *"grand and solemn beauty":* Pearson, *The Sealed Train,* pp. 126–131; Krupskaya, *Memories,* pp. 295–296.

300 *"this is the revolution":* Konstantin Eremeev, "Vstrechi s Il'ichem," *Leningradskaya Pravda,* January 30, 1924.

300 *armored car:* Drabkina, "Priezd tovarishch Lenina," p. 156.

300 *implacable rage against the old order:* Ariadna Tyrkova-Williams, *From Liberty to Brest-Litovsk* (London: Macmillan, 1919), p. 62; Possony, *Lenin,* p. 240.

300 *didn't yet know what to make of him:* Payne, *Life and Death,* pp. 311–312.

301 *Long live the worldwide socialist revolution!":* The accounts of Lenin's return on the "sealed train" are numerous; many were published in Soviet newspapers on the occasion of his death in 1924. For English accounts, see especially Pearson, *The Sealed Train,* and a vivid account that encapsulates some of the best eyewitnesses in Payne, *Lenin,* pp. 301–313. Nadezhda Krupskaya's memoir is disappointingly dull and unrevealing but see Krupskaya, *Memories,* pp. 293–296. Radek's brief account—originally published in *Pravda* in 1924 and an English variant in the *New York Times* in 1922—is particularly interesting. See also accounts by Suliashvili in Moskovsky, *Lenin v Shvetsii,* pp. 85–141; Zinoviev, *Lenin,* pp. 289–294; Hanecki and Drabkina in *Proletarskaya Revolyutsiya;* Lilina, in *Leningradskaya Pravda.* Locomotive 293 is enshrined under glass at St. Petersburg's Finland Station.

Epilogue: Good-bye Lenin

304 *"dustbin of history":* Trotsky's remark came at a meeting of the Council of Soviets in October 1917, when Martov registered his disgust at the Bolshevik seizure of power. "You are pitiful isolated individuals; you are bankrupts; your role is played out. Go where you belong from now on—into the dustbin of history!" See Trotsky, *History of the Russian Revolution* (1933), 3; chap 10; Volkogonov, *Lenin,* p. 102.

304 *Stepa Zinoviev perished:* See Orlando Figes, *The Whisperers* (London: Allen Lane, 2007), p. 248.

304 *"crumbled and died":* Ana Siljak, *Angel of Vengeance* (New York: St. Martin's, 2008), p. 311.

305 *she contracted cholera:* See "Inessa Armand," *Svobodnaya mysl'*, p. 835; Pearson, *Inessa*, pp. 217–221.

305 *Lenin, "propped up" by Nadya:* Vasilieva and Porter, *Kremlin Wives*, pp. 23–24; Porter, *Alexandra Kollontai*, p. 345.

305 *she was poisoned:* Rappaport, *Stalin: A Biographical Companion*, pp. 156–157. For an excellent summary of the Leninist legacy, see Service, *Lenin: The Biography*, pp. 481–494.

306 *insane, fixed stare:* Information from Professor Ronald Chaplain, formerly of Oxford University, who in his bona fide position as a deputy head of Professor Manfred von Ardenne's pioneering cancer hospital in Berlin in the 1970s, was told by top medical advisers to the Soviet leadership that Lenin had died of syphilis. It is possible that the red rash Lenin suffered in April 1903, which he and Nadya self diagnosed as "holy fire," was in fact the classic rash that is a second stage symptom of syphilis. This rash usually appears between six weeks to six months after initial infection. If so, it substantiates rumors that Lenin had contracted syphilis on a trip to Paris around 1902, cited in Lina, *Under the Sign,* p. 129 (see chap. 13 n. 32; Lenin was in Paris in the summer of 1902 and again in early 1903).

In exile Lenin suffered ill temper, headaches, irritability, and sleeplessness, as well as periodic loss of appetite and excruciating headaches, all of which are characteristic of second stage syphilis and were often noted in her memoirs by his wife. After his physical collapse in 1922 these symptoms became much more pronounced, and while they can also be symptomatic of arteriosclerosis of the brain, taking into account Lenin's cumulative medical history they can also be read as manifestations of the brain damage leading to dementia, progressive paralysis, and aphasia characteristic of neurosyphilis, which develops after a ten- to twenty-year incubation period from initial infection. According to Professor Chaplain, the autopsy on Lenin's brain after his death showed up massive sclerosis of the blood vessels and areas of cystic change in both left and right hemispheres consistent with a diagnosis of neurosyphilis in its meningovascular form. Lenin's terminal neurosyphilis was an open secret from the Soviet minister for health, Professor Boris Petrovsky, down through to the elite Kremlin doctors with whom Chaplain conversed. After the collapse of the Soviet Union, evidence emerged that the chief pathologist, Alexey Abrikosov, who had performed Lenin's autopsy, had been specifically instructed to falsify the record to cover up the diagnosis of syphilis. In March 1923 eminent Swedish neuropathologists Salomon and Folke Henschen—both communist sympathizers—were brought in to examine Lenin and refute the syphilis diagnosis. The results of the Wasserman test, used for the early diagnosis for syphilis, that were made on Lenin's blood in May 1922, have, according to Robert Service (*Lenin: A Biography,* p. 444), "gone missing." They would have been irrelevant at the terminal stage of Lenin's disease.

Linora Lawrence, "Cold War Memories," an interview by Professor Chaplain published in *Oxfordshire, Limited Edition,* the magazine of the *Oxford Times,* June 2008, pp. 15–19; V. Lerner et al., "The Enigma of Lenin's (1870–1924) Malady," *European Journal of Neurology* 11 (2004): 371–376, which features the photograph of Lenin mentioned on p. 306 of the epilogue on its front cover; Juri Lina, *Under the Sign of the Scorpion: The Rise and Fall of the Soviet Empire* (Stockholm: Referent), 2002. The only discussion of the possible diagnosis of syphilis in published Lenin biographies is found in Service, *Lenin: A Biography,* pp. 443–446. See also notes in chapter 13, note 32.

306 *around 14 million copies:* "Leniniana," *World Marxist Review* 12, no. 4 (April 1969): 8–9.

307   *a Lenin memorial:* "Lenin's London Home," *Times,* March 16, 1942, p. 6; and "The Shadow of Lenin on a 'Budget' Hotel," *Times,* April 16, 1970, p. 4.

307   *Lenin and Nadya's long Swiss hike:* Elwood, "Lenin on Holiday."

308   *priceless communist relics:* "We Rented to the Lenins," p. 28; *Time,* November 19, 1951; *New York Times,* June 1924, p. E5.

309   *their struggle for independence:* Joni Krekola, "Lenin Lives in Finland," in *The Cold War and the Politics of History* (Department of Social Science History, University of Helsinki/Edita Publishing, 2008).

309   *a different story:* Much of the information in this section comes from conversations with Poles in Kraków, Poronin, Biały Dunajec, and Zakopane. I am indebted to Piotr Bąk, former mayor of Zakopane, for a long and illuminating discussion.

310   *9 million Poles:* "Eyewitness Reports," *News from Behind the Iron Curtain,* p. 28. The news items in this section of the journal were based on information regarding conditions behind the Iron Curtain from refugees interviewed by Radio Free Europe. See also Sobczak, "Two Years in Poland," p. 18.

310   *"the Polish people's aspirations":* Sobczak, "Two Years in Poland," p. 16.

313   *celebrate Lenin:* Information from Piotr Bąk in Zakopane.

313   *Stanisław suddenly stopped talking:* Ibid.

314   *"confessed" to the crime:* Marek Bartosik, "Wódz obalony lebiodką," *Gazeta Krakowska,* September 5, 2008, pp. 8–9.

BIBLIOGRAPHY

―⦾―

1. Archives

Islington Local History Library, London. Box YJ853 09 BRO

PRO Ramsay-MacDonald Papers, 30/69/1753

PRO Lenin File KV2/585

Hoover Institution, Report of Y. A. Litkens on Lenin in Munich, 1900–1902, Boris Nicolaevsky Collection

2. Lenin: Family Background, Life, and Works

Akhapkin, Yuri. *Lenin–Krupskaya–Ulyanovy: Perepiska, 1883–1900*. Moscow: Mysl', 1981.

Alexinsky, Gregory. "Lenin v deistvitel'nosti: Ego roman s Elizavetoi K***." *Illyus-trirovannaya Rossiya*, October 31, 1936; November 7, 14, 21, 1936.

Ascher, A. *Pavel Axelrod and the Development of Menshevism*. Cambridge: Harvard University Press, 1972.

Balabanoff, Angelica. *Impressions of Lenin*. Ann Arbor: University of Michigan Press, 1964.

Beucler, André, and Grigory Alexinsky. *Les amours secrètes de Lénine*. Paris: Editions Baudinière, 1937.

Bonch-Bruevich, Vladimir. *Vospominaniya o Lenine*. Moscow: Izd. Nauka, 1969.

Clark, Ronald. *Lenin: The Man Behind the Mask*. London: Faber, 1988.

Deich, Lev. *Rasskazy o Lenine i Leninskoi Iskry*. Sverdlovsk: Sredne-ural'skoe knizhnoe izdatel'stvo, 1987.

Deutscher, Isaac. *Lenin's Childhood*. London: Oxford University Press, 1970.

Deutscher, Tamara. *Not by Politics Alone: The Other Lenin*. London: Allen & Unwin, 1973.

Donald, Moira. *Marxism and Revolution: Karl Kautsky and the Russian Marxists, 1900–24*. New Haven: Yale University Press, 1993.

Dovring, Folke. *Leninism: Political Economy as Pseudoscience*. Westport: Praeger, 1996.

_____."To the Editor." *Slavic Review* 29, no. 3 (1970): 570–573. Dovring refutes Robert H. McNeal, "Lenin and Lise de K . . . A Fabrication." *Slavic Review* 28, no. 3 (1969): 471–474.

Drabkina, Feodosiya. "Priezd Tov: Lenina." *Proletarskaya revolyutsiya* 4 (1927): 150–163.

Elwood, R. Carter. "Lenin and Armand: New Evidence of an Old Affair." *Canadian Slavonic Papers*, March 2001, pp. 49–66.

_____. "Lenin on Holiday." *Revolutionary Russia* 21, no. 2 (2008): 115–134.

_____. "What Lenin Ate." *Revolutionary Russia* 20, no. 2 (2007): 137–149.

Erokhin, A. S. *Shushenskii Arsenal–O lichnoi biblioteke V. I. Lenina.* Moscow: Izd. Kniga, 1971.

Fedirko, P. S. *V. I. Lenin i Krasnoyarskii Krai.* Krasnoyarsk: Krasnoyarskoe knizhnoe izdatel'stvo, 1986.

Fischer, Louis. *The Life of Lenin.* London: Phoenix, 2002.

Fotieva, Lydia. *Pages from Lenin's Life.* Moscow: Foreign Languages Publishing House, 1960.

Fox, Ralph. *Lenin: A Biography.* London: Gollancz, 1933.

Ganetsky [Hanecki], Yakov. "Priezd tovarishcha Lenina iz Shveitsarii v Rossiyu." In Fritz Platten, *Lenin iz emigratsii v Rossiyu*, pp. 134–140.

Gernet, M. N. *Istoriya tsarskoi tyur'mi.* Vol. 3, *1870–1900.* Moscow: Gos. izd. yuridicheskoi literaturoi, 1963.

Golikov, Georgy Nazarovich. *Vladimir Il'ich Lenin: Biograficheskaya Khronika, 1870–1924.* 12 vols. Moscow: Izd. politicheskoi literatury, 1970–1982.

_____. *Vospominaniya o V. I. Lenine.* 5 vols. Moscow: Politizdat, 1968–1970. Abbreviated as Golikov, *VoVIL.*

Gorky, Maxim. *Days with Lenin.* London: M. Lawrence, 1933.

Haimson, L. *Russian Marxists and the Origins of Bolshevism.* Cambridge: Harvard University Press, 1955.

Hill, Elizabeth, ed. *The Letters of Lenin.* London: Chapman & Hall, 1937.

Institut Marksizma-Leninizma. *Vospominaniya oVladimire Il'iche Lenine.* 3 vols. Moscow: Izd. politicheskoi literatury 1956–1960. Abbreviated as *VoVIL.*

"Inessa Armand: Neizvestnoe pis'mo Leninu. Iz dnevnikov." *Svobodnaya Mysl'* 3 (1992): 80–88.

Ivanskii, A. I. *Lenin v Sibirskoi ssylke.* Moscow: Izd. politicheskoi literatury, 1946.

Ivansky, A., ed. *Comet in the Night: The Story of Alexander Ulyanov's Heroic Life and Tragic Death.* Honolulu: University Press of the Pacific, 2004.

Krasnovsky, A. *In the Footsteps of Lenin: Ul'yanovsk, Kazan, Krasnoyarsk, Shushenskoe.* Moscow: Progress, 1975.

Krupskaya, Nadezhda. *Memories of Lenin.* London: Panther, 1970.

_____. "O Vladimire Il'iche." In Golikov, *VoVIL* 2: 581–585.

Krzhizhanovsky, G. *O Vladimire Il'iche.* Moscow: Partiinoe izdatel'stvo, 1924.

Latyshev, Anatoly. *Rassekrechennyi Lenin.* Moscow: Izd. "Mart," 1996.

Lenin, *Collected Works.* 45 vols. Moscow: Progress, 1963–1970. Abbreviated as *CW.*

Lenin. *Perepiska V. I. Lenina s redaktsiei gazety Iskra.* 3 vols. Moscow: Mysl', 1969–1970.

"Lenin and Libraries." *IFLA Annual 1970.* Moscow Centenary Conference, Copenhagen: Scandinavian Library Centre, 1970.

Lepeshinskaya, Ol'ga. *Vstrechi s Il'ichem.* Moscow: Izd. politicheskoi literatury, 1966.

Levine, Isaac Don. *The Man Lenin.* New York: Thomas Seltzer, 1924.

Lied, Jonas. *Prospector in Siberia.* New York: Oxford University Press, 1945.

Lilina [Zinov'eva], Zina. "Tov: Lenin edet v Rossiyu." *Leningradskaya Pravda*, April 16, 1924.

Lyudvinskaya, T. F. *Velikii, blizkii, prostoi.* Moscow: Znanie, 1969.

McNeal, Robert. *Bride of the Revolution: Krupskaya and Lenin.* London: Gollancz, 1973.

McNeal, Robert H. "Lenin and Lise de K . . . A Fabrication." *Slavic Review* 28, no. 3 (1969): 471–474.

Marcu, Valeriu. *Lenin.* London: Gollancz, 1928.

McNight, David. "Lenin and the Reinvention of the Russian Conspiratorial Tradition." In *Espionage and the Roots of the Cold War.* London: Frank Cass, 2002.

Mel'nichenko, Vladimir. *Ya tebya ochen' lyubila: Pravda o Lenine i Armand.* Moscow: Voskresen'e, 2002.

Meshalkin, Petr. *Sibirskaya ssylka V. I. Lenina.* Krasnoyarsk: Krasnoyarskoe knizhnoe izdatel'stvo, 1987.

Mirsky, D. S. *Lenin.* London: Holme, 1931.

Mushtukov, V. E. *Zdes' zhil i rabotal Lenin.* Leningrad: Lenizdat, 1967.

Novikov, V. *Lenin i deyatel"nost" iskrovykh grupp v Rossii, 1900–1903.* Moscow: Mysl', 1978.

Novorussky, Mikhail. *Zapiski shlissel'burzhtsa, 1887–1905.* Petrograd: Gosudarstvennoe izdatel'stvo, 1924.

Petrov, F. N., et al. *O Vladimire Il'iche Lenine: Vospominaniya, 1900–1922 gody.* Moscow: Izd. politicheskoi literatury, 1963. Abbreviated as *OVIL 1900–1922.*

Payne, R. *The Life and Death of Lenin.* London: Grafton, 1964.

Pearson, Michael. *Inessa: Lenin's Mistress.* London: Duckworth, 2001.

Perris, G. H. *Russia in Revolution.* London: Chapman & Hall, 1905.

Pipes, Richard. "The Intellectual Evolution of Lenin." In *Revolutionary Russia.* London: Oxford University Press, 1968.

———. *The Unknown Lenin.* New Haven: Yale University Press, 1998.

Possony, Stefan T. *Lenin: The Compulsive Revolutionary.* London: Allen & Unwin, 1966.

Potresov, Alexander N. "Lenin." In *Posmertnyi sbornik proizvedenii,* pp. 293–304. Paris: Maison du Livre Etranger, 1927.

Radek, Karl. "Lenin's Sealed Train." *New York Times,* February 19, 1922, p. 92.

———. "V plombirovannom vagone." In Fritz Platten, *Lenin iz emigratsii v Rossiyu,* pp. 127–133.

Read, Christopher. *From Tsar to Soviets: The Russian People and Their Revolution,* New York: Oxford University Press, 1996.

———. *Lenin: A Revolutionary Life.* London: Routledge, 2005.

———. "Retrieving the Historical Lenin." In Ian D. Thatcher, ed., *Reinterpreting Revolutionary Russia: Essays in Honour of James D. White.* Basingstoke: Palgrave Macmillan, 2006.

Rice, C. *Lenin: Portrait of a Professional Revolutionary.* London: Cassell, 1990.

Schapiro, L., and P. Reddaway. *Lenin the Man, the Theorist, the Leader: A Reappraisal.* London: Pall Mall, 1967.

Service, Robert. *Lenin: A Biography.* London: Macmillan, 2000.

———. *Lenin: A Political Life.* 3 vols. Basingstoke: Macmillan, 1985–1995.

Shtein, Mikhail. *Ulyanovy i Leniny: Semeinye tayny.* St. Petersburg: Neva, 2004.

Shtein, M., and G. Sidorovnin. *Vozhd': Lenin, kotorogo my ne znali.* Saratov: Slovo, 1992.

Shub, David. "Fact or Fiction on Lenin's Role." *New International* 16, no. 2 (March–April 1950): 86–91.

———. *Lenin.* Harmondsworth: Penguin, 1966.

Simsova, Sylva. *Lenin, Krupskaya, and Libraries.* London: Bingley, 1968.

Solomon, G. A. *Lenin i ego sem'ya, Ul'yanovy.* Paris: Imprimerie des travailleurs intellectuels, 1931.

Struve, Petr. "My Contacts and Conflicts with Lenin." *Slavonic and East European Review,* April 1934, pp. 573–595.

_____. "My Meeting with Lenin." *Slavonic and East European Review,* July 1934, pp. 66–84.

Suliashvili, D. "Vstrechi s Leninym v emigratsii." *Neva* 2 (1957): 135–144.

Theen, Rolf, and H. W. Theen. *Lenin.* London: Quartet Books, 1974.

They Knew Lenin: Reminiscences of Foreign Contemporaries. Honolulu: University of the Pacific, 2005.

Treadgold, Donald. *Lenin and His Rivals: The Struggle for Russia's Future, 1898–1906.* London: Methuen, 1955.

Trotsky, Leon. *On Lenin: Notes Towards a Biography.* London: Harrap, 1971.

_____. *Portraits: Political and Personal.* New York: Pathfinder, 1977.

_____. *The Young Lenin.* Harmondsworth: Penguin, 1972

Turton, Katy. *Forgotten Lives: The Role of Lenin's Sisters in the Russian Revolution, 1864–1937.* Basingstoke: Palgrave Macmillan, 2007.

Ulam, Adam B. *Lenin and the Bolsheviks.* London: Fontana, 1965.

Usievich, Elena. "Iz vospominanii o V. I. Lenine." In Fritz Platten, *Lenin iz emigratsii v Rossiyu,* pp. 141–155.

Valentinov, Nikolay. *The Early Years of Lenin.* Ann Arbor: University of Michigan Press, 1968.

_____. *Encounters with Lenin.* London: Oxford University Press, 1969.

Vasilieva, Larisa, and Kathy Porter. *Kremlin Wives.* London: Weidenfeld, 1994.

Volkogonov, Dmitri. *Lenin, Life, and Legacy.* New York: Free Press, 1994.

Vol'ner, I. N. *Psevdonimy V. I. Lenina.* Leningrad: Lenizdat, 1968.

Weber, G., and H. Weber. *Lenin: Life and Works.* New York: Facts on File, 1980.

White, James. *Lenin: The Practice and Theory of Revolution.* Basingstoke: Palgrave Macmillan, 2001.

Williams, Beryl. *Lenin.* London: Longman, 2000.

Williams, Robert C. *The Other Bolsheviks: Lenin and His Critics.* Bloomington: Indiana University Press, 1986.

Wolfe, Bertram D. "Lenin and Inessa Armand." *Slavic Review,* March 1963, pp. 96–114.

_____. *Three Who Made a Revolution.* Harmondsworth: Penguin, 1964.

Zinov'ev, Grigory. *Lenin.* Leningrad: Gosudarstvennoe izdatel'stvo, 1924.

3. The Revolutionary Movement and Its Surveillance

Allason, Rupert. *The Branch: A History of the Metropolitan Police Special Branch, 1883–1983.* London: Secker & Warburg, 1983.

Ascher, Abraham. *The Revolution of 1905.* 2 vols. Stanford: Stanford University Press, 1988–1992.

Baedeker's Russia. London: G. Allen & Unwin, 1971. Facsimile of 1914 edition.

Balabanoff, Angelica. *My Life as a Rebel.* London: Hamish Hamilton, 1938.

Baron, Samuel H. *Plekhanov: The Father of Russian Marxism.* London: Routledge & Kegan Paul, 1963.

Bergman, Jay. *Vera Zasulich: A Biography.* Stanford: Stanford University Press, 1983.

Bobrovskaya, Cecilia. *Twenty Years in Underground Russia: Memoirs of a Rank and File Bolshevik.* San Francisco: Proletarian, 1934.

Brust, Harold. *I Guarded Kings.* London: Stanley Paul, 1935.

_____. *In Plain Clothes*. London: Stanley Paul, 1937.

Bunyan, Tony. *History and Practice of the Political Police in Britain*. London: J. Friedmann, 1976.

Burenin, N. E. *Pamyatnye gody: Vospominaniya*. Leningrad: Lenizdat, 1961.

Chernyshevsky, Nikolay. *What Is to Be Done?* New York: Vintage, 1961.

Clements, Barbara Evans. *Bolshevik Women*. Cambridge: Cambridge University Press, 1997.

Conrad, Joseph. *The Secret Agent*. Harmondsworth: Penguin, 1986.

_____. *Under Western Eyes*. London: Penguin, 2007.

Crisp, Olga, and Linda Edmondson. *Civil Rights in Imperial Russia*. Oxford: Clarendon, 1989.

Daly, J. W. *Autocracy Under Siege: Security Police and Opposition in Russia, 1860–1905*. De Kalb: Northern Illinois University Press, 1998.

Deutscher, Isaac. *The Prophet Armed: Trotsky, 1879–1921*. London: Verso, 2003.

Drabkina, Elizaveta. *Chernye sukhari*. Moscow: Khudozhestvennaya literatura, 1970.

Ehrenburg, Ilya. *People and Life: Memoirs of 1891–1917*. London: MacGibbon & Kee, 1961.

Elwood, R. Carter. *Inessa Armand: Revolutionary and Feminist*. Cambridge: Cambridge University Press, 1992.

_____. *Roman Malinovsky: A Life Without a Cause*. Newtonville, Mass: Oriental Resource Partners, 1977.

_____. *Russian Social-Democracy in the Underground (1907–14)*. Assen: Van Gorcum, 1974.

Figes, Orlando. *A People's Tragedy: The Russian Revolution, 1891–1924*. London: Cape, 1996.

Figner, Vera. *Polnoe sobranie sochinenii*. Vol. 3, *Posle Shlissel'burga*. Moscow: Izd. vsesoyuznogo obshchestva politkatorzhani i ssylno-poslentsev, 1932.

_____. *Memoirs of a Revolutionist*. De Kalb: Northern Illinois University Press, 1991.

Fischer, Ben B. *Okhrana: The Paris Operations of the Russian Imperial Police*. Washington: Center for the Study of Intelligence, 1997.

Fitch, Herbert. *Traitors Within*. London: Hurst & Blackett, 1933.

Fomicheva, L. N. *N. K. Krupskaya: Zhizn' i deyatelnost' v fotografiyakh i dokumentakh*. Moscow: Plakat, 1988.

Garnett, Richard. *Constance Garnett: A Heroic Life*. London: Sinclair-Stevenson, 1991.

Geifmann, Anna. *Thou Shalt Kill: Revolutionary Terrorism in Russia 1894–1917*. Princeton: Princeton University Press, 1993.

Getzler, Israel. *Martov: A Political Biography*. Cambridge: Cambridge University Press, 1967.

Goldman, Emma. "The Tragedy of the Political Exiles." *The Nation*, October 10, 1934, pp. 401–402.

Gorelov, I. E. *Bol'sheviki: Dokumenty po istorii bol'shevizma, 1903–1916*. Moscow: Izd. Politicheskoi literatury, 1990.

Haupt, Georges, and Jean-Jacques Marie. *Makers of the Russian Revolution*. London: Allen & Unwin, 1974.

Hingley, Ronald. *The Russian Secret Police, 1565–1970*. London: Hutchinson, 1970.

Holmes, Colin. "Government Files and Privileged Access." *Social History* 6, no. 3 (1981): 335–350.

Hulse, J. W. *Revolutionists in London*. Oxford: Clarendon, 1970.

Kahn, David. *The Codebreakers: The Story of Secret Writing*. London: Sphere, 1977.

Kalmykov, A. G., ed. *Boevaya tekhnicheskaya gruppa pri PK i TsK RSDRP*. St. Petersburg: Gosudarstvennyi muzei politicheskoi istorii Rossii, 1999.

Keep, J. H. L. *The Rise of Social Democracy in Russia*. Oxford: Clarendon, 1963.

Kimball, Alan. "The Harassment of Russian Revolutionaries Abroad." *Oxford Slavonic Papers,* n.s., 6 (1973): 48–65.

Kropotkin, Peter. *Memoirs of a Revolutionist*. London: Smith Elder, 1899.

Lauchlan, Iain. *Russian Hide and Seek: The Tsarist Secret Police in St. Petersburg, 1906–1914*. Helsinki: Vammalan Kirjapaino Oy, 2002.

Lepeshinskaya, Ol'ga. *Vstrechi s Il'ichem*. Moscow: Izd. politicheskoi literaturoi, 1971.

Lepeshinsky, Panteleimon. *Na povorote: ot kontsa 80-kh godov k 1905 g*. Moscow: Nauka, 1922.

Lih, Lars T. "The Organization Question: Lenin and the Underground." In *Lenin Rediscovered*, pp. 433–488. Boston: Brill, 2005.

Lyadov, Mikhail. *Iz zhizni partii: Nakanune i v gody pervoi revolyutsii*. Moscow: Izd. kommunisticheskogo universiteta, 1926.

MacNaughton, Melville. *Days of My Years*. London: Arnold, 1914.

Meijer, Jan. *Knowledge and Revolution: The Russian Colony in Zuerich, 1870–3*. Assen: Van Gorcum, 1955.

Montefiore, Simon Sebag. *Young Stalin*. London: Weidenfeld & Nicolson, 2007.

Naarden, Bruno. *Socialist Europe and Revolutionary Russia: Perception and Prejudice, 1848–1923*. Cambridge: Cambridge University Press, 1992.

O'Connor, T. E. *The Engineer of the Revolution: L. B. Krasin and the Bolsheviks, 1870–1926*. Boulder: Westview, 1992.

Piatnitsky, Osip. *Memoirs of a Bolshevik*. London: Martin Lawrence, 1925.

Pipes, Richard. *The Russian Revolution*. London: Fontana, 1992.

_____. *Social Democracy and the St. Petersburg Labour Movement*. Cambridge: Harvard University Press, 1963.

_____. *Struve: Liberal on the Left, 1870–1905*. 2 vols. Cambridge: Harvard University Press, 1970–1980.

Pope, Arthur Upham. *Maxim Litvinoff*. London: Secker & Warburg, 1943.

Porter, Bernard. "The British Government and Political Refugees, 1880–1914." In John Slatter, *From the Other Shore: Russian Political Emigrants in Britain, 1880–1917*. London: Cass, 1984.

_____. *The Origins of the Vigilant State: The London Metropolitan Police Special Branch Before the First World War*. Woodbridge: Boydell, 1991.

Porter, Cathy. *Alexandra Kollontai*. London: Virago, 1980.

Pozner, S. M. *Pervaya boevaya organizatsiya bol'shevikov 1905–07 gg*. Moscow: Staryi bol'shevik, 1934.

Rappaport, Helen. *Joseph Stalin: A Biographical Companion*. Santa Barbara: ABC-Clio, 1999.

Ruud, Charles A. *Fontanka 16: The Tsar's Secret Police*. Stroud: Sutton, 1999.

Salisbury, Harrison E. *Black Night, White Snow: Russia's Revolutions, 1905–1917*. London: Cassell, 1977.

Sheinis, Maxim. *Maximovich Litvinov*. Moscow: Izd. politicheskoi literaturoi, 1989.

Shotman, Aleksandr. *Zapiski starogo bol'shevika*. Moscow: n.p., 1930.

Shukman, Harold, ed. *The Blackwell Encyclopedia of the Russian Revolution*. Oxford: Blackwell, 1988.

Shuranov, N. P. *Soratniki V. I. Lenina v Sibiri*. Kemerovo: Kemerovskoe knizhnoe izdatel'stvo, 1981.

Slatter, John. *From the Other Shore: Russian Political Emigrants in Britain, 1880–1917*. London: Cass, 1984.

Stasova, Elena. *Vospominaniya*. Moscow: Izd. Mysl', 1969.

Stepniak, Sergey. *Underground Russia: Revolutionary Profiles and Sketches from Life*. New York: Scribner's, 1883.

Sukhanov, N. N. *Zapiski o revolyutsii*. Vol. 2. Moscow: Izd. politicheskoi literaturoi, 1991.

Sweeney, John. *At Scotland Yard*. London: Grant Richards, 1904.

Thompson, W. H. *Guard from the Yard*. London: Jarrolds, 1938.

Trotsky, Leon. *My Life: An Attempt at Autobiography*. New York: Pathfinder, 1970.

Ulam, Adam B. *Prophets and Conspirators in Pre-Revolutionary Russia*. New Brunswick: Transaction, 1998.

Venturi, Franco. *Roots of Revolution: A History of the Populist and Socialist Movements in 19th Century. Russia*. London: Phoenix, 2001.

Wildman, A. "Lenin's Battle with Kustarnichestvo: The *Iskra* Organization in Russia." *Slavic Review* 23 (1964): 479–503.

Woodall, Edwin T. *Secrets of Scotland Yard*. London: John Lane, 1936.

Zuckerman, Fredric S. *The Tsarist Secret Police in Russian Society, 1880–1917*. London: Macmillan, 1996.

_____. *The Tsarist Secret Police Abroad*. Basingstoke: Palgrave Macmillan, 2003.

Zeman, Z. A. B. *The Merchant of Revolution: The Life of Alexander Israel Helphand (Parvus)*. London: Oxford University Press, 1965.

3. Lenin in Exile

Capri

Andreevna, Mariya. "Vstrechi s Leninym." In *Perepiska, vospominaniya, stat'i, dokumenty*. Moscow: Iskusstvo, 1961.

Byalik, Boris. *V. I. Lenin i A. M. Gor'ky: Pis'ma, vospominaniya, dokumenty*. Moscow: Nauka, 1969.

Caruso, Bruno. *Lenin a Capri: Intelletuali, marxismo, religione*. Bari: Dedalo Libri, 1978.

Cerio, Edwin. *That Capri Air*. London: Heineman, 1929.

_____. *The Masque of Capri*. London: Thomas Nelson, 1957.

Desnitsky, Vasilii. *A. M. Gor'ky: ocherki zhizni i tvorchestva*. Moscow: Izd. khudozhestvennoi literatury, 1959.

Guseva, Zinaida. *Svidaniya na Kapri*. Moscow: Izd. Sovetskaya Rossiya, 1968.

Hazzard, Shirley. *Greene on Capri*. London: Virago, 2000.

Levin, Dan. *Stormy Petrel: Life and Work of Maxim Gorky*. New York: Appleton-Century, 1965.

Moskovsky, R. V. *Lenin v Italii: Chekhoslovakii, Pol'she*. Moscow: Izd. politicheskoi literatury, 1986.

Ross, Alan. *Reflections on Blue Water: Journeys in the Gulf of Naples*. London: Harvill, 1979.

Tamborra, Angelo. *Esuli Russi in Italia dal 1905 al 191*. Rome: Tamborra, 1977.

Troyat, Henri. *Gorky*. London: Allison & Busby, 1989.

Wolfe, Bertram D. *The Bridge and the Abyss: The Troubled Friendship of Gorky and Lenin*. London: Pall Mall, 1968.

Yedlin, Tova. *Maxim Gorky: A Political Biography*. Westport: Praeger, 1999.

Finland, Sweden, and Denmark

Dashkov, Yuri. *Po leninskim mestam Skandinavii: Zhurnalistskii poisk*. Moscow: Sovetskaya Rossiya, 1971.

_____. *U istokov dobrososedstva: Iz istorii rossiisko-finlyandskikh revolyutsionnykh svyazei*. Moscow: Mysl', 1980.

Egede-Nissen, Adam. *Et Liv i Strid*. Oslo: J. W. Kappelen, 1945.

Futrell, Michael. *Northern Underground: Episodes of Russian Revolutionary Transport and Communications Through Scandinavia and Finland, 1863–1917*. London: Faber & Faber, 1963.

Koivisto, Mauno. *Itsenaiseki Imperiumin Kainalossa*. Helsinki: Kustanusosakehytiö Tammi, 2004.

Koronen, M. M. *V. I. Lenin i Finlyandiya*. Leningrad: Lenizdat, 1977.

Lenin v vospominaniyakh finnov. Moscow: Izd. Politicheskoi Literaturoi, 1979.

Lindström, Ludvig, "På flykt Vladimir Uljanov mera bekant som Lenin." In *All-svensk samling*, pp. 14–16, 44–48. Gothenburg, 1946.

Malmberg, Ikka. "What If Lenin Had Drowned Here?" *Helsingin Sanomat*, December 8, 2004. www.hs.fi/english/article/What+if+Lenin+had+drowned+here/1101977945887.

Moskovsky, Pavel. *Lenin v Shvetsii*. Moscow: Izd. politicheskoi literaturoi, 1972.

Nerman, Ture. *Allt Var Rott*. Stockholm: Kooperativa förbundets bökforlag, 1950.

Numminen, J., ed. *Lenin ja Suomi*. Helsinki: Opetusministeriö Valtion Painatuskeskus, 1987.

Semenov, V. G. *Lenin v Finlyandii*. Moscow: Izd. politicheskoi literaturoi, 1977.

Ström, Fredrik. *I Stormig Tid: Memoarer*. Stockholm: P. A. Norstedt, 1942.

Thomsen, Carl. *Lenin's Visits to Denmark*. Copenhagen: Royal Library, 1970.

Willers, Uno. *Lenin i Stockholm*. Stockholm: Rabén & Sjögren, 1970.

France

Aline, A. *Lénine à Paris*. Paris: Les Revues, 1929.

Boulouque, Sylvain. "Mardochée Brunswick." *Archives Juives* 30, no. 2 (1997): 119–120.

Elwood, R. Carter. "Lenin and the Social Democratic Schools for Underground Party Workers, 1909–11." *Political Science Quarterly*, September 1966, pp. 370–391.

Feld, Charles. *Quand Lénine vivait à Paris*. Paris: Editions Cercle d'Art et Club Messidor, 1967.

Fotieva, L. N. "Vstrechi s Leninym v Zheneve i Parizhe." In Golikov, *Vo VIL* 2:140–157.

Fréville, Jean. *Lénine à Paris*. Paris: Editions socials, 1968.

Gabrilovich, Evgeny, and Sergei Yutkevich. "Lenin in Paris." In *A Film Trilogy About Lenin*. Moscow: Progress, 1985.

"His Paris Concierge Pays Tribute to Lenin." *New York Times*, April 25, 1921.

Kaganova, R. Yu. *Lenin vo Frantsii Dek, 1908-Iyun' 1912*. Moscow: Mysl', 1972.

Kataev, Valentin. "Malen'kaya zheleznaya dver' v stene." *Sobranie sochinenii* 6 (1984): 54–69.

"Les refugiés révolutionnaires russes à Paris." *Cahiers du Monde russe et soviétique*, July-September 1965, pp. 419–436.

Lyudvinskaya, T. F. "Parizh." In Lyudvinskaya, *Velikii, blizkii, prostoi*. Moscow: Izd. Znanie, 1969.

Moskovsky, P. V., and V. G. Semenov. *Lenin vo Frantsii, Bel'gii i Danii*. Moscow: Izd. Politicheskoi Literatury, 1982.

Rappoport, Charles. "Lénine à Paris." *Russie d'aujourdhui*, January 1938. Reprinted in Rappoport, *Une vie révolutionnaire, 1883–1940*. Paris: Maison des sciences de l'homme.

Shaginyan, M. "Retracing Lenin's Steps." In Mariya Prilezhaeva, *A Remarkable Year*. Moscow: Progress, 1980.

Toussaint, Franz. *Lénine inconnu*. Paris: Les Éditions Universelles, 1952.

Galicia (now Poland)

Adamczewski, Jan. *Polskie Dni Lenina, 1912–14.* Warsaw: Wydawnictwo Interpress, 1970.

Adamczewski, Jan, and Jozef Pociecha. *Lenin w Krakowie.* Kraków: Wydawnictwo Literackie, 1974.

Bagotsky [Bagocki], Sergey. "V. I. Lenin v Krakove i Poronine." In *VoVIL* 1: 438–456.

Bartosik, Marek. "Wódz obalony lebiodka." *Gazeta Krakowska,* September 5, 2008, pp. 8–9.

Bernov, Y., and A. Manusevich. *Lenin v Krakove.* Moscow: Izd. politicheskoi literaturoi, 1972.

———. *V krakovskoi emigratsii: Zhizn' i deyatel'nost' V. I. Lenina. 1912–14.* Moscow: Izd. politicheskoi literaturoi, 1988.

Dubacki, Leonard, et al. *Polacy o Leninie: Wspomnienia.* Warsaw: Ksi ka i Wiedza, 1970.

"Eyewitness Reports." *News from Behind the Iron Curtain* 5, no. 2 (1956): 28.

Gabrilovich, Evgeny, and Sergei Yutkevich. "Lenin in Poland." In *A Film Trilogy About Lenin.* Moscow: Progress, 1985.

Ganetsky [Hanecki]. "S Leninym." *Voprosy istorii KPSS* 3 (1970): 96–101.

Goncharova, S. M. "Iz istorii krakovsko-poroninskogo arkhiva V. I. Lenina." In *Lenin i Pol'sha,* pp. 392–401. Moscow: Nauka, 1970.

Hartig, Edward. *Krakow.* Warsaw: Wydawnictwo "Sport i Turystyka," 1980.

Little, Frances Delanoy. *Sketches in Poland.* London: Andrew Melrose, 1915.

Najdus, Walentyna. *Lenin i Krupska w Krakowskim Zwiazku Pomocy dla Wiezniow Politycznych.* Kraków: Wydawnictwo Literackie, 1965.

Sieradzki, Jozef. *Pol'skie gody Lenina.* Moscow: Izd. politicheskoi literatury, 1966.

Sobczak, Jan. "Two Years in Poland." *World Marxist Review,* December 1969, pp. 16–19.

Trepper, Leopold. *The Great Game: The Story of the Red Orchestra.* London: Michael Joseph, 1977.

"Upheaval in the East: Lenin Statue in Mothballs." *New York Times,* December 11, 1989.

Watson, Peggy. "Nowa Huta: The Politics of Postcommunism and the Past." In J. Edmunds and B. S. Turner, eds., *Narrative, Generational Consciousness, and Politics.* Lanham, Md.: Rowman & Littlefield, 2002.

Germany and Austria-Hungary

Amort, Cestir. 'Lenin in Prague." *World Marxist Review* 13, no. 6 (1970): 19–21.

Baeumler, Ernst. *Verschwörung in Schwabing: Lenins Begegnung mit Deutschland.* Düsseldorf: Econ, 1972.

Baur, Johannes. *Die russische Kolonie in München, 1900–1945.* Wiesbaden: Harrassowitz, 1998.

Brachmann, B. *Russische sozialdemokraten in Berlin, 1895–1914.* Berlin: Akademie-Verlag, 1962.

Haimson, Leopold. *The Making of Three Russian Revolutionaries.* Cambridge: Cambridge University Press, 1987.

Hitzer, Friedrich. *Lenin in München.* Munich: Bayerischen Gesellschaft, 1977.

Huber, Gerdi. *Das klassische Schwabing.* Munich: Neue Schriftenreihe des Stadtarchivs, 1973.

Ivanov, Miroslav. *Lenin v Praze.* Prague: n.p., 1960.

Moskovsky, P V. *Lenin v Italii, Chekhoslovakii, Pol'she.* Moscow: Izd. politicheskoi literatury, 1986.

Muraveva, L. L., et al. *Lenin v Myunkhene: Pamyatnye mesta.* Moscow: Izd. politicheskoi literaturoi, 1976.

Onufriev, Evgeny. *Vstrechi s Leninym–vospominaniya delegata Prazhskoi konferentsii.* Moscow: Izd. politicheskoi literatury, 1966.

Ortmann, F. *Revolutionäre im Exil, 1888–1903.* Stuttgart: Steiner, 1994.

Sackett, Robert Eben. *Popular Entertainment, Class, and Politics in Munich, 1900–1923.* Cambrdge: Harvard University Press, 1982.

Schorske, Carl. *German Social Democracy, 1905–1917.* New York: Harper & Row, 1972.

Swain, G. "The Bolsheviks' Prague Conference Revisited." *Revolutionary Russia,* June 1989, pp. 134–140.

Williams, Robert C. *Culture in Exile: Russian Emigrés in Germany, 1881–1941.* Ithaca: Cornell University Press, 1972.

_____. "Russians in Germany: 1900–1914." *Journal of Contemporary History* 1, no. 4 (1966): 121–149.

London

Aldred, Guy. *No Traitor's Gate.* Glasgow: Strickland, 1957.

Alekseev, N. A. "V. I. Lenin v Londone." In Golikov, *VoVIL,* pp. 86–91.

Armfelt, Count E. "Russia in East London." In George Robert Sims, *Living London.* Vol. 1. London, 1906.

Balabanoff, Angelica. 'Lenin and the London Congress of 1907." In *Impressions of Lenin,* pp. 17–25.

Bassalygo, D. "Nezabyvaemye vstrechi." In *VoVIL* 3:1960.

Beer, Max. Interview with Lenin. In *Fifty Years of International Socialism.* London: Allen & Unwin,1935.

Bergman, Jay. *Vera Zasulich: A Biography.* Stanford: Stanford University Press, 1983.

Bowman, William J. "Lenin in London." *Contemporary Review,* January-June 1957, pp. 336–338.

Brailsford, Henry. "The Russian Congress." *Daily News,* June 4, 1907, p. 6.

_____. "When Lenin and Trotsky Were in London." *Listener,* January 1948.

Briggs, Asa, and Anne Macartney. *Toynbee Hall: The First 100 Years.* London: Routledge & Kegan Paul, 1984.

Coates, Zelda Kahan. "Memories of Lenin." *Labour Monthly,* November 1968, pp. 506–508.

Daily Express, January 5, 1950.

Daily Mirror, May 10–11, 13–18, 22, 1907.

Deutsch, Leo. "The Russian Social Democratic Congress." *Justice,* June 8, 1907.

Drabkina, F. *Vospominaniya o vtorom s'ezde RSDRP.* 1934.

Dudden, A. P. *Joseph Fels and the Single Tax Movement.* Philadelphia: Temple University Press, 1971.

Dudden, A. P., and T. H. von Laue. "The RSDLP and Joseph Fels: A Study in Intercultural Contact." *American Historical Review* 61 (1955–1956): 21–47.

Fishman, William J. *East End Jewish Radicals, 1875–1914.* London: Duckworth, 1975.

_____. "Lenin in London." *Anglia,* October 1967.

_____. "Millie Sabel: Yiddish Anarchist." *East London Arts Magazine* 4, no. 1 (1967).

Free Russia: The Organ of the English Society of Friends of Russian Freedom, May–June 1907.

Gandurin, K. *Epizody podpol'ya: Vospominaniya starogo bol'shevika*. Moscow: Molodaya gvardiya, 1934.

Henderson, Bob. "Lenin and the British Museum Library." *Solanus*, n.s., 4 (1990): 3–15.

———. "Lenin at the British Library." The British Library, Slavonic & East European Collections, 1990.

Higgins, A. G. *A History of the Brotherhood Church*. Stapleton, UK: Brotherhood Church, 1982.

Hollingsworth, Barry. "The Society of Friends of Russian Freedom: English Liberals and Russian Socialists, 1890–1917." *Oxford Slavonic Papers*, n.s., 3 (1970): 45–64.

Justice: The Organ of Social Democracy, March 7, 1903; May 2, 1903; July 15, 1905; March 30, 1907; June 1, 15, 1907.

Kadish, Sharman. *Bolsheviks and British Jews*. London: Cass, 1992.

Karachan, N. V. *V. I. Lenin v Londone*. Leningrad: Izd. Prosveschchenie, 1969.

Karzhansky, N. S. "V. I. Lenin na s'ezde RSDRP." In *VoVIL* 1: 356–363.

Kendall, Walter. *The Revolutionary Movement in Britain, 1900–21*. London: Weidenfeld & Nicolson, 1969.

———. "Russian Emigration and British Marxist Socialism." *International Review of Social History* 8 (1963): 351–378.

Kochan, Lionel. "Lenin in London." *History Today* 20, no. 4 (1970): 229–235.

Lee, H. W., and E. Archbold. *Social-Democracy in Britain*. London: Social-Democratic Federation, 1935.

Lenin. Obituary for Harry Quelch. In *CW* 19: 369–371.

"Lenin and His Wife Were Good, Quiet Tenants." Letter to the editor, *Islington Gazette*, October 15, 1963.

"Lenin Was Their Lodger." *Socialist Commentary*, May 1970, pp. 14–15.

"Lenin's Clerkenwell Home: Recollections of his Landlady." *Guardian*, July 20, 1939, p. 15.

Lepeshinsky, Panteleimon. *Protokoly vtorogo s'ezda RSDRP*. Leningrad: Priboi, 1924.

Leventhal, F. M. *The Last Dissenter: H N Brailsford and His World*. Oxford: Clarendon, 1985.

Levin, Elia. "Conference of the Russian Socialists in London." *Justice*, May 18, 1907.

London Landmarks: Marx, Engels, and Lenin. London: Communist Party, n.d.

Lyadov, Martyn. *Iz zhizni partii nakanune i v gody pervoi revolyutsii*. Moscow: Izd. Kommunisticheskogo Universiteta, 1926.

Maisky, Ivan. *Journey into the Past*. London: Hutchinson, 1960.

Masefield, John. *Letters to Reyna*. London: Buchan & Enright, 1983.

Meacham, Standish. *Toynbee Hall and Social Reform, 1880–1914*. New Haven: Yale University Press, 1987.

"Memoirs of a Meeting with Lenin." *Islington Gazette*, January 31, 1964.

Mikhailov, I. K. "Vospominaniya o V. I. Lenine." In *VoVIL* 3:1960.

Morning Post, May 11, 18, 1907.

Muraveva, Lyudmila. *Lenin in London: Memorial Places*. Moscow: Progress, 1983.

Murray-Browne, Caroline. "Richter, Alias Lenin, the Forgotten Exiles of Finsbury." *Islington Gazette*, March 23, 1978, p. 33.

Pimlott, J. A. R. *Toynbee Hall: Fifty Years of Social Progress*. London: J. M. Dent, 1935.

Quelch, Tom. Interview, *Evening Standard*, August 30, 1941, p. 2.

Rocker, Fermin. *The East End Years*. London: Freedom, 1998.

Rocker, Rudolf. *The London Years*. London: Robert Anscombe, 1956.

Rothstein, Andrew. *A House on Clerkenwell Green*. London: Lawrence & Wishart, 1966.

_____. *Lenin in Britain.* London: Communist Party, 1970.

"Russian Labour Party: Their Congress in London." *Pall Mall Gazette,* May–June, 1907.

Scott, L. "When the Lenins Lived in Holford Square." *Islington News,* November 21, 1960.

Semenov, V. M. "Lenin in London." *Soviet Weekly,* April 21, 1960.

_____. *Po Leninskim mestam v Londone.* Moscow: Gospolitizdat, 1959.

Schapiro, Leonard. "Lenin and the Russian Revolution." *History Today,* May 20, 1970, pp. 324–330.

Slatter, John. *From the Other Shore: Russian Political Emigrants in Britain, 1880–1917.* London: Frank Cass, 1984.

_____. "Our Friends from the East: Russian Revolutionaries and British Radicals." *History Today,* October 2003, pp. 43–49.

Stalin, Joseph. *Notes of a Delegate.* London: Lawrence & Wishart, 1941.

Stracey, John. "The Great Awakening." *Encounter* no. 5. London, 1961.

Surovtseva, N. N., et al. *Vospominaniya o II s'ezde RDSRP.* Moscow: Izd. politicheskoi literatury, 1983.

Thomas, Kay. "History Was Made in London." *Soviet Weekly,* April 18, 1970, pp. 16–17.

Vernitsky Anatoly. "Russian Revolutionaries and English Sympathizers in 1890s London." *Journal of European Studies* 35 (2005): 299–314.

"The Visitor from Russia Who Wasn't Welcomed in Finsbury." *Islington Gazette,* October 8, 1963.

Willats, Eric A. "Lenin and London." *Islington Gazette,* June 18, 25, 1968; July 2, 9, 1968. Original T/S in Islington LHL, Y J853.09 BRO.

Switzerland

Baedeker, Karl. *Switzerland and the Adjacent Portions of Switzerland, Savoy, and Tyrol.* London: K. Baedeker, 1907.

Ball, Hugo. *Flight out of Time: A Dada Diary.* New York: Viking, 1974.

Essen, Mariya. "Vstrechi s Leninym." In *VoVIL* 1:244–261.

Feuer, Lewis S. *Einstein and the Generations of Science.* New Brunswick: Transaction, 1982. See especially "Zurich: The Peaceful Cradle of European Revolution," pp. 4–14.

Fotieva, L. N. "Vstrechi s Leninym v Zheneve i Parizhe." In *VoVIL* 2:140–157.

Gautschi, Willi. *Lenin als Emigrant in der Schweiz.* Zurich: Benziger, 1973.

Haas, Leonhard. "Lenins Frau als Patientin bei Schweizer Ärtzen." *Jahrbucher für Geschichte Osteuropas,* n.s., 17 (1969): 420–436.

Hardy, Deborah. "The Lonely Emigré: Peter Tkachev and the Russian Colony in Switzerland." *Russian Review,* October 1976, pp. 400–416.

Kammerer, Titus. "We Rented to the Lenins." *Partisan Review* 6, no. 3 (1939): 26–28.

Kudryavtsev, A. S., et al. *Lenin v Berne i Tsyurikhe: pamyatnye mesta.* Moscow: Izd. Politicheskoi literaturoi, 1972.

_____. *Lenin's Geneva Addresses.* Moscow: Progress, 1969.

Leuning, Otto. *Odyssey of an American Composer.* New York: Scribner's, 1980. See especially chapter 6, "Refugees and Dadaists in Zurich, 1917–1920."

Ley, J. "A Memorable Day in April." *New Statesman,* April 19, 1958, pp. 496–498.

Marcu, Valeriu. "Lenin in Zurich: A Memoir." *Foreign Affairs* 21, no. 1 (1942–1943): 548–559.

Meijer, J. M. *Knowledge and Revolution: The Russian Colony in Zuerich, 1870–1873.* Assen: Van Gorcum, 1955.

Münzenberg, Willi. "Lenin and We." In *They Knew Lenin*, pp. 79–87.

Nation, Craig. *War on War: Lenin, the Zimmerwald Left, and the Origins of Communist Internationalism.* Durham: Duke University Press, 1986.

Noguez, Dominique. *Lenin Dada–Essay.* Zurich: Le dilettante, 1990.

Novikov, Viktor. *S imenem Lenina svyazano.* Leningrad: Lenizdat, 1987.

"Ou est la table de Lénine?" *Tribune de Genève,* August 3, 2006, p. 28.

Pearson, Michael. *The Sealed Train.* Newton Abbot: Readers Union, 1975.

Pianzola, Maurice. *Lenine en Suisse.* Geneva: Librairie Rousseau, 1965.

Platten, Fritz. *Lenin iz emigratsii v Rossiyu.* Moscow: Moskovskii rabochii, 1990.

Richter, Hans. *Dada: Art and Anti-Art.* London: Thames & Hudson, 1965.

Rozental, E. "Lenin in Switzerland." *World Marxist Review,* June 1969, pp. 11–13.

Schazmann, Paul-Emile. "Sur les traces en Suisse du chef de la révolution russe." *Tribune de Genève,* April 21, 1970.

Senn, Alfred. *The Russian Revolution in Switzerland, 1914–1917.* Madison: University of Wisconsin Press, 1971.

Solzhenitsyn, Alexander. *Lenin in Zurich.* London: Bodley Head, 1975.

Tyrkova-Williams, Ariadna. *Na putyakh k svobode.* New York: Izd. im. Chekhova, 1952.

Ybarra, T. R. "Lenin Lived Poorly in Days of Exile." *New York Times,* June 15, 1924.

Zweig, Stefan. "The Sealed Train." In *The Tide of Fortune: Twelve Historical Miniatures.* London: Cassell, 1927.

INDEX